Peace Psychology Book Series

Series Editor
Daniel J. Christie

More information about this series at http://www.springer.com/series/7298

Stephen Gibson

Editor

Discourse, Peace, and Conflict

Discursive Psychology Perspectives

 Springer

Editor
Stephen Gibson
School of Psychological and Social Sciences
York St John University
York, United Kingdom

ISSN 2197-5779   ISSN 2197-5787 (electronic)
Peace Psychology Book Series
ISBN 978-3-319-99093-4   ISBN 978-3-319-99094-1   (eBook)
https://doi.org/10.1007/978-3-319-99094-1

Library of Congress Control Number: 2018957269

This Springer imprint is published by the registered company Springer Nature Switzerland AG
The registered company address is: Gewerbestrasse 11, 6330 Cham, Switzerland

Acknowledgements

I would like to thank Daniel J. Christie for encouraging me to put together this collection in the first place and for his useful feedback as the volume developed. I would also like to thank Morgan Ryan and Sara Yanny-Tillar of Springer for their support, encouragement and (perhaps most importantly of all) patience.

Contents

Contributors

Peter J. Adams University of Auckland, Auckland, New Zealand

Dimitra Anagnostopoulou Aristotle University of Thessaloniki, Thessaloniki, Greece

Martha Augoustinos University of Adelaide, Adelaide, SA, Australia

Joseph Burridge University of Portsmouth, Portsmouth, UK

Jovan Byford The Open University, Milton Keynes, UK

Peta Callaghan University of Adelaide, Adelaide, SA, Australia

Clemence Due University of Adelaide, Adelaide, SA, Australia

Lia Figgou Aristotle University of Thessaloniki, Thessaloniki, Greece

W. Mick L.Finlay Anglia Ruskin University, Cambridge, UK

Stephen Gibson York St John University, York, UK

Simon Goodman Coventry University, Coventry, UK

Dávid Kaposi The Open University, Milton Keynes, UK

Laura Kilby Sheffield Hallam University, Sheffield, UK

Steve Kirkwood The University of Edinburgh, Edinburgh, UK

Henry Lennon Sheffield Hallam University, Sheffield, UK

Kevin McKenzie Independent Researcher (formerly at University of Cyprus and Qatar University), Brooklyn, New York, USA

Chris McVittie Queen Margaret University, Edinburgh, UK

Kyoko Murakami University of Copenhagen, Copenhagen, Denmark

Bethany Perry Coventry University, Coventry, UK

Rahul Sambaraju Trinity College Dublin, Dublin, Republic of Ireland

Antonis Sapountzis Democritus University of Thrace, Komotini, Greece

Martina Sourvinou Aristotle University of Thessaloniki, Thessaloniki, Greece

Elizabeth Stokoe Loughborough University, Loughborough, UK

Cristian Tileagă Loughborough University, Loughborough, UK

Alison J. Towns University of Auckland, Auckland, New Zealand

Maria Xenitidou Democritus University of Thrace, Xanthi, Greece
University of Surrey, Surrey, UK

About the Editor

Stephen Gibson is based at York St John University, UK, where he has taught psychology since 2005. In his research, Stephen uses discursive and rhetorical approaches to explore a range of social psychological topics, including citizenship, national identity, dis/obedience and representations of peace and conflict. He is editor of *Representations of Peace and Conflict* (Palgrave Macmillan, 2012; with Simon Mollan) and *Doing Your Qualitative Psychology Project* (Sage, 2012; with Cath Sullivan and Sarah Riley).

Chapter 1
Discursive Psychology and Peace Psychology

Stephen Gibson

Introduction

The aim of this volume is to illustrate the potential for discursive psychologists to contribute to peace psychology. In doing so, it is hoped that the encounter between peace psychology and discursive psychology will be of mutual benefit. In this introductory chapter, I will map out some core features of both peace psychology and discursive psychology, focussing in particular on the conceptual and analytic principles of discursive psychology. As will be explained below, discursive psychology is a diverse field, and any attempt to offer a single definition is fraught with difficulty. We might, however, be on safer ground if we begin with a definition of *discourse*, which can be drawn from Potter and Wetherell's (1987, p. 7) classic text which introduced the discourse analytic perspective in psychology: 'We will use "discourse" in its most open sense … to cover all forms of spoken interaction, formal and informal, and written texts of all kinds'. Even here, however, objections might be raised that this prioritises what is sometimes called 'little d' discourse—actual examples of language-in use—over 'big D' discourse, which refers to the more diffuse ways of talking about, and making sense of, objects, events, and phenomena that circulate within a society. For example, we might talk about the 'discourse of neoliberalism' or the 'discourse of populism'. Rather than resolving such tensions at the outset, I will return to them below, and indeed many of the contributors to this volume will, in their own way, seek to wrestle with these tensions, either by focussing on one or the other, or by seeking some form of synthesis. If this begins to hint at the sorts of conceptual debates that make discursive psychology such a fascinating and contested field, let us begin with some rather more prosaic matters concerning the origins and development of discursive psychology. Discursive psychologists emphasize that accounts are always constructed

S. Gibson (✉)
York St John University, York, UK
e-mail: s.gibson@yorksj.ac.uk

in order to perform particular functions in particular contexts, and my account here is, of course, no different. Others would construct different versions, and indeed on other occasions, for different purposes, I would also construct different versions. But for the sake of introducing some key ideas for a peace psychology audience, let me attempt to map out the development of discursive psychology over the last 30 years or so.

Discursive psychology was originally developed within social psychology (e.g. Potter & Wetherell, 1987) and has continued to have a strong orientation to a variety of social psychological issues (see McKinlay & McVittie, 2008 for an overview). In this respect, its development has been closely intertwined with a much broader set of ideas that might loosely (if rather unsatisfactorily) be described as 'critical social psychology' (e.g. Gough, 2017; Gough, McFaddden, & McDonald, 2013; Hepburn, 2003; Ibáñez & Íñiguez, 1997; Tuffin, 2005). Critical social psychology, as part of a wider 'critical psychology' (Fox, Prilleltensky, & Austin, 2009), scrutinizes the ways in which psychology has functioned to shore up oppressive practices, as well as aiming to develop approaches that uncover and seek to redress inequalities and injustice more broadly. A great deal of early discourse analytic work in social psychology (e.g. Parker, 1992; Wetherell & Potter, 1992) was explicitly aimed at contributing towards such an endeavour, and it remains prominent in discursive psychology to this day, with a particular strand, sometimes labelled 'critical discursive psychology', foregrounding issues of power and ideology (e.g. Parker, 2015; Wetherell, 1998, 2015).

Throughout the 1990s, discursive psychology was also notably worked out in part through a critical dialogue with cognitive psychology (e.g. Edwards, 1997; Edwards & Potter, 1992; and see the debate in volume 5, issue 10 of *The Psychologist* [1992] on memory and discourse). Drawing on the wider 'turn to discourse' within the social sciences (Kroger & Wood, 1998), this led some to declare the onset of a 'second cognitive revolution' (Harré, 1992), and the advent of 'post-cognitive psychology' (Potter, 2000). The 'revolution' never really happened, with the alternative to cognitivism being more fully followed through in disciplines other than psychology (te Molder, 2016). However, the recent so-called replication crisis in psychology (e.g. Earp & Trafimow, 2015; Lilienfeld, 2017; Maxwell, Lau, & Howard, 2015) highlights the continued centrality of language and interaction to the discipline. For all that the apparent crisis has swiftly been heavily circumscribed through its labelling as being specifically related to replication, this arguably obscures the much more fundamental failure to appreciate the contextual contingency of psychological research practices, including the extent to which psychological research is fundamentally interactional in nature (Gibson, in press). Moreover, for all the talk of crisis and revolution, there has been a more incremental process whereby discourse analytic research has gradually come to prominence in various parts of the discipline. As such, one can now find a rich literature in areas such as health psychology (e.g. Seymour-Smith, 2015), the psychology of gender (e.g. Wetherell & Edley, 2014), clinical psychology (e.g. Stokoe & Wiggins, 2005), sport psychology (e.g. Locke, 2008; Miller, 2012), psychotherapy/counselling psychology (Avdi & Georgaca, 2007; O'Reilly, Kiyimba, & Lester, 2018), work/organizational psychology (e.g. Dick, 2013; Symon, 2000), and political psychology (e.g. Condor, Tileagă, & Billig, 2013; Demasi, in press; Tileagă, 2013). Recent retrospectives (Augoustinos & Tileagă, 2012; Tileagă & Stokoe, 2016), a major collection of seminal papers (Potter, 2007), and the publication of the first dedicated textbook on discursive psychology (Wiggins, 2017) have contributed to the sense that discursive psychology has matured into a distinct specialism. Yet these developments have also given rise to a critical examination of the field, which in increasingly coming to be seen as having coalesced around a core set of assumptions and research practices has been challenged on the grounds that, essentially, it risks losing its critical edge (e.g. Billig, 2012).

Whilst there are some recent examples of discursive work within peace psychology (e.g. Cameron, Maslen, & Todd, 2013; Gibson, 2011; Karlberg, 2012; Kiguwa & Ally, 2018; Kilby, 2017), there is, as yet, no real systematic attempt to map out the potential for a discursive peace psychology, and indeed it is precisely this task which the present volume aims to undertake. This is not, however, to say that there has been no discursive research on matters of peace and conflict. Many of the core analytic focal points of discursive psychologists deal with issues that peace psychologists would consider in terms of structural (or indirect) violence, such as racism (e.g. Augoustinos & Every, 2007; Goodman, 2014; Wetherell & Potter, 1992) and gender inequalities (e.g. Edley & Wetherell, 1995; Speer & Stokoe, 2011; Wetherell, Stiven, & Potter, 1987). In relation to direct violence, both within discursive psychology (e.g. Billig & MacMillan, 2005; Durrheim, 1997; Finlay, 2018; Gibson, 2012a, 2012b, 2012c; Kilby, 2017; McKinlay, McVittie, & Sambaraju, 2012) and in the wider inter-disciplinary field of discourse studies (e.g. Gavriely-Nuri, 2010; Hodges & Nilep, 2011; Jackson, 2005; Leudar, Marsland, & Nekvapil, 2004; Schäffner & Wenden, 1995) there have been myriad studies that have drawn on one form or another of discourse analysis to address matters of concern to peace psychologists. However, with few exceptions, these analyses are not positioned in terms of the concerns of peace psychology, nor do they seek to address a peace psychology readership.

We should not, of course, get too concerned with disciplinary boundaries; from its earliest statements (e.g. Potter & Wetherell, 1987), discursive research in psychology has drawn heavily on developments across the humanities and social sciences including ethnomethodology, conversation analysis, semiotics, post-structuralism, critical linguistics, sociology of scientific knowledge, and literary theory. However, it remains the case that, within discursive psychology, studies focussed on matters of peace and conflict have rarely engaged directly with the field of peace psychology; and similarly, in the wider discourse studies literature authors have—understandably—only rarely been concerned with psychological matters. There remains, therefore, plenty of scope for a fuller integration of the concerns of peace psychology and discursive psychology, yet there are also potential obstacles to such a development. To begin the process of mapping the possibilities for a discursive peace psychology, it is useful to start with a brief consideration of some of the foundational statements of peace psychology, and of the broader field of peace studies (Christie, 1999), before turning to a fuller outline of discursive psychology itself.

Peace Psychology

Just as discursive psychology has grown in prominence in recent decades, so too has peace psychology. The publication of major textbooks (Blumberg, Hare, & Costin, 2006; Christie, Wagner, & Winter, 2001; MacNair, 2012) and a comprehensive encyclopedia (Christie, 2012), together with the establishment of Division 48 (Peace Psychology) of the American Psychological Association (Wessells, 1996), and the founding of *Peace and Conflict: Journal of Peace Psychology*, mark the field out as one that has established a place in the disciplinary apparatus of psychology, particularly within North America, but also elsewhere (e.g. Boehnke, Fuss, & Kindervater, 2005; Bretherton & Balvin, 2012; Montiel, 2003; Montiel & Noor, 2009; Seedat, Suffla, & Christie, 2017; Simić, Volčič, & Philpot, 2012).

Arising from the Cold War, US Peace Psychology was initially focussed around matters relating to the prevention of nuclear war (Morawski & Goldstein, 1985; Wessells, 1996), but in the post-Cold War era a focus on wider structural processes has emerged (Christie, 2006). In this respect, Christie notes three trends in peace psychology from the 1990s onwards: First, there has been a broadening of the geopolitical purview of peace psychology, expanding from the north American disciplinary base to engage with matters of peace and conflict in a much wider range of contexts, and particularly in the 'global south' (e.g. Montiel, 2018). Second, peace psychology has increasingly taken a systems approach to explanation, combining a focus on individual-level psychology with a more macro perspective than might typically be found in other areas of the discipline. Third, peace psychology has drawn on the wider peace studies literature in order to develop a differentiated perspective on the nature of peace and violence. Indeed, the key distinctions between direct and structural violence, and positive and negative peace (Galtung, 1969) can in many respects be considered foundational for peace psychology.

'Violence' has typically been held simply to refer to acts that lead to direct physical harm, either to individuals or the physical environment. However, Galtung (1969) argued that this *direct* form of violence should be accompanied by the concept of *structural* violence. By this, he meant the systemic, political, and social factors that sustain inequality, and he explicitly noted that structural violence can be understood as being synonymous with social injustice. This distinction between forms of violence was accompanied by an equivalent distinction between different forms of peace. Whereas *negative peace* involves the absence of direct violence, *positive peace* refers to the absence of structural violence. Peace psychology has increasingly been geared towards the wider, structural issues that need to be addressed in order to achieve positive peace, and—following Galtung's (1990) articulation of *cultural violence*, has begun to focus on 'those aspects of culture … that can be used to sustain or legitimize direct or structural violence' (Galtung, 1990, p. 291). This can be seen, for instance, through the development of work that has sought to build *cultures of peace* (e.g. Anderson & Christie, 2001; de Rivera, 2004, 2008). In addressing itself to these tasks, peace psychology has developed as a conceptually and methodologically eclectic field that prioritises the goals of overcoming violence and working towards peace (Christie et al., 2001).

As Christie (2006) notes, as an eclectic and inter-disciplinary field, peace psychology is marked by a large degree of overlap with the related fields of political psychology and social psychology. However, as Vollhardt and Bilali (2008) have argued, whilst there is a great deal of research in social psychology that can be characterized as being oriented towards peace, it has not always been the case that social psychologists have framed their research explicitly in this way. Moreover, whilst Vollhardt and Bilali outline myriad potential and actual examples of what they describe as 'social psychological peace research', they do not consider discursive approaches. This perhaps reflects the split within social psychology (see, for example, Rijsman & Stroebe, 1989) following the so-called crisis of the 1960s–1970s (Faye, 2012), which was effectively resolved by the development of two parallel streams of social psychology, one rooted in experimental-cognitivist paradigms, the other in more interpretivist-qualitative approaches. Whilst peace psychology is characterized by a greater methodological and conceptual eclecticism than much of psychology (Bretherton & Law, 2015; Opotow & Luke, 2013; Vollhardt & Bilali, 2008), there has nevertheless been a much greater interchange with the broadly experimental-cognitive tradition, which has remained dominant in North America.

This has begun to change, with consideration of discursive psychology in Bretherton and Law's (2015) overview of research methods in peace psychology, and Karlberg's (2012) entry on discourse theory in Christie's (2012) *Encyclopedia of Peace Psychology*. Similarly, my own initial sketch of the possibilities of a critical discursive peace psychology (Gibson, 2011) highlighted the potential for cross-pollination between discursive and peace psychology. The present volume represents a continuation of this process, which in drawing together a range of chapters by discursive psychologists engaged in the study of issues relating to direct and structural violence aims more fully than has been attempted before to map out the potential for a discursive psychology of peace and conflict. In order to begin this process, let me now turn to providing a fuller overview of discursive psychology itself.

Discursive Psychology

Discursive psychology (hereafter sometimes DP) is a diverse and complex field characterized—as all fields are—by its own internal debates, divisions, and disagreements. Some may be reluctant to describe it as a singular 'field' at all. Others may prefer to conceive of it in terms of a particular perspective or approach that can be brought to bear within the wider field of psychology, and its various sub-fields (e.g. social psychology, health psychology, peace psychology). For readers new to DP, this can be somewhat bewildering, especially given the range of fundamental challenges that DP presents to what might be described as more conventional ways of thinking about the subject matter of psychology.

My view is that we can distil from all these debates about discursive psychology two broad ways in which the term itself is used. First, discursive psychology is often used to refer to a specific form of discursive approach within psychology that has developed directly from the early work of Potter and Wetherell (1987), but which draws much more heavily on the related tradition of conversation analysis (Sacks, 1995; Schegloff, 2007). This is particularly closely associated with the work of Edwards and Potter (e.g. 1992), and focuses on the way in which psychological matters are made relevant in, oriented to, and managed in discourse. A second usage of the term is somewhat looser and refers to a whole range of perspectives that, whilst they cohere together in having a central concern with the discursive constitution of reality and are focussed on issues that have typically been conceived as falling within the disciplinary purview of psychology, take rather different positions on some key philosophical and analytic issues. These would include discursive psychology in the first sense identified here, critical discursive psychology (e.g. Parker, 2015; Wetherell, 1998), rhetorical psychology (Billig, 1991, 1996), Foucauldian discourse analysis (e.g. Willig, 2008) and, simply, discourse analysis (Potter & Wetherell, 1987). This picture is further complicated by the existence of a range of perspectives beyond psychology that go by the name of discourse analysis (e.g. Brown & Yule, 1983) or critical discourse analysis (e.g. Fairclough, 2013), and related perspectives on which discursive psychological approaches have drawn, but which are not equivalent to them (e.g. conversation analysis; ethnomethodology). To avoid over-complicating matters, let me therefore set out some considerations that might be seen as foundational to any attempt to begin to grasp the discursive psychological approach.

To do this, I will return to Potter and Wetherell's (1987) original statement of the discourse analytic approach in psychology. To be sure, both these authors have subsequently moved to occupy slightly different positions from that which they jointly articulated in this classic book, but equally the core elements of the position they outlined can be seen to underpin much of the work done under the banner of discursive psychology to this day. In particular, their outlining of the constructive, functional, and variable nature of discourse is fundamental to an appreciation of the way in which this approach has challenged some long-held assumptions within psychology.

Discourse as constructive: Discursive psychology is a social constructionist approach that emphasizes the importance of studying how people—in a whole range of contexts—go about their business, and in so doing how they *construct* the world. This follows in part from the conceptual arguments advanced by scholars such as Kenneth Gergen (e.g. 1999, 2001) and John Shotter (e.g. 1993), but DP foregrounds the empirical working through of the implications of such arguments to a much greater extent than some other varieties of constructionism (Potter & Hepburn, 2008). Moreover, whereas constructionism (sometimes labelled as constructi*vism*) is sometimes taken to mean the way in which language constructs underlying mental/cognitive processes, for discursive psychologists the psychological is something that is invoked, made relevant for, and attended to in discourse, rather than something that exists apart from, behind, or as a product of discourse.

Discourse can be understood as constructive in two broad senses. First, discourse is constructed from the available words, metaphors, and broad patterns of description (sometimes called interpretative repertoires; Potter & Wetherell, 1987) available to language users. Second, discourse is used to construct versions of the world, including the mental (psychological) world. Thus, rather than seeing the objects of psychological enquiry (attitudes, identities, personality, motivations, categories, memories, and so on) as standing outside of discourse, DP is interested in how these are worked up discursively, in how they become a live issue for people in the course of going about their day-to-day business.

Discourse as functional: When people use language, they do so in order to get some sort of business done. Discourse is thus *functional*, or *action-oriented*. The functions performed by discourse need not be related to any formal grammatical properties of language. For example, if I walk into a seminar room and say that 'it's rather warm in here', what may appear to be a simple statement concerning temperature may function as a request insofar as one or more of my students rises from their seat to open a window. What grammatically appears to be mere description thus *functions* as a request.

Discourse as variable: In their original statement of the discourse analytic position, Potter and Wetherell (1987) foregrounded the idea of variability. Because the constructive work done by discourse is contingent on the function being performed, and because the function may vary from context to context, empirical analysis demonstrated the variability of discourse. When I explain this to students, I use the example of telephone or social media conversations that they might have had concerning their social lives at university. One can readily imagine that different versions of, say, a particular evening out might be constructed if one is speaking to one's parents as compared with one's friends. We have no way of knowing which description is 'true', and in any case this does not matter since truth is an insufficient warrant for analytic claims. Many things might be true, but that does not determine which things will be constructed on any given occasion (Schegloff, 1972).

In summary then, for Potter and Wetherell (1987, p. 33), 'the principle tenet of discourse analysis is that function involves construction of versions, and is demonstrated by language variation'. More recently, however, the focus on variation—whilst still being important in analytic terms—has been replaced conceptually by the more fundamental idea that discourse is *situated* in particular contexts (Potter & Edwards, 2001; Potter & Hepburn, 2008). This means that the variation observed in discourse arises due to the way in which interactions are bound up with particular situations—so, for example, my statement 'it's rather warm in here' should be understood as being situated in the context of the specific interactional sequence in which it occurs, and in this respect our analytic warrant for saying that it functions as a request comes from the way in which it is oriented to by those to whom it is addressed. When a student replies by saying 'I'll open a window', this is our evidence for the claim that it functions not as a mere statement but as a request. In this respect, the initial utterance cannot be considered in isolation, but needs to be considered in context.

Moreover, this situatedness takes place at a number of levels, including at the level of the basic interactional sequence in which something is said, the broader institutional context in which the interaction takes place, or even the wider cultural/ideological context. So we might also want to explore, for example, the extent to which the institutional context of the university is made relevant for the window-opening interaction, and to do this we might look to see if the institutionally relevant identities of lecturer and student were made relevant by participants in the interaction themselves. This is not always straightforward, and there are tensions between analysts who have tended to emphasize the local-interactional context and those who have tended to emphasize more distal contexts of culture and ideology, which might allow for some 'reading in' of context even where it does not appear explicitly in the discourse of participants in an interaction themselves. These positions would therefore differ on questions such as, for example, the extent to which we would be justified in asserting the relevance of the lecturer-student power dynamics implicit in the window-opening interaction if these identities were not specifically oriented to by speakers themselves (see Schegloff, 1997, 1998; Wetherell, 1998 for a seminal debate; and see Weatherall, 2016, for a recent overview).

It is worth outlining how these conceptual arguments can be worked through in an analytic example that has particular relevance to matters of peace and conflict. The example deals with issues that might typically be understood in terms of attitudes to war, and in this respect I will highlight how we might re-specify some of the assumptions that can be identified in the psychological study of attitudes (Potter, 1998). This should not be taken to indicate that discursive psychology is uniquely well suited to exploring matters typically conceived of in terms of attitudes rather than other psychological constructs. Examples abound of DP work in relation to a whole range of psychological phenomena, such as categorization (e.g. Edwards, 1991), memory (e.g. Middleton & Edwards, 1990), social representations (e.g. Potter & Edwards, 1999; Gibson, 2012b); attribution (e.g. Antaki, 1994; Edwards & Potter, 1993), prejudice (e.g. Augoustinos & Every, 2007), identity (e.g. Antaki, Condor, & Levine, 1996; Antaki & Widdicombe, 1998), emotion (e.g. Edwards, 1999; Wetherell, 2012), social influence (e.g. Gibson, 2013; Hepburn & Potter, 2011), repression (e.g. Billig, 1999), scripts and schemas (e.g. Edwards, 1994). Rather, in providing this extended example, the aim is to provide a more detailed orientation both to how DP differs from some of the standard assumptions taken by psychology, and how the position outlined above is not simply arrived at through a conceptual analysis, but through empirical analyses of specific materials.

The extract below is taken from a study of televised political debates concerning whether or not the UK should take military action against Iraq in 2003 (Gibson, 2012a). The specific stretch of talk to be examined is taken from an episode of the British Broadcasting Corporation's *Question Time* programme, broadcast on 13th February 2003. Each episode of *Question Time* features a panel of around five politicians and other commentators who discuss questions relating to topical political issues posed by members of the studio audience. In this extract, we see the chair,

David Dimbleby (DD), invite a question from an audience member (A7), and then begin the discussion by inviting the columnist Simon Heffer (SH) to speak[1]:

```
 1 DD le-t let's move on let's move on to that
 2 subject a question from ((name deleted))
 3 please
 4 (.)
 5 A7 er if Hans Blix says tomorrow that er (.)
 6 Iraq is in material breach of Resolution
 7 one four four one (.hh) would the panel
 8 support a U S led invasion (.h) or the
 9 Franco-German inspection plan
10  DD Simon Heffer
11 (1.0)
12  SH well I'm not a war monger (.) but we have
13  to accept that for (.h) twelve years (.)
14  Saddam Hussein has been taking the mickey
15  (.) out of (.) the western (.) alliance
16  that defeated him in 1991 (.hh) there was a
17  specific (.) peace treaty at that stage we
18  (.) the alliance stopped (.) um fighting in
19  Iraq (.) in return in part for him
20  disarming (.) and he has refused to do
21  that and there have been sporadic bombings
22  of Iraq in (.h) retaliation for his refusal
23  to do it (.hh) if the (h) western powers
24  are to have any (.h) moral authority >an'
25  that is a very< tall order (.h) that
26  authority has to consist in part (.) of
27  the alliance being able to enforce (.h)
28  that peace treaty (.) it has to be able to
29  say look you cannot go on indefinitely (.h)
30  taking the mickey out of us you can't go on
31  concealing weapons refusing to (.) ah
32  cooperate with our inspectors (.) ah you
33  can't go on terrorising your own people er
34  against cooperating with these inspectors
35  (.h) and (.) reluctantly I think that if
36  he is going to (.hh) er refuse to do that
37  and Doctor Blix tomorrow is going to say
38  that they're in breach of Resolution one
39  four four one (.) then (.) after twelve
40  years (.) and no one can accuse us of doing
41  this hastily or impatiently (.) after
42  twelve years and I think (.) reluctantly we
43  have to take (.hh) force (.) against him
44  (.) ah I hope concentrating purely on
45  military targets and er (.h) not civilian
```

---

[1] The transcript uses the transcription conventions developed by Gail Jefferson (e.g. 2004). These conventions, typically labelled *Jeffersonian*, were originally developed for use in conversation analysis, but have increasingly been used by many—but by no means all—discursive psychologists. An overview of the transcription conventions can be found in the Appendix.

```
46 targets at all (.) but we have to go in
47 and make our will known that that treaty
48 will be enforced
```

What we see in this extract is a very careful articulation of an argument in favour of taking military action in Iraq. Heffer begins his turn by disclaiming the identity of 'war monger', and goes on to construct his argument in such a way that the military action is framed as an unfortunate necessity, placing the responsibility for this on Saddam Hussein, and working through the details of the case for war. Notably, however, in his own terms he does not argue for *war* but for the enforcement of a peace treaty. It is useful to set out more systematically how he does this in relation to the key concepts of construction, function, and situation.

Construction: When psychologists measure attitudes to war (or indeed, to anything), they typically use a scale of some sort. This involves an attitude object (e.g. war) and a numeric evaluative scale (e.g. 1 = strongly disagree; 2 = agree, and so on). This entails the separation of the attitude object from the dimension of judgement. As Potter and Wetherell (1987) observed, however, when we explore how evaluations are done in discourse such a separation rarely takes place, and instead the evaluation is *built into* the way in which the object is constructed. In our example, therefore, it is notable that, even before Heffer speaks, the terms of the question on lines 5–9 carry with them an evaluative position. The audience member provides the panel with two options: 'a US led invasion' or 'the Franco-German inspection plan'. Consider hypothetical alternative ways of framing the terms of this question. The speaker could have said 'a US led *liberation*' or 'the Franco-German *appeasement* plan' (elsewhere in the corpus of data from which this example is taken, other speakers did indeed provide such alternative glosses on the respective options; see Gibson, 2012b).

Subsequently, when Heffer outlines his position, he constructs the action of which he is in favour not as *war*, nor as *military action* or *intervention*, but rather as *the enforcement of a peace treaty*. He sets this up on lines 16–20 by invoking a 'specific peace treaty' that came into force following the 1991 Gulf War which set certain conditions on Hussein (i.e. 'disarming'). Heffer then proceeds to outline Hussein's refusal to comply with the terms of this treaty in a way that places the responsibility for this squarely on Hussein himself, with the 'western powers' having being patient over a significant period of time (lines 13 & 42: 'twelve years'), meaning that 'no one can accuse us of doing this hastily or impatiently' (lines 40–41). The action is thus to be undertaken 'reluctantly', and—importantly—is not *war*, but is to 'make our will known that that treaty will be enforced' (lines 47–48; see Gibson, 2012a, for a fuller analysis).

We could try and work out what Heffer's *real* attitude to war is, or perhaps his attitude to this specific war; and to do that we might suggest using the sort of scale that is common in peace-psychological research that studies attitudes to war (e.g. Cohrs & Moschner, 2002; Cohrs, Moschner, Maes, & Kielmann, 2005; Saucier et al., 2018; Sundberg, 2014). However, to do this would involve selecting the terms of the object(s) to be evaluated ourselves, and we would thus miss all the delicate constructive work that Heffer does here. For discursive psychologists, therefore, scaling techniques represent the outcome of a process of construction undertaken by researchers, which necessarily obscures the constructive work that speakers do in the course of formulating evaluations on a routine basis. The question is, quite simply, why would we want to design our research in such a way as to miss all this?

Function: If attitude scales typically neglect the constructive work done by speakers formulating evaluations, they also miss the functional nature of such evaluations. If we focus on Heffer's initial statement, 'I'm not a war monger' (line 12), we might say that this is a good example of an attitudinal statement. He makes clear where he stands in terms of what the literature would consider to be his general attitude to war—he is not, typically, inclined to be in favour of war. However, this misses the *function* that this statement performs in the context of his argument as a whole. As a disclaimer (Hewitt & Stokes, 1975), 'I'm not a war monger but' functions to deny that he is pre-disposed to favour military solutions to international disputes, and in particular to ward off the potential accusation that he may be pursuing war with an unseemly, irrational haste. Similarly, the careful construction of his position as one that is taken reluctantly further functions to anticipate and ward off potential accusations of undue haste. Thus, when people make evaluative statements they are always *doing* something; the problem with traditional techniques of studying attitudes is that the thing people are doing when they indicate their evaluation of something is filling in a questionnaire, an activity that is disconnected from the business of everyday life, except insofar as filling in questionnaires has itself become a particular activity to be found in everyday life.

This points to a further key concern of DP, which is in the way in which discourse is oriented to deal with *dilemmas of stake and interest* (Edwards & Potter, 1992). Heffer's disclaimer anticipates the possibility that his position may lead to accusations of warmongering, and in so doing he attends to his stake in the debate. If he can be characterized as someone who is habitually in favour of war, as someone who has an *interest* in seeing a military solution to this particular problem of international relations, his argument can be more readily dismissed. It is in this sense, therefore, that his initial disclaimer, and the subsequently more elaborate discursive work through which he constructs his position as reluctant, can be understood as attending to matters of stake and interest.

Situation: Heffer's argument is situated in a number of ways. First, it is important to note that the most obvious candidate for what psychologists would typically see as an unambiguous statement of his attitudinal position ('I'm not a war monger') is situated in the context of an argument in favour of military action (or, to use Heffer's own terms, *the enforcement of a peace treaty*). If we abstract the attitudinal statement from this context, we thus miss the important rhetorical work that it does in warding off potential accusations of being overly eager to press for military action. In this respect, the fundamentally rhetorical nature of discourse can be highlighted (Billig, 1991, 1996; Potter, 1996).

Heffer's argument is also situated in a specific institutional context: that of the conventions of the televised political debate in general, and of *Question Time* in particular. In very broad terms, the different roles on *Question Time* carry with them very different entitlements to speak. David Dimbleby, as chair, is able to manage the allocation of speaking turns, as he does on lines 1–3 by inviting an audience member to pose a question, and on line 10 by inviting Simon Heffer to respond. But Dimbleby, in a manner similar to news anchors and others in analogous positions (Clayman, 1988), is typically careful to avoid being heard as articulating *his own views* and thus maintains a neutral footing. Audience members are allowed to pose questions of the panel, as on lines 5–9 here, and on other occasions are allowed to contribute to the debate. But audience members' speaking turns are typically much shorter than the turns allocated to panellists, who are allowed to speak at greater length on the subjects under discussion. The panellists are introduced with reference to their specific *category entitlement* to speak on topical political issues (e.g. Heffer was introduced as a 'historian and columnist for the Daily Mail'). Thus speakers are not free to articulate their evaluations in any straightforward sense, but rather they are enabled and constrained in doing so by the specific institutional structure of the context in which they are speaking, and which they contribute to reproducing through their very participation in it.

Heffer's argument is also situated in the context of a debate that we can understand as operating on at least two levels: first, there is the explicit debate within the television studio in which his arguments are addressed at (anticipated) counter-arguments from fellow panellists as well as members of the studio audience; second his arguments also need to be understood as being addressed to the wider television audience who are what Goffman (1981) terms *ratified overhearers*. In this respect, his discourse is shaped not only in response to, and for the benefit of, those immediately co-present, but also for the imagined audience-at-home who are observers of, and at least potential participants in, the broader debate that was going on at the time concerning the appropriateness of military action. He thus not only presents himself as a reasonable and reluctant advocate of military action for the purpose of managing the local interactional concerns of the television studio, but for the purpose of persuading the wider audience of the necessity of intervention.

This stands in stark contrast to the more typical way in which psychologists have tended to conceive of, and to study, attitudes. The scaling techniques that are typically used to study attitudes effectively design out any possibility of attending to the *constructive* work done by speakers in formulating evaluations because the terms in which attitudes can be expressed are set by the researchers. The *functional* nature of evaluative statements is neglected as participants responding to attitude scales are doing little more than performing the function of completing a survey, an activity that they will have, at best, only a minimal stake in. Similarly, when we think of the *situation* of much psychological research, it would not be unfair to characterise it as being situated simply in the context of participating in psychological research. Thus, it is more typical for psychologists to see people's everyday activities as a potential obstacle and thus seek to abstract people from the world in which they are ordinarily located. In contrast, discursive psychology seeks to explore people's practices in the context of their occurrence. Rather than seeking to abstract some hypothetical essence of an activity such as evaluating, persuading, blaming, and so on, DP thus seeks to explore how these activities are accomplished in the course of ordinary activity. This is not, incidentally, a matter of simply arguing that a qualitative approach is preferable to more statistically oriented research; one of the key debates in DP in recent years has centred around the over-reliance on interviews in some qualitative research (e.g. Griffin, 2007; Potter & Hepburn, 2005, 2007, 2012; Rapley, 2016), and whilst interviews are still used widely in discursive research, there is a well-developed critique of the practice of exploring people's *accounts* of their lives rather than exploring how life itself is lived. Instead, this issue concerns the extent to which, if we see practices as fundamentally bound up with the contexts in which they are situated, why would we seek to study those practices as divorced from their context?

This necessarily brief and partial analytic example hopefully provides the beginnings of an orientation to the approach taken by discursive psychologists. Much more could be said, and it should be noted that, as indicated above, there are different shades of discursive psychological analysis. For some my approach may pay insufficient attention to the detail of the turn-by-turn unfolding of the interaction; for others, I may stick too closely to the text when I should be moving outwards into the realms of culture and ideology. I could, of course, provide alternative analyses of this example, or perhaps attempt a more fuller, integrated analysis, but in the hope that what little I have provided here has served to whet the appetite, let me instead allow the contributors to the volume to take up the baton and develop their own analyses of their own analytic materials. I will therefore now conclude this introductory chapter by providing an overview of the contributions that follow.

Structure of the Book

The book is organized into four broad sections. The first focuses on what we might loosely term interpersonal and intergroup conflicts, though we should be careful to note that the boundaries between these should not be seen as absolute. Incidents of domestic violence might, for example, be seen as interpersonal in that they are typically between two people, with one seeking to exert power over, and use violence against, another. However, the inevitably gendered nature of such interpersonal violence highlights the extent to which conflicts between individuals can often be traced to wider issues of intergroup conflict and ideology. Indeed, the very assertion of a conflict as being interpersonal should in itself be seen as a political act, with the suggestion that an episode of violence can be understood in purely interpersonal terms functioning to individualize and depoliticize the violence.

In Chap. 2, Elizabeth Stokoe considers a form of conflict that has only rarely been the subject of sustained attention: disputes between neighbours. Stokoe argues that whilst such disputes have been studied only infrequently, they allow us to explore one of the fundamental relationships underpinning social life: that between people who live in close proximity to one another. Stokoe outlines findings from her studies of telephone calls to mediation services for such disputes, and shows how a number of interactional strategies used by call-takers can lead callers either closer to, or further away from, agreeing to sign up for mediation. These findings have important implications for practice, and in this respect Stokoe concludes with an overview of her path-breaking Conversation Analytic Role-play Method (CARM), an approach to communication training that emphasises the value of using real-life examples of interaction as the basis for training, rather than the highly artificial role-playing exercises that are commonly used in professional training.

If Stokoe's chapter shows the potential applications of a micro-interactional focus informed by conversation analysis, in Chap. 3 Alison J. Towns and Peter J. Adams outline a more macro-oriented approach informed by a Foucauldian perspective. Towns and Adams provide an overview of their work on discourse and domestic violence, highlighting the ways in which the justifications used by men who perpetrate violence against women function to perpetuate gendered forms of direct and structural violence. Concentrating on a single extended example, Towns and Adams draw attention to two broad discourses that function to reproduce domestic violence: a 'colonizing' discourse, in which a violent male's version of interpersonal relationships comes to *colonize* the way in which a woman makes sense of her own existence; and a 'natural order' discourse, in which male power (and male abuse of power) over women comes to be naturalized—as being just the way the world is.

In Chap. 4, Simon Goodman and Bethany Perry provide a DP analysis of political speeches concerning the debate over gun control in the USA. Focussing on speeches by President Barack Obama and Wayne LaPierre of the National Rifle Association, Goodman and Perry highlight the way in which both speakers frame their arguments in terms of protection: For Obama, gun control is a matter of protecting children, whereas for LaPierre, opposing gun control is a matter of protecting freedom. Their analysis highlights the extent to which debates over increased restrictions on gun ownership not only involve contestation over the desirability or otherwise of gun control itself, but also involve debates over psychological matters. For example, Goodman and Perry show that whereas Obama constructs the motives of those who have taken steps to introduce gun controls as laudable, and indeed frames them as acting against their own self-interest, LaPierre constructs them as opportunistic and as being motivated by self-interest. Similarly, the debates revolve around questions of identity; specifically around what it is to be American. Obama constructs compassion and a desire to protect children who may be victims of gun violence as something that all Americans will identify with, and in linking this to attempts to introduce legislation aimed at restricting gun ownership, works up gun control itself as something that all Americans will be able to identify with. By contrast, LaPierre draws on notions of freedom—particularly as enshrined in the US constitution—in order to frame gun ownership as an inalienable right, and thus to position legislative restrictions on gun ownership as fundamentally incompatible with American identity.

In Chap. 5, Mick Finlay considers the way in which group members discredit opponents *within* their own group. Finlay highlights how conflict relies not only on the construction of distinctions between an in-group and an outgroup, but also on distinctions at the intragroup level between the 'good', 'genuine', and/or 'true' representatives of the group, and those other group members characterised as an obstacle and/or as 'enemies within'. Indeed, Finlay shows that this intragroup distinction is itself an intergroup distinction in that a further intergroup conflict is constructed within a group that is involved in intergroup conflict at a higher level. Finlay maps out some of the discursive strategies through which these distinctions are constructed, and focuses in particular on a distinction between 'mild' and 'strong' discrediting practices. Whereas the former constructs one's in-group opponents as misguided and/or deceived, and ultimately as less accountable for their position, the latter involves more overt attempts to frame opponents as actively disruptive and intentionally subversive.

The second section focuses specifically on what we might loosely describe as intractable and international *military* conflicts. Again, we should be cautious of making too hard-and-fast a distinction: many of these can, for example, also be understood in terms of intergroup conflict. However, in framing the section in this way I want to signal the extent to which these chapters are dealing with contexts that have not typically been foregrounded by discursive psychologists, and the key unifying feature of these is that they deal with conflicts that are of a specifically *military* nature.

In Chap. 6, Chris McVittie and Rahul Sambaraju explore the discursive construction of peace and conflict in the context of the Palestine-Israeli conflict. Drawing on classic discursive critiques of psychological models of categorization, they argue for the traditional analytic aim of codifying peace and conflict (e.g. Galtung, 1969) to be re-specified by attending to the ways in which social actors themselves (in this case, Palestinian and Israeli political leaders) discursively construct certain actions and events in terms of either peace or conflict. Efforts at conflict resolution should therefore focus less on trying to establish what actually would constitute 'peace' in any absolute sense, and instead take into account the flexible and action-oriented nature of 'peace' (and conflict) discourse.

In Chap. 7, Dávid Kaposi explores British conservative newspapers' coverage of the first Gaza War of 2008–2009. Kaposi consider the ways in which two 'quality' newspapers—*The Times* and *The Daily Telegraph*—which are generally considered to be sympathetic towards Israel—construct the nature of the war. Whereas *The Daily Telegraph* was unequivocally pro-Israel from the outset, *The Times* initially offered a potentially more nuanced position. In particular, Kaposi's analysis draws attention to the way in which a distinction between *ius ad bellum* (the legality of war) and *ius in bello* (legality in war) is constructed by *The Times* in order to manage an apparent tension between support for the war itself, with the raising of potentially critical comments of the conduct of the war. However, just at the point at which criticism of Israel's actions appear to be possible, Kaposi shows how *The Times'* editorial line shifts to a position much more akin to *The Daily Telegraph's*, which involves the construction of both Hamas and 'liberal' critics of Israel as being beyond rationality, and thus as being unworthy of any attempt at engagement other than with the aim of military defeat. It is through such constructions that the intractable nature of the Israeli-Palestinian conflict is thus perpetuated. In outlining this analysis, Kaposi also raises some critical points for consideration for discursive psychologists, particularly around the relationship between discourse, truth, and morality.

In Chap. 8, Joseph Burridge focuses on the core DP concern with how speakers and writers manage dilemmas of stake and interest (Edwards & Potter, 1992). Analysing data from UK media and parliamentary debates on the invasion of Iraq in 2003, Burridge explores how the categories of 'pacifist' and 'warmonger' are invoked in attempts to disqualify opponents as 'interested'—as having pre-existing motivations to be either for or against the war, and therefore as not having being persuaded solely by the facts of the matter. These categorisations were, in turn, resisted: those arguing against war oriented to the problematic status of pacifism, emphasizing that they were open to the use of force when necessary, but that the present context was not such an occasion; whilst those arguing for war emphasized that they were *not* warmongers, but rather had come reluctantly to the conclusion that war was necessary. Indeed, Burridge argues that when those arguing against military intervention level the accusation of warmongering at their opponents, they actually make things *easier* for them. The accusation that one is a warmonger—that one is dispositionally inclined to favour war, and/or that one has rushed to war with unseemly haste—is relatively easy for those favouring military action to rebut by emphasizing the patient, evidence-based approach that one has taken. In this respect, Burridge's analysis provides some useful suggestions for those engaging in such debates, as well as raising the question of how best to rehabilitate the ideology of pacifism in public discourse.

In Chap. 9, Kyoko Murakami considers the implications of taking a discursive approach to reconciliation. Exploring a narrative from an interview with a former prisoner of war, Murakami considers how perspectives that have considered the psychological processes involved in reconciliation at the individual level might be augmented by an approach which highlights the dialogical production and repro-duction of reconciliation. Drawing on conceptual and analytic resources from posi-tioning theory and narrative analysis, as well as discursive psychology, Murakami shows how reconciliation is performed in the storying of the narrator's experience of seemingly mundane events from his post-war life.

Section three explores a specific—but hugely significant—consequence of both direct and structural violence: the movement of people across territories. Whether officially classified as refugees fleeing direct violence, or as migrants seeking an alternative to structural inequalities, population movement has become ever more contentious in recent years, with the ongoing 'refugee crisis' (Goodman, Sirriyeh, & McMahon, 2017) in Europe being a particularly acute example of the scale of human tragedy involved, and of the difficulties that political leaders seem to have in identifying and enacting effective solutions.

In Chap. 10, Steve Kirkwood and Simon Goodman review discursive psycho-logical research on refugees. In considering the ways in which refugees construct their own position, Kirkwood and Goodman highlight a dilemma whereby refugees orient to the difficulties of appearing to be either too happy or too unhappy in their host country. If they appear to be doing very well and enjoying a good standard of living, they risk being characterised as economically motivated; by contrast, if they appear to be too critical of their treatment by their host country, they risk appearing ungrateful. Turning to examine the way in which refugees are constructed by both the media and the host population, Kirkwood and Goodman map out the ways in which refugees are constructed as a threat. They highlight three different types of threat construction: Refugees as posing an economic threat; refugees as posing a criminal and/or terrorist threat; and refugees as posing a threat to community cohesion. Across the discourse of both refugees and the host population, Kirkwood and Goodman highlight how racism is seemingly made to disappear, with refugees orienting to the delicacy of being heard to accuse members of the host population of being racist, and members of the host population themselves constructing racism as being restricted to an extreme minority. Thus, the more subtle ways in which refugees are constructed as problematic are normalised, and Kirkwood and Goodman conclude by suggesting that—ironically—it is the construction of refugees as threatening 'our' peace that ultimately makes it difficult for refugees to find the peace that they seek.

In Chap. 11, Martha Augoustinos, Clemence Due, and Peta Callaghan explore the ways in which asylum seekers are dehumanized by the media. Focussing on the case of Australia, they show how media constructions of asylum seekers constitute them as *homo sacer*; as existing in a state of exception, outside the law, and therefore as subject to whatever measures the state judges to be appropriate. In constructing asylum seekers as less-than, or other-than, human, Augoustinos et al. argue that the media contributes to the creation of an environment in which the idea that asylum seekers can be treated in dehumanizing ways has become increasingly normalised. Thus, the construction of asylum seekers as existing in a 'state of exception' outside the law functions to legitimate both direct and structural violence towards those who are fleeing conflict.

These themes are explored further in Chap. 12, in which Lia Figgou, Martina Sourvinou and Dimitra Anagnostopoulou analyse the way in which a sense of 'crisis' has been constructed in relation to the reception of refugees in Europe in recent years. Using data from Greek parliamentary debates, Figgou and colleagues consider the way in which politicians' mobilization of 'crisis', and the attendant ways in which they sought to manage accountability and attribute blame, constituted the situation as being outside of the norm; as literally *extra*ordinary. Again drawing upon the idea of the 'state of exception', Figgou and colleagues argue that 'crisis' narratives highlight the extent to which structural violence is built into international socio-economic systems.

In Chap. 13, Antonis Sapountzis and Maria Xenitidou consider legal frameworks that function to constrain citizenship rights of migrants as forms of structural violence. Focussing on the case of Greece, which introduced a new law concerning the process through which immigrants would be eligible to apply for Greek citizenship in 2010, Sapountzis and Xenitidou provide an overview of their findings from an interview study with both Greek nationals and immigrants. They note a dilemma between making Greek citizenship contingent upon an ineffable sense of connection to Greece, or feelings of 'Greekness', whilst nevertheless not being seen to be depriving migrants of the rights needed to function in Greek society on a day-to-day basis. Sapountzis and Xenitidou's analysis shows how their participants—both members of the Greek majority and immigrants—construct citizenship as *more than* merely a technical process of meeting certain legal requirements. This allows for an essentialized sense of citizenship as requiring *Greekness* to remain intact.

In section four, we turn to explore some of the conceptual issues raised through a consideration of the intersection of discursive and peace psychology. For example, the extent to which *that which is not said* can be incorporated within the purview of discursive psychological analysis is considered, as are the tensions between discursive psychology and the ethnomethodological tradition from which it draws. The final two chapters also consider the important issue of the extent to which analysis of the visual can be built into discursive analyses of peace-psychological issues.

In Chap. 14, Cristian Tileagă explores attempts at reconciliation through the explicit construction of collective memory, a key process through which positive peace can be promoted. Using the specific example of the Tismăneanu Report into Romania's Communist past, Tileagă focuses in particular on what he terms *social practices of avoidance*: the ways in which an emphasis upon certain aspects of the Romanian Communist regime entails the neglect, or avoidance, of other elements. For example, in framing Communism as something *other*, associated with the Soviet Union and therefore non-Romanian, the specifically *Romanian* nature of Romanian Communism is avoided. Communism can thus be understood in the collective memory as something that was *done to* Romania rather than being Romanian; as something perpetrated by the other, rather than being something in which 'we' were complicit.

In Chap. 15, Kevin McKenzie draws on ethnomethodology to interrogate what he argues is the way in which the distinction between direct and structural violence maps onto the classic distinction between agency and structure. Drawing on his research with humanitarian aid workers in Israel-Palestine, McKenzie explores how this distinction is made relevant by social actors in the course of accounting for their activities in relation to matters of peace and conflict, in much the same way as it has been highlighted in peace psychology. His analysis shows how the relationship between efforts aimed at ameliorating the direct effects of conflict and attempts at political action aimed at effecting change at the structural level is managed by participants themselves in the process of accounting for the moral status of aid work. The way in which they do this varies—for some, the possibility of political/structural change is framed as a warrant for aid work, whereas for others humanitarian work is treated as a necessary pre-condition to positive (i.e. structural) peace.

In Chap. 16, Jovan Byford considers the role of images in discursive psychological analysis, arguing for a movement from studying talk *about* images to the study of the communicative functions of images in their own right. Drawing on the long-standing discursive psychological concern with emotion discourse, Byford explores the powerful images of Alan Kurdi, a dead child washed up on the beaches of Turkey during the European 'refugee crisis' in 2015. Identifying the ways in which these images represented a recognisable genre of photo-journalism, Byford argues that the analysis of discourse should not restrict itself to the analysis of words: 'Focusing simply on what participants *say* about an image leads us to miss the complex dynamic by which that image became visible to them, and instituted as something worth talking about.'

In Chap. 17, Laura Kilby and Henry Lennon present a multi-modal critical discourse analysis of the cartoon that appeared on the front cover of the 'survivors' issue' of the French satirical magazine, *Charlie Hebdo*, published in the aftermath of the mass murder of 12 people at the magazine's offices in January 2015. In providing a detailed analysis of the meanings woven into a single image, Kilby and Lennon go some way beyond the parameters of much discursive psychology, but in so doing they raise fundamental questions about the extent to which discursive psychology can and should be expanded into the visual realm. Such analyses are necessarily more difficult to warrant with reference to endogenous features of the text itself, but equally to neglect the non-textual is to neglect an important part of the way in which meaning is constructed. Moreover, in engaging with a key aspect of visual culture, their analysis points to the significance of images in the performance of cultural violence, and ultimately to the ways in which images—as much as text—can function as the instantiation of ideological dilemmas of peace and conflict.

Finally, in Chap. 18 I draw together what I take to be some common threads in the analyses presented in the book, and highlight some potential ways forward for the development of a discursive peace psychology, as well as drawing attention to possible conceptual stumbling blocks that remain to be fully addressed. In particular, I will first consider the essentially contested nature of the objects of peace psychology, most notably 'peace' itself, and suggest that the focus on analysts' definitions of peace (and violence) might usefully be complemented by a greater concern with participants' constructions. Second, I will consider the potential for discursive peace psychology to contribute to the analysis of cultural violence (and, by extension, to the achievement of cultures of peace), as well as suggesting that a unique contribution might come in terms of the analysis of *discursive violence*. Third, I will consider the practical implications for discursive psychology, with the encounter with peace psychology encouraging a more interventionist (in the non-military sense) form of practical engagement. Fourth, I will sketch out some potential obstacles to an integration of discursive and peace psychology, focussing in particular on the incompatibilities between the structural focus of peace psychology and the post-structural orientation of discursive psychology. Fifth, and relatedly, I will suggest that a post-structural position has advantages in enabling peace psychology to overcome a residual individualism that it shares with much of the broader discipline of psychology.

Taken together, the contributions to this volume illustrate a range of empirical findings that bear directly on matters of direct, structural, and cultural violence, and highlight a range of potential ways forward for the application of discursive psychology to issues of concern to peace psychologists. It is by no means the intention that these contributions—diverse though they are—should be taken to represent an exhaustive overview of the possibilities for a discursive peace psychology. Rather, in drawing together these various analyses, it is hoped that they will act as a stimulus to further research and to the further development of practical peace initiatives that draw on the ideas of discursive psychology. In this respect, much of the work of establishing a discursive peace psychology remains to be done.

Appendix

Transcription Conventions (adapted from Hutchby & Wooffitt, 1998, *pp. vi–vii)*

(1.0)   The number in parentheses indicates a time gap to the nearest tenth of a second.

(.)   A dot enclosed in parentheses indicates a pause in the talk of less than two-tenths of a second.

[ ]   Square brackets between adjacent lines of concurrent speech indicate the onset and end of a spate of overlapping talk.

.hh   A dot before an 'h' indicates speaker in-breath. The more h's, the longer the in-breath.

hh   An 'h' indicates an out-breath. The more h's, the longer the breath.

(( ))   A description enclosed in double parentheses indicates a non-verbal activity. For example, ((pointing)). Alternatively double parentheses may enclose the transcriber's comments on contextual or other features.

-       A dash indicates the sharp cut-off of the prior word or sound.

:   Colons indicate that the speaker has stretched the preceding sound. The more the colons, the greater the extent of stretching.

!   Exclamation marks are used to indicate an animated or emphatic tone.

that   Underlined fragments indicate speaker emphasis.

° °   Degree signs are used to indicate that the talk they encompass is spoken noticeably quieter than the surrounding talk.

> <   'More than' and 'less than' signs indicate that the talk they encompass was produced noticeably quicker than the surrounding talk.

References

Anderson, A., & Christie, D. J. (2001). Some contributions of psychology to policies promoting cultures of peace. *Peace and Conflict: Journal of Peace Psychology, 7*, 173–185.

Antaki, C. (1994). *Explaining and arguing: The social organization of accounts.* London: Sage.

Antaki, C., Condor, S., & Levine, M. (1996). Social identities in talk: Speakers' own orientations. *British Journal of Social Psychology, 35*, 473–492.

Antaki, C., & Widdicombe, S. (Eds.) (1998). *Identities in talk.* London: Sage.

Augoustinos, M., & Every, D. (2007). The language of "race" an prejudice: A discourse of denial, reason, and liberal-practical politics. *Journal of Language and Social Psychology, 26*, 123–141.

Augoustinos, M., & Tileagă, C. (2012). Twenty five years of discursive psychology [Special issue]. *British Journal of Social Psychology, 51*(3), 405–412.

Avdi, E., & Georgaca, E. (2007). Discourse analysis and psychotherapy: A critical review. *European Journal of Psychotherapy and Counselling, 9*, 157–176.

Billig, M. (1991). *Ideology and opinions: Studies in rhetorical psychology.* London: Sage.

Billig, M. (1996). *Arguing and thinking: A rhetorical approach to social psychology* (2nd ed.). Cambridge: Cambridge University Press.

Billig, M. (1999). *Freudian repression: Conversation creating the unconscious.* Cambridge: Cambridge University Press.

Billig, M., & MacMillan, K. (2005). Metaphor, idiom and ideology: The search for 'no smoking guns' across time. *Discourse & Society, 16*, 459–480.

Billig, M. (2012). Undiscipline beginnings, academic success, and discursive psychology. *British Journal of Social Psychology, 51,* 413–424. https://doi.org/10.1111/j.2044-8309.2011.02086.x

Blumberg, H. H., Hare, A. P., & Costin, A. (2006). *Peace psychology: A comprehensive introduction.* Cambridge: Cambridge University Press.

Boehnke, K., Fuss, D., & Kindervater, A. (2005). Peace psychology in Germany. *Peace and Conflict: Journal of Peace Psychology, 11*, 229–237.

Bretherton, D., & Balvin, N. (Eds.). (2012). *Peace psychology in Australia.* New York: Springer.

Bretherton, D., & Law, S. F. (Eds.). (2015). *Methodologies in peace psychology: Peace research by peaceful means.* New York: Springer.

Brown, G., & Yule, G. (1983). *Discourse analysis.* Cambridge: Cambridge University Press.

Cameron, L., Maslen, R., & Todd, Z. (2013). The dialogic construction of self and other in response to terrorism. *Peace and Conflict: Journal of Peace Psychology, 19*, 3–22.

Christie, D. J. (1999). Peace studies: The multidisciplinary foundations of peace psychology. *Peace and Conflict: Journal of Peace Psychology, 5*, 95–99.

Christie, D. J. (2006). What is peace psychology the psychology of? *Journal of Social Issues, 62*, 1–17.

Christie, D. J. (Ed.). (2012). *The encyclopedia of peace psychology.* New York: Wiley.

Christie, D. J., Wagner, R. V., & Winter, D. D. (2001). *Peace, conflict, and violence: Peace psychology for the 21st century.* Englewood Cliffs, NJ: Prentice Hall.

Clayman, S. E. (1988). Displaying neutrality in television news interviews. *Social Problems, 35*, 474–492.

Cohrs, J. C., & Moschner, B. (2002). Antiwar knowledge and generalized political attitudes as determinants of attitude toward the Kosovo war. *Peace and Conflict: Journal of Peace Psychology, 8*, 139–155.

Cohrs, J. C., Moschner, B., Maes, J., & Kielmann, S. (2005). Personal values and attitudes toward war. *Peace and Conflict: Journal of Peace Psychology, 11*, 293–312.

Condor, S., Tileagă, C., & Billig, M. (2013). Political rhetoric. In L. Huddy, D. O. Sears, & J. S. Levy (Eds.), *The Oxford handbook of political psychology* (2nd ed., pp. 262–297). Oxford: Oxford University Press.

de Rivera, J. (2004). Assessing cultures of peace. *Peace and Conflict: Journal of Peace Psychology, 10*, 95–100.

de Rivera, J. (Ed.). (2008). *Handbook on building cultures of peace.* New York: Springer.

Demasi, M. (in press). Facts as social action in political debates about Great Britain and the European Union. *Political Psychology.*

Dick, P. (2013). The politics of experience: A discursive psychology approach to understanding different accounts of sexism in the workplace. *Human Relations, 66*, 645–669.

Durrheim, K. (1997). Peace talk and violence: An analysis of the power of 'peace'. In A. Levett, A. Kottler, E. Burman, & I. Parker (Eds.), *Culture, power and difference: Discourse analysis in South Africa* (pp. 31–43). London: Zed Books.

Earp, B. D., & Trafimow, D. (2015). Replication, falsification, and the crisis of confidence in social psychology. *Frontiers in Psychology, 6*, 621.

Edley, N., & Wetherell, M. (1995). *Men in perspective: Practice, power and identity.* London: Prentice Hall-Harvester Wheatsheaf.

Edwards, D. (1991). Categories are for talking: On the cognitive and discursive bases of categorization. *Theory and Psychology, 1*, 515–542.

Edwards, D. (1994). Script formulations: A study of event descriptions in conversation. *Journal of Language and Social Psychology, 13*, 211–247.

Edwards, D. (1997). *Discourse and cognition.* London: Sage.

Edwards, D. (1999). Emotion discourse. *Culture & Psychology, 5*, 271–291.

Edwards, D., & Potter, J. (1992). *Discursive psychology.* London: Sage.

Edwards, D., & Potter, J. (1993). Language and causation: A discursive action model of description and attribution. *Psychological Review, 100*, 23–41.

Fairclough, N. (2013). *Critical discourse analysis: The critical study of language* (2nd ed.). Abingdon: Routledge.

Faye, C. (2012). American social psychology: Examining the contours of the 1970s crisis. *Studies in History and Philosophy of Biological and Biomedical Sciences, 43*, 514–521. https://doi.org/10.1016/j.shpsc.2011.11.010

Finlay, W. M. L. (2018). Language and civilian deaths: Denying responsibility for causalities in the Gaza Conflict 2014. *Political Psychology, 39*, 595–609.

Fox, D., Prilleltensky, I., & Austin, S. (2009). *Critical psychology: An introduction.* London: Sage.

Galtung, J. (1969). Violence, peace, and peace research. *Journal of Peace Research, 6*, 167–191.

Galtung, J. (1990). Cultural violence. *Journal of Peace Research, 27*, 291–305.

Gavriely-Nuri, D. (2010). The idiosyncratic language of Israeli 'peace': A cultural approach to critical discourse analysis (CCDA). *Discourse & Society, 21*, 565–585.

Gergen, K. J. (1999). *An invitation to social construction.* London: Sage.

Gergen, K. J. (2001). *Social construction in context.* London: Sage.

Gibson, S. (2011). Social psychology, war and peace: Towards a critical discursive peace psychology. *Social and Personality Psychology Compass, 5*, 239–250.

Gibson, S. (2012a). 'I'm not a war monger but…': Discourse analysis and social psychological peace research. *Journal of Community and Applied Social Psychology, 22*, 159–173.

Gibson, S. (2012b). History in action: The construction of historical analogies in televised debates concerning the Iraq War. *Papers on Social Representations, 21*, 13.1–13.35.

Gibson, S. (2012c). Supporting the troops, serving the country: Rhetorical commonplaces in the representation of military service. In S. Gibson & S. Mollan (Eds.), *Representations of peace and conflict* (pp. 143–159). Basingstoke: Palgrave Macmillan.

Gibson, S. (2013). Milgram's obedience experiments: A rhetorical analysis. *British Journal of Social Psychology, 52*, 290–309.

Gibson, S. (in press). *Arguing, obeying and defying: A rhetorical perspective on Stanley Milgram's obedience experiments.* Cambridge: Cambridge University Press.

Goffman, E. (1981). *Forms of talk.* Oxford: Basil Blackwell.

Goodman, S. (2014). Developing an understanding of race talk. *Social and Personality Psychology Compass, 8*, 147–155.

Goodman, S., Sirriyeh, A., & McMahon, S. (2017). The evolving (re)categorisations of refugees throughout the "refugee/migrant crisis". *Journal of Community & Applied Social Psychology, 27*, 105–114.

Gough, B. (Ed.). (2017). *The Palgrave handbook of critical social psychology.* London: Palgrave Macmillan.

Gough, B., McFaddden, M., & McDonald, M. (2013). *Critical social psychology* (2nd ed.). Basingstoke: Palgrave Macmillan.

Griffin, C. (2007). Being dead and being there: Research interviews, sharing hand cream and the preference for analysing 'naturally occurring data'. *Discourse Studies, 9*, 246–269.

Harré, R. (1992). Introduction: The second cognitive revolution. *American Behavioral Scientist, 36*, 5–7.

Hepburn, A. (2003). *An introduction to critical social psychology.* London: Sage.

Hepburn, A., & Potter, J. (2011). Threats: Power, family mealtimes, and social influence. *British Journal of Social Psychology, 50*, 99–120.

Hewitt, J. P., & Stokes, R. (1975). Disclaimers. *American Sociological Review, 40*, 1–11.

Hodges, A., & Nilep, C. (Eds.). (2011). *Discourse, war and terrorism.* Amsterdam: John Benjamins.

Hutchby, I., & Wooffitt, R. (1998). *Conversation analysis: Principles, practices and applications.* Cambridge: Polity.

Ibáñez, T., & Íñiguez, L. (Eds.). (1997). *Critical social psychology.* London: Sage.

Jackson, R. (2005). *Writing the war on terrorism: Language, politics and counter-terrorism.* Manchester: Manchester University Press.

Jefferson, G. (2004). Glossary of transcription symbols with an introduction. In G. H. Lerner (Ed.), *Conversation analysis: Studies from the first generation* (pp. 13–31). Amsterdam: John Benjamins.

Karlberg, M. (2012). Discourse theory and peace. In D. J. Christie (Ed.), *The encyclopedia of peace psychology.* New York: Wiley.

Kiguwa, P., & Ally, Y. (2018). Constructed representations of street protest violence: Speaking violence, speaking race. *Peace and Conflict: Journal of Peace Psychology, 24,* 36–43.

Kilby, L. (2017). Social representations of peace in terrorism talk: A United Kingdom talk-radio analysis. *Peace and Conflict: Journal of Peace Psychology, 23,* 106–116.

Kroger, R. O., & Wood, L. A. (1998). The turn to discourse in social psychology. *Canadian Psychology, 39,* 266–279.

Leudar, I., Marsland, V., & Nekvapil, J. (2004). On membership categorisation: 'Us', 'them' and 'doing violence' in political discourse. *Discourse & Society, 15,* 243–266.

Lilienfeld, S. O. (2017). Psychology's replication crisis and the grant culture: Righting the ship. *Perspectives on Psychological Science, 12,* 660–664.

Locke, A. (2008). Managing agency for athletic performance: A discursive approach to the *zone. Qualitative Research in Psychology, 5,* 103–126.

MacNair, R. M. (2012). *The psychology of peace: An introduction* (2nd ed.). Santa Barbara, CA: Praeger.

Maxwell, S. E., Lau, M. Y., & Howard, G. S. (2015). Is psychology suffering from a replication crisis? What does "failure to replicate" really mean? *American Psychologist, 70,* 487–498.

McKinlay, A., & McVittie, C. (2008). *Social psychology and discourse.* Chichester: Wiley-Blackwell.

McKinlay, A., McVittie, C., & Sambaraju, R. (2012). 'This is ordinary behaviour': Categorization and culpability in Hamas leaders' accounts of the Palestinian/Israeli conflict. *British Journal of Social Psychology, 51,* 534–550.

Middleton, D., & Edwards, D. (Eds.). (1990). *Collective remembering.* London: Sage.

Miller, P. K. (2012). Arsene didn't see it: Coaching, research and the promise of a discursive psychology. *International Journal of Sports Science and Coaching, 7,* 615–628.

Montiel, C. J. (2003). Peace psychology in Asia. *Peace and Conflict: Journal of Peace Psychology, 9,* 195–218.

Montiel, C. J. (2018). Peace psychologists and social transformation: A global south perspective. *Peace and Conflict: Journal of Peace Psychology, 24,* 64–70.

Montiel, C. J., & Noor, N. M. (Eds.). (2009). *Peace psychology in Asia.* New York: Springer.

Morawski, J. G., & Goldstein, S. E. (1985). Psychology and nuclear war: A chapter in our legacy of social responsibility. *American Psychologist, 40,* 276–284.

O'Reilly, M., Kiyimba, N., & Lester, J. N. (2018). Discursive psychology as a method of analysis for the study of couple and family therapy. *Journal of Marital and Family Therapy, 44*(3), 409–425. https://doi.org/10.1111/jmft.12288.

Opotow, S., & Luke, T. J. (2013). Diverse contexts and approaches in peace psychology research. *Peace and Conflict: Journal of Peace Psychology, 19,* 1–2.

Parker, I. (2015). *Critical discursive psychology* (2nd ed.). New York: Palgrave Macmillan.

Parker, I. (1992). *Discourse dynamics: Critical analysis for social and individual psychology.* London: Routledge.

Potter, J. (1996). *Representing reality: Discourse, rhetoric and social construction.* London: Sage.

Potter, J. (1998). Discursive social psychology: From attitudes to evaluative practices. *European Review of Social Psychology, 9,* 233–266. https://doi.org/10.1080/14792779843000090

Potter, J. (2007). *Discourse and psychology* (Vols. I-III). London: Sage.

Potter, J., & Edwards, D. (1999). Social representations and discursive psychology: From cognition to action. Culture & Psychology, 5, 447–458. https://doi.org/10.1177/1354067X9954004

Potter, J. (2000). Post-cognitive psychology. *Theory & Psychology, 10,* 31–37.

Potter, J., & Edwards, D. (2001). Discursive social psychology. In W. P. Robinson & H. Giles (Eds.), *The new handbook of language and social psychology* (pp. 103–118). Chichester: Wiley.

Potter, J., & Hepburn, A. (2005). Qualitative interviews in psychology: Problems and possibilities. *Qualitative Research in Psychology, 2*, 281–307.

Potter, J., & Hepburn, A. (2007). Life is out there: A comment on Griffin. *Discourse Studies, 9*, 276–282.

Potter, J., & Hepburn, A. (2008). Discursive constructionism. In J. A. Holstein & J. F. Gubrium (Eds.), *Handbook of constructionist research* (pp. 275–293). New York: Guilford Press.

Potter, J., & Hepburn, A. (2012). Eight challenges for interview researchers. In J. F. Gubrium, J. A. Holstein, A. B. Marvasti, & K. D. McKinney (Eds.), *The Sage handbook of interview research: The complexity of the craft* (2nd ed., pp. 555–570). London: Sage.

Potter, J., & Wetherell, M. (1987). *Discourse and social psychology: Beyond attitudes and behaviour.* London: Sage.

Rapley, T. (2016). Questions of context: Qualitative interviews as a source of knowledge. In C. Tileagă & E. Stokoe (Eds.), *Discursive psychology: Classic and contemporary issues* (pp. 70–84). London: Routledge.

Rijsman, J., & Stroebe, W. (1989). The two social psychologies or whatever happened to the crisis? *European Journal of Social Psychology, 19*, 339-344. https://doi.org/10.1002/ejsp.2420190502

Sacks, H. (1995). *Lectures on conversation.* Oxford: Blackwell.

Saucier, D. A., Webster, R. J., McManus, J. L., Sonnentag, T. L., O'Dea, C. J., & Strain, M. L. (2018). Individual difference in masculine honor beliefs predict attitudes toward aggressive security measures, war, and peace. *Peace and Conflict: Journal of Peace Psychology, 24*, 112–116.

Schegloff, E. A. (2007). Sequence organization in interaction: A primer in conversation analysis (Vol. 1). Cambridge: Cambridge University Press.

Schäffner, C., & Wenden, A. L. (1995). *Language and peace.* London: Routledge.

Schegloff, E. A. (1972). Notes on a conversational practice: Formulating place. In D. Sudnow (Ed.), *Studies in social interaction* (pp. 75–119). New York: The Free Press.

Schegloff, E. A. (1997). Whose text? Whose context? *Discourse & Society, 8*, 165–187.

Schegloff, E. A. (1998). Reply to Wetherell. *Discourse & Society, 9*, 413–416.

Seedat, M., Suffla, S., & Christie, D. J. (Eds.). (2017). *Enlarging the scope of peace psychology: African and world-regional contributions.* New York: Springer.

Seymour-Smith, S. (2015). Applying discursive approaches to health psychology. *Health Psychology, 34*, 371–380.

Shotter, J. (1993). *Conversational realities: Constructing life through language.* London: Sage.

Simić, O., Volčič, Z., & Philpot, C. R. (2012). *Peace psychology in the Balkans: Dealing with a violent past while building peace.* New York: Springer.

Speer, S. A., & Stokoe, E. (Eds.). (2011). *Conversation and gender.* Cambridge: Cambridge University Press.

Stokoe, E., & Wiggins, S. (2005). Discursive approaches. In J. Miles & P. Gilbert (Eds.), *A handbook of research methods for clinical & health psychology* (pp. 161–174). Oxford: Oxford University Press.

Sundberg, R. (2014). Violent values: Exploring the relationship between human values and violent attitudes. *Peace and Conflict: Journal of Peace Psychology, 20*, 68–83.

Symon, G. (2000). Everyday rhetoric: Argument and persuasion in everyday life. *European Journal of Work and Organizational Psychology, 9*, 477–488.

te Molder, H. (2016). What happened to post-cognitive psychology? In C. Tileagă & E. Stokoe (Eds.), *Discursive psychology: Classic and contemporary issues* (pp. 87–100). Abingdon: Routledge.

Tileagă, C. (2013). *Political psychology: Critical perspectives.* Cambridge: Cambridge University Press.

Tileagă, C., & Stokoe, E. (Eds.) (2016). *Discursive psychology: Classic and contemporary issues.* London: Routledge.

Tuffin, K. (2005). *Understanding critical social psychology*. London: Sage.

Vollhardt, J. K., & Bilali, R. (2008). Social psychology's contribution to the psychological study of peace: A review. *Social Psychology, 39*, 12–25.

Weatherall, A. (2016). Interpretative repertoires, conversation analysis and being critical. In C. Tileagă & E. Stokoe (Eds.), *Discursive psychology: Classic and contemporary issues* (pp. 15–28). Abingdon: Routledge.

Wessells, M. G. (1996). A history of Division 48 (peace psychology). In D. A. Dewsbury (Ed.), *Unification through division: Histories of the Divisions of the American Psychological Association (Volume 1)* (pp. 265–298). Washington, DC: American Psychological Association.

Wetherell, M. (1998). Positioning and interpretative repertoires: Conversation analysis and post-structuralism in dialogue. *Discourse & Society, 9*, 387–412.

Wetherell, M. (2012). *Affect and emotion: A new social science understanding*. London: Sage.

Wetherell, M. (2015). Discursive psychology: Key tenets, some splits, and two examples. In I. Parker (Ed.), *Handbook of critical psychology* (pp. 315–324). Hove: Routledge.

Wetherell, M., & Edley, N. (2014). A discursive psychological framework for analysing men and masculinities. *Psychology of Men and Masculinity, 15*, 355–364.

Wetherell, M., & Potter, J. (1992). *Mapping the language of racism: Discourse and the legitimation of exploitation*. London: Harvester Wheatsheaf.

Wetherell, M., Stiven, H., & Potter, J. (1987). Unequal egalitarianism: A preliminary study of discourses concerning gender and employment opportunities. *British Journal of Social Psychology, 26*, 59–71.

Wiggins, S. (2017). *Discursive psychology: Theory, method and applications*. London: Sage.

Willig, C. (2008). *Introducing qualitative research in psychology: Adventures in theory and method* (2nd ed.). Maidenhead: Open University Press.

Part I
Interpersonal and Intergroup Conflicts

Chapter 2
How to Increase Participation in a Conflict Resolution Process: Insights from Discursive Psychology

Elizabeth Stokoe

Introduction

In this chapter, I describe the history and development of a discursive psychology project that began with research about neighbour disputes and evolved into communication training for the professionals who try to resolve such disputes. In particular, I describe how the study of encounters between members of the public and mediation services culminated in training mediators to better engage their prospective clients. The chapter will start by locating this project in the context of research on neighbour relationships and disputes, as well as discursive and interactional work on conflict in interaction. Next, I will describe the collection of the large-scale qualitative dataset that underpinned the project, including telephone calls to mediation services, environmental health services, and police interviews with arrested suspects in neighbour conflict cases. I will also outline how the data were analysed using conversation analysis (CA), in the discursive psychological (DP) tradition pioneered by Edwards (e.g. 1995; Edwards & Stokoe, 2004) and Potter (e.g. Potter & Hepburn, 2003). The chapter will report the findings from the project that showed how mediators fail and succeed to attract potential clients to mediation. I describe how research findings about what works to engage clients has underpinned national and international mediation training, using the Conversation Analytic Role-play Method (CARM). In sum, the chapter will show how discursive psychological research can have big pay-offs in terms of the impact of its findings in real-life settings that matter for people in conflict.

E. Stokoe (✉)
Loughborough University, Loughborough, UK
e-mail: E.H.Stokoe@lboro.ac.uk

© Springer Nature Switzerland AG 2018
S. Gibson (ed.), *Discourse, Peace, and Conflict*, Peace Psychology Book Series,
https://doi.org/10.1007/978-3-319-99094-1_2

The Neighbours Project

In the late 1990s, neighbour disputes became a familiar social problem and a focus for the broadcast and news media. In the United Kingdom, television schedules were populated with programmes called "Neighbours from Hell" and "Neighbours at War"; aggrieved callers spoke to radio phone-in or television chat show hosts to air their neighbour grievances; newspapers reported neighbours doing damage to each other's properties, minds, and bodies. "Neighbours from Hell" became a video game; "Neighbors from Hell" an American sitcom. Twenty years later, public discourse about toxic neighbour relationships is as buoyant as ever. However, psychologists, now as then, have been slow to try to understand this relationship. Despite the wealth of research on interpersonal relationships of all kinds—from family, romantic, workplace, and virtual relationships—there remains an absence of scholarly work on the most mundane of relationships that occur in the small routines of social life as we say "good morning" while walking to the car, up our paths or shutting our gates (Stokoe & Wallwork, 2003, p. 554). While social, community, and environmental psychologists have examined neighbour-related topics, such as people's experiences of, and attitudes toward, various aspects of their neighbourhoods, communities, and places (for an overview, see Stokoe, 2006), there remains remarkably little explication of what it means to be a "neighbour" (Painter, 2012), or how everyday neighbour relationships are managed.

It was in this context—of a gap between public and psychological discourse—that my interest in neighbour relationships and disputes was piqued. As a researcher working in the discursive psychology (DP) and conversation analytic (CA) traditions, I wanted to collect episodes of "life as it happens" (Boden, 1990); data that would pass Potter's (2002, p. 541) famous "dead social scientist test". In other words, following Garfinkel (1967), I wanted to capture episodes of social life in which neighbour disputes and relationships became the articulated concern of real people. To understand neighbour relationships, I realized that my best chance was to study them as they became somewhat public; somewhat accountable—which meant capturing disputes, rather than interaction over the garden fence. In this way, I would be able to interrogate the "seen but unnoticed" organization of social life; "the normally hidden, socially constructed conventions that are the foundations for intersubjectivity" (Goldman, 1982). For Schegloff, one of the founders of conversation analysis, the comprehensibility of "normal scenes" was illuminated "by considering disruption of them" (Schegloff, 1968, p. 1077). To this end, I began to analyse recordings of neighbour dispute documentaries, newspaper reports, and radio call-ins (Stokoe, 2003). Alongside these data, I pursued unedited, non-broadcast datasets which began with recordings of community mediation and evolved from there.

Community Mediation and Neighbour Disputes

When conflict between neighbours becomes unmanageable, external organizations may become involved, either at the request of one or both parties or at the instigation of public agencies, the courts, or the organizations themselves. For example, in the

United Kingdom (with similar options around the world), police become involved if disputants engage in criminal activities (e.g. assault, criminal damage, public order offences). One neighbour may contact environmental health services, for example, about the problematic behaviour of another (e.g. noise). They may contact a lawyer to start proceedings to legally constrain the behaviour of the other neighbour. A neighbour may call community mediation services who will then contact the other neighbour. Or housing officers may initiate contact with community mediation services on behalf of residents, with or without their explicit request to do so.

In the United Kingdom and elsewhere, no single national organization offers mediation; they are provided by a variety of services (both non-profit and commercial) with varied funding sources (local authorities, grants, charities) and staff (volunteer and paid). Mediators may pursue a variety of different training programmes, from short professional development courses, service-run to year-long postgraduate university degrees on conflict resolution, but there is no nationally recognized qualification or accreditation for mediators as there is for, say, lawyers, doctors, or teachers. As a profession and a practice, "mediator" and "mediation" are unfamiliar to most people. As we will see later, this lack of knowledge can be a problem in intake calls because people have seldom heard of the service they are being offered and do not seem to know what to expect from it.

While there is little research on neighbour disputes themselves, there is a great deal of work on mediation as a service designed to resolve disputes of all kinds. Much of the literature focuses on participants' experiences of mediation, their evaluations of mediators and the mediation process, or on mediators' reports about their strategies for (un)successful mediation (e.g. Barlow, Hunter, Smithson, & Ewing, 2017; Goldberg, 2005). Mediation research has generally been conducted via the collection of self-report data, survey responses, and/or interviews, with less attention paid to tracking the "moment-to-moment activities that shape meaning, realities, and outcomes" (Glenn & Susskind, 2010, p. 118). Some studies have, however, examined actual encounters between mediators and clients, their organizational structure, and constituent actions (e.g. Greatbatch & Dingwall, 1997; Jacobs & Aakhus, 2002; Trinder, Firth, & Jenks, 2010).

As I will show in this chapter, mediators often meet resistance from their prospective clients to get involved in mediation at all. Mediation services are impartial by design, unlike the police and other services listed above, which generally work to gather evidence against one party in the dispute and act on it (e.g. arrest or evict a neighbour; move them to another house; issue a noise abatement order). We will see that prospective clients doubt the usefulness of mediation compared to the other organizations that are more explicitly on the client's side in a conflict.

From Mediation to Pre-mediation

The research findings that were to later underpin communication training for mediators were generated in a study funded by the UK Economic and Social Research Council which explored identities and neighbour conflict (e.g. Stokoe & Edwards,

2009). As described above, the project was designed around collecting data from contexts in which neighbours might talk to one another and engage in defining what counted as a "good neighbour relationship". In addition to police-suspect investigative interviews in cases of neighbour crime, and calls into various local authority council offices, I approached community mediation services to ask if they might record encounters between mediators and clients. Although some mediators agreed, many did not. Instead, services offered to record their initial inquiry calls into their offices. For mediators, these calls were not "mediation proper", and so they were less concerned about a researcher studying them. From my perspective, the data were ideal for a study of neighbour disputes because they comprised a "naturally occurring survey" of the causes of disputes, as well as an opportunity to examine the ways that neighbour complaints were formulated (e.g.Edwards, 2005; Stokoe, 2009).

Toward the end of the project, however, my focus turned away from analysing the design of neighbour complaints and their identity features and toward the organization of initial inquiries (or "intake calls"), and, in particular, whether or not callers became clients of community mediation organizations by the end of their encounter with a mediator. Such intake calls are treated as separate from and outside of an actual mediation and have received no attention from either researchers or mediation training. But because mediation services secure funding partly on the basis of recognized need—on the size of their client base—it is crucial that mediators successfully convert callers to the service into clients of their service; into clients of mediation "proper". As Charkoudian (2010, p. 141) points out, "to justify continued public or philanthropic funds in a tight economic environment, it is incumbent on community mediation centers to demonstrate their value".

As we will see, analysis of intake calls revealed clients' doubt about the usefulness of mediation compared to other services such as going to the police, lawyers, or court; in other words, institutions that are more explicitly on the client's side in a conflict. Given that the outcome of intake calls is a bottom-line issue for mediation services, it was surprising that both research and training had focused, prior to this project, on what happens *once clients have been secured*, rather than on what happens to secure them (or not) in the first place. The project's findings were, therefore, to be of direct relevance to mediation organizations.

Project Data and Methods

The dataset for the project comprised a large corpus of audio-recorded intake calls from community mediation services (and, later, family mediation services also), all based in the United Kingdom. All participants consented to have their calls recorded for research purposes, and all names and other identifying features of the calls were anonymized. The data were transcribed using Jefferson's (2004) system for conversation analysis (CA). This transcription system includes information about the delivery of talk, such as its pacing, overlapping talk, and intonation.

The analytic approach was conversation analytic, drawing on CA's principles of turn design, action formation, and sequence organization as well as discursive psychology's compatible concerns with "the ways in which talk manages subject-object relations, or mind-world relations" and other psychological considerations such as identity and motive (Edwards, 2007, p. 31). CA examines the overall structure of interaction, in terms of its constituent actions, as well as the specifics of, and patterns in, turn design (how a turn of talk is designed to do something), turn-taking (who talks when), action formation (how actions are formed within and across turns of talk), and sequence organization (how actions are organized in a sequence) (Schegloff, 2007).

With Derek Edwards (e.g. Edwards & Stokoe, 2007) and, later, Rein Sikveland (e.g. Sikveland & Stokoe, 2016), I analysed approximately 600 audio-recorded encounters between organization mediators and the public. These intake calls to community mediation services, that is, calls from mediators to neighbours or from neighbours to mediation services, were the first point of contact between members of the public and mediation as a process. During these calls, potential clients first describe their problems and request (or receive an offer for) mediation. The mediator's job is to elicit a description of the problem from the potential client, explain what mediation is and offer mediation services to her or him, and arrange a visit between the mediator and potential client. In the next section, I will summarize the main findings of the project regarding features of calls in which callers agreed or did not agree to mediate. In the final section, I will describe how mediators were able to engage with these findings in CARM training workshops.

Identifying and Overcoming Barriers to Participation in Conflict Resolution

Conversation analysis and discursive psychology can, unlike other "qualitative" methods, identify "repetitive, uniform, typical and cohort-independent" practices (Heap, 1990, p. 46). Our qualitative yet large-scale datasets provide the basis for *naturally occurring experiments* which can generate evidence about the effectiveness or otherwise of communicative practices (Stokoe & Sikveland, 2017). In the sections that follow, I will show how certain turn designs were more likely than others to result in a positive outcome for the mediator (i.e. convert a caller into a client). By identifying endogenous features of talk (e.g. delayed or dispreferred responses), CA provides evidence of the outcomes achieved with "interactional nudges", from uncovering how customers are encouraged to pay "gift aid" on their entrance fee in an art gallery (Llewellyn, 2015) to the difference one word can make to reduce patients' unmet concerns in consultations with GPs (Heritage, Robinson, Elliott, Beckett, & Wilkes, 2007). The first section establishes a key problem for mediation services: the public do not know about them. The second shows how asking a particular question of callers results in immediate problems for the progress of calls. The third section reports on the different ways of explaining mediation that were more or less effective, and the final one shows how clients' resistance can be overcome with a particular verb selection.

"I've Just Been Given This Number"

Extract 1 (below) is from the opening of a call between a member of the public and a mediation service. The extract headings indicate the particular dataset that the extract comes from (e.g. "DC" refers to calls from a town whose first letter is D) and call number. "M" is the mediation service call-taker (often mediators themselves); "C" is the caller and potential client.

Extract 1: DC-12[1]

```
1   M:   Mediation in We̲stborough g'mo↑rning,
2        (0.6)
3   C:   Hello:: I'm ju- I've ↑just been given this numbe̲r↓
4        an' I just wanted to ta̲lk a↓bout like
5        we've got re̲ally terrible ne̲ighbours.
```

This extract contains several features that were typical of call openings to mediation services. First, despite the fact that C reports having "really terrible neighbours," the stock-in-trade for community mediation services, she did not initially intend to call a mediation service. She has, in fact, called elsewhere and "been given this number" (line 3). C does not know, therefore, that people with neighbour problems can seek out community mediation, the way that a person with a broken arm seeks out a hospital. Across the data, calls rarely started with callers requesting a service that they *already knew* about and *wanted*. Rather, they came to mediation second-hand via another organization, and there was often a match between the first organization the person called (e.g. housing association or police department) and the kind of intervention he or she sought (e.g. eviction or arrest of their neighbour).

Second, in Extract 1 we see components that suggest C's lack of knowledge of who, and what type of organization, she is calling: note the 0.6 s delay between M's institutional identification and greeting and C's response, and C's hesitant start to, and "repair" or "restart" of, her response ("I'm ju- I've just been"). Third, C formulates a *one-sided* problem: "we've got really terrible neighbours" rather than describing a dispute involving more than one party. Instead, she has *already* placed the blame with her "really terrible neighbours". This becomes relevant later in this and other calls, in which the *two-sided*, impartial approach of mediation fails to appeal to callers who perceive that they are blameless and that their neighbours are at fault, who see themselves not as participants in a conflict but as victims of other people's bad behaviour.

---

[1] In transcripts, the punctuation symbols used refer to pitch movement up (↑) and down (↓), stretching sounds (::), timed pauses to the nearest tenth of a second (e.g. 0.6), a "cut-off" sound (-), and emphasis (underlining). Full stops indicate a falling intonation; commas indicate a slightly rising intonation.

Analysis of call openings therefore revealed that mediation is an *unknown institution*. For mediators, the first barrier to participation is basic awareness of their services. The second barrier is to stop treating initial encounters with potential clients as unimportant. I mentioned earlier that, while mediators were reluctant to record actual mediation meetings, they were happier to record intake calls. This tells us something about the status of the calls in mediators' eyes: they are not worth training for; people just call for an appointment; they are not mediation "proper". Mediation openings contrasted starkly with, say, calling the doctor to make an appointment, in which people know what to do (e.g. Stokoe, Sikveland, & Symonds, 2016). Showing mediators examples like Extract 1 was something of a revelation, and the starting point for further training about what works and does not work to convert callers to clients.

Have You Tried Talking to Your Neighbour?

When members of the public call service providers and other organizations, they give a reason for the call. And a feature of any service provision is what has been called, variously, *doctorability*, *policeability*, and so on, where it is established that the reason for calling (with a problem) is fitted to the service being called upon (e.g. Heritage & Robinson, 2006; Meehan, 1989; Whalen & Zimmerman, 1990). Seeking medical attention or reporting a police emergency are situations in which resolving the problem oneself is usually beyond an ordinary person's competence. Nevertheless, people typically must establish that they are ill enough or in a sufficiently risky situation to warrant calling for help (Sacks, 1992, p. 113ff). So, for example, for a headache to be "doctorable", a patient must establish that it is sufficiently painful and of sufficient duration, and that self-help (e.g. taking over-the-counter painkillers) has failed. And it is incumbent on the doctor to offer something other than the self-help solution; that is, something more than the painkillers the patient has already used.

For a neighbour dispute to be "mediatable", we found that the relevant self-help was to "try talking to the neighbours" (Edwards & Stokoe, 2007). Callers reported that attempts at self-help failed, either because their neighbour was unwilling or unable to talk with them in a way that resolved the conflict, or because they had not tried talking for fear of making the situation worse. Either way, callers were involved in a situation *bad enough* to warrant outside intervention but, crucially, one that they presented as of their neighbours' making. Becoming enmeshed in a neighbour dispute is a delicate matter. Like in counselling or therapy, the focus in mediation is on mundane relationship matters that most people presumably handle for themselves. Reporting a relationship problem, then, can imply that the caller is the kind of person who cannot get on with others (Edwards, 2005).

To solve these problems of "mediatability" and self-help, callers typically reported problems in extreme terms, placed the blame for the problem entirely on their neighbours, and sought to get the mediator on their side. It is not surprising, then, that callers resisted using a service that is, *on principle*, not on their side, and offers a talk-based solution (Edwards & Stokoe, 2007). In Extract 2, the problems of self-help and "mediatability" are acute. After explaining her problem, M asks C what she has done to try to "resolve the issue". After explaining that she has called the environmental health services and the police, M asks C whether she has spoken to her neighbour about the problem.

Extract 2: DC-71

```
1    M:   .hhh And have you spoken to ↓he:r?
2              (1.3)
3    M:   About this,= H've you spoken to your ↓neighbor
4            abou[t it?
5    C:              [>If I< went round (.) she wouldn't live.
6                     (0.6)
7    C:   [Believe] me.
8    M:   [.tch.] HHhh >Yeh but-< bu- ha-have you actually tried
9            to speak with he:r.
10                    (0.4)
11   C:   No I have[↑n't ↓spoken to 'er]
12   M:            [ No:.  Cos   you- ]
13                 (.)
14   M:   Cos [y- cos
15   C:        [I ↑don't wanna ta:lk to 'e[r.
16   M:                                    [Yeh. .hhh u:m
17          .h all r- c'n I just really explain to you brief↓ly
18          what mediation: (.) i- how mediation wo:rks
```

Here, C offers an account that also functions as a negative response to M's question: no, she has not spoken to her neighbour because if C went "round (.) she wouldn't live". (line 5). Note also the initial delay in answering (line 2) and M's subsequent reformulation of the question (lines 3–4). At lines 8–9, M treats C's response as an insufficient or non-literal answer to her question, and repeats it once more. At line 11, C states explicitly that she has not spoken to her neighbour and offers a further account that she does not want to "talk to 'er". (lines 11, 15). It is at this point in the sequence, after C has produced such an account, that M begins to explain mediation as a *talk-based* offer of help. It is unsurprising that C does not go ahead.

We also identified three solutions to the problems of self-help and "mediatability". The first is to ensure that mediation is formulated as an activity that offers a *different* solution to the self-help already tried by callers; that is, not a "talk-based" solution. The second is to offer some affiliation with (or empathy toward) callers and display some shared understanding of the problem. The third is to not ask questions about self-help—"have you tried talking to your neighbour"—at all, thus avoiding opening up a slot for callers to say that they "do not want to talk to their neighbour". Extract 3 illustrates all three strategies:

Extract 3: EC-37

```
1    C:   Um::: .hhh an' I phon- I phoned them up an' reported it, it was
2            quite late at ni:gh," (0.3) a:nd then nobody sort- (.) again
3            nobody came rou:nd.
4    M:   Myeh: yeh.
```

```
5   C:   U::m,
6   M:   .aheh Agai:n very frustratin' for you: I s'pose you feel like
7        you- (.) you wanna se:e something being done. .hh [about it yeh,
8   C:                                                     [I do:. Ye:s.
9            (1.0)
10  M:   Mmm.
11           (0.4)
12  M:   .hhh okay, w'll do you know anything at all about us?
```

At lines 1–3, C concludes her explanation of her problem. Rather than ask a self-help question, however, or launch immediately into an explanation of mediation, M takes a different turn. First, she empathizes with C, suggesting that the situation must be "very frustratin" (line 6). The inclusion of "for you" permits M to make empathic assessments while also remaining somewhat impartial: it is frustrating for C, not M. The second part of M's turn, "I s'pose you feel like you…you wanna see something being done…about it" is also empathic, as it suggests an understanding of C's point of view. Furthermore, it prefaces M's forthcoming explanation of mediation, which begins at line 12. More precisely, it formulates C's need not for talk, but for *action*, just at the point where mediation, as the thing that C may be able to "see being done", is about to be explained and offered.

"We Don't Take Sides"

As we saw in the first analytic section, unlike telephoning one's general practice, callers to mediation services do not know what is on offer. This means that mediators, unlike GP receptionists, must explain what mediation is. I found that these explanations generally took one of two formats, and that one was more successful than the other in engaging prospective clients. Extract 4 is an example of one type of explanation.

Extract 4: HC-2

```
1   M:   What we do as a mediation service we: um: (1.1) we help
2        people: (.) sort out- (0.4) their own uh differences so .hhh
3        we wouldn't take si:des, we wouldn't- (0.7) try an' decide
4        who's right or wrong but would- .hh would try to help you
5        both um:: (0.8) sort out uh: the differences between: (0.2)
6        between you.
7            (2.5)
8   C:   Well I-hh (1.2) to be qui:te honest I don't think she'd
9        cooperate.
```

M is explaining a fundamental principle of mediation: its impartiality with regard to both parties to a dispute. C's unenthusiastic response begins with a long delay at line 7, followed by the turn-initial "Well" at the start of line 6. That C's response is a dispreferred one is suggested further by the phrase "to be quite honest" (Edwards & Fasulo, 2006). C indicates that she will reject mediation because she thinks her neighbour would not "cooperate" (lines 6–7). The phrase "to be quite honest" also suggests that C is reluctant to criticize a neighbour; that she is another "blameless caller" with a "blameworthy neighbour". As noted earlier, resisting mediation on the basis that *callers' neighbours* rather than *callers themselves* would be unlikely to participate was one of the most common explanations for rejecting offers.

Extract 5 illustrates both findings: responding negatively to explanations of impartiality and resisting mediation on the basis of the neighbour's likely unwillingness.

Extract 5: DC-57

```
1    M:    ↑Wh- ↑wha- what usually ha:ppens↓ i:s that the
2          mediators would come out an' (0.5) uh- see you fi:rst
3          an' hear your side o'the story. .hhh=
4    C:    =°Yeh°
5:   M:    =um: I'mean if still:* wanted to continue we'd write
6          out t'y'r neighbor,=.hh an' offer 'im a similar
7          appointment, (.) .hhh (.) uh: t'hear what's hap'nin'
8          from 'is point of view .hhh
9                       (.)
10   M:    Um:: (1.0) I mean he can say no: but *you- y- y-* (.)
11         .pt *uh-or-:* or there is a chance that he- y'know he
12         will see the mediators .hhh an' put his side of the
13         story str- uh: t'them, Uh:nd the mediators will
14         (back) um: (0.5) pass on your concerns [to him.
15   C:                                          [↑Is there
16         uh anyone e:lse that I c'n call.=is there anything
17         else that I c'n do:..hh becau- I really don't think
18         that's goin't'work, .hhh
19                (0.2)
20   C:    Y'know: he- he makes it very plain that he's doin'
21         what he wants to do:?
```

As M finishes explaining that mediators will visit C to hear her "side o'the story", C's response at the first "transition relevance place" (TRP) (i.e. the point at which some kind of response is appropriate) is "Yeh". Here, C aligns with M's project to explain mediation. At the next TRP, however, after M adds that mediators will also hear "what's hap'nin' from [C's neighbour's] point of view", C does not align with M (line 9). That is, at that point C stops supporting M's project. As M continues to explain mediation, her turn is increasingly littered with hesitations, pauses, and repair initiators (lines 10–14), perhaps orienting to this lack of alignment from C. Then, at line 15, C interrupts the end of M's turn, and rejects explicitly mediation as a possible course of action. Like the callers in other extracts, she also starts to explain this rejection on the basis of her neighbour's character (lines 20–21).

Benjamin (2010) has argued that people are generally reluctant to negotiate a dispute or accept that there are two sides to a story; that human beings are "predictably irrational" in this regard that they want a third party to establish that they are right and that the target of their complaint is wrong. As Jacobs and Aakhus (2002, pp. 177–178) have argued:

> Ordinary people bring to mediation a commonsense vision that their dispute will be resolved through reasonable argumentation ... by bringing in the facts of the matter, establishing who is in the right and who is in the wrong, determining relevant evidence, and so on ... So there is characteristic tension between the conduct of mediators and the conduct of disputants.

Whether or not these authors are correct, I found that the "two-sided" explanation of mediation deters callers from the process. Callers and mediators therefore have a fundamental mismatch of expectations (see Tracy, 1997). However, I found that a different way of explaining mediation was more likely to engage prospective clients. Extract 6 is an example:

Extract 6: EC-37

```
1    M:   We're a mediation projec- (0.4) project in the:: (.) Stockham area, (0.2)
2    C:   Ye[h.
3    M:   [.hhh and what - (0.2) we try t'help neighbours that are in dispute::, [.hhh what=
4    C:                                                                           [Uhuh.
5    M:   =we do first um: .pt send a letter out to your neighbour straight away .hh t'say that:
6         y- we've been in touch with you, .h[hh and hm- ask 'em (0.2) whether they would=
7    C:                                        [Yeh,
8    M:   =(0.4) .hhh get in touch with us so that we can discuss it with them? Hh=
9    C:   =Yeh,
10   M:   If they sa::y- if they phone up an' say yes then we make an arrangement t'come
11        an' see you both separately, .hhhhh [but with (0.3) but with the aim of: (0.2)=
12   C:                                        [Yes.
13   M:   =<eventually,> gettin' (0.3) round a table an' discussing matters with you all,
14   C:   M[m:.
15   M:   [.hhh to try an' come t'some sort of an agree:ment of: ways you can go fo:rward.
```

In contrast to Extract 5, the mediator in Extract 6 explains mediation as a *process*, and in terms of what it does, rather than what it does not do. The evidence that this explanation is effective is in the caller's regular responses as each component of the explanation is produced. Note that the mediator does not hide from the caller that they will talk to their neighbour; but neither do they invoke notions of "sides". They describe the process as impartial, in a way, but do not explicitly articulate impartiality as an ideology or as the mediator's *raison d'etre*. Across the data, *procedural* rather than *ideological* explanations of mediation were more effective in getting callers to become clients of their service.

Are You Willing?

Across the collection of intake calls, callers regularly offered one reason for turning down offers of mediation: that their neighbour is the "kind of person" who will not mediate. Extract 7 provides an example:

Extract 7: HC-30

```
1    M:   So as I say the mediators would visit you,=hear your side of
2         the story, (0.4) the::n if you wa:nted them to: we:'d get in
3         touch with your neighbors an' ask- [them if they wanted t-=
4    C:                                       [°Mmm°
5    M:   =[uh:: mediation. hh]
6    C:    [  °Yeh. °  ]
7    C:   Yeh- I don't think you'll get very fa:r with 'em.
8              (0.8)
```

```
9   M:  D'you not.
10          (0.6)
11  C:  .hhh No::.
12          (0.7)
13  M:  Ri::ght. [right.
14  C:           [Ver- she's very aggressive.
```

Again, in response to a description of mediation as a two-sided or impartial service, callers express resistance toward the process at the point at which mediators tell callers that they will talk to their neighbours. In Extract 7, C produces a weakly aligning response at line 4, "Mmm" (Gardner, 1997). At line 6, C begins to supply an account that will become the reason for not engaging further in the mediation process, "I don't think you'll get very far with 'em", adding at line 14 the further detail that "she's very aggressive". Like Extract 5, in which M stated that mediation would work only if the caller's neighbours were "willing" to be involved, here M states that they would see if C's neighbours "wanted" mediation.

Such descriptions *provide for* the account that immediately follows, that problematic neighbours will not, *of course*, be willing or want mediation. Indeed, to minimize their own culpability, to save face in having requested outside help in a mundane relationship matter, and in pursuit of affiliation from the mediator, callers take every opportunity to characterize their neighbour in negative ways. By implication, if callers' neighbours are the kinds of people who will not mediate, callers are the kinds of people who will. Some mediators invoke, subtly, the way callers present themselves as morally superior to their neighbours in creative and productive ways. In Extract 8, M has explained the mediation process and is now asking C if it sounds "helpful".

Extract 8: EC-37

```
1   M:  Does that sound .hhh like it might be helpful to you?
2          (0.7)
```

We know from line 2—a gap of 0.7 s—that it is likely that the caller is about to produce a rejection-implicative turn. By examining talk in such forensic detail, we are able to pin-point key moments in interaction that show trouble ahead. If the caller was enthusiastic about mediation, this would reveal itself at line 2 (e.g. "that sounds great!"; "yes it does"). Let us see the caller's response.

Extract 8 (contd.): EC-37

```
1   M:  Does that sound .hhh like it might be helpful to you?
2          (0.7)
3   C:  I- uh- (0.2) it might be but um:: (0.3) I'm not too sure at this stage about
4          (0.6) you know, how long- y- seein' this: gi:rl, [at all,
```

The caller's response is indeed a classic "dispreferred" response (Pomerantz, 1984), in that it is delayed, it includes an appreciation "it might be" and an account which, in this case, starts to invoke the other party ("this girl"). Revealing an unfolding interaction in this way, turn by turn, is fundamental to the training methodology that I will explain in the final section of this chapter. In CARM workshops, we ask mediators to consider what they might do to nevertheless encourage the caller to become their client in situations like the above. Ninety-five percent of mediators do not come up with what actually works, even though the practice appears regularly across the data corpus. This suggests that people are not good at recalling their experience sufficiently to know what works in these crucial moments, even if they may use it in practice. What works is revealed next.

Extract 8 (Contd.): EC-37

```
1  M:  Does that sound .hhh like it might be helpful to you?
2              (0.7)
3  C:  I- uh- (0.2) it might be but um:: (0.3) I'm not too sure at this stage about
4       (0.6) you know, how long- y- seein' this: gi:rl, [at all,
5  M:                                              [W'yeah.=↓yeh, but you'd be
6       willin' t'see two of our media[tors jus' t'talk about it all. .hhhh]
7  C:                                 [Oh of course.   Yeah. Yeah] definitely.
```

When mediators ask if callers are "willing", or propose that they are—as in this case—callers' responses were marked: they were fast (note the overlap at line 7 where the caller begins to respond before she has heard all of what is being proposed that she is willing to do!) and they were "more than"—she does not just say "yes". The mediator's proposal about the caller is a *moral* one: the caller, unlike the caller's neighbour (cf. Extracts 4 and 5—"if your neighbour was unwilling..."), *is* the kind of person who will mediate.

In the past five years, I have expanded my interest in mediation from community to family mediation. We established that the pattern illustrated in Extract 8 held across both settings (Sikveland & Stokoe, 2016). Here are some examples of callers' strong uptake of family mediation in response to questions including the word "willing".

Extract 9: DG-1

```
1  M:  I'm sure he would be will:ing t'come in and see our mediat[or:?
2  C:                                                            [Oh yeah:
```

Extract 10: CFM-3

```
1  M:  I just- wanted to see if you would be willing to attend a: a session as well.
2  C:  I'm more than happy to go down that route.
```

Extract 11: DG-19

```
1  M:  =Is that something that you would be willing to [do:.   ]=
2  C:                                                  [I would-]=
3  C:  =I ↑would be willing to ↓do it.=ye[s:.   ]
4  M:                                    [.ptk (th)at]'s grea:[t.   ]
5  C:                                                         [Just-] (.) do anything just
6       to try and get to see my son,=you know,
```

In each case, note that the caller responds immediately and with more than a "yes" response ("Oh yeah"; "I'm more than happy"; "I'm more than willing"; "I would..."). Indeed, the "Oh" indicates the caller's position preceded the question; that they—unlike their partner—were *pre-disposed* to mediate.

Here, then, we have seen how certain linguistic interventions make it more or less likely that callers will engage in a particular behaviour—or at least take the first step of saying "yes" on the phone and making an appointment. Conversation analysis and discursive psychology provide insights into what works and what is not effective in these and other environments. On the basis of this research, I was consulted by the UK Ministry of Justice to change the language used to describe family mediation in government promotional materials online, in posters and on leaflets. This intervention demonstrates the impact of CA-DP research in surprising settings, and how one might translate findings about effective spoken interaction to the written word. How does one best learn the effectiveness of a published explanation of a service like mediation? One could run focus groups with potential users, but these participants do not have the same stake in evaluating an explanation as a caller, live, on the phone, deciding in the context of calling for help. One could ask other professionals, who may give an opinion. Or one can test, live, the effectiveness of an explanation by seeing the outcome in a call such as those illustrated above. Spoken interaction, as a "naturally occurring experiment", provides the best evidence about what works, in a setting that matters.

Training Mediators to Engage Parties in Conflict Resolution

I want to conclude this chapter by discussing the evolution of the neighbours' project into a communication training method called the Conversation Analytic Role-play Method, or CARM. CARM is, first and foremost, an approach based on CA and DP evidence about the sorts of problems and roadblocks that can occur in interaction, as well as the techniques and strategies that best resolve and overcome them. Historically, mediation training—and communication training more generally—is based largely on one of two methods: post-hoc reflections on strategy or best practice that are formalized into texts and guidelines, and/or role-play.

Writing about the first approach, Glenn and Susskind (2010, p. 118) stated that while "training materials are rich with suggestions for managing such talk", "prescriptions tend to skew either toward global strategic considerations or toward isolated individual behavior". They further argue that "written accounts of successful or problematic practices" are subject to "temporal and perceptual limitations … [and] the vagaries of memory". Similarly, I have found that the sorts of effective practices revealed by analysis of transcripts are seldom the same as mediators' post-hoc reporting of what they think does or does not work (Stokoe, 2013a). I believe this is because people often have a normative, rather than an empirical, understanding of interaction. One job of conversation analysis is to yield "empirically grounded results at variance with our commonsense intuitions about how some action is accomplished or what action some utterance is to be understood to have accomplished" (Schegloff, 1996, p. 169).

The second type of training method is role-play or simulation. Role-play typically involves mediators (or mediation students) interacting with other mediators playing the part of clients, using hypothetical scenarios or adaptations of actual scenarios as the basis for the simulated encounter. As Glenn and Susskind pointed out, however, role-play leaves "open the question of how 'real life' might differ" (p. 118). I have addressed this question elsewhere, by comparing role-play training talk to the actual interactions that the training was designed to mimic (Stokoe, 2013b). I found that people do things in training that they do not do in actual encounters, such as including "rapport-building" actions in exaggerated ways that are made explicit for the overhearing trainer. Consequently, assessing people's skills on the basis of what they do in role-play is problematic and calls into question the value of role-play as a training tool.

In contrast to traditional role-play, I have developed what I call the "Conversation Analytic Role-play Method" (CARM). CARM takes best practice findings from research about actual interaction as a basis for training. Although Susskind (2010, p. 165) suggested that CA researchers "may not be the best people to figure out how their insights (however quickly or slowly they emerge) should be used by negotiation analysts and instructors", CARM provides an effective method for disseminating such insights (Stokoe, 2011, 2014). The method works by transcribing and anonymizing extracts from recordings that demonstrate different ways that mediators formulate and organize particular actions (e.g. offering mediation). The audio and/or video files and transcripts are presented synchronously, such that students experience encounters without knowing what will happen next. Next, as illustrated in Extract 8, workshop participants role-play what they might do next to handle the situation. For example, if party A makes a particular sort of comment, how might party B respond most appropriately? Sometimes participants discuss their likely responses in small groups, other times they respond individually by taking the next turn without time for discussion (which is what would happen in a real interaction). Finally, party B's actual response is revealed and discussed, and the workshop moves on. Participants develop insights about best practices on the basis of what mediators actually do and say and on what actually works.

During the past ten years, I have delivered CARM workshops to many tens of mediation organizations in the United Kingdom, Ireland, and the United States, at more than 300 workshops to thousands of mediators. The workshops have focused not only on intake calls but also on such varied topics as opening mediation, asking solution-focused questions, and dealing with racism in conflicts—all based on CA-DP research (e.g.Stokoe, 2009, 2015; Stokoe & Edwards, 2007; Stokoe & Sikveland, 2016). There is an emerging tradition in conversation analytic research to disseminate findings to practitioners, with the aim of improving practice. From doctor–patient encounters to midwifery education, from improving response rates to telephone interviews to examining the way choice is delivered to people with intellectual disabilities (see Antaki, 2011), studying actual practice with a view to informing people about practice is proving fertile ground for understanding what institutions are to the people who encounter them, and what practitioners do, for the people who engage with them.

In the last few years, CARM's reach and impact has proliferated. CARM workshops were accredited by the UK College of Mediators and the Royal College of

Paediatricians and Child Health, meaning that participants are awarded "Continuing Professional Development" points ("CPD") which practitioners must accrue each year. The route to CPD is one way of developing wider audiences and demand for training interventions, as well as to generating interest in CA research and changing the culture of communication training (see Emmison, 2013; Meagher, 2013, on the impact of CARM). Furthermore, CARM has recently been commercialized as a not-for-profit social enterprise (www.carmtraining.org), securing private as well as public sector clients and generating income to employ researchers and cross-subsidize workshops for third sector organizations. It has been the subject of a number of public engagement invitations including TED (2014), Royal Institution (2015), New Scientist Live (2016), Latitude Festival (2016), Risky Business (2017), Google (2017), and Cheltenham Science Festival (2018) talks and lectures. It also won a WIRED Innovation Fellowship (2015). And the public appetite to hear about neighbour disputes remains; at the time of writing I appeared on BBC Radio 4's series "How To Disagree" (2018)[2], talking about effective dispute resolution.

Such enterprise activities might be steps too far for some. Yet, in a world of limited research funding, CARM generates income to support research and researchers. It has provided CA-DP researchers ("CARM Affiliates") with a tried-and-tested method for intervention that was developed with blue-chip research council funding, providing leverage for further funding. It shows how what I refer to as "designedly large-scale qualitative research" can create impact. It also brings CA-DP to wide audiences who begin to understand the power of studying interaction. In this chapter, I hope to have shown that research about conflict can be useful to the organizations that work to resolve it.

References

Antaki, C. (Ed.). (2011). *Applied conversation analysis: Intervention and change in institutional talk.* Basingstoke: Palgrave Macmillan.
Barlow, A., Hunter, R., Smithson, J., & Ewing, J. (2017). *Mapping paths to family justice: Resolving family disputes in neoliberal times.* London: Palgrave.
Benjamin, R. (2010). *Selling mediation: The 9 ½ best guerrilla marketing strategies and techniques drawn from neuroscience.* Retrieved from http://www.mediate.com/articles/benjamin50.cfm
Boden, D. (1990). The world as it happens: Ethnomethodology and conversation analysis. In G. Ritzer (Ed.), *Frontiers of social theory: The new synthesis* (pp. 185–213). New York: Columbia University Press.
Charkoudian, L. (2010). Giving police and courts a break: The effect of community mediation on decreasing the use of police and court resources. *Conflict Resolution Quarterly, 28,* 141–155. https://doi.org/10.1002/crq.20017
Edwards, D. (1995). Sacks and psychology. *Theory & Psychology, 5,* 579–596. https://doi.org/10.1177/0959354395054006
Edwards, D. (2005). Moaning, whinging and laughing: The subjective side of complaints. *Discourse Studies, 7,* 5–29. https://doi.org/10.1177/1461445605048765

[2] https://www.bbc.co.uk/programmes/b0bf56gk

Edwards, D. (2007). Managing subjectivity in talk. In A. Hepburn & S. Wiggins (Eds.), *Discursive research in practice: New approaches to psychology and interaction* (pp. 31–49). Cambridge: Cambridge University Press.

Edwards, D., & Fasulo, A. (2006). "To be honest": Sequential uses of honesty phrases in talk-in-interaction. *Research on Language and Social Interaction, 39*, 343–376. https://doi.org/10.1207/s15327973rlsi3904_1

Edwards, D., & Stokoe, E. H. (2004). Discursive psychology, focus group interviews, and participants' categories. *British Journal of Developmental Psychology, 22*, 499–507. https://doi.org/10.1348/0261510042378209

Edwards, D., & Stokoe, E. (2007). Self-help in calls for help with problem neighbours. *Research on Language and Social Interaction, 40*, 9–32. https://doi.org/10.1080/08351810701331208

Emmison, M. (2013). 'Epistemic engine' versus 'role-play method': Divergent trajectories in contemporary conversation analysis. *Australian Journal of Communication, 40*, 5–7.

Gardner, R. (1997). The conversation object *Mm*: A weak and variable acknowledging token. *Research on Language and Social Interaction, 30*, 131–156. https://doi.org/10.1207/s15327973rlsi3002_2

Garfinkel, H. (1967). *Studies in ethnomethodology*. Englewood Cliffs, NJ: Prentice-Hall.

Glenn, P., & Susskind, L. (2010). How talk works: Studying negotiation interaction. *Negotiation Journal, 26*, 117–123. https://doi.org/10.1111/j.1571-9979.2010.00260.x

Goldberg, S. B. (2005). The secrets of successful mediators. *Negotiation Journal, 21*, 365–376. https://doi.org/10.1111/j.1571-9979.2005.00069.x

Goldman, R. (1982). Hegemony and managed critique in prime-time television: A critical reading of 'Mork and Mindy'. *Theory & Society, 11*, 363–388.

Greatbatch, D., & Dingwall, R. (1997). Argumentative talk in divorce mediation sessions. *American Sociological Review, 62*, 151–170.

Heap, J. L. (1990). Applied ethnomethodology: Looking for the local rationality of reading activities. *Human Studies, 13*, 38–72.

Heritage, J., & Robinson, J. D. (2006). Accounting for the visit: Giving reasons for seeking medical care. In J. Heritage & D. W. Maynard (Eds.), *Communication in medical care: Interaction between physicians and patients* (pp. 48–85). Cambridge: Cambridge University Press.

Heritage, J., Robinson, J. D., Elliott, M. N., Beckett, M., & Wilkes, M. (2007). Reducing patients' unmet concerns in primary care: The difference one word can make. *Journal of General Internal Medicine, 22*, 1429–1433. https://doi.org/10.1007/s11606-007-0279-0

Jacobs, S., & Aakhus, M. (2002). What mediators do with words: Implementing three models of rational discussion in dispute mediation. *Conflict Resolution Quarterly, 20*, 177–203. https://doi.org/10.1002/crq.19

Jefferson, G. (2004). Glossary of transcript symbols with an introduction. In G. H. Lerner (Ed.), *Conversation analysis: Studies from the first generation* (pp. 13–31). Amsterdam/Philadelphia: John Benjamins.

Llewellyn, N. (2015). Microstructures of economic action: Talk, interaction and the bottom line. *British Journal of Sociology, 66*, 486–511. https://doi.org/10.1111/1468-4446.12143

Meagher, L. R. (2013). *Research impact on practice: Case study analysis: Report on ESRC grant number RES-189-25-0202 mediating and policing community disputes: Developing new methods for role-play communication skills training*. Swindon: ESRC.

Meehan, A. J. (1989). Assessing the 'police-worthiness' of citizen's complaints to the police: Accountability and the negotiation of 'facts'. In D. T. Helm, W. T. Anderson, A. J. Meehan, & A. W. Rawls (Eds.), *The interactional order: New directions in the study of social order* (pp. 116–140). New York: Irvington.

Painter, J. (2012). The politics of the neighbour. *Environment and Planning D: Society and Space, 30*, 515–533. https://doi.org/10.1068/d21110

Pomerantz, A. (1984). Agreeing and disagreeing with assessments: Some features of preferred/dispreferred turn shapes. In J. M. Atkinson & J. Heritage (Eds.), *Structures of social action: Studies in conversation analysis* (pp. 57–101). Cambridge: Cambridge University Press.

Potter, J. (2002). Two kinds of natural. *Discourse Studies, 4*, 539–542. https://doi.org/10.1177/14614456020040040901

Potter, J., & Hepburn, A. (2003). "I'm a bit concerned": Early actions and psychological constructions in a child protection helpline. *Research on Language and Social Interaction, 36*, 197–240. https://doi.org/10.1207/S15327973RLSI3603_01

Sacks, H. (1992). *Lectures on conversation* (Vol. 1). Oxford: Blackwell.

Schegloff, E. A. (1968). Sequencing in conversational openings. *American Anthropologist, 70*, 1075–1095.

Schegloff, E. A. (1996). Confirming allusions: Toward an empirical account of action. *American Journal of Sociology, 102*, 161–216.

Schegloff, E. A. (2007). *Sequence organization in interaction: A primer in conversation analysis*. Cambridge: Cambridge University Press.

Sikveland, R. O., & Stokoe, E. (2016). Dealing with resistance in initial intake and inquiry calls to mediation: The power of 'willing'. *Conflict Resolution Quarterly, 33*, 235–253. https://doi.org/10.1002/crq.21157

Stokoe, E. H. (2003). Mothers, single women and sluts: Gender, morality and membership categorization in neighbour disputes. *Feminism & Psychology, 13*, 317–344. https://doi.org/10.1177/0959353503013003006

Stokoe, E. (2006). Public intimacy in neighbour relationships and complaints. *Sociological Research Online, 11*(3). Retrieved from www.socresonline.org.uk/11/3/stokoe.html

Stokoe, E. (2009). Doing actions with identity categories: Complaints and denials in neighbour disputes. *Text and Talk, 29*, 75–97. https://doi.org/10.1515/TEXT.2009.004

Stokoe, E. (2011). Simulated interaction and communication skills training: The 'Conversation Analytic Role-play Method'. In C. Antaki (Ed.), *Applied conversation analysis: Changing institutional practices* (pp. 119–139). Basingstoke: Palgrave Macmillan.

Stokoe, E. (2013a). Overcoming barriers to mediation in intake calls to services: Research-based strategies for mediators. *Negotiation Journal, 29*, 289–314. https://doi.org/10.1111/nejo.12026

Stokoe, E. (2013b). The (in)authenticity of simulated talk: Comparing role-played and actual conversation and the implications for communication training. *Research on Language and Social Interaction, 46*, 1–21. https://doi.org/10.1080/08351813.2013.780341

Stokoe, E. (2014). The Conversation Analytic Role-play Method (CARM): A method for training communication skills as an alternative to simulated role-play. *Research on Language and Social Interaction, 47*, 255–265. https://doi.org/10.1080/08351813.2014.925663

Stokoe, E. (2015). Identifying and responding to possible '-isms' in institutional encounters: Alignment, impartiality and the implications for communication training. *Journal of Language and Social Psychology, 34*, 427–445. https://doi.org/10.1177/0261927X15586572

Stokoe, E., & Edwards, D. (2007). "Black this, black that": Racial insults and reported speech in neighbour complaints and police interrogations. *Discourse & Society, 18*, 337–372. https://doi.org/10.1177/0957926507075477

Stokoe, E., & Edwards, D. (2009). Accomplishing social action with identity categories: Mediating neighbour complaints. In M. Wetherell (Ed.), *Theorizing identities and social action* (pp. 95–115). London: Sage.

Stokoe, E., & Sikveland, R. O. (2016). Formulating solutions in mediation. *Journal of Pragmatics, 105*, 101–113. https://doi.org/10.1016/j.pragma.2016.08.006

Stokoe, E., & Sikveland, R. O. (2017). The Conversation Analytic Role-play Method: Simulation, endogenous impact and interactional nudges. In V. Fors, T. O'Dell, & S. Pink (Eds.), *Theoretical scholarship and applied practice*. Oxford: Berghahn Books.

Stokoe, E., Sikveland, R. O., & Symonds, J. (2016). Calling the GP surgery: Patient burden, patient satisfaction, and implications for training. *British Journal of General Practice, 66*, e779–e785. https://doi.org/10.3399/bjgp16X686653

Stokoe, E. H., & Wallwork, J. (2003). Space invaders: The moral-spatial order in neighbour dispute discourse. *British Journal of Social Psychology, 42*, 551–569. https://doi.org/10.1348/014466603322595284

Susskind, L. (2010). Looking at negotiation and dispute resolution through a CA/DA lens. *Negotiation Journal, 26*, 163–166.

Tracy, K. (1997). Interactional trouble in emergency service requests: A problem of frames. *Research on Language and Social Interaction, 30*, 315–343.

Trinder, L., Firth, A., & Jenks, C. (2010). 'So presumably things have moved on since then?' The management of risk allegations in child contact dispute resolution. *International Journal of Law, Policy and the Family, 241*, 29–53.

Whalen, M. R., & Zimmerman, D. H. (1990). Describing trouble: Practical epistemology in citizen calls to the police. *Language in Society, 19*, 465–492.

Chapter 3
Discursive Psychology and Domestic Violence

Alison J. Towns and Peter J. Adams

This chapter explores ways in which discursive psychology sheds light on how language justifies, conceals, and works to produce the dominance of men in intimate relationships. We demonstrate two ways language can be deployed to achieve these effects. First, the close examination of discourses about violence can reveal much about the way violence against women is justified, minimized and ignored. Second, attention to rhetorical devices deployed in these discourses, such as metaphor, ambiguity, and marking strategies, can help in understanding how they are anchored and reinforced in everyday conversations. These forms of discursive enquiry, and other possibilities, open up ways of better understanding the dynamics of men's violence against women and opportunities for intervention to produce more equitable practices.

Our work in this area has been concerned with informing population-based interventions that would assist in the primary prevention of domestic violence thereby producing a more gender conscious and socially just society. Within this model, violence prevention is understood to occur at three levels: primary prevention, secondary prevention, and tertiary prevention (Wolfe & Jaffe, 1999). Primary prevention involves developing the socio-cultural environment that would stop violence before it starts. For example, promoting gender equity is known to be one way to effectively prevent men's domestic violence towards women (World Health Organization, 2004) and requires the development of critical reflection on gender practices. Secondary prevention involves working with those people at risk of becoming victims or perpetrators of violence in the future, through, for example, good parenting programs or ensuring that the environment where they are raised is free of violence. Tertiary prevention involves intervening to ensure the safety and recovery of the victims of such violence and that perpetrators are held accountable for their actions and given the opportunity to change.

A. J. Towns (✉) · P. J. Adams
University of Auckland, Auckland, New Zealand

© Springer Nature Switzerland AG 2018
S. Gibson (ed.), *Discourse, Peace, and Conflict*, Peace Psychology Book Series,
https://doi.org/10.1007/978-3-319-99094-1_3

The ecological model has been used to explain the prevention of domestic violence (World Health Organization, 2004) and resonates with models described in peace psychology. In the ecological model, interventions are possible at the individual level (challenging gendered beliefs), at the interpersonal level (couple and family therapy), at the social and community level (e.g., community development), and at the societal level (e.g., addressing norms). Primary prevention of domestic violence is predominantly concerned with the social and community level and societal level interventions.

This model of prevention is consistent with the model of peace psychology described by Christie, Tint, Wagner, and Winter (2008), particularly their description of positive peace, in which the socio-cultural context is understood to be pivotal to the promotion of peace. In their three-stage model, negative peace is described as addressing existing conflicts through nonviolent peace management prior to the eruption of any incident, de-escalating violence once it occurs, and then peace building after the violence. Positive peace is described as follows:

> We use the term positive peace to refer to transformations within and across institutions that rectify structural inequities. Positive peace is promoted when political structures become more inclusive and give voice to those who have been marginalized in matters that affect their well-being. Economic structures become transformed when those who have been exploited gain more equitable access to material resources that satisfy their basic needs (Galtung, 1996). Culturally violent narratives that support structural violence are transformed when, for example, "just world thinking" (M.J. Lerner, 1980) is replaced with "conscientization," or an awakening of a critical consciousness, a shared subjective state in which the powerless begin to critically analyze and challenge the oppressive narratives of the powerful (Freire, 1970).
> (Christie et al., 2008, p. 547)

Such transformations are consistent with those required in the primary prevention of violence against women and discursive psychology has an important role here.

Critical discursive psychology brings greater awareness to the language that supports men's domestic violence against women and silences women's talk of such violence, thereby marginalizing them. As language is pivotal to socio-cultural understandings, raising awareness of the language that supports such violence provides victims, advocates, and others with the linguistic and socio-cultural resources that assist with the mobilization of action towards socio-cultural and political change. Such research can be used to challenge and counter the commonsense language and socio-cultural norms, which work against gender equity, and assists with promoting more inclusive political structures, gender consciousness, and equity.

Critical Discursive Psychology's Unique Contribution

The discipline of psychology is a broad church with many sub-disciplines drawing on a variety of academic traditions. At the center is a desire to better understand why we think, feel, and behave in the ways we do. Such a focus naturally foregrounds us as discrete individuals and this leads, understandably, to calling on concepts that characterize what is going on for us as individuals; concepts such as attitudes, motivations, cognitions, and mental sets. What this risks doing, however, is confining psychological understandings to what is going on in terms of individuals, almost as though each of us are discrete particles behaving in absolute space. But individuals are never behaving in absolute space. We are at all times surrounded by our relationships to others: other objects, other people, and the discourses and social systems in which we move.

We could reduce a study of men who engage in violence against women to focusing on aspects of them as individuals and concentrate our efforts on the psychological dynamics that contribute to that behavior: the violence is explained in terms of the beliefs, cognitions, attitudes, emotions, and motivations that he carries. Such an orientation provides a limited understanding of the psychology involved. A broader focus that includes a man's understanding and experiences of gender, men and women, the role of men and women in his world and his ideals, dilemmas, and concerns might yield a greater connection of his actions with the broader and/or localized socio-cultural context and the associated collective of men. Moreover, when the focus is widened to the socio-political context, one type of behavior can be seen as interacting with other types of behavior.

By broadening the focus, discursive psychology offers a way of integrating the psychology of the individual with the intertwined dynamics of the socio-political context. For example, the key beliefs that enable violence are not only located within the individual but also located in the discursive environment in which the individual is participating. By including ways of speaking, discursive psychology offers the opportunity to examine what is happening for individuals in the context of the broader social and political milieu.

Men's domestic violence against women is understood as a reflection of the gendered power relationships between men and women, which is supported by power practices performed and endorsed in social norms and perpetuated in interpersonal conversations, local and national political discourses and structures. Gendered power practices are scripted into commonsense language and understandings that are accepted as normal. Accordingly, unpacking how language is deployed around domestic violence opens up a vantage point for exposing the gendered power practices that contribute to such violence.

We have used critical discursive psychology informed by feminist post-structuralism and Foucault's understandings of power in our qualitative research on men's domestic violence against women. When this methodology was developed in the early 1990s, we were part of the inaugural Discourse Research Unit at the Psychology Department of the University of Auckland, whose members also included Nicola Gavey, Timothy McCreanor, and Raymond Nairn. Tim McCreanor and Ray Nairn had for years been concerned with the ways media represented the aspirations of indigenous Māori in Aotearoa/NewZealand, requiring their research to move beyond the standard quantitative methodologies endorsed by university psychology departments at the time into the ways language was employed to trivialize, disempower, and immobilize Māori from raising matters to do with social justice and the impact of colonization (e.g., Nairn & McCreanor, 1990, 1991). Nicola Gavey was involved in the exploration of qualitative methodologies and feminist approaches to understanding sexual coercion. Her work on feminist post-structuralism (e.g.,

Gavey, 1989, 2005) was pivotal to the methodologies we subsequently used in our research on domestic violence. The early influences she described in articulating this approach (Gavey, 2011) were also those that influenced us:

> *feminist* poststructuralist scholarship requires (careful and wise) theoretical impurity; it requires us to work simultaneously with two theoretically contradictory understandings of language – as descriptive on one hand and constitutive on the other
>   (Gavey, 2011, p. 187, italics in original)

When listening to and reading women's accounts of the violence they have experienced, we understand these to be describing their experienced reality, whereas when seeking the socio-cultural understandings that inform violent practices we turn to the language that enables those practices to be performed.

Foucault's writings on power practices and how they work discursively have played a key role in developing the methods we have used to try to make sense of men's violence against women (Foucault, 1977, 1982, 1988, 1991). He argued that power did not reside within individuals but rather in the relations people had with each other. Power would not exist without someone on whom to practice power. He highlighted how power practices were evident in the overarching discourses present in everyday conversations, language, media representations, official and judicial documentation, and texts of government policies as well as practices. Such discourses are often difficult to identify from within the socio-cultural context. Discourses may be understood to be the rhetoric, metaphors, maxims, and statements that coalesce around a particular meaning.

Foucault (1980) argued that certain discourses become dominant through governance practices that favor some discourses over others. These discourses are written into policy documents and institutional practices as if commonsense. People regulate their behavior depending on how they are positioned by these socio-cultural discourses leading Foucault to describe power practices associated with language as "technologies of the self" (Foucault, 1988). Identifying the language that supports these power mechanisms allows people to resist or disrupt and transform the discourses and socio-cultural norms that are harmful to them, promoting alternative discourses and governance practices. Our work has been concerned with identifying the socio-cultural discourses that are embedded in everyday language and employed by men and others to justify and excuse domestic violence and silence talk of it with a view to resisting and challenging these influences. Always at the center of our work are women's lived experiences of such violence and associated coercive control.

Why Is the Prevention of Domestic Violence Important to Peace?

Violence against women by a heterosexual partner or ex-partner accounts for a disproportionate number of culpable homicides of women in many countries and impacts on their ability to be able to contribute to society. In New Zealand, for example, approximately half of all murders have been found to be "family violence" related, with most victims being women and children, with indigenous Māori women and children over-represented (FVDRC, 2015; Martin & Pritchard, 2010). In the United Kingdom, 44% of all women killed through homicide in the year ending March 2015 were killed by a partner or ex-partner (Office for National Statistics, 2017). In the USA, 62% of female homicide victims were killed by intimate partners or ex-partners in 2013 (VPC, 2016).

Internationally, around 30% of women are expected to experience physical or sexual violence from a partner at some time in their partnered lifetime. In a World Health Organization (WHO) survey of 24,097 women in ten countries between 2000 and 2003 (Bangladesh, Brazil, Ethiopia, Japan, Namibia, Peru, Samoa, Serbia and Montenegro, Thailand, and the United Republic of Tanzania), Garcia-Moreno, Jansen, Ellsberg, Heise, and Watts (2006) found that life-time prevalence rates of such violence varied from 15 to 75%, with two countries having less than 25%, seven between 25 and 50% and six more than 50%. Lifetime prevalence in 33 OECD countries of physical and sexual violence ranged from 6% in Canada to 47% in Mexico. Lifetime prevalence in Anglo-western countries was 36% for the USA, 29% for the United Kingdom, 25% for Australia, and 33% for New Zealand. Prevalence rates vary between ethnic groups within countries possibly reflecting the marginalization of certain groups. In New Zealand, for example, Fanslow, Robinson, Crengle, and Perese (2010), using the same methodology as the WHO study, found life-time prevalence of physical and sexual violence experienced was 34% for women of European ethnicity, 58% for women of Māori ethnicity, 32% for women of Pasifika ethnicity, and 12% for women of Asian ethnicity.

A consistent finding across countries is that those women who had experienced domestic violence had partners who were more controlling than those who had not experienced such violence (Garcia-Moreno et al., 2006). Stark (2007) described coercive control as the pervasive daily experience of women who lived with a violent partner, with physical violence often minor but sufficient to maintain the man's control of the woman and limit her agency. Such violence impedes the woman's ability to act independently through the man's enforcement of gender-based rules, surveillance of the woman to ensure her compliance (Hand, Chung, & Peter, 2009), restriction of her movements, and isolation of the woman from her supportive family and community. Punishment of the woman for transgressions can involve limitations on the essentials of life (such as food, drink, and sleep), and various other forms of emotional, physical, or sexual violence perpetrated against her and her children.

Men's domestic violence against women has substantial health impacts and economic costs to communities and nations. Physical and sexual violence can result in external and internal injuries to women, while the emotional violence experienced can affect women's mental health. Physical injuries range from minor injuries such as burst ear-drums or bruises, which may prevent women from leaving the home, to permanent disabilities, brain injuries, and death (Black, 2011). Many women do not seek help fearing further violence but of those who do most had received blunt force trauma to the head, face, or neck. Injuries to the facial bones in women have been attributed to domestic violence (Zeitler, 2007) raising the question of intentional facial disfigurement. Brain injuries and strangulation, both extremely dangerous, are often missed in medical settings (Glass et al., 2008; Jackson et al., 2002). The primary mental health impact on women is through traumatic stress symptoms or disorders, suicidality, anxiety, depression, and alcohol and drug use (Briere & Jordan, 2004; Dutton et al., 2006; Ellsberg, Jansen, Heise, Watts, & Garcia-Moreno, 2008; Ludermir, Schraiber, D'Oliveira, Franca-Junior, & Jansen, 2008; Taft, Murphy, King, Dedyn, & Musser, 2005). Mental health effects continue long after the violence has ended (Bergman & Brismar, 1991).

The violence can impact on women's sexual health, their pregnancy and their children. Sexual violence can result in genital injuries, chronic pelvic pain, pelvic inflammatory disease, and pain during menstruation and intercourse (Black, 2011). Reproductive control—involving control of whether the woman has contraception resulting in unintended pregnancies and whether she has or does not have an abortion—has also been documented (de Bocanegra, Rostovtseva, Khera, & Godhwani, 2010). Pregnancy outcomes such as low birth weight, preterm delivery, and premature labor have been attributed to domestic violence, as have the loss and death of the fetus, and induced abortions (Alio, Nana, & Salihu, 2009; Fanslow, Silva, Whitehead, & Robinson, 2008; Garcia-Moreno, 2009). Longitudinal studies of children, such as the Adverse Childhood Experiences studies have shown the poor outcomes for children of exposure to such traumatic events, these children being much more susceptible to social and cognitive difficulties, chronic diseases later in life and premature death.

The economic cost of such violence is not only to the women and their children but also to communities and to society. Homelessness can result when women attempt to leave their violent partners, and such homelessness can result in a downward spiral of poverty and hardship (Breckenridge, Hamer, Newton, & Valentine, 2013; Towns, 2014; Tutty, Ogden, Giurgiu, & Weaver-Dunlop, 2013). Women's employment ability, their education, and their training is affected by domestic violence, as the abuser attempts to confine them to the house and prevent contact with others thereby silencing talk of such violence (Lloyd & Taluc, 1999; Swanberg & Logan, 2005; Towns, 2014). The economic cost to nations of such violence has been put at billions of dollars annually (Snively, 1995). Some children exposed to such violence are likely to go on to harm their partners (Ehrensaft et al., 2003) and be responsible for violent crime, setting the stage for community and societal violence (World Health Organization, 2002). Interrupting such violence and constituting gender equitable and peaceful relationships as normative will assist in producing the climate that is required for peaceful societies.

In the following, we will describe two discourses that are employed to justify men's domestic violence against women and the rhetorical devices utilized to this end in men's accounts of their violence. These discourses support the continued dominance of men over women and their entitlement to privileges, enabling the subordination of women and the continued harm towards them through men's domestic violence. They reinforce male dominance through various rhetorical devices, some of which we will describe here. The discourses we discuss are "colonizing discourses" and "natural order discourses".

Colonizing Discourses

Colonizing discourses suggest that there is a correct way of acting in the world, that others need to understand this way and act accordingly and that any problems in the relationship are a product of others not understanding or acting according to the colonizer's particular worldview. The colonizer's task becomes to educate others to behave according to his right way of being.

In these colonizing discourses, the man works to re-educate the woman into his view of the world and she is successfully subjugated when she comes to believe his constitution of the world or is silenced from questioning it and acts accordingly. Cahill (2015) described this process as the "derivitization" of a woman's experience because how she must be in the world is derived from a man's worldview. Stark (2007, p. 274) used the terms "micromanagement" and "microregulation" of the woman to articulate the minutiae of coercive control practices employed by the man to control the woman. Adams (2012) used the term "masculine empire" and described the colonizing discourses men employed to conceal their violence and to construct their controlling practices towards the woman as normative or commonsense.

We have previously written about the rhetorical devices used to justify and support the colonizing effects of domestic violence (Adams, Towns, & Gavey, 1995; Towns, Adams, & Gavey, 2003; Towns & Adams, 2009; Towns & Adams, 2016). For example, we have explored the use of pronouns, particularly the use of the second person plural ("we" and "us") to absorb and appropriate the experience of female partners ("we shouldn't be arguing"). We have also examined how marking strategies (such as terms like "it's a fact of life", "that's it pure and simple") are employed to set boundaries on what a partner can legitimately talk about ("women should know their place, that's the way it is"). However, out of an available toolkit of many different rhetorical devices, we have found metaphors to be the most commonly employed rhetorical device to bolster the colonizing practices associated with violence.

Our research has identified the common use of a wide range of metaphors. Some help in justifying silence ("don't air your dirty washing in public"), others are used to justify violent behavior ("pressure just builds and I explode"), and some help in repositioning abuse as some form of equal combat ("she provoked me", "she hurts me just as much with her words as I do to her with my fists"). But at the heart of any colonizing enterprise lies a strong belief that the colonizer's way of looking at the world is superior to that of the colonized (Adams, 2012). Accordingly, it is those social metaphors that position women as occupying inferior positions to those of men that play a key role in establishing the entitlement to colonize. Such metaphors include: women as childlike ("over-emotional", "unable to see the broader picture"), women as military subordinates ("keeping her in line", "obeying orders"), women as less educated ("irrational", "not in touch"), and women as employees ("needing direction", "complying with procedures").

In the following, we look at one example of a social metaphor of inferiority and explore some of its complexities. By portraying a female partner in the role of a child, a man is then able to weave in ways of speaking that highlights why it is important for women to conform to what her male partner sees as the correct order of things. In the excerpt below, Peter Adams asks "Grant", a New Zealand man of European descent, about his violence towards his partner. Prior to this excerpt he had explained that some of his violence had occurred following disputes with his partner over finances. Both he and his partner worked and contributed to the household finances:

Peter: You said that "there's a part of me that connects with that", women are like children.

Grant: Yeah. Um.

Peter: Can you explain that?

Grant: I think males grown up that if you did something wrong there was um, there was punishment of some type. Whether it was a smack or if you did something in the schoolyard, you got punched or- you know, and we've learnt wrong and right. Whereas I don't think [women] have a good grasp of wrong and right. ...

Peter: ... how do you see that?

Grant: ... I think the sort of things like, um, men are sort of expected to be able to cook, vacuum clean, do the washing, mow the lawns, ah look after children, provide- fix cars, you know do all of the sort of man things- I think men have a greater grasp of ah skills than a lot of women. You know, women aren't expected to be able to repair a car or clean a fish, or you know, do sort of what you term male things. Whereas males are expected to do women things, and I think males can- most men can do, you know- are very- a lot more versatile. Um sort of getting a little bit back about the feminism thing, um, with females perhaps not knowing- having such a good grasp of right and wrong, they now have been put in a position where they're getting a lot more power, um, and I don't know if they have the capabilities of grasping this power. Um, the, I'm sure the money thing, you wouldn't be so much of an issue if women were still living in the regime where you got marr ... you got married, had a child sort of within the first year of the marriage. The wife stayed at home, um I think you know, the money thing would be quite a bit different. Um with women out there working now they've-

Peter: ... I was wondering how that [money] was... linked to yourself to um- in your guts, get the feeling that women perhaps don't have as good an understanding of right or wrong or as good as a connection with that (Grant: Yeah, yeah) basically.

Grant: The money thing, I'm perhaps a bit unorthodox to mainstream thinking with the way I (unclear) handle money. Um, but it works for me and I do it quite well. So that's sort of- is something that I'm not intending to be like that for the rest of my life. I'm just doing it for this period. I'm accumulating as much as I can so I can draw out later. I don't want to work all my life, and I think that's one that- ...

Peter: Did she feel that you controlled a lot of these things in the relationship at all? Did you have a sense of that?

Grant: Yeah I think that she probably did. Um, it got to the stage with um, basically when I started- I paid ... Sue's debt ... She had more money in her bank account, um, and I would have liked to have seen that money then being put into more debt clearing. But Sue took it that it was spending money. Um I would not have cleared those debts in the first place if I had known that that money was then going to become frivolous spend money (Peter: Mmmm) ... Sue, from my side of the fence, Sue seemed to want all the um, all the benefits of having money, but didn't want to take the responsibility or the hard work of getting it there. She just wanted to- you know obviously that's probably quite a generalization, you know, um there's a lot more involved in that than just what I've said, but overall that was sort of the picture that I was getting out of it.

Peter: That was like, you would say about a child.
Grant: Yes.
Peter: Talking that way?
Grant: Yeah, it's um- give a child a box of lollies, um, some of them will eat the whole lot, others will um, eat half of them and put half aside, and you know, and then you sort of, then you get into the money sort of thing, um some will blow the whole lot and others will um put some of it aside.

Here Grant describes having a particular way of managing the finances in the home that "works" for him. Although the full details of the criticisms he had of his partner Sue's managing of their finances are not provided here, he represents his way of managing money as superior and indicating his preference for executive control of any spending by constituting Sue as financially irresponsible. He constantly speaks in ways that position Sue as childlike, enabling him to conceptualize his controlling behavior as acceptable and aimed at helping Sue recognize the way things ought to operate. Moreover, the metaphor also enables him to link the common practices of disciplining children and educating children as normal and understandable ways of managing home environments.

Colonizing discourses contribute to the man's control of material resources in the home: his control of labor, finances, food, clothing, and other essentials of living. By accessing such discourses the man is able to justify and excuse his violence, coercive control, and dominance of the woman. Women who had experienced men's domestic violence described the use of such rhetorical devices that support colonizing discourses as follows:

They're [men who use violence against women] the ones who are right, their behavior is okay, their reasons for their behavior are the true reasons behind whatever it was that created that behavior, whatever situation it was, whatever the argument was or what will- I mean there's not even arguments all the time. They are right, they have a right to be right, they have a right to have what they want- nothing else comes into it. (Casie)
I was starting to get so frustrated. I couldn't get this man to even hear what I was saying. It was just simply his way and that was it and so the frustration started building in me. (Liz)

There is no room for diversity or difference in these colonizing discourses. The construction these women survivors portray is of a man who sets up a world of binaries, where he is right and all others are wrong, and where any challenges will not be met with negotiation or reflection but with conflict and aggression. The phrase "their behavior is okay" suggests the man constitutes his practices as normative or acceptable within the local community and therefore unable to be challenged. The use of phrases such as "nothing else comes into it" and "it was just simply his way *and that was it*" (emphasis added) enabled the women to highlight the man's colonizing practices.

Foucault (1980) considered that a singular monolithic construction of the world was the avenue to sovereign power: totalitarian power exercised through top down practices and reinforced with violence if necessary. He was interested in identifying these power practices with a view to interrupting those designed to subjugate or oppress. Colonizing discourses may be understood as a mechanism of power, as a means to conceal violence by impressing on the victim of such violence (and others) that the abuser's way is the right way, that there is a correct way of being, that there is no other way, and that his abusive practices are normal and acceptable. Resistance would require challenging these discursive practices at all levels from the individual to the relational to the societal.

In those communities that actively accept diversity or gender equity promoting a man's singular view of the world is likely to be more difficult. In Sweden, for example, sustaining the discursive construction of the man's dominance and control of the woman as normal and commonsense is difficult because gender equity is accepted and is valued by men and women, and violence against women is considered to be shameful (Gottzen, 2016). Constituting coercively controlling male practices as normative and acceptable would be more readily subjected to challenge than in those countries or communities where gender equity is not well established or accepted.

In the long excerpt above Grant contributes again to colonizing discourses by employing the rhetoric of moral authority to endorse the "rightful" leadership of men:

> Um sort of getting a little bit back about the feminism thing, um, with females perhaps not knowing- having such a good grasp of right and wrong, they now have been put in a position where they're getting a lot more power, um, and I don't know if they have the capabilities of grasping this power.

Earlier Grant had argued that men are punished physically more than girls and therefore learn right from wrong at an early age in a way girls do not. Having laid the ground for men's greater moral authority, he uses this reasoning in the above excerpt to argue against feminist aspirations for women's leadership. By positioning men as having greater moral authority, Grant is then able to argue that women do not have the "capabilities of grasping this power". Control of the finances is a source of power in the home and by dismissing women's ability to lead he is able to justify his "better" financial management and to position Sue's financial management as like that of a child.

Maintaining moral authority in the face of an immoral act is difficult, but men who employ violence against women use discursive strategies to promote their moral authority in these circumstances. Our research has revealed the work language accomplishes to allow the man to shift responsibility for his violence and maintain his moral authority in the face of his violence. Ambiguity was employed to obfuscate the man's responsibility, conceal his violence, and to shift focus to the woman's responsibility (Towns & Adams, 2016). We described the various socio-cultural influences that were drawn on to create ambiguity and contribute to confusion around responsibility for violence. Commonly these socio-cultural influences were highly gendered and had very old historical roots. For example, Christian beliefs of Eve bringing evil into the world by eating the forbidden fruit and of Pandora opening the locked box and releasing evil in the world are evocative of women holding lesser moral authority than men. These very old Western narratives form part of the socio-cultural landscape that supports the accounts of men who use violence: that women do not have the moral authority that men have and that they should therefore not hold equivalency in any decision-making.

LeCouteur and Oxlad (2011) used a discursive analysis and found that men from South Australia, who either denied or did not deny violence towards their partners, constructed their woman victims as having breached the gendered normative moral order to justify their violence. Using identity categorization to analyze their data, they stated:

> when men were asked to describe their abused female partners, they regularly drew on categorizations that highlighted her exclusion from the commonsense, moral order of proper gendered behaviour. (LeCouteur & Oxlad, 2011, p. 11)

Ultimately these colonizing discourses, and the rhetorical devices that support them, contribute to the socio-cultural landscape that allows men to justify their physical violence against women. Countering these mechanisms of power by clearly placing the culpability for men's domestic violence against women with the man is a way to resist ambiguity and associated shifts in responsibility.

Natural Order Discourses

Deep within colonizing discourses lies a belief in the natural superiority of men with respect to women and how that is part of the natural order of things. Sometimes, this is religiously referenced by talking of it as part of God's grand design ("it's the way men are created"); sometimes, it is supported with reference to biology or evolution ("men are stronger than women"); sometimes, appeal is also made to the need for social order ("without men in charge everything would be chaotic"). But for many men the belief in natural order is a given, something intrinsic to the fabric of the world that does not need to be discussed, questioned, or analyzed. Men in charge is simply part of the natural order of what it means to be human. Consider, for example, the following passage from the interview with Grant:

> they [women] now have been put in a position where they're getting a lot more power, um, and I don't know if they have the capabilities of grasping this power…

Grant draws from natural order discourses to question women's capabilities to lead and in doing so portrays a highly gendered notion of who has entitlement to positions of power, privileging men. Such discourses are also apparent in our interviews with women, such as in the following account:

> They say that it's god's rule that the man rules the house… I used to hear that from my husband although he wasn't a religious person. "I am the head of this house, that is god's rule". (Michelle)

In this extract, Michele illustrates her husband's positioning as "ruler" of the house with the use of active voicing in which she reconstructs the words of her husband in order to lend weight to her account.

Adams et al. (1995) identified the rhetorical devices men who had used violence against women used to endorse men's dominance and entitlement including reference ambiguity (such as pronoun ambiguity), axiom markers (as discussed above), synecdoche (a reference which substitutes a part for a whole or a whole for a part), metaphor and metonymy (substituting something that has become associated with the object). An example of reference ambiguity is "that is god's rule" to justify male dominance or "it takes two to tango" to implicate the woman in the man's violence; an example of metaphor is "she presses my buttons" to suggest provocation, or "I just exploded" to suggest a loss of control or responsibility for violence; an example of synecdoche is "it was just a bit of *push and shove*" when referring to physical violence; and an example of metonymy is "she is too *lippy*" to refer to what a woman says.

The commonsense use of rhetoric rendered these male discourses as simply part of the normative socio-cultural climate in New Zealand, making them resistant to challenge. The men who we interviewed drew on these discourses to justify and explain their violence and support their accounts that men were naturally dominant in heterosexual relationships. In their accounts, men's entitlement to dominance was just part of the natural order and therefore unquestionable.

Grant employed natural order discourses to support his argument that men should be in control and in charge. He criticized "the feminism thing" and argued that money wouldn't be an issue if "women were still living in the regime where you … got married, had a child within the first year of the marriage. The wife stayed at home." He draws on patriarchal values making nostalgic reference to traditional sex roles as a solution to having to navigate gender equitable practices.

Other discourse analysts have worked to uncover the language employed to justify and excuse men's domestic violence against women thereby assisting the identification of the norms that support such violence (Towns, 2015). For example, Dragiewicz (2008) examined the antifeminist backlash rhetoric of USA fathers' rights groups responding on web sites to the Violence Against Women Act. The primary themes she identified were demands for "formal equality" or gender obfuscating language in law, calls for the reaffirmation of patriarchy, and objections to women's authority or voice. These themes were connected to child custody and support issues. Van Niekirk and Boonzaier (2016) found that South African men who had been violent to their partners employed masculinity discourses of male dominance and promoted the subordination of women.

A man's enactment of natural order discourses creates ideological dilemmas (Billig et al., 1988) for women. Towns and Adams (2009) explored the accounts of women who had been raised in a community that advocated women's equity, has women in leadership roles, and encourages women to do anything. Women described being caught between ideologies of patriarchy—demonstrated through the man's enforcement of male privilege—and feminist ideologies of gender equity. Intellectually, they might adhere to ideologies of gender equity, but their lived experience of their partner was of patriarchal practices, denigration, criticism, and punishment if they strayed beyond the boundaries of his expected traditional gendered roles. In this context, the woman can either remain silent, thereby being complicit with his patriarchal expectations, or be constructed by the man as "unlovable," "ball-breaking," or "man-hating" if she confronts him. In the face of this dilemma, many women remained silent.

Natural order discourses work by shaming the woman and wearing her down with criticism, which is typically gendered in its origins (Enander, 2010; Hyden, 2005). In commonsense understandings, the home is constituted as a place of love and happiness, consequently love is difficult to reconcile with violence and coercive control. Those men who use violence against women work to redefine this commonsense meaning of the love/violence distinction by exploiting gendered assumptions and traditional narratives and beliefs. Traditionally, women's role has been to promote the home as a loving environment for the man and their children and to selflessly ensure loving relationships. Her inability to manage this expectation in the context of the man's domestic violence is constituted by the man, her, and others as a failure on her part. The effect is to diminish the woman, and shame and silence her from talking of the violence.

Jack (1991) has described women as having a critical "over-eye" that maintains oversight of their actions and criticizes them according to whether they comply with expected gendered norms or were the "good woman." This critical gendered internal scrutiny was particularly harsh when the woman was in a relationship with a man who used violence against her. In her silencing theory of women's depression, she described the ways in which gendered norms influenced women to be silent and self-sacrificing rather than speak of the gendered matters that contributed to their depression. In Towns and Adams (2016), we elaborated more on this silencing theory in relation to men's domestic violence and described the rhetoric and associated gendered norms that contribute to the man's blaming of the woman and the obfuscation of his violence.

The results of the study showed how colonizing and natural order discourses were employed by men to shift the blame for the violence towards the woman and to justify and excuse their violence. The man depicts the woman as never meeting his exemplary gendered standards. The implication is that if she had met such standards he would not have needed to be violent. In these discourses, she is the one who needs to change and had she done so his violence would not have occurred. Women described working hard on housework, having the meals on time and keeping the children well behaved in order to comply with the man's expectations. For example, Ann described the expectations on her to carry out all the housework when she was also working:

> The dynamics are: 'Okay if you're going to want to work, make sure that you still keep- you know, carry on the housework as well.' … It's almost as if 'Well if I don't do it it's not going to get done and I don't want a hassle.' You know 'I don't want to create anymore hassle.' So they almost emotionally have us at odds, so that it just too much trouble to bother them.

Foucault's (1977) term "docile bodies" refers to the ways in which those subjected to power practices comply with the expectations of those exercising power, who are able to assert control whether present or not, due to unpredictable surveillance and punishment for non-compliance. Under such power practices, people become docile and compliant in order to avoid unpredictable punishment. Some women used language that suggested their self-regulation produced "docile bodies" of them: a consequence of the man's violence and coercive control and the women's attempts to provide the perfect love that would comply with his natural order expectations. For example, some women described themselves as becoming "puppets" and "robots" manipulated and controlled by the man, who was never satisfied with the woman's actions, decisions, and choices. In their accounts, the woman loses agency and becomes as if a tool of the man.

Conclusion

Discursive psychology has enabled a much more nuanced interpretation of the dynamics of domestic violence, situating the actions of men and women in this context within a broader socio-cultural, discursive, and ideological framework. Our work in this area suggests that men who use violence draw on commonsense understandings to silence talk of the violence, avoid responsibility, and shift the blame onto the woman. Men's coercive control of women and intermittent violence is enabled by various discursive strategies, which allow men to maintain control over important resources in the home: financial and material resources, emotional resources, moral authority, and leadership. In these respects, men's violence against women is not markedly different from violence in other contexts. Such discursive control, however, causes harm to women and children. Many men remain invested in such control and this investment is demonstrated by the prevalence of such violence towards women, their actions to attempt to obfuscate and degender such violence and by their inactions and therefore complicity with men's violence against women.

The Canadian context stands out as different because of the substantially smaller prevalence of such violence in this country. Canadian men introduced the White Ribbon Day following the mass killing by Marc Lépine, who claimed to be fighting feminism prior to killing 14 women and injuring 10 other women and four men, then killing himself, at the École Polytechnique in Montreal on 6 December 1989. White Ribbon Day, which has spread internationally, provides an opportunity for men to commit to never using violence against a woman and to reflect on what sort of society they want, how they want the women in their lives to be treated and what future they want for their daughters. Canada has shown how men can collectively act to reduce such violence if they are prepared to look to the future for the women in their lives and enable women to access the same resources that they enjoy.

Cultural norms reinforced and produced through discursive strategies account for whether victims/survivors of men's domestic violence can speak up publicly. In Sweden, Gottzen (2016) described gender equity as a value that both men and women were proud of and violence against women as transgressing this cultural value. He described men's shame about their violence as a consequence of these cultural norms, which contributed to their concealment of their violence, but these cultural norms were also valuable in bringing about disclosure. In many countries, however, women are silenced from talking of such violence. Erez, Ibarra, and Gur (2015) described the ways cultural norms and structural inequities contributed to the concealment of violence against women within minority Palestinian communities living in Israel. Some women from these Palestinian communities described violence against women as normative within their culture, and some preferred the local community response to this violence over the legal interventions of a state that they regarded as oppressive and prejudiced against them. Towns et al. (2003) described the ways language was employed to silence talk of such violence in New Zealand when the men who were violent towards their women partners knew that others were aware of their violence and when friends and family had knowledge of their violence.

Theismeyer (2003) described such silence and awareness as a "secret non-secret" enabled by the utilization of discursive resources. Outlining a discursive silencing theory she described the layers of concealment of gender-based violence from the discourses employed between individuals, to those discourses drawn on to support gender normative values and hide the violence within communities, to those used to conceal violence at the political level to ensure that the status quo remains and that changes that would stop the violence do not occur. Discourses and other linguistic resources may be understood to provide the "cultural scaffolding" for the concealment of gender-based violence against women (Gavey, 2005) as they articulate and inform the values and normative beliefs that contribute to the ways in which such violence is hidden, justified, and enabled.

However, as the Canadian and Swedish contexts show, by raising consciousness of the norms and discourses that support violence against women, by working against the discourses that silence women's talk of such violence, and by acting to counter colonizing and natural order discourses, the normative climate that enables violence against women can be resisted, with the ultimate outcome being to reduce such violence. These transformative changes will happen more quickly when there is the political and societal will for change enabled by global movements towards gender equity.

References

Adams, P. J. (2012). *Masculine empire: How men use violence to keep women in line*. Auckland: Dunmore.

Adams, P. J., Towns, A., & Gavey, N. (1995). Dominance and entitlement: The rhetoric men use to discuss their violence towards women. *Discourse & Society, 6*, 387–406.

Alio, A. P., Nana, P. N., & Salihu, H. M. (2009). Spousal violence and potentially preventable single and recurrent spontaneous fetal loss in an African setting: Cross-sectional study. *The Lancet, 373*, 318–324.

Bergman, N., & Brismar, B. (1991). A 5-year follow-up study of 117 battered women. *American Journal of Public Health, 81*, 1486–1489.

Billig, M., Condor, S., Edwards, D., Gane, M., Middleton, D., & Radley, A. (1988). *Ideological dilemmas: A social psychology of everyday thinking*. London: Sage.

Black, M. C. (2011). Intimate partner violence and adverse health consequences. *American Journal of Lifestyle Medicine, 5*, 428–439.

Breckenridge, J., Hamer, J., Newton, B., & Valentine, K. (2013). *NSW homelessness action plan extended evaluation: Final evaluation report for long-term accommodation and support for women and children experiencing domestic and family violence*. Sydney: NSW Government.

Briere, J., & Jordan, C. E. (2004). Violence against women: Outcome complexity and implications for assessment and treatment. *Journal of Interpersonal Violence, 19*, 1252–1276.

Cahill, A. (2015). Bodies, sex work and ethics: Thinking beyond objectification. Psychology Department Gender and Sexual Politics Symposium, Engineering School, University of Auckland, 28 January.

Christie, D. J., Tint, B. S., Wagner, R. V., & Winter, D. D. (2008). Peace psychology for a peaceful world. *American Psychologist, 63*, 540–552.

de Bocanegra, H. T., Rostovtseva, D. P., Khera, S., & Godhwani, N. (2010). Birth control sabotage and forced sex: Experiences reported by women in domestic violence shelters. *Violence Against Women, 16*, 601–612.

Dragiewicz, M. (2008). Patriarchy reasserted: Fathers' rights and anti-VAWA Activism. *Feminist Criminology, 3*, 121–144.

Dutton, M. A., Green, B. L., Kaltman, S. I., Roesch, D. M., Zeffiro, T. A., & Krause, E. D. (2006). Intimate partner violence, PTSD, and adverse health outcomes. *Journal of Interpersonal Violence, 21*, 955–968.

Ehrensaft, M. K., Cohen, P., Brown, J., Smailes, E., Chen, H., & Johnson, J. G. (2003). Intergenerational transmission of partner violence: A 20 year prospective study. *Journal of Consulting and Clinical Psychology, 71*, 741–753.

Ellsberg, M., Jansen, H. A. F. M., Heise, L. L., Watts, C. H., & Garcia-Moreno, C. (2008). Intimate partner violence and women's physical and mental health in the WHO multi-country study on women's health and domestic violence: An observational study. *The Lancet, 371*, 1165–1172.

Enander, V. (2010). "A fool to keep staying": Battered women labeling themselves stupid as an expression of gendered shame. *Violence Against Women, 16*, 5–31.

Erez, E., Ibarra, P. R., & Gur, O. M. (2015). At the intersection of private and political conflict zones: Policing domestic violence in the Arab community in Israel. *International Journal of Offender Therapy and Comparative Criminology, 59*, 930–963.

Fanslow, J., Robinson, E., Crengle, S., & Perese, L. (2010). Juxtaposing beliefs and reality: Prevalence rates of intimate partner violence and attitudes to violence and gender roles reported by New Zealand women. *Violence Against Women, 16*, 812–831.

Fanslow, J., Silva, M., Whitehead, A., & Robinson, E. (2008). Pregnancy outcomes and intimate partner violence in New Zealand. *Australian and New Zealand Journal of Obstetrics and Gynaecology, 48*, 391–397.

Foucault, M. (1977). *Discipline and punish: The birth of the prison*. New York: Pantheon.

Foucault, M. (1980). Two lectures: Lecture one 7 January 1976, Lecture two 14 January 1976. In C. Gordon (Ed.), *Power/knowledge: Selected interviews and other writings 1972–1977 by Michel Foucault* (pp. 79–108). Brighton: Harvester Press.

Foucault, M. (1982). Afterword: The subject and power. In H. L. Dreyfus & P. Rabinow (Eds.), *Michel Foucault: Beyond structuralism and hermeneutics* (pp. 208–226). Chicago, IL: University of Chicago Press.

Foucault, M. (1988). Technologies of the self. In L. H. Martin, H. Gutman, & P. H. Hutton (Eds.), *Technologies of the self: A seminar with Michel Foucault* (pp. 16–49). London: Tavistock.

Foucault, M. (1991). Governmentality. In G. Burchell, C. Gordon, & P. Miller (Eds.), *The Foucault effect: Studies in governmentality* (pp. 86–104). London: Harvester Wheatsheaf.

Freire, P. (1970). *Pedogogy of the oppressed*. New York: Seabury Press.

FVDRC. (2015). *Family Violence Death Review Committee fourth annual report: December 2012-December 2013*. Wellington: Health Quality and Safety Commission New Zealand.

Galtung, J. (1996). *Peace by peaceful means: Peace and conflict, development and civilization*. London: Sage.

Garcia-Moreno, C. (2009). Intimate partner violence and fetal loss. *The Lancet, 373*, 278–279.

Garcia-Moreno, C., Jansen, H. A., Ellsberg, M., Heise, L. L., & Watts, C. (2006). Prevalence of intimate partner violence: Findings from the WHO multi-country study on women's health and domestic violence. *The Lancet, 368*, 1260–1269.

Gavey, N. (1989). Feminist poststructuralism and discourse analysis. *Psychology of Women Quarterly, 13*, 459–475.

Gavey, N. (2005). *Just sex? The cultural scaffolding of rape*. London: Routledge.

Gavey, N. (2011). Feminist poststructuralism and discourse analysis revisited. *Psychology of Women Quarterly, 35*, 183–188.

Glass, N., Laughon, K., Campbell, J., Block, C. R., Hanson, G., Sharps, P., et al. (2008). Non-fatal strangulation is an important risk factor for homicide of women. *Journal of Emergency Medicine, 35*, 329–335.

Gottzen, L. (2016). Displaying shame: Men's violence towards women in a culture of gender equality. In M. Hyden, M. Wade, & A. Gadd (Eds.), *Response based approaches to the study of interpersonal violence* (pp. 156–175). London: Palgrave MacMillan.

Hand, T., Chung, D., & Peter, M. (2009). *The use of information and communication technologies to coerce and control in domestic violence and following separation*. Retrieved from www.adfc.unsw.edu.au

Hyden, M. (2005). 'I must have been an idiot to let it go on': Agency and positioning in battered women's narratives of leaving. *Feminism & Psychology, 15*, 171–190.

Jack, D. C. (1991). *Silencing the self: Women and depression*. New York: Harvard University Press.

Jackson, H., Philp, E., Nuttall, R. L. & Diller, L. (2002). Traumatic brain injury: A hidden consequence for battered women. *Professional Psychology, Research and Practice, 33*, 39–45.

LeCouteur, A., & Oxlad, M. (2011). Managing accountability for domestic violence: Identities, membership categories and morality in perpetrators' talk. *Feminism & Psychology, 21*, 5–28.

Lerner, M. J. (1980). *The belief in a just world: A fundamental delusion*. New York: Plenum.

Lloyd, S. & Taluc, N. (1999). The effect of male violence on female employment. *Violence Against Women, 5*, 370–392.

Ludermir, A. B., Schraiber, L. B., D'Oliveira, A. F. P. L., Franca-Junior, I., & Jansen, H. A. (2008). Violence against women by their intimate partner and common mental disorders. *Social Science & Medicine, 66*, 1008–1018.

Martin, J., & Pritchard, R. (2010). *Learning from tragedy: Homicide within families in New Zealand 2002-2006*. Wellington: Ministry of Social Development.

Nairn, R. G., & McCreanor, T. N. (1990). Insensitivity and hypersensitivity: An imbalance in Pakeha accounts of racial conflict. *Journal of Language and Social Psychology, 9*, 293–308.

Nairn, R. G., & McCreanor, T. N. (1991). Race talk and common sense: Patterns in Pakeha discourse on Maori/Pakeha relations in New Zealand. *Journal of Language and Social Psychology, 10*, 245–262.

Office for National Statistics. (2017). *Compendium: Focus on violent crime and sexual offences, England and Wales, year ending March 2016: Homicide*. Retrieved from https://www.ons.gov.uk/peoplepopulationandcommunity/crimeandjustice/compendium/focusonviolentcrimeandsexualoffences/yearendingmarch2016/homicide#how-are-victims-and-suspects-related

Snively, S. (1995). The New Zealand economic cost of family violence. *Social Policy Journal of New Zealand,* (4). Retrieved from https://www.msd.govt.nz/about-msd-and-our-work/publications-resources/journals-and-magazines/social-policy-journal/spj04/04-the-new-zealand-economic-cost-of-family-violence.html

Stark, E. (2007). *Coercive control: How men entrap women in personal life*. Oxford: Oxford University Press.

Swanberg, J. E., & Logan, T. K. (2005). Domestic violence and employment: A qualitative study. *Journal of Occupational Health Psychology, 10*, 3–17.

Taft, C. T., Murphy, C. M., King, L. A., Dedyn, J. M., & Musser, P. H. (2005). Posttraumatic Stress Disorder symptomatology among partners of men in treatment for relationship abuse. *Journal of Abnormal Psychology, 114*, 259–268.

Theismeyer, L. (2003). Introduction. In L. Theismeyer (Ed.), *Discourses and silencing: Representation and the language of displacement* (pp. 1–42). Amsterdam: John Benjamins.

Towns, A. J. (2014). *"It's about having control back, freedom from fear." An evaluation of the Shine safe@home programme for victims/survivors of domestic violence*. Auckland: Mt Albert

Psychological Services Ltd. Retrieved from https://library.nzfvc.org.nz/cgi-bin/koha/opac-detail.pl?biblionumber=4680

Towns, A. (2015). *Discursive and coercive control: Theorizing men's domestic violence against women using the language control wheel as a training tool.* Paper presented at the NZ Psychological Society Conference, 'Te Ao Turoa—The World In Front of Us', Waikato University, Hamilton, New Zealand. Retrieved from https://www.researchgate.net/publication/311648495

Towns, A. J., & Adams, P. (2016). "I didn't know whether I was right or wrong or just bewildered." Ambiguity, responsibility, and silencing women's talk of men's domestic violence. *Violence Against Women, 22*, 496–520.

Towns, A. J. & Adams, P. J. (2009). Staying quiet or getting out: Some ideological dilemmas faced by women who experience violence from male partners. *British Journal of Social Psychology, 48*, 735–754.

Towns, A., Adams, P. J., & Gavey, N. (2003). Silencing talk of men's violence towards women. In L. Theismeyer (Ed.), *Discourse and silencing: Representation and the language of displacement* (pp. 43–77). Amsterdam: John Benjamin.

Tutty, L. M., Ogden, C., Giurgiu, B., & Weaver-Dunlop, G. (2013). I built my house of hope: Abused women and pathways into homelessness. *Violence Against Women, 19*, 1498–1517.

Van Niekirk, T. J. & Boonzaier, F. (2016) "The only solution there is to fight": Discourses of masculinity among South African domestically violence men. *Violence Against Women, 22*, 271–291.

VPC. (2016). *When men murder women: An analysis of 2014 homicide data.* Violence Policy Centre. Retrieved from http://www.vpc.org/studies/wmmw2016.pdf

Wolfe, D. A., & Jaffe, P. G. (1999). Emerging strategies in the prevention of domestic violence. *The Future of Children, 9*, 133–144.

World Health Organization. (2002). *World report on violence and health.* Geneva: WHO.

World Health Organization. (2004). *Preventing violence: A guide to implementing the recommendations of the World Report on Violence and Health.* Geneva: World Health Organisation. Retrieved from http://apps.who.int/iris/bitstream/10665/43014/1/9241592079.pdf

Zeitler, D. (2007). The abused female oral and maxillofacial surgery patient: Treatment approaches for identification and management. *Oral and Maxillofacial Surgery Clinics of North America, 19*, 259–265.

Chapter 4
The American Gun Control Debate: A Discursive Analysis

Simon Goodman and Bethany Perry

Introduction

The debate about gun control in the USA has enormous implications for peace and conflict because many thousands of people are killed or injured in gun-related violence each year. For example, in 2016 15,078 people were killed by firearms and twice as many were injured (Gun violence archive, 2017). Discursive psychology therefore has a major role to play in understanding this debate because it is due to the present impasse that guns remain easily accessible. Our position is that gun control is necessary to end these preventable deaths, and it will only be as a result of a shift in this debate that additional controls may become law. In this chapter, we will first briefly outline the scale of gun violence in the USA; we will then demonstrate the potential role of discursive psychology by showing how an action-oriented approach to the gun control debate can allow for a greater understanding of how arguments for and against gun controls are made, illustrated with speeches from President Barack Obama, who aimed to control gun ownership, and Wayne LaPierre, the executive vice president of the pro-gun lobby group the National Rifle Association (NRA). The benefits of taking a discursive approach to this issue of peace and conflict are shown to be an understanding of (1) the flexible ways that values such as 'protecting' can be used by opposing sides of the debate, (2) the ways in which national identity and history are drawn upon to both support *and* oppose gun controls, and (3) how distinct speeches are positioned against both existing arguments and anticipated counterarguments.

In the USA in 2016 there were 15,078 homicides by firearms (an average of over 41 each day). Approximately 270 million firearms are possessed by civilians (McDonald, LeBrun, Berman, & Krause, 2012). Mass shootings often result in calls for tighter gun controls; however, such calls are challenged with the Second

S. Goodman (✉) · B. Perry
Coventry University, Coventry, UK
e-mail: simon.goodman@coventry.ac.uk

© Springer Nature Switzerland AG 2018   67
S. Gibson (ed.), *Discourse, Peace, and Conflict*, Peace Psychology Book Series,
https://doi.org/10.1007/978-3-319-99094-1_4

Amendment of the US constitution which states that 'the right of the people to keep and bear Arms, shall not be infringed'. Gun control laws do currently exist; the National Firearms Act of 1934 and the Gun Control Act of 1968 both restrict the buying and owning of a firearm, prohibiting mail-order sales of weapons and knowingly selling to a minor, or an individual with prior criminal records and/or mental health issues. However, for some, these restrictions are not enough.

The ease with which American citizens can access guns remains central to the debate. The restrictions placed on the selling of weapons to individuals with a history of violence and/or mental health problems are cited by supporters of gun control as necessary to prevent shootings (Winkler, 2013). However, these restrictions appear not to be working, as demonstrated by high-profile examples such as the Virginia Tech shootings of 2007 ('25 Deadliest U.S. Mass Shootings' 2017) and the Gerald Hume case of 2013 (Christensen, 2013), in which a person with schizophrenia purchased numerous weapons and went on to kill his own mother. For pro-gun campaigners, it is these cases of shootings perpetrated by people with mental health problems that are cited as the grounds for allowing greater gun ownership so that people can protect themselves from events such as these (Winkler, 2013). So while President Obama called for Mental Health First Aid Training as a tool for teachers to identify signs of mental health problems in young people, the NRA highlights the existence of these shootings as the very reason why gun ownership should be encouraged as it is 'sick people' that are the problem, rather than the amount of guns privately owned in the USA (The Economist, 2013).

A particular focal point for debate in recent years was the aftermath of the Sandy Hook shooting. On the 14th December 2012, 20-year-old Adam Lanza entered Sandy Hook elementary school in Newtown, Connecticut. He proceeded to shoot and kill 20 children and 6 adults before shooting himself. A former student at Sandy Hook, Lanza had entered the school carrying an assault rifle and two handguns; all of which he used to open fire on the unarmed classrooms. Following this high-profile event, new calls for gun controls were made; however, all of the proposed gun controls that were suggested after the Sandy Hook shooting were defeated. Instead, the debate continues with no end in sight, resurfacing with each successive tragedy.

Gun Control Research

Research exploring gun control tends to favour positivistic methods that are used to assess factors such as the role of mental illness in mass shootings (e.g. McGinty, Webster, & Barry, 2013). Attitudes and opinions of American citizens have also been assessed. For example, Kleck, Gertz, and Bratton (2009) found that only 30% of US adults supported a law to ban handgun possession. Seate, Cohen, Fujioka, and Hoffner (2012) examined the perceived effects of news coverage of the Virginia Tech shooting using online surveys. Here 'gun owner' was shown to be a strong social identity, with gun owners appearing more dismissive of the message of news coverage surrounding the shootings than non-gun-owners. Wintemute (2014) surveyed 1601 licenced dealers and pawnbrokers in 43 states regarding support for tighter background checks. It was found that the majority of respondents supported tighter control. Patten, Thomas, and Wada (2013) showed that 70% of students opposed the option of carrying concealed guns to class whereas Bouffard, Nobles, Wells, and Cavanaugh (2012) argued that potentially all classrooms would be likely to contain a concealed handgun if carrying handguns on campuses was made legal. Braman and Kahan (2003) argue that attitudes to gun control can be explained in terms of valuing collectivism and equality, which is associated with support for controls, and valuing individualism and hierarchy, which predicts opposition to controls.

While this research provides a useful overview of attitudes towards gun control, it overlooks the way in which the debate itself is conducted. Researchers have highlighted how important the debate is, with Blendon, Young, and Hemenway (1996) demonstrating that it can be a deciding factor at presidential elections. O'Grady, Parnaby, and Schikschneit (2010) conducted an analysis of a mass shooting in Canada and found that the ideas presented in the media persisted for almost a year, suggesting that what is discussed in the media has a lasting impact. Yet despite this, there is limited research concentrating on the actual debate itself. The notable exceptions however, are discussed here. Downs (2002) argues that the media coverage of the debate is problematic, as it can silence public debate and polarise the debate which prevents common ground being found. McKinlay and Dunnet (1998, p. 37) summarised this polarisation as follows: 'Gun-control proponents view gun ownership as something which makes society less safe and more violent. Gun ownership proponents view gun ownership as something which makes "normal" citizens safer from the violence perpetrated by criminals'. Winkler (2013) demonstrated that this is exactly what happened following the Sandy Hook massacre. However, Winkler argued that the Democratic Party's usual avoidance of gun control (based on the potential damage this can do to electoral success) changed as a direct response to the shooting when President Obama began supporting gun control. In contrast, the NRA responded in their usual way, by saying that more, rather than fewer, guns are needed to prevent gun crime. However, despite the attention that has been given to the gun control debate, what is lacking is a detailed focus on the ways in which the arguments in the debate are made and what impact these may have. It will now be shown how discursive psychology can overcome this current gap in knowledge.

Discursive Psychology and the Gun Control Debate

As discursive psychology (DP, Edwards & Potter, 1992) is explicitly concerned with talk, in the gun control debate DP would advocate not focusing on what participants in the debate think or feel, but on what such talk can *accomplish* in the debate. There is now a wealth of discursive psychological work focusing on political debates, where the focus is on public debates that are designed to persuade members of the public to behave differently (see Tileagă, 2013 for a review). For example, Gibson (2012) argues for a discursive approach to peace research by focusing on televised debates in the lead up to the Iraq war of 2003. While the current research has a different focus, Gibson clearly demonstrated the ways in which talk in political discussions should not be seen to represent neutral and accurate representations of what participants think, but that this talk is designed to perform social actions; in Gibson's study this was to argue for or against the war in Iraq, in the current study therefore the focus will be on how arguments for and against tighter gun controls are made.

However discursive research has tended to focus on European and Australasian contexts, with limited analysis of American politics. One notable exception is McKinlay and Dunnet's (1998) analysis of gun-owner identities. McKinlay and Dunnet (1998) looked at how gun-owners presented themselves as reasonable and average and attempted to resist any suggestions that being a gun-owner may be a problematic identity. This analysis provides an example of the way in which a discursive approach can focus on how talk about guns can be used to perform social actions; in their case to show that gun-owners position themselves as normal and reasonable. However, what is lacking is an analysis of both sides of the debate over gun control. This chapter seeks to provide this, with a particular focus on the debates that followed the Sandy Hook massacre, in which President Obama failed to impose tighter gun controls.

The analysis focuses on key figures in the debate whose talk is analysed to see how their arguments are presented in a way that best promotes the policy they are aiming to promote. The specific research question addressed is therefore: In light of the failed attempt to impose tighter gun control following the Sandy Hook school shooting, how did President Obama and Wayne LaPierre argue for and against gun control in the USA?

Method

Data Corpus

Data were selected to reflect the opposing positions in the attempt to legislate for tighter gun control in the wake of the Sandy Hook massacre. While there were many speeches and commentaries made at this time, the present analysis focuses on a single speech from each 'side'. As the most prominent figures on each 'side' were President Obama, who proposed gun controls, and Wayne LaPierre, who opposed them, it was decided that a high-profile speech from each would be most appropriate to analyse. Obama's speech in favour of gun control, lasting 14 min, was delivered on April 17, 2013, following the failure of measures to increase gun control.[1] LaPierre's speech, lasting 23 min, was delivered on March 15, 2013 at a point where increased gun controls were looking like a possibility.[2] Both speeches are available as videos and transcripts for readers to engage with. It is these publicly available transcripts that were used for analysis. It is worth noting that these transcripts represent specific texts themselves that were provided to the public to present a particular version of the speech (each produced by representatives of the speaker), but which do not necessarily perfectly match the speeches that were given. Data of this kind can be considered 'naturally occurring' (e.g. Potter, 2004) in that they exist independently of the researcher which means that the issues being discussed are those topicalized by the speakers rather than by the researchers.

Analytic Strategy

Discourse analysis is ideal for focusing on what is accomplished through talk and is used to identify rhetorical strategies, or ways of talking that are designed to perform specific actions. An example of this can be seen in McKinlay and Dunnet's (1998) analysis of gun-owners in which speakers construct a normal (rather than violent or other problematic) identity by positioning themselves as 'average'. Following Wetherell's (1998) critical discursive social psychological approach, the analysis was conducted by focusing on speakers' talk regarding the invoking of psychological concepts, identities, and wider social discourses. The analysis is organised by dealing with a short extract of each speech in turn.

Analysis

The speeches demonstrate two polarised dichotomies. The first of these sees both speakers present themselves as working to protect something important. Obama presents his measures as in the service of protecting lives, whereas LaPierre presents his opposition to the same measures as designed to protect freedom. A second dichotomy can be seen where Obama constructs those who support gun control as 'courageous', whereas for LaPierre these same people are constructed as villains.

---

[1] A video of the Obama's speech is available here: http://www.nytimes.com/video/us/politics/100000002177815/president-obama-on-the-gun-vote.html. A transcript of Obama's speech is available here: http://swampland.time.com/2013/04/17/president-obamas-speech-on-gun-control-bill-defeat-transcript/#ixzz2j88uLhPc

[2] A video of LaPierre's speech is available here: http://www.nranews.com/a1f/video/cpac-2013-nra-ceo-evp-wayne-lapierre/list/lapierre-speeches A transcript of LaPierre's speech is available here: http://home.nra.org/pdf/Wayne_LaPierre_3_15_13.pdf

Both speakers state that their campaigns will continue into the future, whatever the outcome of the current attempt to bring about tighter gun controls.

Protecting Lives vs. Protecting Freedom

This opening portion of President Obama's speech serves to introduce the topic by directly referring to previous high-profile shootings:

Extract 1: 'Protecting lives' (Obama)
1. A few months ago, in response to too many tragedies — including
2. the shootings of a United States Congresswoman, Gabby Giffords, who's here
3. today, and the murder of 20 innocent schoolchildren and their teachers –this
4. country took up the cause of protecting more of our people from gun violence.
5. Families that know unspeakable grief summoned the courage to petition their
6. elected leaders – not just to honour the memory of their children, but to protect
7. the lives of all our children.

There are a number of noteworthy features of this section. First gun crime is presented as a serious problem through the references to 'tragedies', (line 1; note the use of the plural here) 'shooting', (line 2) 'murder' of 'innocent children' (line 3), and the reference to Giffords, whose shooting became a major news story. Obama's reference to her physical presence adds an extra potency to his words. It is this serious problem from which Obama claims people need protection (line 4). The response, which is presented as offering that protection, is not attributed to him individually, but instead to the whole country (line 4); by doing this Obama is able to present support for gun control as a sensible response to the issues that he has just referred to and, importantly, as consensual. Obama positions himself as speaking on behalf of the entire nation, but the action of taking 'up the cause' is positioned as being independent of him. The further reference to 'our people' (line 4) once more serves to position Obama as a typical American, who is speaking on behalf of everyone. The victims of gun crime are presented as vulnerable and in need of protection throughout this extract. In addition to the reference to schoolchildren, Obama also refers to 'families' (line 5) and again to 'children' (lines 6 and 7) which gives a specific moral identity worthy of protection. For Obama then, this is an issue of protecting American citizens. As can be seen in the next extract taken from LaPierre's speech, the notion of protection remains, but for him it is freedom that is presented as in need of protection so that people are able to defend themselves:

Extract 2: 'Protecting freedom' (LaPierre)
1. The political elites may not like it. The liberal media can keep hating
2. on me. But I'm still standing, unapologetic and unflinching in defence of our
3. individual freedom. They can call me crazy and whatever else they want, but
4. NRA's nearly 5 million members and America's 100 million gun owners will
5. not back down — not now, not ever. The Second Amendment is not just
6. words on parchment. It's not some frivolous suggestion from our Founding
7. Fathers to be interpreted by whim. It lies at the heart of what this country
8. was founded upon. Our Founding Fathers knew that without Second

9. Amendment freedom, all of our freedoms could be in jeopardy. Our
10. individual liberty is the very essence of America. It is what makes America
11. unique. If you aren't free to protect yourself — when government puts its
12. thumb on that freedom — then you aren't free at all.

This extract occurs immediately after his opening remarks. He immediately starts by presenting himself as the underdog who is challenging the establishment (lines 1–2). This is similar to talk of the far right, in which speakers present themselves as bravely challenging the 'elite' (e.g. the former leader of the far right British National Party presented himself as opposing the British elite [Johnson & Goodman, 2013]; also see Berlet and Lyons [2000] on right-wing populism in the USA). LaPierre explicitly states that he makes no apologies for his beliefs (line 2) which are attributed to the importance of 'individual freedom' (line 3). While LaPierre refers to himself (e.g. 'keep hating on me' lines 1–2) in a way that Obama does not, LaPierre (like Obama) nevertheless presents himself as speaking on behalf of a very large group; at least all (100 million) gun-owning Americans, and possibly all Americans ('our' line 2).

For LaPierre, it is individual freedom that is under threat, and this is something that is presented as extremely serious. He draws upon the Second Amendment rights (lines 5–9) as being an extremely important part of American history, that is worthy of defending, and yet under threat. Indeed, it is his appeal to personal freedom that is presented as allowing the freedom 'to protect yourself' (line 11). This means that LaPierre, like Obama, displays a concern for personal protection, but what is different is that for LaPierre individual protection (signalled through the use of 'protect *yourself*') is only possible if individual freedoms are protected (see O'Neill [2007] for a discussion of how the NRA develop the rhetoric of individual protection through gun ownership). LaPierre therefore presents himself as taking on a government that is set on reducing individual freedom. He goes on to construct what it is to be American, by drawing on the notion of personal freedoms (line 10). Those who oppose individual freedoms therefore are presented as being un-American, and working against protecting individuals, especially if it is the government that is doing this. LaPierre therefore presents his opposition to gun control as necessary because it is about protecting what it is to be American, which is to be free. He is presenting himself as the archetypal American, which puts him in direct competition with the government which is presented as threatening.

Protecting is clearly a positive action, and it would be difficult for opponents of gun control to be presented as not interested in protecting, especially when children are being highlighted as an example of those in need of protection. For LaPierre then it is perhaps not surprising that protection is also a key part of the argument, but here a different value—freedom—is presented as in need of protection because according to LaPierre this is necessary to allow for personal protection yet gun controls are presented as directly violating this. By focussing on protecting liberty in this way, it is sometimes difficult to see that LaPierre's speech is about guns at all, so to some extent the focus of the debate is shifted and the potential harm caused by guns is discursively removed.

Overcoming Political Differences vs. Pushing Their 'Political Agenda'

In the following extract, we see Obama continue his speech and also refer to the Second Amendment. This indicates that, although the two speeches are of course separate and discrete, each is designed to deal with and address the previous—and anticipated—arguments that have been, and will be, made in relation to gun control. In this respect, we can understand the speeches as part of a dialogical network (Leudar & Nekvapil, 2004) in which seemingly isolated events are organised in response to, and in anticipation of, counterarguments. In this case, Obama refers to those that have worked on the (now unsuccessful) attempt to bring in further gun controls as courageously bridging political differences to support gun control, precisely because of their support for the Second Amendment.

Extract 3: 'Courageously overcoming political differences' (Obama)
1. I'm going to speak plainly and honestly about what's happened here because
2. the American people are trying to figure out how can something have
3. 90 percent support and yet not happen. We had a Democrat and a Republican
4. – both gun owners, both fierce defenders of our Second Amendment,
5. with 'A' grades from the NRA — come together and worked together to
6. write a commonsense compromise on background checks. And I want to
7. thank Joe Manchin and Pat Toomey for their courage in doing that. That
8. was not easy given their traditional strong support for Second Amendment rights.

Once more, Obama positions himself as speaking as, and on behalf of, a 'typical' American, which is shown through the use of 'American people' (line 2) and then 'we' in the following line. Obama presents the defeat of the measure as surprising and unfair (signalled through the reference to '90% support' and 'trying to figure out'). The explicit reference to 'common sense' (line 6) to describe the proposal does a number of things: first it works to support the proposal, second it works to suggest that opposing it does not make sense (which strengthens the notion of surprise signalled through 'trying to figure out'), and third it further strengthens the idea that Obama is representing normal people, who share this 'common' sense. Common sense has been shown to be a feature of political talk because it constructs consensus (Capdevila & Callaghan, 2008) when attempts are made to put forward a potentially problematic policy.

Next comes Obama's portrayal of politicians who are explicitly referred to as coming from across the political divide (line 3), as NRA members and, importantly, as supporters of the Second Amendment (which is highlighted through the repeated reference to this, lines 4 and 8). This works to manage his stake and interest because he is aligning with people that may be expected to disagree with him. It is also noteworthy that these politicians are presented as 'defenders' (line 4) of the Second Amendment because by so doing Obama is aligning himself with the Second Amendment and presenting it as something that he is not attacking, but respects and wants to maintain. This is in direct opposition to LaPierre's suggestion (as seen in the previous extract) that the government is attacking these rights and therefore the freedom of American people and provides further evidence for how the two speeches featured in this analysis can be seen to be linked in a dialogical network and share the same argumentative backdrop. These politicians are presented as brave precisely because they value the Second Amendment, but are also working for the majority of American citizens, and against what could be presented as their own interest, in protecting citizens' safety. This works to present protection of safety and protection of the Second Amendment as compatible, rather than in conflict, as LaPierre suggests.

Obama presents his allies as courageous for overcoming political boundaries, and in so doing works to construct a political consensus and to avoid potential conflict. LaPierre however does the opposite and presents his opponents—politicians seeking tighter gun control—as villains and enemies. LaPierre presents himself as different from politicians, who are presented as attempting to curtail individual freedoms:

Extract 4: Pushing their 'political agenda' (LaPierre)
1.   Senator Dianne Feinstein admitted that she had her gun ban bill ready
2.   to go A YEAR AGO, tucked away in a drawer, just waiting for the right opportunity.
3.   Really? Waiting for unspeakable tragedy to push her political agenda?
4.   And they wonder why most Americans don't trust Congress. They are simply not
5.   serious about making our kids or our country safer. If they were serious,
6.   they'd arrest, prosecute and imprison felons with guns, gangs with guns and
7.   drug dealers with guns — as many as they can find. But they don't do that.
8.   They let them go free.

Here, LaPierre criticises a senator who proposed a gun bill. Feinstein is presented as opportunistically waiting for the change to bring in gun control, which allows LaPierre to present her as the villain. Rather than responding to a mass shooting (which is how Obama presents gun control) those favouring gun control are presented as using the shooting for their own ends. This allows LaPierre to go on to suggest that they do not really care about safety, which, as shown in extract one, is a key thrust of the gun control position, therefore undermining a key gun control argument. Instead, in an example of stake attribution (Edwards & Potter, 1992), LaPierre positions Feinstein as using the Sandy Hook massacre opportunistically for her own ends. Again, LaPierre presents himself as speaking on behalf of all American people (through the use of 'most Americans' (line 4) and the repetition of 'our' (line 5)), who are again presented as distinct from, and not represented by, politicians. This serves to present LaPierre and the NRA as political outsiders and underdogs (rather than as a major lobbying force) and as more representative of American citizens than politicians, who are presented as untrustworthy. This is an important rhetorical move for LaPierre as he is now able to present those supporting gun control, who are glossed as politicians through the reference to 'Congress' (line 4) as failing to protect victims of crime. This is brought about through the use of a three part list of those that politicians are failing to properly deal with (felons, gangs, and drug dealers).

The authorities (who are proposing gun control) are presented as weak on crime, whereas those supporting gun rights are presented as tough on crime. This means that, in common with the NRA members studied by McKinlay and Dunnet (1998), LaPierre presents himself as normal and typical by contrast with criminal others who are seen as the problem. However, in this case a reference is made to the criminal other to highlight and criticise politicians who are accused of not properly dealing with these criminals because they are interested only in controlling guns rather than controlling crime.

We Are Going to Get This Right/Stand and Fight

Returning to Obama's speech, towards the end he summarises and concludes his points and uses this to make a call for a continuation of the campaign for tighter gun control:

Extract 5: 'we are going to get this right' (Obama)
1. And I'm assuming that the emotions that we've all felt since Newtown, the
2. emotions that we've all felt since Tucson and Aurora and Chicago — the pain we
3. share with these families and families all across the country who've lost a loved
4. one to gun violence — I'm assuming that's not a temporary thing. I'm assuming
5. our expressions of grief and our commitment to do something different to
6. prevent these things from happening are not empty words.
7. I believe we're going to be able to get this done. Sooner or later, we are going to get
8. this right. The memories of these children demand it. And so do the American
people.

Reminiscent of a speech preparing troops for battle, Obama's language suggests that the campaign has only just started and will continue until the objective is met. Graham, Keenan, and Dowd (2004) identified a strategy of constructing a thoroughly 'evil Other' in historical 'call to arms' speeches. Obama's 'evil Other' is not Wayne LaPierre himself or even the NRA, but guns. This means that Obama can attempt to unify the American people against an object rather than take on any individuals or organisations. The objective isn't presented as gun control for the sake of it, but again Obama returns to the idea of protection, and in particular protecting 'families' (mentioned twice on line three) and 'children' (line 8). As with the previous extracts, Obama positions himself as speaking on behalf of all American citizens, signalled through the use of 'we' (lines 1, 2 and 7) and the final explicit mention of 'the American people' (line 8).

This closing statement is full of references to psychological categories (such as 'emotions', 'felt', and 'grief') that are designed to perform actions. As Edwards (1997) argues, such talk about emotions (which are explicitly introduced and referred to by Obama) does not offer an insight into what speakers 'truly' feel, but instead can be used to do things. Here, Obama is using this emotion talk in an attempt to galvanise the American public, which he is claiming to speak on behalf of, into supporting gun controls. Of particular note is Obama's reference to shared pain (lines 2 and 2–3) which works to position Obama again as typical of the American people who he not only understands, but shares feelings with. This works to normalise Obama so that he is presented as an ordinary person (which challenges a potential counterargument that he is an out of touch member of the elite, as implied by speakers such as LaPierre) who is representative of American people. By talking about shared pain in this way, Obama makes opposition to his plans sound particularly unreasonable; this makes it extremely difficult for an opponent to say that they do not share this pain and are happy for it to continue. Rather than admitting defeat, Obama suggests that his 'campaign' will continue so a 'march of progress' repertoire is drawn upon (lines 7–8) where gun control is presented as the only sensible outcome and something that will eventually be reached.

In this final extract, we can see that LaPierre's talk also contains a call to continue the campaign; however, unlike Obama who refrains from using battle metaphors, LaPierre is explicit about this being a fight. He does this by returning to the pro-freedom and anti-elite strategies identified above:

Extract 6: 'Stand and Fight' (LaPierre)
1. You are here because you want to make your own
2. difference, take your own stand. Plant your feet firmly in the foundation of
3. freedom, don't be swayed by the winds of political insanity, and no matter
4. what, let the elitists who scorn you be damned. Fill your heart with pride.
5. Clear your eyes with conviction. This is your time to Stand and Fight — now
6. and in the next election and the one after that. Now and for the rest of your
7. life. Always stand and always fight for freedom!

As in extract two, LaPierre is highlighting freedom as the reason for fighting; again no explicit mention of guns is made, but instead freedom (lines 3 and 7) is repeated. Reflecting Obama's call to continue the challenge, LaPierre refers to taking a stand (line 2). LaPierre turns this theoretical debate into a physical one, not just through the battle analogies (lines 2, 5, and 7) but through two three part lists, first: 'Plant your feet firmly in the foundation of freedom' (lines 2–3), 'don't be swayed by the winds of political insanity' (line 3), and 'no matter what, let the elitists who scorn you be damned' (3–4) which is followed immediately be the second list: 'Fill your heart with pride' (line 4), 'Clear your eyes with conviction' (line 5), 'This is your time to Stand and Fight' (line 5). The enemy for this fight is presented as being politicians and the elite, and their actions are presented as being particularly offensive, as signalled through the reference to 'insanity' (line 3) which works to present them as irrational. This sets up a clear distinction in which the elite enemy 'them' shows contempt for 'us', who are being called upon to fight this contempt.

The reference to the elite is again reminiscent of far right talk in the UK (Johnson & Goodman, 2013) where a vaguely defined elite is constructed as doing harm against the majority of the country for reasons that are never explained, so there is a similar conspiratorial argument here. However, while LaPierre's elite is presented as a somewhat homogenous group (line 4: 'the elitists'), acting against those the speech is directed towards, the listeners are presented rather differently, as individuals. Rather than referring to 'us' or even members of the NRA, references are made to 'you' (lines 1 and 4) and 'your' (lines 1, 2, 4, 5, and 6). This matches the references he makes to 'I' in extract two and gives an overall impression of individualism rather than group action. This may be designed to enforce the NRA's presentation of the Second Amendment as representing an individual, rather than collective, right to gun ownership. Finally, the fight against political elites is presented as an ongoing one. This is achieved through the call to fight in all upcoming elections and for life.

Discussion

This analysis, the first to apply discursive psychology to opposing sides of the American gun control debate, has demonstrated the ways in which two key figures representing each side of the debate construct the notion of protection and those who campaign for gun safety. In terms of protection it has been shown that both sides refer to protection as a positive value and they invoke this in their arguments. Where they differ is regarding what protection involves, so that for Obama this means a straightforward protection from the risk of guns, for LaPierre and the NRA protection refers to the individual right to protect oneself from government interference, which is the only way to ensure personal protection. This demonstrates the flexible way in which concepts and values—here protection—can be used by different speakers to aid very different arguments.

Gun Control, Discourse, and Identity

Throughout the speeches, much of the rhetorical work that is done is focused on what exactly it means to be American and how typical of American citizens the speaker is. Obama frequently talks on behalf of 'the American people', 'this country', and more simply 'we'; he does not refer to himself as the president of the country, but instead as a prototypical citizen in the country. Such a strategy helps to both position Obama as a legitimate leader but also works to present the American public as homogenous and united in their desire to control guns, which attempts to remove the controversial nature of the gun control debate. LaPierre too presents himself as a prototypical American citizen with regular references to 'us' and 'our' as well as to the large numbers of NRA members and gun-owners. This also works to normalise gun ownership and make it average and moderate in the way McKinlay and Dunnet (1998) found.

It therefore seems that the battle is not just over controlling guns, but what it means to be American and indeed what the 'real' USA is. For Obama, the USA is a country defined by compassion and unity with a representative government, whereas for LaPierre it is one of individual freedom and necessary mistrust of the government. This is consistent with Ricento's (2003) work on American identity in which it was shown that different contradictory versions of American history were drawn upon to construct different American values, in this case in debates about immigration. For both, the Second Amendment is a significant part of American history that must be respected. However, it is nevertheless interpreted differently, with LaPierre using this as a cornerstone of the argument about individual freedom from government intervention in the form of gun controls. Conversely, Obama presents it is something worthy of defending, but also as a potential barrier to necessary controls.

The Benefits of a Discursive Approach

This analysis has demonstrated a number of benefits of utilising a discursive psychological approach to explore the American gun control debate. First, the analysis has demonstrated how the ways key figures present their arguments are of great importance. Both of the speeches addressed in this analysis, and the many more contributions to the dialogical network of the gun control debate, represent 'discourse which is argumentative and which seeks to persuade' (Billig, 2001, p. 214). This analysis has highlighted some of the ways in which talk about gun control is designed to persuade, for example, in extract one Obama highlights the presence of a high-profile victim of gun crime in an attempt to highlight problems associated with inadequate gun controls and in extract two LaPierre draws upon the will of the Founding Fathers to present gun control as anti-American.

Second, it has allowed for a detailed understanding of the ways in which key aspects of the debate, such as the notion of protection, are presented. As discussed above, both Obama and LaPierre claim to support protection, indeed it seems unlikely that anyone could oppose this notion. However, on closer inspection while there may be universal support for protection, exactly how protection can be achieved—and from what people need protecting—is a point of contention, and the discursive approach offers a means of capturing the flexible and action-oriented ways in which this concept is used in the debate.

Third, the discursive approach allows for an understanding of how American identity, history, and values are both invoked and constructed in the debate. The discursive approach to identity maintains that identities are drawn upon so as to perform social actions (e.g. Abell & Stokoe, 2001). In this case, different versions of what it means to be an American and different versions of American history are drawn upon to support conflicting arguments. In doing so, different versions of American history and values are simultaneously constructed.

Finally, by using a discursive approach it has been shown how distinct speeches are positioned against both existing arguments and anticipated counterarguments. There are numerous examples of this throughout the extracts featured here. For example, in extract four LaPierre implies that supporters of gun control don't really value safety, which clearly responds to, and pre-empts, the counter point that gun control is all about safety, in an attempt to undermine this argument. Another example, in extract three, sees Obama pre-empt potential accusations that he does not support the second amendment, by invoking it himself. This provides support for Leudar and Nekvapil's (2004) notion of the dialogical network in which they claim that seemingly distinct events (such as individual speeches) are part of a much larger ongoing discussion and as such can be viewed as interactional. All of this provides a case for applying a discursive approach more widely to the gun control debate.

Implications for the Gun Control Debate and Policy

We now know the outcome of this round of the gun control debate as Obama's attempts to tighten gun control failed. However, as both speakers suggest, it is likely that the gun control debate will continue. What this analysis has taught us about the debate is that what counts as 'protection', as 'American' and who is working for the common good are all contentious issues. In terms of gun policies, it is not possible to determine which side is 'correct' as both can be seen attempting to present their viewpoint as reasonable and justifiable and better than the alternative. In the debate, those seeking to oppose gun controls will have to continue to convince the public that controlling guns is anti-American and that gun ownership is necessary in order to protect individuals, whereas those seeking to impose tighter gun controls will need to overcome the suggestion that gun controls are being imposed by an uncaring elite on American people. Further, as freedom is so persuasive in the debate, supporters of gun control may need to promote freedom from gun-related violence as more important than the individual freedom to own guns.

Conclusion

This chapter has demonstrated the way in which the same value—protection—is used by opposing sides of the debate for opposing ends. It has been shown how protection is used in the debate so that who or what (children and freedom) needs protecting is at the heart of the debate, as is whether the actors attempting to bring about gun controls are heroes or villains. By treating these speeches as social actions, the analysis has been used to identify the ways in which both speakers attempt to present their arguments as legitimate. It has been shown that both speakers present themselves as speaking on behalf of the nation, and in doing so they attempt to construct their own version of what that nation is; it is not just gun control that is being debated, but the essence of what it means to be American.

References

25 Deadliest Mass Shootings in U.S. History Fast Facts. (2017, June 28), *CNN*. Retrieved from http://edition.cnn.com/2013/09/16/us/20-deadliest-mass-shootings-in-u-s-history-fast-facts/

Abell, J., & Stokoe, E. (2001). Broadcasting the royal role: Constructing culturally situated identities in the Princess Diana *Panorama* interview. *British Journal of Social Psychology, 40,* 417–435.

Berlet, C., & Lyons, M. N. (2000). *Right-wing populism in America: Too close for comfort.* New York: Guilford Press.

Billig, M. (2001). Discursive, rhetorical and ideological messages. In M. Wetherell, S. Taylor, & S. J. Yates (Eds.), *Discourse theory and practice: A reader* (pp. 210–221). London: Sage.

Blendon, R. J., Young, J. T., & Hemenway, D. (1996). The American public and the gun control debate. *The Journal of the American Medical Association, 275,* 1719–1722.

Bouffard, J. A., Nobles, M. R., Wells, W., & Cavanaugh, M. R. (2012). How many more guns? Estimating the effect of allowing licensed concealed handguns on a college campus. *Journal of Interpersonal Violence, 27,* 316–343.

Braman, D., & Kahan, D. M. (2003). More statistics, less persuasion: A cultural theory of gun-risk perceptions. *University of Pennsylvania Law Review, 51,* 1291–1327.

Capdevila, R., & Callaghan, J. (2008). 'It's not racist. It's common sense'. A critical analysis of political discourse around asylum and immigration in the UK. *Journal of Community & Applied Social Psychology, 18,* 1–16.

Christensen, J. (2013, February 5). How the violent mentally ill can buy guns. *CNN.* Retrieved from http://edition.cnn.com/2013/01/30/health/mental-illness-guns/index.html

Downs, D. (2002). Representing gun owners: Frame identification as social responsibility in news media discourse. *Written Communication, 19,* 44–75.

Edwards, D. (1997). *Discourse and cognition.* London: Sage.

Edwards, D., & Potter, J. (1992). *Discursive psychology.* London: Sage.

Gibson, S. (2012). 'I'm not a war monger but…': Discourse analysis and social psychological peace research. *Journal of Community & Applied Social Psychology, 22,* 159–173.

Graham, P., Keenan, T., & Dowd, A.-M. (2004). A call to arms at the end of history: A discourse-historical analysis of George W. Bush's declaration of War on Terror. *Discourse and Society, 15,* 199–221.

Gun Violence Archive. (2017). *Past summary ledgers.* Retrieved from http://www.gunviolencearchive.org/past-tolls

Johnson, A. J., & Goodman, S. (2013). Reversing racism and the elite conspiracy: Strategies used by the British National Party leader in response to hostile media appearances. *Discourse, Context and Media, 2,* 156–164.

Kleck, G., Gertz, M., & Bratton, J. (2009). Why do people support gun control? Alternative explanations of support for handgun bans. *Journal of Criminal Justice, 37,* 496–504.

Leudar, I., & Nekvapil, J. (2004). Media dialogical networks and political argumentation. *Journal of Language and Politics, 3,* 247–266.

McDonald, G., LeBrun, E., Berman, E., & Krause, K. (Eds.). (2012). *Small arms survey 2012: Moving targets.* Cambridge: Cambridge University Press.

McGinty, E. E., Webster, D. W., & Barry, C. L. (2013). Effects of news media messages about mass shootings on attitudes towards persons with serious mental illness and public support for gun control policies. *American Journal of Psychiatry, 170,* 494–501.

McKinlay, A., & Dunnet, A. (1998). How gun-owners accomplish being deadly average. In C. Antaki & S. Widdicombe (Eds.), *Identities in talk* (pp. 34–51). London: Sage.

O'Grady, W., Parnaby, P. F., & Schikschneit, J. (2010). Guns, gangs, and the underclass: A constructionist analysis of gun violence in a Toronto high school. *Canadian Journal of Criminology and Criminal Justice, 52,* 55–77.

O'Neill, K. L. (2007). Armed citizens and the stories they tell: The National Rifle Association's achievement of terror and masculinity. *Men and Masculinities, 9,* 457–475.

Patten, R., Thomas, M. O., & Wada, J. C. (2013). Packing heat: Attitudes regarding concealed weapons on college campuses. *American Journal of Criminal Justice, 38,* 551–569.

Potter, J. (2004). Discourse analysis as a way of analysing naturally occurring talk. In D. Silverman (Ed.), *Qualitative analysis: Issues of theory and method* (2nd ed., pp. 200–221). London: Sage.

Ricento, T. (2003). The discursive construction of Americanism. *Discourse and Society, 14*, 611–637.

Seate, A. A., Cohen, E. L., Fujioka, Y., & Hoffner, C. (2012). Exploring gun ownership as a social identity to understanding the perceived media influence of the Virginia Tech news coverage on attitudes toward gun control policy. *Communication Research Reports, 29*, 130–139.

The Economist. (2013). *Why the NRA keeps talking about mental illness, rather than guns.* Retrieved from http://www.economist.com/blogs/lexington/2013/03/guns-and-mentally-ill

Tileagă, C. (2013). *Political psychology: Critical perspectives.* Cambridge: Cambridge University Press.

Wetherell, M. (1998). Positioning and interpretative repertoires: Conversation analysis and post-structuralism in dialogue. *Discourse and Society, 9*, 387–412.

Winkler, A. (2013). *Gunfight: The battle over the right to bear arms in America.* New York: W. W. Norton & Company.

Wintemute, G. J. (2014). Support for a comprehensive background check requirement and expanded denial criteria for firearm transfers: Findings from the firearms licensee survey. *Journal of Urban Health, 91*, 303–319.

Chapter 5
Disloyal, Deluded, Dangerous: How Supporters of Violence or Separatism Discredit Their Political Opponents

W. Mick L. Finlay

Introduction

> Naturally the common people don't want war... But after all, it is the leaders of the country who determine the policy, and it is always a simple matter to drag the people along, whether it is a democracy or a fascist dictatorship or a Parliament or a Communist dictatorship....
> ...the people can always be brought to the bidding of the leaders. That is easy. All you have to do is tell them they are being attacked and denounce the pacifists for lack of patriotism and exposing the country to danger. It works the same way in any country. (Herman Goering, April 18, 1946, in Gilbert, 1947, pp. 278–9)

Where there is debate over a group's relations with other groups, members argue with each other over the correct course of action. Some claim that violence or separation is the best strategy, while others argue for peace, negotiation, and interdependence. In these disputes, we would expect to find that issues of identity come to the fore, and there has been much research into the discursive construction of the outgroup, the ingroup, and the intergroup context (e.g. Bar-Tal, Halperin, & Oren, 2010; Billig, 1995; Finlay, 2018; Hodges, 2013; Lazar & Lazar, 2004; Oddo, 2011; Reicher, Haslam, & Rath, 2008). However, these often bitter and fierce debates also involve representations of the identities of, and divisions between, ingroup members. Central to these internal disputes are claims about who is the most loyal and authentic group member, who is entitled to speak for the group, and who perceives the intergroup situation most accurately. In this chapter, I will examine how this is done by those advocating violence and/or separation ('hawks', 'separatists', 'extremists', the far right, nationalists, and so on), and how this involves a range of representations designed to discredit ingroup opponents (e.g. 'moderates', 'doves', 'peaceniks', human rights activists, multiculturalists). These representations fulfil a number of functions: they delegitimize ingroup opponents and negate their rights to

W. M. L. Finlay (✉)
Anglia Ruskin University, Cambridge, UK
e-mail: Mick.Finlay@anglia.ac.uk

© Springer Nature Switzerland AG 2018
S. Gibson (ed.), *Discourse, Peace, and Conflict*, Peace Psychology Book Series,
https://doi.org/10.1007/978-3-319-99094-1_5

speak on behalf of the group, they convey and enforce political norms, and they act as a form of social pressure against opposition and dissent. This chapter will examine the discursive practices used to discredit opponents in a range of current and historical conflict situations.

Two fundamental understandings underlie this chapter. The first is that group relations are made up of myriad social practices, structures, and beliefs, and that if we are to contribute something that will help tackle conflict, we need to understand what these are and how they work. Following Galtung's (1969) distinction between direct and structural violence, social practices that contribute to intergroup conflict include direct acts of violence, subjugation, discrimination, and separation as well as all the social processes that support these practices, and which occur in meetings, education, entertainment, offices, the legal system, police forces, the military, politics, and journalism, just to name a few. Linguistic practices that encourage and sustain conflict and inequality are central to many of these processes and practices.

The second understanding is that groups are not homogenous: they are made up of people and organizations that take up different stances and argue over them. With regard to intergroup relations, people who share the same group identity argue over the nature of the intergroup context, the characteristics of 'them' and 'us', what the best course of action is to create a better future, who has the right to speak for the group, and so on. For example, there is disagreement about norms concerning contact with non-Muslims among UK Muslims with different political, theological, and cultural backgrounds (Hopkins & Kahani-Hopkins, 2006), and research on schisms in other religious and political groups has shown how members of each sub-group claim their own faction represents the true essence of the group (Sani & Reicher, 1998, 2000).

These arguments often involve conflicting claims about identity. As Reicher, Hopkins, and Condor (1997) point out, people define groups and identities in such a way as to legitimate their own political projects, and political argument often involves depictions of opponents as unrepresentative of the group (e.g. Bar-Tal, 1997; Finlay, 2005, 2007, 2014; Leudar, Marsland, & Nekvapil, 2004; Rapley, 1998; Reicher & Hopkins, 1996, 2001; Rooyackers & Verkuyten, 2012; Wood & Finlay, 2008; Yildiz & Verkutyen, 2012). As Hopkins, Kahani-Hopkins and Reicher (2006, p. 55) put it, 'Reconstructions of identity … are produced to explain situations and organize actions … Particular identity constructions arise to counter alternative definitions'.

Debates over whether to fight or negotiate, whether to form alliances or remain separate, or whether one group has unfair advantages over another are found in many different political and social contexts, and their content and form differs as a result. They happen in situations where members of one group who occupy a defined territory want to form a separate nation state or join an existing one; where a violent minority who do not have political power claim to be fighting on behalf of a much larger group against groups they define as enemies; where the far right campaign against immigrants, asylum-seekers, and other minority groups; where governments overtly persecute and subjugate minorities; where there is civil or inter-state war; and where a nation wishes to join or withdraw from a multi-nation union.

Silencing Opponents

Efforts to suppress the voice of those advocating peace, co-existence, or further integration with other groups can take many forms. In totalitarian regimes, the law and threat of imprisonment or death is often used. In Nazi Germany, those who associated with Jews, had relations with Poles, or opposed racial policy could be publicly pilloried, imprisoned under the Enabling Act, thrown into concentration camps, or executed. A number of terms were used to refer to such people and their offences such as 'rassenschende' (race defilement), 'judenknechte' (slave to the Jews), and 'judenfruende' (friend of the Jews) (Burleigh & Wippermann, 1991), and historical research shows that the Gestapo relied on denunciations from the general public to help them enforce racial policy (Gellately, 1990). Whites who protested against the apartheid regime in South Africa were often arrested and interrogated, and in many countries we have seen journalists imprisoned for exposing injustice or speaking out against government policy. When militias, killing squads, or violent insurgents are operating in a country, those who object become targets themselves. For example, in Rwanda, Hutus who tried to aid the Tutsis during the genocide of 1994 were likely to be slaughtered themselves by the Interahamwe (Berkeley, 2001).

Silencing opponents is also involved in the maintenance of sectarian segregation. Shirlow (2003), writing on the Northern Ireland conflict, concludes that 'the violent, cultural and political acts which aid the reproduction of segregation should not be read as being supported by all residents of segregated communities … The fear of entering areas dominated by the "other" ethnosectarian group can be influenced by threats, both imagined and real, that are set against people by members of their "own" community.' (p. 76). In his study, interviews with residents of two neighbouring areas of Belfast, Ardoyne (Protestant/Unionist), and Upper Ardoyne (Catholic/Republican), revealed two approaches to mixing with the other group. Sectarians were more likely to be adults of working age. They would avoid going into the neighbouring area or using its shops and community facilities, tended to talk about members of the other group in negative terms, and represented their own community as victimized. They also tended to view those who had cross-group contacts as disloyal.

Non-sectarians, who were more likely to be older and to have had cross-community friends and relatives before the start of the Troubles, rejected segregation. They were more likely to use facilities in the neighbouring area, maintain social relations and activities with those in the other group, and were more likely to acknowledge that both groups shared blame for violence. However, they were also more likely to suffer physical attacks from, or be berated by, members of their own community due to their non-sectarian or anti-paramilitary attitudes. Non-sectarians reported being distrusted to such an extent that they felt they had to hide their cross-group contacts and their political views from other members of their own community unless they knew they could trust them. Shirlow claimed that these social pressures effectively silenced those voices who could have challenged ethnosectarian discourses.

In many contexts, exerting pressure on opposing voices occurs without the threat of violence, and here the danger to dissenters is more about public shaming, ridicule, or social ostracism. However, in all these situations advocates of violence or separation use forms of discourse that discredit their ingroup opponents, in which they claim to represent the true interests and spirit of the group while their opponents are dismissed as selfish, disloyal, subservient, evil, weak, or ignorant.

Discrediting Statements: Form and Function

Discrediting statements have a range of functions which are more or less explicit. They are an attempt to claim what the normative beliefs, behaviours, and identifications of group members are or should be. At the same time, they imply the speaker/writer is a loyal, authentic member of the group who sees the intergroup situation and the interests of the group most clearly, while the target who is discredited should not be listened to, has no right to speak for the group, and should either change their position, keep quiet, or have some punitive actions applied to them. For the audience, the discrediting statement acts as an implicit warning that this is how they will be talked about or seen if they were to adopt a similar position.

In terms of form, several distinctions can be drawn. Characterizing opponents as people whose opinions should not be trusted or who are dangerous involves depictions designed to discredit their identities using social categorizations, personality traits, emotions, psychological complexes, and motivations. Often social-psychological explanations are also given of why these people have such 'wrong-headed' opinions. That is, the opponents are not just wrong but they are wrong for a reason which is further discrediting. They are also discredited through descriptions of their actions, which might imply ideas of sabotage, violence, or subservience to outsiders. A second distinction will be drawn in this chapter between 'strong' (blaming, accusing, threatening) and 'mild' (forgiving, persuading, non-blaming) discounting practices.

Analytic Approach

My approach to the examples here is broadly based on the types of discursive and rhetorical analysis mainly developed in Social Psychology (e.g. Billig, 1987, 1995; Edwards & Potter, 1992; Potter, 1996; Potter & Wetherell, 1987; van Dijk, 1987; Wetherell & Potter, 1992). That is, I am interested in how these accounts are put together, the wider sets of meanings and ideas they draw on, and the functions relevant to group relations which are served by these types of discourse. While each of the extracts could have been analysed in more detail, my aim is only to make analytic points directly relevant to how opponents are discredited in these contexts, and to illustrate variations across a range of contexts where intergroup relations are contested.

The examples below come from situations in which intergroup relations are at issue. They were selected principally to illustrate how discrediting is carried out in situations of conflict. While some come from a full analysis of particular datasets (e.g. the Party for Islamic Renewal and Jewish self-hate examples) others were collected in the course of reading historical materials and news media. There is no implication that the contexts drawn on below are morally or historically comparable. In cases such as Scottish independence, for example, there is no implication that either side holds the moral high ground. However, the problem the speaker/writer faces is basically the same: how to account for opposing views in such a way as to present them and their proponents as wrong, while at the same time presenting the speaker as a more trustworthy representative of the group. We will start by looking at several examples of milder discrediting practices.

Mildly Discrediting Accounts and Descriptions of Opponents

In 2014, there was a referendum in Scotland about whether the country should become an independent nation ('Yes') or remain part of the UK ('No'). While the main UK parties supported remaining in the Union, the Scottish National Party (SNP) argued for independence, and public opinion remained fairly evenly split in the run up to the referendum. SNP discourse contained explanations as to why some Scottish people were in favour of the Union, and why they were wrong in this belief.[1] Since this was not a violent situation and the SNP wanted to persuade voters to turn away from the 'No' camp, they gave these accounts in ways that did not insult or threaten those who disagreed with them, but still functioned to discount the unionist position. For example, in 2010 the then leader of the SNP, Alex Salmond, said in his SNP conference speech:

> Delegates – one of our party founders Robert Cunningham Graeme once said: "The problem for Scotland is not the English who are a great and noble people. The problem for Scotland is those Scots who are born without imagination." In one sense, he was wrong. People are not born without imagination – it is drummed out of them – often by political parties, who have a vested interest in lowering the expectations of the people. (Salmond, 2010)

The extract begins with a quote from a party founder. By using this, Salmond immediately does some rhetorical work. Billig (1987) points out that when analysing what people say we often need to understand how their accounts are put together to resist alternative versions. In this case, the relevant context is that the SNP are often accused by opponents of being driven by anti-English sentiment. Salmond wards this off by praising the English—they are 'a great and noble

---

[1] Thanks to Ruaridh McDermott for finding these three SNP extracts.

people'. The next part of the quote accuses Scottish opponents of independence of lacking imagination. Since it is important not to insult those you want to persuade to vote for you, Salmond immediately disagrees. He modifies Graeme's statement by saying a lack of imagination is not their own fault, but is 'drummed out of them—often by political parties'. The function of this section of his speech is that it allows him to portray the opposition as wrong due to a lack of imagination and low expectations. However, it is not Scottish voters who are to blame, but political parties with vested interests. He reinforces this later in the speech:

> Just think of it. Labour, the party which brought the country to its financial knees, unites with the Tories, the party of omnishambles, to tell Scotland that we are uniquely incapable as a nation. (Salmond, 2012)

Again, blame for the 'No' position is not placed on Scottish voters, but the two main UK political parties. What we also see here is the 'No' position portrayed as the belief that 'we are uniquely incapable as a nation'. Scottish nationhood (whether or not associated with a nation state) is asserted as given in this formulation, as is the idea that all other nations are capable. Since it is only Scotland that these parties think is incapable, the 'No' position is an insult to the Scottish people. Both of these constructions, that it is politicians driving the 'No' camp, and that they believe Scotland is incapable, are also found in a 2012 conference party speech by Nicola Sturgeon, the deputy leader at the time:

> Friends, there is no country in the world—big or small—that is guaranteed success. But the combination of our natural resources and the skills and intelligence of our people make us just as capable as any other nation (...) That Scotland could thrive as an independent nation is not, never has been, never should be in doubt. And shame on any politician who ever suggests that it is. (Sturgeon, 2012)

We can also find these milder types of discrediting accounts in violent, totalitarian contexts. The following is from a propaganda article written by Goebbels in 1941 for the Nazi magazine Das Reich:

> The Jews (...) have recently found a new trick. They knew the good-natured German Michel in us, always ready to shed a sentimental tear for the injustice done to them. (...) The Jews send out the pitiable. They may confuse some harmless souls for a while, but not us. We know exactly what the situation is. (...) The Jews are a parasitic race that feeds like a foul fungus on the cultures of healthy but ignorant peoples. (Goebbels, 1941)

This extract attempts to account for the behaviour of non-Jewish Germans who supported the Jews. They are presented in positive terms as 'good-natured', 'sentimental', and 'harmless', but also as easily fooled when the Jews 'send out the pitiable'. It is initially their good nature, and then their ignorance, which makes them confused. However, the Nazis are presented as seeing through this ploy: 'We know exactly what the situation is'. Of course, much more aggressive denunciations were also used against those who rejected Nazi racial policy, and this was often accompanied by imprisonment, brutality, and execution.

Strongly Discrediting Accounts and Descriptions of Opponents

More strongly discrediting accounts and descriptions are those in which opponents are disparaged and their arguments discounted using moral condemnation, pejorative character descriptions, and references to war and violence which impute evil and destructive intentions. Examples of this can be found in both right-wing politics and in violent conflicts.

Strongly Discrediting Accounts and Descriptions of Opponents in Right-Wing Political Discourse

Aggressive and belittling discourse is often used by those on the far right to attack their liberal opponents (Copsey, 2004; Finlay, 2007). The British National Party (BNP) is a political party which in 2005 claimed on its website 'exists to secure a future for the indigenous peoples of these islands in the North Atlantic which have been our homeland for a millennia'. The extract below comes from an article on its website (www.bnp.org.uk) shortly after the London tube and bus bombings which killed 52 people in 2005 (see Wood & Finlay, 2008, for a more comprehensive analysis). The article, by Lee Barnes (then Legal Director of the BNP and writer of the Brimstone column on the website), argues that Muslims pose a threat to Britain because there is a programme to infiltrate non-Muslim societies and destroy them from within. The article warns that it is not just Muslims who are dangerous to British society, but all those who support multiculturalism:

> The Multi-Cultural nightmare of Britain is the sea in which the terrorist can swim. The era of the liberal Consensus is over. The time when deluded and apathetic liberals, New Left fascists, tolerance freaks and diversity nazis, sycophantic vicars and various other white witless female version of Charles Dickens Mrs Jellyby were listened to is over. They should all now be despised for the utter idiots they all are and for the danger they have placed us all in. (Barnes, 2005)

The extract starts by declaring that the terrorist attacks in London mean that the political consensus on multiculturalism has changed. Barnes dismisses those who promote multiculturalism and liberal values with a range of pejorative terms: *deluded and apathetic liberals*, *New Left fascists*, *tolerance freaks and diversity nazis*, *sycophantic vicars*, *white witless female version of Charles Dickens Mrs Jellyby*. Each of these identities is constructed negatively either by the use of adjectives (e.g. deluded, witless, sycophantic) or categorical nouns with negative connotations (e.g. fascists, Nazis, freaks, idiots). Mrs Jellyby is a fictional character in Dickens' novel 'Bleak House' whose philanthropic concern for Africa led to a neglect of herself and her family. It is interesting that these attacks on liberals present them as both strong and weak. Describing those who speak up for multiculturalism as fascists depicts them as authoritarians and is a common way that extreme-right parties counter accusations of fascism levelled against themselves (Copsey, 2004).

Fig. 5.1 *Daily Mail* front pages

Presenting them as deluded, witless, utter idiots, and sycophantic presents them as ignorant and weakly subservient to others. Either way, Barnes blames these types of people for the terrorist attacks. The ways in which supporters of multiculturalism are discredited make the proposed actions towards them logical—they should 'be despised' and should not be listened to.

More recent examples from mainstream right-wing discourse suggest that political opponents are deliberately and/or violently threatening 'the people'. One case comes from political debate in the UK over whether to remain in or leave the European Union in 2016. During the referendum campaign, those arguing for leaving the EU ('Brexiters') claimed that this would allow the UK to 'take back control' and reclaim its lost sovereignty and independence. Leave voters thus saw themselves as more patriotic than 'remain' voters ('Remainers'). After the UK voted by a narrow majority to leave in a referendum, there were several legal challenges asserting that, for constitutional reasons, the result of the referendum had to be ratified in Parliament. The popular right-wing newspaper Daily Mail, strongly anti-EU and anti-immigrant, ran two front pages denouncing both the High Court judges and those who supported the legal challenge (Fig. 5.1).

In the first example, the newspaper labels those supporting the legal challenge 'unpatriotic Bremoaners'. *Bremoaners* is a play on the terms *Brexit* and *Remainers*, portraying Remainers as bad losers since they continue to *moan* about leaving after narrowly losing the vote. This is coupled with the adjective 'unpatriotic', and then reinforced by describing them as engaging in a 'plot to subvert the will of the British people' with the implications of sabotage, treachery, and a failure to respect/love the nation.

In the second example, the paper brands the High Court judges who ruled in favour of the legal challenge 'enemies of the people'. Both headlines discredit their targets, but they do it using discourse more appropriate to war than to peace-time political debate. The judges and those mounting the legal challenge are depicted as hostile to the British people and as actively engaged in covert actions against the nation.

US President Donald Trump has used similar discourse in his Twitter attacks. For example, shortly after becoming president, he attacked a range of mainstream news organizations who did not give him positive reviews or support his early attempts to bring in measures against Muslim immigrants:

> The FAKE NEWS media (failing @nytimes, @NBCNews, @ABC, @CBS, @CNN) is not my enemy, it is the enemy of the American People! (@realDonaldTrump, February 17, 2017).

This notion of an internal enemy is found in other current right-wing political discourse in the USA. The following extracts are from the Chief Executive of the National Rifle Association,[2] Wayne LaPierre, in a speech made at the Conservative Political Action (CPA) Conference in February, 2017 (Bump, 2017). The speech as a whole warns of a dangerous and deliberate threat to American people from those who oppose Trump and/or his policies (through street protests, in the media, in Washington, and in the courts), and we see an interesting discursive feature: the use of the term 'violence' to cover a range of non-violent opposition. LaPierre begins by describing protests by the 'far left' on Inauguration Day:

> They tomahawk beer bottles and rocks at police, putting multiple police in the hospital. They smashed business' plate-glass windows while customers cowered inside.

This is followed by two alleged examples of violence against Trump supporters, one in which a schoolgirl was beaten up, and one in which a group was attacked with eggs and had their hats stolen. He uses these examples to make the claim:

> Right now, we are facing a gathering of forces that are willing to use violence against us. Think about it. The leftist movement in this country is enraged. Among them and behind them are some of the most radical political elements there are. Anarchists, Marxists, communists and the whole rest of the left-wing Socialist brigade. Many of these people hate everything America stands for. Democracy. Free-market capitalism. Representative government. Individual freedom. They want to tear down our system and replace it with their collectivist, top-down, global government-knows-best utopia.

Here, LaPierre describes Trump's opponents as a collective 'leftist movement' and discredits them with the claim that 'behind them' (i.e. controlling them) are 'some of the most radical political elements there are'. This is followed by a list of category labels historically seen as enemies of the country (anarchists, Marxists, communists), which he explicitly characterizes as hating fundamental American political values (democracy, capitalism, representative government) and wanting to tear down the system. The discourse takes an interesting form: while not claiming all those on the left want to do those things, the quote implies that those directing it do. The danger posed by those opposing Trump is implied in another way later on:

---

[2] At the time of writing, the NRA website claimed nearly five million members in the USA although this figure is disputed.

So, if you are a member of the leftist media or a soldier for the violent left, a violent criminal, a drug cartel gang member or would-be terrorist, hear this: You're not going to win and
you will not defeat us.

Here, LaPierre discredits Trump's opponents by grouping the 'leftist media' along
with the 'violent left', drug cartels, and criminals, and suggesting this collectivity
wants to defeat 'us'. This construction implies the media is a threat on the level of,
or morally associated with, these other actors. The use of the term 'violent left' is
usefully vague. It could either mean elements of the left which protest using violence, or it could simply imply the left are violent, with echoes of the way Trump
often uses adjectives to modify the names of his opponents so that every mention of
the person becomes an opportunity to discredit them (e.g. lying Ted; crooked
Hillary; little Marco; crazy Bernie; low-energy Jeb; failing @nytimes [ABC News,
2016]).

It becomes apparent that LaPierre is applying the term 'violent' to Trump opponents in general later in his speech. The media is referred to as 'leftist' in the extract
above, a description justified by his claim elsewhere in the speech that the 'national
media machine' is 'biased almost entirely one-way'. When talking about media
criticism of Trump, he also discredits it through constructions of hostile activity,
saying 'the leftist media is responsible for blowing the winds of violence'. Later in
the speech, he says 'our country is under siege from a media carpet-bombing campaign' aimed at 'maliciously destroying the Trump presidency'. LaPierre also
broadens the concept of violence to include legal challenges to Trump's executive
order 13769 which tried to ban people from seven Muslim countries from entering
the USA for 90 days:

The left's violence against America has taken many forms. For example, left-wing judicial
activism can be a form of violence against our constitutional system. Look at judicial efforts
to block President Trump's executive order to take a longer look at people coming from
countries that sponsor terrorism.
    …they might as well throw a Molotov cocktail at the U.S. Constitution. They do vio-
lence to the Constitution's separation of powers and the U.S. code. And they do violence to
the checks and balances that keep government under control.

Here, the victim of the left's violence is not the people, but the Constitution. LaPierre
reinforces the idea of violent revolution and threat by repetition of the word 'violence' four times in these two extracts, and by his comparison of the legal challenge
to throwing a 'Molotov cocktail'. The prejudicial aspects of Trump's executive
order banning residents of seven Muslim countries from entry are also minimized
by the lack of detail: it is described as simply designed to 'take a longer look at
people coming from countries that sponsor terrorism'. Despite the fact that the order
overwhelmingly targets Muslims, there is no mention of Muslims (they are simply
referred to as 'people').

LaPierre uses references to violence and war actions (carpet-bombing, under
siege, destroying, throwing Molotov cocktails) in order to present mainstream
media criticism and non-violent legal opposition to Trump's policies as essentially
violent. Opposition in all arenas has become simply an expression of 'the violent
left,' allowing for the following rallying cry to Trump supporters:

> We'll fight the violent left on the airwaves, the Internet, and on TV. We'll fight the violent left in Congress and in the Washington Bureaucracy.

Later in the speech, the 'violent left' becomes terrorist:

> Make no mistake, if the violent left brings their terror to our communities, our neighborhoods or into our homes, they will be met with the resolve and the strength and the full force of American freedom in the hands of the American people, and we will win because we are the majority in this country.

In the two extracts above, we see LaPierre talk about 'we' (see Billig, 1995, for discussion of the construction of national communities using pronouns), which seems to refer at the same time both to the listening audience (Trump supporters/the NRA/the CPA attendees) and the American people more generally. Not only is the left attacking 'our' communities and homes, but 'we' will win because 'we are the majority in this country'. Elsewhere, 'we' refers to those who support the politics of the NRA and the CPA, and who are presented as the saviours of America:

> We're the nation's largest gathering of lawful, peaceful, right-thinking people who are absolutely determined to live our lives without fear. (…) We stand ready and resolved to defend our freedom and secure our safety against any enemy.

LaPierre implies it is he and his audience who truly represent America in these extracts, both as under threat from the 'violent left' and as those who will fight against them. At the same time, the left (including the liberal media and the courts) is discredited by numerous claims that it is a violent danger to both the principles of the nation (freedom, democracy) and the safety of its people. The function of such constructions is to present opposition to Trump as not emanating from reasonable consideration of the issues by ordinary Americans, but rather as the expression of a violent hatred of America, its principles and its people. This is achieved through a loose use of the term 'violent' to refer to a range of non-violent political, media, and legal activities and institutions, through the conflation of all opposition under the noun phrase 'violent left', and through grouping the opposition with criminals and terrorists. What is striking about this type of talk is that it is a discourse of war rather than one of peaceful, reasoned democratic argument. It is all about violence.

Strongly Discrediting Accounts and Descriptions of Opponents in Violent Conflicts

So far we have seen examples of the ways people argue against fellow group members through depictions of them in various negative ways—as lacking confidence, being ignorant and easily fooled, being subservient, or, more severely, as being authoritarian, hating the nation and its principles, and engaging in sabotage. This section will examine some ways this is done in violent conflicts.

This first example comes from the Middle Eastern conflict, where there are important debates among Jews across the world over the policies of the Israeli government towards the Palestinians. In these debates, we often find arguments over who best understands the conflict, what the best strategy is, what the ultimate goals should be for the land, and who therefore has the right to represent the Jewish people. The notion of 'self-hate' is often used in hawkish Zionist discourse to discredit Jews who speak up for the plight of Palestinians and criticize the actions of the Israeli government (Finlay, 2005). The notion of Jewish self-hatred is a social-psychological one, where it is claimed that living in anti-Semitic cultures can lead Jews to internalize anti-Semitism and thus hate their own identity and cultural heritage. It is a powerful rhetorical move in the argument because it declares that the political views of Jewish opponents of Israeli government policy are due to a hatred of Jews, the Jewish state and Jewish culture, rather than due to a set of moral principles or historical/political understandings. For example, in 1992 Ariel Sharon, the defence minister during the 1982 massacre of Palestinian civilians at Sabra and Shatilla and later the prime minister, wrote a piece in the Jerusalem Post describing the Jewish left-wing who criticized the invasion of Lebanon as 'consumed by self-hate and the tendency to kowtow to the enemy, and the Arab nationalist parties'. In a later article in the same paper, he criticized the then Labour government for their participation in the Oslo peace process and for accepting the idea of an independent Palestinian Authority:

> But history marches on. Terrible self-hate engulfs us. The terrorist organization's flag is unfurled in Tel Aviv's Malchei Yisrael Square. We plead with Arafat by phone, dispatch couriers post-haste. Our leaders talk to Arafat about disarming Jews and dismantling Jewish settlements. (Sharon, 1994)

The notion of self-hate is powerful. The concept is well-known in Jewish narratives about history and identity and is laden with negative meanings about authenticity, loyalty, and psychological health, and it is all the more powerful in the context of a long-term violent conflict which has taken many lives (for further examples of its use in discrediting the Jewish peace movement see Finlay, 2005, 2007).

Other forms of discrediting discourse can be seen in the analysis of email communications sent out by the Party for Islamic Renewal, a UK-based Al-Qaeda-supporting group (see Finlay, 2014 for a full analysis). The emails, sent to the organization's distribution list, contained mainly news articles and commentaries on current events. Overall, they were anti-Western, anti-Semitic, against the rulers of Muslim countries and also against Western involvement in those countries. A number of emails clearly supported Al Qaeda and its attacks. The so-called 'moderate' Muslims, who either condemned terrorist attacks, worked with the UK government, or joined with non-Muslims in political organizations, were subject to a great deal of derogatory and discrediting commentary in the emails. The emails describe them as dangerous for supporting governments engaged in wars in Iraq and Afghanistan, and therefore as contributing to the deaths of Muslims. A number of discrediting explanations for their behaviour were given. These included that they were doing it for financial and personal gain, they were unmanly, weak, and psychologically subservient to former colonial rulers, and that they were apostates (i.e. had chosen to leave Islam and thus the Muslim community). The following extract refs to a member of the Muslim Council of Britain who was also chair of a government taskforce on extremism, and who allegedly said that Muslims could fight in the British armed forces:

> Numerous verses in the Quran have clearly stated that the believers are prohibited from allying with the non-Muslims and most definitely if the alliance is against fellow Muslims (...) I would sincerely advise everyone to treat this 'man' as if 'he' is a belligerent apostate! I would not pray behind 'him' nor would I permit any Muslim female to marry him. (...) I would strongly advise his wife to leave the joint home because apostasy annuls marriage automatically.

The extract begins by using evidence from the Quran ('numerous verses') as the basis for the ensuing judgement that, by breaking Quranic injunctions on allying with non-Muslims, the man is an apostate. We also see his manhood questioned with the use of quotation marks around 'man', 'he', and 'him'. The function of this is clearly to discredit him by questioning his masculinity and suggesting he is no longer a Muslim, and therefore has no right to speak on behalf of Muslims. The action that follows this is clearly stated—other Muslims should shun him and his wife should leave him.

'Moderate' Muslims are also accused of feeling inferior and seeking validation from non-Muslims. The next two extracts come from emails that attack Muslims who joined the Respect Party, a political party established by George Galloway (an ex-Labour MP) and which campaigned against the Iraq war and for Muslim rights. The party was an alliance of Muslims and non-Muslims, and targeted constituency seats in areas with large Muslim populations. In the first extract, the 'he' refers to George Galloway:

> He's figured that the British Muslims are so mentally colonised from the days of the old British Empire that if they see a white man showing sympathy for them then they'll be flocking to him.
> Yet we see self-appointed moderate Muslims nuzzling his Kafir backside for validation by a white man! That sums up these eunuchs of the Ummah.

The writer here discredits moderates by drawing on historical examples. Other scholars have shown how history (and 'serial connectedness'—Condor, 1996) is often used in debates about identity and political action (Condor, 2006; Hopkins, Reicher, & Kahani-Hopkins, 2003; McKinlay, McVittie, & Sambaraju, 2012). In this data set, the Crusades, the Inquisition, and the UK's history of racism and colonialism were often used to discredit opponents. In a similar type of account to that of Jewish self-hatred, the two extracts above suggest that domination by the British (historically and through being in a minority in Britain) has led to 'moderates' being 'mentally colonised' and suffering from an 'inferiority complex'. This social-psychological explanation, that they are desperate for approval from non-Muslims, is used to explain why they work with non-Muslims. Other explanations, for example that they share common values or aspirations for peaceful relations between groups, are not considered.

Another way of discrediting 'moderates' was to suggest they were only engaging with non-Muslims for personal gain. This writer characterizes Muslims who participate in a government taskforce on extremism as "Opportunist Muslim Parliamentarians" who,

> ... use the task force to promote themselves as Blair loyalists, hence working their way up the ladder at the expense of British Muslims. There will be plenty of work for consultants and Muslims seeking to establish their careers, and places on 'influential' committees.

Here, we see them described as working against the interests of British Muslims and supporting the prime minister Tony Blair in order to further their own careers ('working their way up the ladder' and gaining 'places on 'influential' committees').

Conclusion

In this chapter, I have used examples from a range of political contexts to illustrate how those arguing for violence against, separation from, or distrust of other groups respond to a common problem: how to persuade fellow group members that they represent the group and its interests, and that those who argue for peace, an end to persecution, co-operation, or unity across boundaries should not be listened to. They do this in a variety of ways which can loosely be categorized as mildly to strongly discrediting accounts and descriptions.

Mildly discrediting accounts and descriptions suggest that opponents are mistaken but not through their own fault. They have been misinformed or manipulated, and they are too trusting or good-natured. These types of discourses do not cast the opponent out of the group, do not call for penalties against them, and leave the way open that they might change their minds.

Strongly discrediting descriptions are more blaming and punitive. They take many forms (and may include milder explanatory accounts such as being 'mentally colonized' by a dominant outgroup), but all suggest opponents are an internal enemy who must be fought: they hate their own kind and its values due to a warped political orientation; they are selfishly pursuing their own interests at the expense of the group; they are psychologically weak and subservient to powerful outsiders; or they are rejecting their faith. Discrediting statements are constructed through derogatory and threatening representations of social categories, psychological traits and complexes, as well as activities. These types of derogatory characterizations are a warning to others about how they might be seen if they adopt similar positions. They also allow for more severe actions to be taken towards opponents, from being shunned and isolated, being silenced in political debate, to being imprisoned, attacked, or killed. Indeed, this type of discourse is often aggressive in ways that are reminiscent of the hostile ways the same speakers and commentators represent outgroups.

One final point can be made with respect to the construction of the intergroup context in situations of conflict or separation. It is well recognized that those arguing for separation from, or hostility towards, a national, ethnic, or religious outgroup construct the other as presenting some level of threat to the ingroup. But here we see a second, finer level of intergroup context asserted *within* the ingroup—that of good, authentic, and loyal members who have a right to speak for the group, as opposed to those treacherous, ignorant, or selfish members who do not. When we try to understand the discursive practices that contribute to conflict, then, we must recognize that constructions of the intergroup context occurs at both levels, one inside the supposed 'ingroup' and one involving the more obvious ingroup/out-group comparison.

References

ABC News. (2016). *From 'Crooked Hillary' to 'Little Marco', Donald Trump's many nicknames*. Retrieved May 11, 2016, from http://abcnews.go.com/Politics/crooked-hillary-marco-donald-trumps-nicknames/story?id=39035114

Barnes, L. (2005). *The Islamic Manchurian candidates*. Retrieved 15/07/2005 from www.bnp.org.uk

Bar-Tal, D. (1997). The monopolization of patriotism. In D. Bar-Tal & E. Staub (Eds.), *Patriotism in the lives of individuals and nations*. Chicago: Nelson-Hall.

Bar-Tal, D., Halperin, E., & Oren, N. (2010). Socio–psychological barriers to peace making: The case of the Israeli Jewish society. *Social Issues and Policy Review, 4*, 63–109.

Berkeley, B. (2001). *The graves are not yet full: Race, tribe and power in the heart of America*. New York: Basic Books.

Billig, M. (1987). *Arguing and thinking: A rhetorical approach to social psychology*. Cambridge: Cambridge University Press.

Billig, M. (1995). *Banal Nationalism*. London: Sage

Bump, P. (2017). The head of the NRA defines his new enemies: The 'violent left' and judges who 'do violence' to the Constitution. *The Washington Post*, Feb 24.

Burleigh, M., & Wippermann, W. (1991). *The racial state: Germany 1933-1945*. Cambridge: Cambridge University Press.

Condor, S. (1996). Social identity and time. In W. P. Robinson (Ed.), *Social groups and identities: Developing the legacy of Henri Tajfel*. Oxford: Butterworth-Heinemann.

Condor, S. (2006). Public prejudice as collaborative accomplishment: Towards a dialogic social psychology of racism. *Journal of Community and Applied Social Psychology, 16*, 1–18.

Copsey, N. (2004). *Contemporary British Fascism: The British National Party and the quest for legitimacy*. Basingstoke: Palgrave MacMillan.

Edwards, D., & Potter, J. (1992). *Discursive psychology*. London: Sage.

Finlay, W. M. L. (2005). Pathologizing dissent: Identity politics, Zionism and the 'self-hating Jew'. *British Journal of Social Psychology, 44*, 1–23.

Finlay, W. M. L. (2007). The propaganda of extreme hostility: Denunciation and the regulation of the group. *British Journal of Social Psychology, 46*, 323–341.

Finlay, W. M. L. (2014). Denunciation and the construction of norms in group conflict: Examples from an Al-Qaeda-supporting group. *British Journal of Social Psychology, 53*, 691–710.

Finlay, W. M. L. (2018). Language and civilian deaths: Denying responsibility for casualties in the Gaza conflict 2014. *Political Psychology, 39*, 595–609.

Galtung, J. (1969). Violence, peace, and peace research. *Journal of Peace Research, 6*, 167–191.

Gellately, R. (1990). *The Gestapo and German society: Enforcing racial policy, 1933-1945*. Oxford: Clarendon Press.

Goebbels, J. (1941). Die Juden sind schuld! (The Jews are guilty!). Das eherne Herz (pp. 85–91). Retrieved 27/11/2005 from the German Propapaganda Archive web-site: http://www.calvin.edu/academic/cas/gpa/goeb1.htm

Hodges, A. (2013). Introduction. In A. Hodges (Ed.), *Discourses of war and peace* (pp. 3–22). Oxford: Oxford University Press.

Hopkins, N., & Kahani-Hopkins, V. (2006). Minority group members' theories of intergroup contact: A case study of British Muslims' conceptualizations of 'Islamophobia' and social change. *British Journal of Social Psychology, 45*, 245–264.

Hopkins, N., Kahani-Hopkins, V., & Reicher, S. (2006). Identity and social change: Contextualizing agency. *Feminism & Psychology, 16*, 52–57.

Hopkins, N., Reicher, S., & Kahani-Hopkins, V. (2003). Citizenship, participation and identity construction: Political mobilization amongst British Muslims. *Psychologica Belgica, 43*, 33–54.

Lazar, A., & Lazar, M. M. (2004). The discourse of the New World Order: 'Out-casting' the double face of threat. *Discourse & Society, 15*, 223–242.

Leudar, I., Marsland, V., & Nekvapil, J. (2004). On membership categorization: 'Us', 'them' and 'doing violence' in political discourse. *Discourse and Society, 15*, 243–266.

McKinlay, A., McVittie, C., & Sambaraju, R. (2012). 'This is ordinary behaviour': Categorization and culpability in Hamas leaders' accounts of the Palestinian/Israeli conflict. *British Journal of Social Psychology, 51*, 534–550.

Oddo, J. (2011). War legitimation discourse: Representing 'us' and 'them' in four US presidential addresses. *Discourse & Society, 22*, 287–314.

Potter, J. (1996). *Representing reality: Discourse, rhetoric and social construction.* London: Sage.

Potter, J., & Wetherell, M. (1987). *Discourse and social psychology: Beyond attitudes and behaviour.* Thousand Oaks, CA: Sage.

Rapley, M. (1998). 'Just an ordinary Australian': Self-categorization and the discursive construction of facticity in 'new racist' political rhetoric. *British Journal of Social Psychology, 37*, 325–344.

Reicher, S., Haslam, S. A., & Rath, R. (2008). Making a virtue of evil: A five-step social identity model of the development of collective hate. *Social and Personality Psychology Compass, 2*, 1313–1344.

Reicher, S., & Hopkins, N. (2001). *Self and nation.* London: Sage.

Reicher, S., Hopkins, N., & Condor, S. (1997). Stereotype construction as a strategy of influence. In R. Spears, P. J. Oakes, N. Ellemers, & S. A. Haslam (Eds.), *The social psychology of stereotyping and group life.* Oxford: Blackwell.

Rooyackers, I. N., & Verkuyten, M. (2012). Mobilizing support for the extreme right: A discursive analysis of minority leadership. *British Journal of Social Psychology, 51*, 130–148.

Sani, F., & Reicher, S. (1998). When consensus fails: An analysis of the schism within the Italian Communist Party (1991). *European Journal of Social Psychology, 28*(4), 623–645.

Sani, F., & Reicher, S. (2000). Contested identities and schisms in groups: Opposing the ordination of women as priests in the Church of England. British Journal of Social Psychology, 39(1), 95–112.

Salmond, A. (2010). *Speech to the SNP Conference.* Retrieved from http://www.bbc.co.uk/news/uk-scotland-11560698

Salmond, A. (2012). *Speech to the SNP Conference.* Retrieved from http://www.heraldscotland.com/news/13077771.In_full__Alex_Salmond_s_speech_to_SNP_conference/

Sharon, A. (1994, March 11). A reality that speaks for itself. *Jerusalem Post*, p. A4.

Shirlow, P. (2003). 'Who fears to speak': Fear, mobility and ethno-sectarianism in the two 'Ardoynes'. *The Global Review of Ethnopolitics, 3*, 76–91.

Sturgeon, N. (2012). *Speech to SNP Conference.* Retrieved from http://www.ukpol.co.uk/nicola-sturgeon-2012-speech-to-snp-party-conference/

van Dijk, T. A. (1987). *Communicating racism: Ethnic prejudice in thought and talk.* Newbury Park, CA: Sage.

Wetherell, M., & Potter, J. (1992). *Mapping the language of racism: Discourse and the legitimation of exploitation.* New York: Harvester Wheatsheaf.

Wood, C., & Finlay, W. M. L. (2008). British National Party representations of Muslims in the month after the London bombings: Homogeneity, threat, and the conspiracy tradition. *British Journal of Social Psychology, 47*(4), 707–726.

Yildiz, A. A., & Verkuyten, M. (2012). Conceptualising Euro-Islam: Managing the societal demand for religious reform. *Identities, 19*(3), 360–376.

Part II
Intractable and International Military Conflicts

Chapter 6
Constructing Peace and Violence in the Palestinian-Israeli Conflict

Chris McVittie and Rahul Sambaraju

Introduction

The Palestinian-Israeli conflict is probably the most intractable conflict in the modern world (Nets-Zehngut & Bar-Tal, 2007). With the roots of the conflict going back for over a century, relations between Palestinians and Israelis over this period have for the most part been marked by warfare, bloodshed, and suffering. A detailed history is beyond the scope of this chapter and, in any case, any such history is open to contestation in terms of how events are to be framed and understood. For present purposes, we confine ourselves to outlining events in the relatively recent past that bear upon attempts at peace and subsequent events. In this respect, a useful starting point is the agreement signed in 1993 by the then leader of the Palestine Liberation Organisation (PLO) Yasser Arafat and the then Israeli Prime Minister Yitzhak Rabin, which came to be known as the Oslo Accords (Declaration of Principles on Interim Self-Government Arrangements, 1993). The primary achievement of the Oslo Accords was to set out principles for cessation of immediate conflict and recognition of the parties' respective positions; the Declaration did not attempt any resolution of the disputed issues of the final status of Palestine and Israel. The subsequent Oslo II Accords (Israeli-Palestinian Interim Agreement on the West Bank and the Gaza Strip, 1995) provided for control of territory in the West Bank and Gaza Strip to pass to The Palestinian Authority. These too however were viewed as interim measures leaving issues of the final status of Palestine and Israel to be determined later.

C. McVittie (✉)
Queen Margaret University, Edinburgh, UK
e-mail: CMcVittie@qmu.ac.uk

R. Sambaraju
Trinity College Dublin, Dublin, Republic of Ireland

© Springer Nature Switzerland AG 2018   101
S. Gibson (ed.), *Discourse, Peace, and Conflict*, Peace Psychology Book Series,
https://doi.org/10.1007/978-3-319-99094-1_6

The years since then, however, have been marked primarily not by further steps towards peace but by continuing outbreaks of conflict and violence. Over this period, the combatants and leaders have changed, the disputes less so. For Palestinians, the death of Arafat in 2004 led to the demise of The Palestinian Authority as then constituted and of unitary Palestinian leadership. There followed a division among Palestinians between Fatah (the Palestinian National Liberation Movement) and rival group Hamas (Harkat Al Mokwama Al Islamia), with each claiming to be the true voice of the Palestinian people. Fatah is led by Mahmoud Abbas, Arafat's appointed successor, and is thus seen as the natural successor to the PLO. Hamas came into being, in its present form, during the first Palestinian Intifada in 1987 and identifies itself as being an Islamist movement based in Palestine (for further discussion, see Milton-Edwards & Farrell, 2010). It is often regarded as a terrorist organisation, being listed as such by the United States since 1995 (American Foreign Policy Council, 2014). Hamas was also listed as a terrorist organisation by the European Union in 2003 (Levitt, 2006) although this listing was subsequently successfully challenged and is destined for annulment (European Union, 2016). Since the most recent Palestinian elections held in 2006, Fatah have held power in the West Bank and Hamas have held power in the Gaza Strip. For many years rivals, Fatah and Hamas in 2011 signed a reconciliation pact and in 2014 announced their agreement to work towards and form a unity government of Palestine, followed by the signing of a final reconciliation agreement between them in October 2017. The outcome of this reconciliation remains to be seen.

As might be expected, Israeli leaders have also changed since the Oslo Accords, with various Prime Ministers adopting different positions in relation to the peace process as envisaged. Some time after the Accords, in 2005 the then Israeli Prime Minister Ariel Sharon enforced the removal of Israeli settlers from occupied Palestinian territory in the Gaza Strip and West Bank, an act widely seen as a move towards resolution of the dispute over Palestinian status. Thereafter however, following Sharon's departure from office, subsequent Israeli governments ceased the dismantling of settlements and indeed countenanced and approved the establishment of further Israeli settlements on occupied Palestinian territory, actions thereafter retrospectively legalised by Israel (Lubell, 2017) despite being condemned by the United Nations (United Nations, 2016). Moreover immediately prior to the most recent Israeli parliamentary election, the subsequently elected Prime Minister, Benjamin Netanyahu, ruled out publicly the possibility that Israel would agree to the establishment of a Palestinian state (Rudoren, 2015). Immediate prospects of the Israeli government returning to the arrangements envisaged in the Oslo Accords therefore appear unlikely at this time. Resolution of the final status issues bound up with the conflict would seem even more remote.

The Palestinian-Israeli conflict, then, to date has encompassed numerous episodes of conflict and violence occasionally interspersed by efforts towards peace that have as yet failed to produce any enduring peaceful outcome. As such, it presents a major challenge on many fronts, not just to the parties immediately involved and their leaders but also to the international community more widely. And, at the same time, it presents a challenge for researchers from a broad range of backgrounds as to how we might usefully begin to understand the elements involved in the conflict, let alone seek to address these. In this chapter, we consider the contribution that discursive psychology might offer to this process.

Categorising Peace and Violence

Categorising and Differentiation

Much of psychology's interest to date in the study of peace and conflict has stemmed from the field of peace psychology. In the post-Cold War era, peace psychology turned its attention from a primary concern with the avoidance of conflict and the critique of US foreign policy to the study of peace and violence more broadly. Writing about the growth of the field over recent decades, Christie et al. (2008, p. 542) noted that the development of peace psychology had been particularly marked by three themes, namely '(a) greater sensitivity to geohistorical context, (b) a more differentiated perspective on the meanings and types of violence and peace, and (c) a systems or multilevel view of the determinants of violence and peace'. In adopting this focus, peace psychology has been influenced by earlier work conducted within the field of peace studies, especially that of Galtung (1969). Galtung, in examining issues of peace and violence, argued that violence could take two distinguishable forms: either direct or personal violence that is occasioned by an identifiable actor or actors and inflicted on the person, or indirect or structural violence that reflects broader social injustice that disadvantages individuals or social groups. Taking peace to comprise the absence of violence, the absence of direct violence is taken to constitute peace in a narrow sense, or negative peace, while the absence of structural violence is bound up with moves towards broader social justice, or positive peace. These distinctions, based upon categorisations of forms of violence on the one hand, and categorisations of forms of peace on the other, provide the basis for peace psychology's search for a more differentiated understanding of types of peace and violence.

From this perspective, attention focuses on the identification of factors associated with peace and violence, for example, processes that lead to fairer social arrangements (Lederach, 2003) or factors that contribute to a context of violence (Christie & Montiel, 2013). The emphasis on greater differentiation, combined with sensitivity to geohistorical context and a more developed view of determinants, is treated as self-evident, pointing the way to more nuanced categorisations of instances of peace and violence. Yet such an approach quickly runs into difficulties when we consider more closely how categorisations of peace and violence operate in real-world contexts, such as the Palestinian-Israeli conflict.

Categorising and Social Action

Instead of seeking clearer differentiation of forms of peace and violence, let us consider more closely what we understand by the term 'peace'. Although 'peace' is routinely taken to denote a positive and desirable state of affairs, what it comprises usually is left unspecified. As Gavriely-Nuri (2010, p. 566) notes, 'in most peace research, "peace" and "peace discourse" are terms whose meanings are usually taken for granted and treated as "common knowledge"'. Closer inspection of the literature, however, shows that there are at least five different possible meanings of 'peace' (see e.g. Galtung, 1969; Gavriely-Nuri, 2010; Hakvoort & Oppenheimer,

1998; Hall, 1993), often with little overlap between them. An outcome of this lack of consistency is that the term 'peace' has been turned into 'a black box or, more precisely, into an attractive but empty box' (Gavriely-Nuri, 2010, p. 566), that is flexible enough to be applied to very different situations.

The variability of peace (and war) can be seen clearly in a set of studies that are pertinent to the current chapter. Gavriely-Nuri (2008, 2009, 2010, 2014) reports that in their political discourse successive Israeli Prime Ministers have commonly described peace and war in particular ways. Rarely, if ever, do they refer simply to peace; instead they use *peace phrases* in which the term 'peace' is accompanied by another term (either noun or adjective) to specify the precise terms of their claims in any instance. Thus, phrases such as 'secure peace' or 'just peace' are used to argue for particular forms of peace while undermining other possibilities. As Gavriely-Nuri (2010) notes, Israeli leaders draw upon these descriptions to legitimise their own claims to be committed to peace (whatever that peace might be). Similarly, recurring talk of 'extending the hand in peace' is commonly used not to signify attempts at peace in themselves but instead to provide a basis for claims that Israel seeks peace and that its efforts are rejected by others. Israeli leaders' descriptions of war also serve a particular function. By drawing on *war-normalising metaphors* such as 'war is women's work' or 'war is sport', speakers downgrade the significance of wars in which Israel was involved and thereby render unexceptional actions that otherwise might be the targets of criticism (Gavriely-Nuri, 2008, 2009, 2014).

What we see from the studies above is that peace and war are certainly amenable to categorisation. Categorisation, however, is not a straightforward process of allocating instances to specific categories (however nuanced) as is proposed by current writings in peace psychology. Findings such as those discussed above demonstrate that speakers actively engage in using categorisations to construct versions of social phenomena rather than (simply) assigning social actions and events to pre-existing categories. Categorisation thus can be understood not as the act of assigning appropriate category labels to external stimuli but as a social process that individuals negotiate in discourse and social interaction. As McKinlay and McVittie (2008, p. 105) note, categorisation comprises three main features. Of these, the first is one of selection, namely that individuals have leeway in selecting the categories that they use in any instance. In the case of Israeli leaders' political discourse, the categorisations of peace or war that they deploy are not the only possibilities available but have been selected for use on these occasions. The second feature of categorisation is that the features relevant to any category cannot be assumed or 'read off'; speakers 'work up' the categories that they use to attend to the immediate context of the description. Thus, for example, the meaning of a categorisation such as 'just peace' or 'war as sport' cannot be assumed but is developed in the local discursive context. Finally, McKinlay and McVittie argue that categorisation is linked to social action: it is an active process and not merely the allocation of labels to people or other phenomena. When, therefore, we see speakers referring to one form of peace instead of another, or seeking to normalise engagement in war, all such categorisations are oriented towards some form of outcome. It is not difficult to see the action-orientation of the categorisations in the instances considered by Gavriely-Nuri (2008, 2009, 2010, 2014), most if not all of which are designed to justify or account for the speaker's own position while deflecting criticism and attributing to others blame for actions that might be treated as blameworthy.

Applying this discursive approach to the topic of this chapter, attention turns to the discourse that the parties involved, their leaders, and all interested others use to describe the actors, actions, and events involved. Here, the focus is on discourse as the topic of study in itself, as 'a phenomenon which has its own properties, properties which have an impact on people and their social interaction' (McKinlay & McVittie, 2008, p. 8). Discursive psychology foregrounds examination of the categories that individuals select and use, how these are developed, and the actions that they achieve in doing so. Descriptions of issues associated with the conflict therefore are treated not as reflections of forms of peace and violence that are distinguishable external phenomena but as versions of the conflict that individuals 'work up' and deploy to accomplish outcomes. These action outcomes are central to understanding the conflict, the issues at stake, and the possibilities (if any) for possible resolution. Understanding peace and violence, then, requires detailed analysis of the categorisations that speakers produce and deploy, how these are developed in specific discursive contexts, and the social actions that speakers accomplish by constructing peace and violence in different ways.

Categorising Violence, Peace, and Peace-Building

The Palestinian-Israeli conflict has attracted attention from discursive researchers as it has from others. We have already seen how discursive work can shed light upon the political discourse of Israeli leaders, and how they seek to legitimate the Israeli position in the conflict (Gavriely-Nuri, 2008, 2009, 2014). Similar findings come from a study by Sambaraju and Kirkwood (2010) who found that Israeli leaders mobilised discourses of moderation and peace to justify Israel taking military action against the Palestinians who were categorised as 'extremists'. By contrast, McKinlay, McVittie, and Sambaraju (2012) showed that political leaders of Hamas constructed the Palestinians as victims of Israeli occupation and aggression and of the indifference of the international community towards their plight, constructions that allowed Hamas leaders to categorise Palestinian actions against Israel as resistance. Relatedly, McVittie, Sambaraju, and McKinlay (2011) found that Hamas leaders discounted the value of pursuing a peace process with Israel and instead directed their arguments for achieving peace at the international community. All such findings are oriented towards action, in each case justifying the actions of the speaker's own side while criticising and blaming the other side for violence and for failure to engage in appropriate peace discussions. They are also bound up with specific constructions of identities of both sides (McKinlay & McVittie, 2011), here most commonly identities of victim and aggressor. The identity of victim was evident also in Jaspal and Coyle's (2014) analysis of speeches by Palestinian

President Mahmoud Abbas and Israeli Prime Minister Benjamin Netanyahu to the UN General Assembly on the topic of a Palestinian bid in 2011 for state membership of the UN. Both leaders constructed their own party as victims of violence committed by the other party, but neither employed the 'language of reconciliation or peace' (Jaspal & Coyle, 2014, p. 211).

The findings point to recurring concerns in Palestinian and Israeli constructions of the conflict and of peace and violence. Here, we extend these findings by examining in detail how leading Palestinian and Israeli politicians construct violence, peace, and the possible resolution of the conflict. To do so, we draw upon available transcripts of speeches given by these politicians and of interviews that they have given to members of the international media, during the period following the Palestinian elections in 2006 to date. These transcripts provide the publicly enduring records of how Palestinian and Israeli politicians construct the conflict and as such provide an especially rich source of data for examining how their discourse functions to present violence and peace in this context. The data extracts presented below span much of the period under consideration and therefore include instances previously examined elsewhere and examples that are derived from recent speeches and interviews on the matters at hand.

Accounting for Violence

We start by considering how the parties themselves describe the acts of violence that occur in the course of the conflict. The extract below is taken from an interview with the then Israeli Foreign Minister Tzipora Livni conducted by Maggie Rodriguez, in Jerusalem, for CBS news on 28 December 2008, during the Gaza war between Israel and Palestine.

```
Extract 1
  1   Rodriguez   We just heard you say that your objective here is to
  2               force Hamas to stop its rocket barrages, and to limit
  3               its military build up. But the extent -- the intensity
  4               of your retaliation has been widely condemned, not
  5               only in the Arab world, but across Europe. Are you
  6               afraid this could be counter-productive?
  7   Livni       This is not retaliation. We are trying to change
  8               realities on the ground, and the realities were --
  9               until this operation -- that Israeli citizens were under
 10               daily attacks from Gaza Strip, a place that we left.
 11               We drew -- took our forces out. We dismantled
 12               settlements in order to create a vision of peace. And
 13               Hamas took Gaza Strip with all its citizens and
 14               abused this in order to target Israel. Now, about
 15               your question -- about the Arab world and so -- it is
 16               important to understand that the world and
 17               description is being divided between extremists and
 18               moderates.
```

19	And Israel stands together with other powers of the
20	Arab and Muslim world together against extremism,
21	which is being represented by Hamas, by Iran, by
22	Hezbollah. They're not fighting for any legitimate
23	rights of the Palestinians, so they are just trying to
24	deprive us from our rights.

(from Sambaraju & Kirkwood, 2010, p.138, original formatting)

Rodriguez's question asks about violence being inflicted by Israel. It should be noted that Rodriquez categorises that violence as being of a specific form, referring to it as 'retaliation'. This description characterises violence originating from Israel in two ways, first as being reactive to other circumstances rather than as proactive, and second as thereby understandable and rational. Thus, Israel is positioned as the responder rather than the aggressor in this instance. Rodriguez suggests, however, that this does not excuse its actions, in that it has been said to have been widely 'condemned' for how it has responded and is therefore treated as accountable for this response.

What we see in Livni's response is a combination of three elements that seek to render invisible, or at least less objectionable, Israeli actions and to introduce a different framework for understanding Israeli and Palestinian acts. First, she seeks to recategorise entirely the Israeli actions to which Rodriquez referred. Instead of constituting 'retaliation', the actions in question are reworked as an attempt 'to change realities on the ground'. The substitution of the verb 'change' for the noun 'retaliation' downgrades the motivation for the actions and consequently the extent to which they might reasonably be challenged. Second, this reformulation leads on to a description of the Israelis that presents them as victims of Palestinian attacks, attacks that are to be understood as especially objectionable in light of the steps that Israelis are said to have taken 'to create a vision of peace'. Third, this description itself is then set within a broader explanatory framework that specifies how issues of peace and violence are more generally to be understood. Here, Livni introduces a distinction between a category that comprises 'extremists' and one of 'moderates'. To the former she assigns Hamas, Iran, and Hezbollah and she characterises their actions as 'not fighting for any legitimate rights of the Palestinians' and as 'just trying to deprive us from our rights'. The latter category of 'moderates' is said to include Israel and 'other powers of the Arab and Muslim world' that she claims stand 'together against extremism'. These categorisations function to argue that Hamas are not genuinely representing the interests of the Palestinians in the conflict and to attribute to Hamas responsibility for the violence that is salient to continuing the conflict. By contrast, Israeli actions in the conflict are presented as being those of 'moderates' who are faced with such violence.

Extract 2 comes from an interview with Khaled Meshaal, then Leader of Hamas, conducted on 31 March 2008 by Tim Marshall, Foreign Affairs editor of Sky News, at an unspecified location in Syria. This extract follows a question relating to the extent of Arab support for Hamas and a response from Meshaal describing the options available to the Palestinian people.

Extract 2
```
 1   Marshall   Nothing is left to them and there'll be even less left to them if you keep
 2              sending what many people believe are brainwashed people to blow
 3              themselves up. Killing small children and then invited the retribution
 4              that then comes.
 5   Meshaal    First of all we do not brainwash anyone. Every Palestinian
 6              spontaneously feels that his land is occupied. That Israel is killing
 7              children and women, demolishing their homes, taking their land,
 8              building the wall, the settlements, that journalism favours Israel, and
 9              digging under the al Aqsa mosque. So the Palestinian finds himself
10              going directly to fight for the resistance. This is his duty. As the French
11              fought the Nazis, and in the American revolution, as the Vietnamese
12              people fought, as did the South African. This is ordinary behaviour it
13              doesn't need brainwashing.
```
                                                        (from McKinlay et al., 2012, p.543)

As with the previous extract, Extract 2 begins with a question that asks about violence. In this case, however, the violence is made out in highly reprehensible terms,
suggesting that Hamas send 'brainwashed people' 'to blow themselves up' and are
'killing small children'. This proposed action of sending people who have been
deprived of the necessary capacity to make their own decisions to commit such acts
attributes accountability to Hamas for extreme violence in the conflict. Here again
Israeli actions are, by contrast, characterised as retribution and presented as being
reactive and not proactive.

Meshaal's response orients to all of these elements. First, he reformulates those
who commit the actions being described in general and all-encompassing terms as
'every Palestinian' and he offers a motivation for such actions by referring to how
Palestinians 'spontaneously feel'. This works to undermine Marshall's suggestion
that Hamas 'brainwash' people to carry out these acts. Thereafter, Meshaal offers an
explanation for why Palestinians feel as they do. This is made out in terms of Israeli
occupation of Palestinian land and Israeli aggressions carried out during the conflict,
all described as proactive and emphasised through the listing of different morally
opprobrious actions. His comparison of Israeli actions against Palestinians to those
of 'the Nazis' presents these actions as being of such a quality that they should be
unhesitatingly condemned. This provides the basis on which he can then
re-characterise the actions of Palestinians in the conflict, constructing their actions
as resistance that is similar in form to what other international actors have done in
similar situations in the past. Moreover, Meshaal's final upshot, 'this is ordinary
behaviour', categorises the actions of the Palestinians not as acts of unwarranted
violence but instead as understandable responses to the situation in which they find
themselves.

There are two main points that we can take from Extracts 1 and 2. First, we
should note that the speakers provide totally divergent versions of how violence
occurring in the conflict is to be understood. Livni in Extract 1 constructs Israeli
actions as the actions of 'moderates' and as unexceptional in that they are attempting
to change what is happening 'on the ground'. In her version, it is the actions of
Hamas, to which Israel has to respond, that should be taken to constitute unreasonable
violence. By contrast, Meshaal in Extract 2 presents the actions of Palestinians as
similar to what others have done in circumstances similar to those in which the

Palestinians find themselves and therefore as wholly understandable in the context of this conflict. For Meshaal it is the Israelis who, through occupation of Palestinian land and by committing acts of aggression to which the Palestinians have to respond, are responsible for proactive and unreasonable violence. Thus, as is evident, there is no single version of how violence should be understood in this context. Second, it is equally clear from these two extracts that the versions of violence that the speakers are providing cannot be treated as straightforward descriptions of any external states of affairs and/or how the speakers understand them. Rather these accounts, as is the case with all discourse, are designed to perform particular actions. More specifically, they are designed to attend to accountability for the violence that occurs. Both Livni and Meshaal produce accounts that render understandable, and thereby excuse, the actions of the party for which they speak, positioning it as the victim in the conflict (Jaspal & Coyle, 2014), and at the same time criticising and rendering the other party accountable for what is portrayed as constituting unreasonable violence.

Constructing Peace

Just as violence occurring during the conflict is open to varying constructions, so too is peace. Extract 3 below comes from an interview with Israeli Prime Minister Benjamin Netanyahu conducted on 19 March 2015 by Steve Inskeep of the US-based National Public Radio (NPR) (NPR, 2015). This interview took place shortly after the success of Netanyahu's Likud Party in Israel's 2015 parliamentary elections:

Extract 3

1	Inskeep	While we were reporting in Israel, we heard people in Israel on the left
2		and on the right openly worry about Israel's increasing international
3		isolation, particularly because the conflict with Palestinians has gone on
4		and on and there has not been the establishment of a Palestinian state.
5		How concerned are you about Israel's international isolation?
6	Netanyahu	Well, look. I think that there is a misperception. Israel has done
7		enormous amount of, for peace. I myself have done things that no prime
8		minister previously had done. I had frozen the settlements. Nobody did
9		that. And I think, you know, the ones that have to be convinced are not
10		only the international communities, the people of Israel will have to be
11		convinced that the Palestinians are ready for peace. The leaders of Iran,
12		just in the last few days have said that they would arm the West Bank
13		and turn it into another Gaza. What the people of Israel are saying,
14		"Hey, make sure that doesn't happen again." And if that is
15		misperceived in some parts of the international community that's
16		unfortunate, but I think that that's the truth.

The question put here to Netanyahu refers to a possible resolution of the conflict, namely 'the establishment of a Palestinian state'. Inskeep, however, introduces this in a specific way by suggesting that failure to achieve this outcome has led to concern that Israel might be internationally isolated, making available the inference that Israel is treated as responsible for this failure.

Netanyahu responds to this suggestion by setting out a claim first for the steps that Israel and he personally have taken towards peace, and second for what is further required for peace. The first of these is advanced through the claim to have 'frozen the settlements'. Here, he maximises his own efforts in stating that he has 'done things that no prime minister previously had done', emphasising the extent of the steps that he personally has taken towards peace. The second element relates to what would be required for moves towards peace to progress. For peace to come closer, he attributes responsibility to the Palestinians who have to be 'ready for peace'. This is made out in terms of the Palestinians having to 'convince' the Israelis of their readiness, a task that is made more difficult by the actions of those who have said they will 'arm the West Bank'. Netanyahu's reference here to 'Iran' as the source of that statement suggests that it is that country rather than the Palestinians who are in control of what happens in 'the West Bank' and, furthermore, that Iranian involvement would inevitably replicate previous problems and dangers for Israel in that this would 'turn it into another Gaza'. This provides the basis for Netanyahu's upshot that Israelis are concerned not to repeat what they see as past mistakes, and that this concern is not appropriately recognised by 'some parts of the international community'.

From Netanyahu's perspective, then, responsibility for progressing peace lies with the Palestinians who have to demonstrate their readiness for peace. As we see in the next extract, the Palestinians do not share this perspective, instead arguing that responsibility for failure to progress towards peace rests with Israel. This extract comes from the address made by Palestinian Authority President Mahmoud Abbas to the United Nations General Assembly on 22 September 2016 (Abbas, 2016):

Extract 4

1	Abbas	We remain committed to the agreements reached with Israel since
2		1993. However, Israel must reciprocate this commitment and must act
3		forthwith to resolve all of the final status issues. It must cease all of its
4		settlement colonization activities and aggressions against our cities,
5		villages and refugee camps. It must cease its policies of collective
6		punishment and its demolition of Palestinian homes. It must cease its
7		extrajudicial executions and cease the arrest of our people, and must
8		release the thousands of our prisoners and detainees. It must cease its
9		aggression and provocations against the Holy Al-Aqsa Mosque. For all
10		of these policies and practices prevent an environment in which peace
11		can be realized in our region. How can anyone seeking peace perpetrate
12		such actions?

Here, we see Abbas begin by describing Palestinian commitment to the agreements comprised in the Oslo Accords. The inference made available by this is that of Palestinian commitment to peace as envisaged there. This is however followed by a list of steps that are required of Israel for peace to come about. These steps comprise first the commencement of moves towards resolving issues of 'final status', that is resolution of disputes over the establishment and recognition of a Palestinian state, and second the cessation of a range of ongoing actions. He categorises these actions as 'settlement colonisation activities and aggressions' and 'provocations', emphasising their proactive nature, and also describes them in ways that can be heard as highly culpable, for instance in being described as 'collective punishment' and 'extrajudicial executions'. Each description in itself refers to Israeli violence, suggesting through the repeated use of 'cease' that these actions are ongoing. Here, the listing of such descriptions serves to emphasise the commonality of these elements (Jefferson, 1990), that is that each sets out an illegitimate and culpable action for which Israel is accountable and that these are exemplars of a broader set of possibilities that could be drawn upon. Thus, Abbas' listing of these different actions carried out against the Palestinians highlights the extent and scope of Israeli aggressions against the Palestinians and thus gives rhetorical emphasis to his claim that Israel is responsible through its actions for a failure to progress towards peace.

As with the accounts of violence seen in Extracts 1 and 2, the descriptions of what is required for peace seen in the two extracts above are totally divergent. Netanyahu, in Extract 3, constructs himself as having taking unprecedented steps towards peace by having 'frozen the settlements', but as unable to proceed further without moves on the Palestinian side to demonstrate that they are 'ready' for peace. While Netanyahu does not draw upon the metaphor of 'extending the hand in peace', his formulation here resembles those commonly used by Israeli leaders as identified by Gavriely-Nuri (2010): the claim is that Israeli efforts have not been recognised by others and that their current stance is thereby warranted. By contrast, Abbas in Extract 4 argues that the Palestinians remain committed to peace as envisaged in the Oslo Accords but that Israel fails to demonstrate a similar commitment. Consistent with previous findings (McKinlay et al., 2012; McVittie et al., 2011), Abbas portrays the Palestinians as unable to make progress towards peace in a situation of occupation and attendant violence. For each, then, it is the in-group who have done all that could reasonably be expected of them towards arriving at peace with further progress being dependant on the actions (or cessation of actions) of the other party.

One further point of interest here lies in the role of external actors in relation to the conflict. In Extract 3, Netanyahu refers to the potential role of Iran in stating that they would 'arm the West Bank', a claim that suggests that Iran rather than the Palestinians is in control of what happens or might happen during the conflict. According to Netanyahu, it is this role of external agents that leads to Israeli concern over moves towards peace. When asked about 'Israel's international isolation', he responds by arguing that Israel's position in this regard is 'misperceived'. The suggestion here is that 'the international community' should recognise and not seek to change Israel's stance towards the conflict and what is needed for peace to result. Abbas in Extract 4 makes no reference to external actors, directing his talk at elements of the conflict more narrowly. At other times, however, the Palestinians too construct a role for the international community in relation to the resolution of the conflict. And, as we will see in the following section, this potential role is somewhat different from that proposed by Netanyahu here.

Negotiating Peace-Building

The different versions of violence and peace seen above are reflected in the parties' respective accounts of how the present conflict might be resolved. Extract 5 comes from an interview with Israeli Prime Minister Benjamin Netanyahu conducted by Leigh Sales of the Australian Broadcasting Corporation and broadcast on 23 September 2014 (Sales, 2014):

Extract 5

1	Sales	The former president, Bill Clinton, was captured on tape last week
2		agreeing with the assertion that you are not the man who is going to
3		make a peace deal. Based on your performance so far he's correct, isn't
4		he?
5	Netanyahu	Well, I will make peace that will hold. I will make a peace that will not
6		crash on the rocks of illusion. We have to make sure that it's a peace
7		that Israel can defend, because if we just walk out as we walked out of
8		Gaza. We just walked out of Gaza; Hamas, backed by Iran, walked in.
9		We got 15,000 rockets on our head. We walked out of Lebanon;
10		Hezbollah, backed by Iran, walked in. We got another 15,000 rockets
11		on our head. Imagine that: imagine 30,000 rockets fired on Australia.
12		So you think there'd be some caution about doing it a third time

The question in the extract above foregrounds Netanyahu's own role in any potential peace process. Specifically, Sales suggests that based on the view of someone who is entitled to speak with authority on such matters, former US President Bill Clinton, Netanyahu's previous actions do not indicate that he is interested in concluding a peace deal.

In response, Netanyahu argues that he is prepared to 'make peace'. This willingness is however associated with a specific form of peace, in that he describes it as a 'peace that will hold' and one that 'will not crash on the rocks of illusion'. He goes on to argue that it has to be 'a peace that Israel can defend'. This statement is developed by reference to previous Israeli actions and their claimed consequences, in that on other occasions when Israel 'walked out' of territory it occupied other parties 'walked in' and rockets were thereafter fired at Israel. As in Extract 3, he develops this claim with reference to 'Iran', arguing that it has previously 'backed' the parties that 'walked in' to land that was given up, leading on both occasions to the firing of '15,000 rockets' at Israel. This description of the claimed consequences of Israeli concessions, and of the role of Iran in backing violence against them, leads him to the upshot that 'there'd be some caution about doing it a third time'.

What we can note from this extract is that, notwithstanding his initial references to peace that he is willing to make, Netanyahu does not specify what that peace would involve. His later description, however, indicates the sort of peace that he and Israel would be reluctant to make, namely one that involves them 'walking away' and giving up land currently occupied by Israel to the Palestinians. Moreover, for Netanyahu the proposed outcome is 'a peace that Israel can defend'. This formulation comprises what Gavriely-Nuri (2010) termed a *peace phrase,* combining the term 'peace' with another lexical item to argue for one version of peace and undermine other possibilities. Netanyahu's reference here to 'defend' envisages the use of force, military force in particular, to maintain established patterns of social relations. Commonly, of course, 'peace' is taken to denote the absence of violence and hostilities. In referring to 'a peace that Israel can defend', Netanyahu proposes that a resolution of the ongoing conflict should provide for Israel retaining the option of deploying force as it deems necessary if it perceives itself to be under threat. The proposed outcome, then, is one that provides for the appearance of peace but which leaves Israeli military options intact.

In the final extract, we see a rather different version of how peace should be built. This extract again comes from an interview with Khaled Meshaal, then Leader of Hamas, in this case conducted by Tom Rayner, Middle East Reporter for Sky News on 4 December 2014 (Rayner, 2014):

Extract 6

1	Rayner	Would it not make sense, if what you really want to do is assist the
2		people of Gaza to rebuild their lives, to take steps that makes it easier
3		for the world to work with you—while there is armed resistance, most
4		governments can't work with you.
5	Meshaal	. . . the question is what Palestinian position required from Hamas or
6		from Fatah or from the other Palestinian factions that will satisfy the
7		international world to help us achieve our goals? We showed every
8		flexibility required to reach a solution when the Palestinian powers all
9		agreed to a resolution based on the 1967 borders, what more do they
10		want? We fixed our Palestinian house according to democratic means
11		since 2006. The West rejected it and the Israelis rejected it and there are
12		parties that conspired against it. What does the international community
13		want? The international community knows that the stubbornness is
14		from the Israeli leadership. And you know that Israel is being over-run
15		by the right-wingers, as we saw in the developments of the Israeli
16		governments recently—the Israeli right-wing is the master of these
17		times, it is the one provoking our people in the Holy sites, it is the one
18		insisting on stealing the lands, and with settlements, which conflicts
19		with the international opinion. And with all this, they don't do anything.
20		We as Palestinians gave everything required to make the just peace a
21		success, but the international community is in-between impotence and
22		pandering or being hypocritical towards Israel, and is biased towards it,
23		at the expense of logic

In Extract 6, Rayner's question introduces the matter of the international community and their potential role in resolving the conflict. The suggestion is that this will not happen as long as the Palestinians engage in 'armed resistance'. The question, however, is framed in such a way as to suggest that Hamas might be more interested in continuing armed resistance than they are in helping the Palestinians and to question whether they seek an outcome that will 'assist the people of Gaza to rebuild their lives'.

Following a brief reference to other issues (not included here) Meshaal begins by claiming that the Palestinians share one unified position on the matters under discussion, referring to the 'Palestinian position required from Hamas or from Fatah or from the other Palestinian factions' as reflected in 'our goals'. The remainder of his response comprises two elements, first a contrast between the attributes and actions of the Palestinians and those of the Israelis and, second, a description of how the outside world in the form of the 'international community' responds to the actions of each side.

As regards the first of these, Meshaal describes the Palestinians as demonstrating what is required for peace to be achieved. This is set out through a listing structure similar to those seen in earlier extracts, with Meshaal arguing that the Palestinians 'showed every flexibility', 'agreed to a resolution', and 'fixed our Palestinian house according to democratic means'. Each part of the list points to the efforts of the Palestinians and together they function to emphasise rhetorically the Palestinians' willingness for peace. This is contrasted with the stance and actions of the Israelis who are described as demonstrating 'stubbornness' and as being controlled by extremist factions in that they are 'being over-run by the right-wingers'. Again, Meshaal lists the actions involved, in this instance actions of 'provoking our people in the Holy sites', 'stealing the lands', and 'with settlements', which together emphasise the illegitimate and culpable nature of what Israelis are doing. The suggestion here is that others are powerless to stop such actions, as 'the Israeli right-wing is the master of these times'.

Meshaal's contrast between the 'flexibility' and 'democratic' moves of the Palestinians and the Israelis' 'stubbornness' and 'stealing the lands' is, at the same time, developed within a framework of how the 'international community' respond to the conflict and what is needed for progress towards peace. Throughout his turn, he presents questions that are directed at the international community, asking what is 'required' of Palestinians and what do they 'want'. Following his descriptions of the actions of both sides, he argues that 'the West' have 'rejected' the reasonable steps taken by the Palestinians and that despite knowing that 'the stubbornness is from the Israeli leadership' they 'don't do anything'. This leads to his final forthright criticisms of the international community, namely that it is 'in-between impotence and pandering' or 'hypocritical towards Israel' and 'biased towards it at the expense of logic'. It is in this context that he argues for 'the international community' to take steps towards the realisation of a 'just peace', a peace that recognises 'everything' that the Palestinians have done towards such an outcome.

In these final extracts, then, we see again totally divergent accounts of how peace might be built from the current conflict. According to Netanyahu in Extract 5, he is willing to move towards peace, a peace however that does not require it to 'walk away' or give up territory to other parties and 'that Israeli can defend'. For Meshaal, the Palestinians have already done whatever could reasonably be asked of them to achieve peace, and it is the intransigence of Israel and the failure of the international community to act appropriately that prevent the realisation of a 'just peace'.

Discussion and Conclusions

What we have seen in Israeli and Palestinian leaders' descriptions of the ongoing conflict is how different versions of what is to count as peace and violence are negotiated in their talk. Specifically, these versions are developed by reference to a range of actions (or absence of action) by the parties involved and how they are to be understood, and in relation to the identities that each side ascribes to themselves and to the other. In their descriptions of the issues, both Israeli and Palestinian leaders justify the actions of their own side while attributing responsibility for unwarranted and unreasonable violence to the opposing side. Similarly, the leaders seek to justify their own side's actions and efforts in terms of attempting to achieve progress towards peace while criticising the other side for its failure to do what is necessary. Indeed, the form that peace should take is equally contested, involving either 'a peace that Israel can defend' or resolution of 'all of the final status issues' depending on the perspective adopted.

Given these competing descriptions and claims, it is clear that there is no single version, of peace on the one hand and violence on the other, by which specific elements of the conflict can be relevantly categorised. The variability of the discourse of peace and violence renders any such attempt futile. From a discursive psychological perspective, this is to be expected: discourse will always vary and the descriptions that speakers produce, of social actors, actions, and events, will inevitably be tailored towards the demands of the immediate interactional context within which the descriptions are produced. And, as we have seen in the speakers' descriptions of the issues relating to this conflict, their discourse is oriented towards specific action outcomes of justifying their own position, criticising the opposing side, and arguing for certain outcomes to the conflict. Thus, a focus on the detail of how the individuals involved themselves categorise and construct aspects of the conflict shows what they accomplish and provides us with insights into how peace and violence are negotiated in this setting.

Of course, the descriptions considered here were produced in contexts of news media interviews. They are therefore not directed solely at the individual interviewer in any one case but are designed also to present particular versions of the conflict to a broader viewing or listening audience. It is for such reasons that we see references to recognisable international figures such as Bill Clinton in Extract 5, to the role of other organisations, states, and conflicts in many of the extracts, and to the less specific 'international community' in Extracts 3 and 6, and other talk that makes relevant the actions and positions of those who are not directly involved in the conflict. And, just as the leaders' descriptions vary in how they describe events so too they vary in terms of the role that is proposed for the international community. Thus, we see Netanyahu in Extract 3 arguing that the international community should re-evaluate their position relating to the status quo and accept Israel's stance, while Meshaal in Extract 6 argues that it is being 'hypocritical' in failing to 'help us achieve our goals'.

We should note that, although Meshaal's argument for the international community to intervene in the conflict might appear reasonable as set out, this argument relies on the claim that, for whatever reason(s), the international community ignores what should be readily apparent to it. In this respect, Meshaal's position is similar to that which underpins mainstream peace psychology: peace and violence are states that are amenable to clear differentiation and categorisation. As we have seen, however, categorisations of peace and violence are not perceptual and cognitive activities: these and other categorisations are developed in context and tailored towards specific actions. Thus, the international community too can construct peace and violence according to the demands of the immediate context. Evidence from studies of international initiatives in other conflicts suggests that often these bear little relation to 'peace-building' and indeed can result in anything but peace. For example, Heathershaw (2008), writing about peace-building in the Central Asian state of Tajikistan following a civil war during the 1990s, notes that international interventions succeeded only in reinforcing pre-existing power structures and became less to do with implementing peace than with being able to construct the mission as successful. On a similar note, Selby (2013) notes that United Nations' interventions in Cambodia in 1992 to 1993 following the civil war failed to secure an enduring peace and that the aim of the intervention turned to one of allowing international powers to disengage from involvement in the region under a 'veneer of UN-sanctioned legitimacy' (2013, p. 72). In these and other instances, international peace-keeping becomes little more than a myth (Selby, 2013), or 'a fantasy space or dreamland of international affairs (where peace-keeping operations are successful, governance is realised, etc.) inside which claims to neoliberalism on a global scale can be made' (Debrix, 1999, p. 216).

On the basis of such experience, it is far from certain that even well-intentioned international intervention would produce a peace that is meaningful for all parties and result in enduring resolution of the conflict. An international initiative that claimed success in producing peace while changing little would certainly be consistent with Netanyahu's argument (Extract 3) that Israel's stance is 'misperceived'. To achieve what Meshaal (Extract 6) refers to as a 'just peace' would however require not just acceptance of the Palestinian version of the conflict but an initiative that is very different to those seen previously in Tajikistan and Cambodia. For Palestinians, the irony is perhaps not that their efforts to date have gone unrecognised but that even recognition of those efforts would not necessarily lead to the outcome they seek. This, as much as anything, demonstrates the variability of the term 'peace', a variability that cannot be resolved by differentiation and categorisation but that can be understood through close attention to the discourse of all those who have an interest in this conflict.

There remains the question of what is to be, or indeed can be, done about the Palestinian-Israeli conflict. One useful starting point would be to reconsider the use of talk of peace and violence in this context. If the term 'peace' is indeed nothing more than 'an attractive but empty box' (Gavriely-Nuri, 2010, p. 566), into which anyone can place and argue for what is to count as peace, then it can achieve little to retain this as the most desirable description of an outcome. Equally, where it becomes bound up with expectations (or lack of expectations) of international actors, then 'peace' potentially does little more than add layers of misunderstanding to existing complexities and to obscure what is at issue. Talk of violence similarly appears to bring little of clarity. A first step then might be for those who participate in interventions or who negotiate conflict to adopt a critical approach to these terms; instead of taking them to represent the individual disposition of the speaker towards achieving a particular outcome or the outcome itself, a recipient of such talk can usefully ask what the speaker is seeking to accomplish in their discourse.

Models and strategies grounded in social psychology (Kelman, 1999, 2007) make use of concepts such as identities and categorisation, which as seen in the analyses above are better understood as discursive constructions used to accomplish social action. Understanding peace and conflict from a discursive perspective offers a radically alternative approach that focuses on the social actions that talk of peace or violence accomplishes. Thus, recipients of such talk, particularly those who seek to offer interventions or engage in conflict resolution at broader international or local levels can more usefully attend to the action outcomes of talk than treat this as avowals of commitment to peace or violence. Much previous research, and the analyses above, show that talk of peace or violence is routinely aimed at justification, criticism, and lack of progress. However, recognition of such by practitioners of conflict resolution might push for alternative forms of discussion such as on the detail of issues in dispute. In view of the history of this most intractable of conflicts, there is of course no certainty that resolution of these issues will come quickly or easily: all evidence over recent decades suggests otherwise. What is more certain, however, is that recognising the role of discourses of peace or violence will, potentially at least, allow for some moves towards progress.

References

Abbas, M. (2016). *Full text of PA President Mahmoud Abbas's speech at the UN*. Retrieved from http://www.timesofisrael.com/full-text-of-pa-president-mahmoud-abbass-speech-at-the-un

American Foreign Policy Council. (2014). *The world almanac of Islamism*. American Foreign Policy Council/Rowman & Littlefield.

Christie, D. J., & Montiel, C. J. (2013). Contributions of psychology to war and peace. *American Psychologist, 68*, 502–513.

Christie, D. J., Tint, B., Wagner, R. V., & Winter, D. D. (2008). Peace psychology for a peaceful world. *American Psychologist, 63*, 540–552.

Debrix, F. (1999). *Re-envisioning UN peacekeeping*. Minneapolis, MN: University of Minnesota Press.

Declaration of Principles on Interim Self-Government Arrangements, Israel-Palestine Liberation Organization, September 13, 1993. Retrieved February 19, 2009, from http://news.bbc.co.uk/1/hi/in_depth/middle_east/israel_and_the_palestinians/key_documents/1682727.stm

European Union. (2016). *Advocate General Sharpston considers that the Court should annul the measures maintaining Hamas and LTTE on the EU list of terrorist organisations on procedural grounds*. Retrieved from https://curia.europa.eu/jcms/upload/docs/application/pdf/2016-09/cp160108en.pdf

Galtung, J. (1969). Violence, peace, and peace research. *Journal of Peace Research, 6*, 167–191.

Gavriely-Nuri, D. (2008). The 'metaphorical annihilation' of the Second Lebanon War (2006) from the Israeli political discourse. *Discourse & Society, 19*, 5–20.

Gavriely-Nuri, D. (2009). Friendly fire: War-normalizing metaphors in the Israeli political discourse. *Journal of Peace Education, 6*, 153–169.

Gavriely-Nuri, D. (2010). The idiosyncratic language of Israeli 'peace': A cultural approach to critical discourse analysis (CCDA). *Discourse & Society, 21*, 565–585.

Gavriely-Nuri, D. (2014). Talking peace—Going to war. *Critical Discourse Studies, 11*, 1–18.

Hakvoort, I., & Oppenheimer, L. (1998). Understanding peace and war: Review of developmental psychology research. *Developmental Review, 18*, 358–389.

Hall, R. (1993). How children think and feel about war and peace: An Australian study. *Journal of Peace Research, 30*, 181–196.

Heathershaw, J. (2008). Seeing like the international community: How peacebuilding failed (and survived) in Tajikistan. *Journal of Intervention and Statebuilding, 2*, 329–351.

Israeli-Palestinian Interim Agreement on the West Bank and the Gaza Strip. (1995). Retrieved from http://www.unsco.org/Documents/Key/Israeli-Palestinian%20Interim%20Agreement%20on%20the%20West%20Bank%20and%20the%20Gaza%20Strip.pdf

Jaspal, R., & Coyle, A. (2014). Threat, victimhood, and peace: Debating the 2011 Palestinian UN State Membership Bid. *Digest of Middle East Studies, 23*, 190–214.

Jefferson, G. (1990). List construction as a task and interactional resource. In G. Psathas (Ed.), *Interactional competence* (pp. 63–92). Washington, DC: University Press of America.

Kelman, H. C. (1999). The interdependence of Israeli and Palestinian national identities: The Role of the Other in Existential Conflicts. *Journal of Social Issues, 55*, 581–600. https://doi.org/10.1111/0022-4537.00134

Kelman, H. C. (2007). The Israeli-Palestinian peace process and its vicissitudes: Insights from attitude theory. *American Psychologist, 62*, 287–303.

Lederach, J. P. (2003). *Conflict transformation*. Intercourse, PA: Good Books.

Levitt, M. (2006). *Hamas: Politics, charity, and terrorism in the service of Jihad*. New Haven, CT: Yale University Press.

Lubell, M. (2017). *Israel legalizes settler homes on private Palestinian land*. Retrieved from http://www.reuters.com/article/us-israel-palestinians-settlements-vote-idUSKBN15L2F3

McKinlay, A., & McVittie, C. (2008). *Social psychology and discourse*. Oxford: Wiley-Blackwell.

McKinlay, A., & McVittie, C. (2011). *Identities in context: Individuals and discourse in action*. Oxford: Wiley-Blackwell.

McKinlay, A., McVittie, C., & Sambaraju, R. (2012). 'This is ordinary behaviour': Categorization and culpability in Hamas leaders' accounts of the Palestinian/Israeli conflict. *British Journal of Social Psychology, 51*, 534–550.

McVittie, C., Sambaraju, R., & McKinlay, A. (2011). 'There will only be lots of chit-chat': How Hamas leaders and media interviewers handle controversial topics. *Research on Language and Social Interaction, 44*, 92–105.

Milton-Edwards, B., & Farrell, S. (2010). *Hamas: The Islamic resistance movement*. Cambridge: Polity Press.

National Public Radio. (2015). *Transcript: NPR's interview with Israeli Prime Minister Benjamin Netanyahu*. Retrieved from http://www.npr.org/2015/03/20/394191261/transcript-nprs-interview-with-israeli-prime-minister-benjamin-netanyahu

Nets-Zehngut, R., & Bar-Tal, D. (2007). The intractable Israeli-Palestinian conflict and possible pathways to peace. In J. Kuriansky (Ed.), *Psychotherapy in a turmoil region: Reconciliation between Palestinians and Israelis from a psychological perspective* (pp. 3–13). Westport, CT: Praeger.

Rayner, T. (2014). *Hamas leader says 'stripping Palestinians of hope' will lead to chaos*. Retrieved from https://medium.com/@RaynerSkyNews/hamas-leader-warns-against-stripping-palestinians-of-hope-20c3aab595c5

Rudoren, J. (2015). *Netanyahu says no to statehood for Palestinians*. Retrieved from https://www.nytimes.com/2015/03/17/world/middleeast/benjamin-netanyahu-campaign-settlement.html?_r=0

Sales, L. (2014). *'We want to make peace' with Palestinians says Israeli PM Benjamin Netanyahu*. Retrieved from http://www.abc.net.au/7.30/content/2014/s4093374.htm

Sambaraju, R., & Kirkwood, S. (2010). 'We represent, here, the interests of the free world': Accountability in Israeli leaders' media talk on the Gaza Crisis (2008-2009). *eSharp, 15*, 133–156.

Selby, J. (2013). The myth of liberal peace-building. *Conflict, Security & Development, 13*, 57–86.

United Nations. (2016). *Israel's settlements have no legal validity, constitute flagrant violation of international law, Security Council reaffirms*. Retrieved from https://www.un.org/press/en/2016/sc12657.doc.htm

Chapter 7
In the Shadow of the Other: Arguments About the First Gaza War in British Conservative Editorials

Dávid Kaposi

Introduction

Truth and morality may be taken to have haunted discursive psychology ever since its inception (Kaposi, 2012). Whilst the doyens of discursive psychology (and conversation analysis, an applied variant of which discursive psychology has increasingly started to resemble) may have been satisfied with their answers to outsiders' queries as to their take on issues such as "truth" and "morality" and "politics", reviewing historical exchanges on these issues one cannot escape the lingering feeling that they brought less light than would be desirable: the discursive (or CA) position converted no one who had not already in the first place been persuaded.

Symptomatically, for instance, Derek Edwards and Jonathan Potter's proposal to focus on the rhetoric of remembering instead of the validity of memories in their classic criticism of Ulric Neisser's study of John Dean's memory might have lead to an exemplary discursive analysis of Dean's mnemonic performance in the courtroom as well as Neisser's rhetoric in his own paper (Edwards & Potter, 1992a, 1992b; Neisser, 1981). But it also led to what sounded as a genuinely puzzled observation by the cognitive psychologist Neisser himself: "[They] do not care [...] what actual people remember: whether John Dean's testimony was accurate, for example, or where the errors came from if it was not. [...] It doesn't matter what Dean actually remembered [...]" (Neisser, 1992, p. 451). Indeed, as Edwards and his colleagues in their rejoinder reasserted, they made "[...] no claim that Dean was lying, any more than that he was telling the truth" (Edwards, Middleton, & Potter, 1992, p. 455). But whilst it appeared quite clear that within the language game they defined for themselves, discursive psychologists could not indeed answer Neisser's question, those who posed such questions continued to display an interest in such issues (which, in the case of John Dean, might be said to be the paramount issues).

D. Kaposi (✉)
The Open University, Milton Keynes, UK
e-mail: David.Kaposi@open.ac.uk

© Springer Nature Switzerland AG 2018
S. Gibson (ed.), *Discourse, Peace, and Conflict*, Peace Psychology Book Series,
https://doi.org/10.1007/978-3-319-99094-1_7

Further exchanges around epistemological, moral, or political issues equally led to impasses, where discursive psychologists or conversation analysts continued to assert the primacy of discourse and a commitment to what at face value looked like a broadly poststructuralist or social constructionist agenda, yet for some reason limited their understanding of both discourse and social construction to whatever immediate piece of discourse (i.e. data) or social construction they happened to have immediately in front of their eyes (Billig, 1999; Conway, 1992; Corcoran, 2009, 2010; Edwards, Ashmore, & Potter, 1995; Edwards, Middleton, & Potter, 1992; Edwards, Potter, & Middleton, 1992; Potter, 2010; Schegloff, 1998, 1999a, 1999b; Wetherell, 1998).[1] This way, in its critics' eyes conversation analysis-informed discursive psychology started to look like a rather mundane, a-theoretical, a-political, a-moral, a-critical, and ultimately curiously positivistic endeavour in the radical constructionist guise (Billig, 1999).

Dilemmas around discourse's relation to intelligibilities beyond (and constituting the understanding of) the immediately observable data are of course less conspicuous if the political and moral significance of the material we are investigating does not at first look obvious. And it might be for this very reason that most contemporary examples of discursive psychology limit our focus to just such kind of material. Yet chapters in the present volume all tackle issues where both political and moral significance are immediately recognisable. For this reason, the dilemma that has been with discursive psychology from its inception (that between discourse and morality, discourse and politics, discourse and truth) will continue to haunt them.

That is to say, even if denying the validity of the discursive psychological/conversation analytic gesture of separating whatever piece of data is in front of us from the rest of the world/mind/heart; in other words, even if we posit a continuity between discourse in the strict sense (i.e. data) and discourse in the broad sense, we still have to ponder the relationship of discourse broadly conceived to what is traditionally posited as non-discursive: truth and morality.

Thus, looking into British conservative broadsheets' editorial arguments on the morality of the First Gaza War (or "Operation Cast Lead"), as this chapter does, a justification is required as to why morality and identity will be examined as emerging from the newspapers' discourse, rather than something which exists prior to this discourse and to which this discourse should be compared. These issues will be re-engaged with in the final section of the chapter—hopefully not any more to haunt us but to substantiate a viable constructionist/discursive/rhetorical position on morality and politics.

---

[1] There is no space here to go into any detail, but the exchanges at the end of the 1990s, first between Margaret Wetherell (1998) and Emanuel Schegloff (1999a), and then as a follow-up between Schegloff (1999a, 1999b) and Michael Billig (1999a), may have formed an important point at which discursive psychology ultimately aligned itself with conversation analysis as opposed to any kind of critical social science. Indicatively, it was a conversation analyst (i.e. Schegloff) who argued from a perspective now dominating discursive psychology, and it was two academics (i.e. Wetherell and Billig) associated with the inception of discursive psychology who argued from recognisably critical perspectives.

Context: Historical and Methodological Considerations

What some call the First Gaza War, others Operation Cast Lead and yet others the Gaza massacre took place between 28 December 2008 and 20 January 2009 between the armed forces of the State of Israel and Hamas (Kaposi, 2014, pp. 1–22; cf., Howoritz, Ratner, & Weiss, 2011; Philo & Berry, 2011). Historical issues in the Israeli-Palestinian conflict are particularly sensitive (cf., Morris, 1999), yet a consensual proximal origin of the war may be located in 2005 when Israel withdrew its soldiers and settlers from occupied Gaza, yet continued to control its airspace and borders. With the triumph of the Islamist militant Hamas (the founding document of which continues to call for the destruction of Israel) in the 2006 Palestinian legislative elections, this control developed into a fully-fledged economic blockade, leading in turn to the intensification of Hamas militants' firing short-range rockets into Southern Israel. Thus, the dynamics of rocket fire and tightening economic blockade changed little in the ensuing years, and when an Egyptian sponsored 6-month ceasefire (which dissatisfied Hamas as it expected the blockade to ease, and Israel as it expected the release of a captive soldier) in 2008 came to an end, first Hamas resumed and intensified the rocket fire and then Israel responded by launching what it called Operation Cast Lead.

The war, where an aerial phase was followed by ground invasion, was a rather one-sided affair and, in a limited military sense, led to an unequivocal Israeli victory: only 5 Israeli soldiers were killed by Hamas (Howoritz et al., 2011; Human Rights Watch, 2009). Yet Israel could not unequivocally declare itself as winner, for two important reasons. First, its campaign resulted in vast devastation of Palestinian infrastructure and civilian life, and was both during the war and in its aftermath severely criticised by human rights organisations (Amnesty International, 2009; The Goldstone Report, 2011; Human Rights Watch, 2009). Second, the military victory could not be matched by any discernible progress on the political front: no solution to the conflict in Palestine-Israel was anywhere near in sight and, following its recuperation from the war, Hamas eventually resumed the periodic firing of its rockets towards civilian areas in Southern Israel.

This chapter is part of a wider project in which the British broadsheets' (*Daily Telegraph, Financial Times, Guardian, Independent, The Times*) full coverage of the war is examined (Kaposi, 2014; cf., Kaposi, 2017). This study had two broad strategies to analyse newspapers' content. With regard to conceptual areas such as fatalities, action and events in war, and historical context, a quantitative study was carried out where around 70 codes were identified and counted in the full output of the newspapers. This was followed by a qualitative study of in-depth analysis of arguments in comments and editorial pieces. These concerned instances when newspapers talked about the act of criticism and argued about the morality of the State of Israel and Hamas.

This chapter is an offshoot of this latter cluster of rhetorical analyses. It will look at the two conservative newspapers' that are commonly considered to be supportive of Israel (*The Daily Telegraph* and *The Times*) and will explore arguments concerning the two traditional moral dilemmas of war: *jus ad bellum* or the legality of a war, and *jus in bello* or legality of the conduct of a war (Walzer, 2000, 2006). That is, the chapter will look at whether conservative newspapers treated the State of Israel's launching of the war and then its conduct of the war as just, and what arguments were marshalled towards this end. In particular, the chapter will focus on how the image of the "other" features in these arguments: how Hamas is depicted in these editorials; and how those who have a critical perspective different from the conservative newspapers' feature there.[2]

What the chapter seeks to argue is that, first, whilst in the *Daily Telegraph* it is from the very beginning of the war that a radical disjuncture exists between Israel and Hamas, *The Times* only adopts such a rhetorical strategy in its arguments regarding *jus in bello*—when it actually seems to start critiquing *Israel*. And second, that an equally radical disjuncture exists—albeit less prominently—in both newspapers regarding political-moral perspectives that evaluate the war from a perspective different from the newspaper's own. The conclusion will then attempt to link these findings to the broader concerns sketched out in the introduction.

Analysis: At War with the "Other"

Jus ad bellum

The standard moral dilemma we face at the beginning of a war is whether the launching of the war is justified or not (Walzer, 2000, 2006). This is the issue of *jus ad bellum*, and it was duly taken up by the conservative newspapers in their accounts of the Gaza war. We will first look at the *Daily Telegraph*'s arguments and constructions regarding war and morality. This will be followed by *The Times*' account.

The *Telegraph*'s first editorial on the war started as follows:

Extract 1
The first reaction of most commentators was that the air attacks on Gaza were unnecessarily savage. The deaths of nearly 300 Palestinians, including civilians, seems disproportionate to the small number of Israelis killed by rocket attacks. Hamas was not expecting retribution on this scale, but we can be sure that it will extract the maximum possible propaganda advantage from the slaughter. Israel's enemies in the liberal West are already pinning the blame squarely on "Zionists'. So are most Muslims.

But, before we jump to conclusions, we should pay close attention to the response of Mahmoud Abbas, chairman of the Palestinian National Authority. He blamed Hamas for triggering the Israeli raids by not extending its truce. His Fatah party is engaged in a vicious feud with Hamas, so this is perhaps what one would expect him to say. But he is right, none

[2] The editorials used in the present analysis are as follows: *Daily Telegraph*, "Hamas and Iran pose a threat to the world" (29 December 2008, p. 17); *Daily Telegraph*, "A ceasefire would be in Israel's interests" (10 January 2009, p. 23); *The Times*, "Bitter Harvest" (29 December 2008, p. 2); *The Times*, "In Defense of Israel" (10 January 2009, p. 2); *The Times*, "Israel's cause is just but some of its tactics are self-defeating" (16 January 2009, p. 2).

the less. Hamas did engineer this crisis, by firing rockets whose range has been increased so
they can reach southern Israeli cities. (Daily Telegraph, 29 December)

The newspaper is unequivocal in its assessment of the outbreak of the war and the
question of the legality of the war. It clearly agrees with the "chairman of the
Palestinian National Authority" in "blaming Hamas for triggering the Israeli raids
by not extending its truce". In fact, what the phrase "triggering" implies is not so
much a reason for Israeli action or a justification for Israel's choice being the right
choice. Rather, it implies a *casus belli* in the strictest of senses: a *cause* which then
automatically led to war. Israel's choice is therefore no real "choice" at all here, and
the deliberation which presumably has led to the launching of the Operation is a
chimera. The Jewish state is without a choice and without a substantive role here.

Yet what exactly did Hamas do to "trigger" this course of events? The passage
above mentions "firing rockets whose range has been increased so they can reach
southern Israeli cities"—but neither here nor elsewhere in *Telegraph* editorials do
we learn more than that these rockets had killed a "small number of Israelis". What
is seemingly left unattended to is how such an act would ever "trigger" a war and its
concomitant destruction of considerably many more "numbers".

Of course, it is not the case that the *Daily Telegraph* would have been blind to
such a moral conundrum. It is rather that it is our analytic strategy that has to account
not simply for the material *consequences* the firing of rockets results in, but the
intentions with which they are fired and the *identity* of those who are firing them. In
other words, the moral judgment regarding *jus ad bellum* may be anchored in the
identity we ascribe to those we are fighting against:

Extract 2
Only one group of people can have derived any satisfaction from the footage of blood-
covered children being pulled from the rubble in Gaza: the fanatics of Hamas. This terrorist
organisation has been firing rockets into Israel ever since the breakdown of the ceasefire, in
the hope of provoking a furious Israeli response. And that is precisely what materialised.
[…] Hamas is not a reasonable political movement. It cannot thrive without crisis; the
blood of innocents is its own lifeblood. These are not Palestinian nationalists who happen
to be Muslims; they are totalitarian Islamists whose Palestinian identity is of secondary
importance. They have nothing but contempt for Arab Muslim states (Daily Telegraph, 29
December)

The image of Hamas and of the intention guiding the rockets we encounter here is
not simply of a terrorist organisation but one of nihilistic total destruction. Hamas
does not fight for "Arab Muslim states" or even for "Palestinians" or for "children
[…] pulled from the rubble of Gaza". Its "fanaticism" is not matched by anything
constructive. It wishes to "wipe out […] eventually, every secular Arab state" too
and "hope[s] to provoke a furious Israeli response" that results in "the footage of
blood-covered children" (Daily Telegraph, 29 December). In this context, regardless of the actual material consequences rockets cause, what determines the political-
moral choices of the situation is the exclusively destructive intention that guides
them towards Israel. Launching the war is predicated on the essentially evil identity
of those the Israelis are fighting. This way, non-engagement and the complete lack
of political-moral relations between Israel and Hamas, between pure victim and

impure perpetrator, becomes not so much a practical impossibility but a *sacred necessity*. Support for Israel is absolute—but only on the equally absolute condition of Israel fulfilling its (non-)role.

Couched in the language of political and moral criticism, it was therefore an ultimately metaphysical argument that the *Telegraph* marshalled in its categorical defence of Israel and equally categorical condemnation of Hamas.

Interestingly, such an account seemed to differ in significant respects from that of the other conservative quality newspaper, *The Times*:

Extract 3
After eight days of rocket attacks from Gaza the Palestinian group Hamas seemed to have left Israel with little choice but to retaliate. On Saturday it did so, launching one of the deadliest series of air assaults in the history of the 60-year-old conflict. As a result, innocent lives are being destroyed. (The Times, 29 December)

Does it matter that *The Times*' judgment is less categorical than the *Telegraph*'s? That whilst the latter wrote of the war having been "triggered" and alluded thereby to a complete lack of choice from Israel's part, the former mentions Israel having been left "with little choice but to retaliate". Is this difference merely rhetorical? Or does the minimal freedom of choice that is assigned to Israel here lead to substantial differences?

Notably, in this respect, the first two editorials of *The Times* are completely devoid of the kind of descriptions of Hamas that were offered by the *Telegraph*. In fact, not only is the *Telegraph*'s vivid construction of Hamas absent, but an alternative perspective is presented. Namely, in none of the editorials the *Telegraph* devoted to the war do we find any reference to the Israeli occupation or the blockade.[3] The reason for this is clear, for inasmuch as Hamas constitutes the manifestation of an evil and destructive *essence*, no external factor is accountable for its conduct. *The Times*, however, offers a rather different perspective:

Extract 4
The latest tragedy is the outcome of a vicious cycle that has gripped Gaza since Hamas seized full control of the territory from the more moderate, secular Palestinian Fatah movement in June 2007. Israel tightened its blockade as a result, and has been demanding that Hamas cease its rocket attacks. Hamas vowed to continue them until Israel opened the border and stopped retaliating. (The Times, 29 December)

A number of points are interesting here. Whilst certainly not depicted in positive terms and not excused for firing rockets at Israeli civilians, at least part of Hamas's *present* rocket-fire may be accounted for by an external factor: Israel "tighten[ing] its blockade". This is how the newspaper's notion of the "vicious cycle" becomes clear: for Israelis, the blockade is the result of Hamas not stopping the rocket-fire; and, for Hamas, the blockade is the *very reason for continuing the rocket fire*. It goes without saying that we cannot learn here whether Hamas would have really stopped the rockets if "Israel [had] opened the border". Yet this possibility cannot be ruled

---

[3] In their general output, the frequency of the two newspapers' references to the blockade was more or less equal (cf., Kaposi, 2014, p. 62).

out either, given that we encounter no other account for the Hamas rocket-fire than the implied effect of Israel's "tightened ... blockade".

In fact, the next paragraph asserts that following the "unravelling" of the "uneasy sixmonth [sic] truce", "Israel has tightened its control of the border, permitting only the intermittent delivery of humanitarian supplies" (The Times, 29 December). That is, Israel did something which had already been known to lead to rocket-fire. It may not be the cause of it, but its conduct most certainly does not help.

The editorial continues in a similar vein:

Extract 5
Both the Israelis and Palestinians have failed in Gaza. The Israelis had hoped to make life intolerable for Hamas, intending either that it would reform and start to co-operate, or that the people of Gaza would decide that they had had enough of their Government. Neither has happened. On the contrary, the bold words of Hamas leaders suggest that they have found renewed strength through the conflict. In their turn, the Palestinians have claimed to want peace. But they have been only occasional partners in the peace process, and sometimes openly hostile. (The Times, 29 December)

The position constructed for Hamas in this extract is, once again, not a black-and-white one. On the one hand, the editorial asserts that the Palestinians have been "only occasional partners in the peace process, and sometimes openly hostile" and what the general category ("the Palestinians") may imply is that it is quite possibly Hamas that actually is *the* element that has been "openly hostile" and not the one that has been an "occasional partner in the peace process". *On the other hand,* whatever Hamas is and does now is not simply springing from its essence. We learn that "Israelis had hoped to make life intolerable for Hamas, intending either that it would reform and start to co-operate, or that the people of Gaza would decide that they had had enough of their Government". This may be understandable as an aim and a political strategy, but it has not had the consequences Israelis would have hoped for: "Neither has happened. On the contrary, the bold words of Hamas leaders suggest that they have found renewed strength through the conflict". For what happened did not just fail to comply with Israeli intentions. It actually went against them as it ended up bolstering Hamas's "bold words" and led to its "renewed strength through the conflict".

Thus, *The Times*'s early engagement with the war is rather different from that of the *Telegraph*. In terms of launching the war, there is some room implicitly constructed for Israeli choice and deliberation rather than a stimulus-response mechanics. Accordingly, Hamas is not depicted in the colours of evil. More importantly, it is not depicted as merely *acting out an essence*. Israeli actions were depicted as being, to some extent, constitutive of Hamas's conduct and identity; certainly not creating either of these *ex nihilo*, but still contributing to their existence.

Thus, whilst by and large accepting the Israeli justification, there is at least space created for potential criticism. And likewise, whilst being rather critical of Hamas's conduct, there is at least recognition that the Palestinian organisation acts and exists in a web of relations and therefore can potentially be engaged with in other than violent ways.

Jus in bello

This second analytic section continues the focus on *The Times'* editorial argumentation. As we saw, in contrast to the *Daily Telegraph, The Times,* whilst by and large supporting Israel's predicament, nonetheless retained a critical perspective towards the actions of the Israeli state. This was, partly, a result of its account of the "other", Hamas, not in terms of a black-and-white essence but of a web of relationships to Israel itself.

What is of interest in this second section is how the editorial arguments covered the second moral dilemma of war: *jus in bello* or law in war. As war soldiered on, needless to say, (left-)liberal newspapers that even in the beginning unequivocally condemned Israel's launching the operation further intensified their criticism (Kaposi, 2014, pp. 139–169). Yet, at this stage, even the *Daily Telegraph* had to voice some criticism: "It cannot be right to seek to protect the innocent victims of southern Israel by the killing of the innocents of Gaza" (Daily Telegraph, 10 January). So how did *The Times* engage with the issue of law in war? How did the newspaper which is on the whole considered "pro-Israel", which in this particular conflict by and large supported Israel's opting for war, yet which retained a nuanced critical perspective and a relatively complex image of Hamas—how did it cover the phase of the conflict that may be characterised as ever more one-sided and bringing on ever more devastation in Gaza (cf., Kaposi, 2016)?

The questions are especially pertinent as, first among British newspapers, *The Times* broke the news of Israel's apparent use of the controversial chemical substance, white phosphorous, in its invasion.[4] The issue was duly taken up in the newspaper's editorials as well:

> Extract 6
> Eleven days ago *The Times* reported that Israel appeared to be using white phosphorus shells over built-up areas of Gaza. Since then, Israeli spokesmen and women have issued a series of increasingly forlorn denials as the number of Palestinian deaths in Gaza has passed 1,000 and many of the injured have been treated for burns caused, apparently, by white phosphorus.
>   It is time to clear the air. (The Times, 16 January)

These are of course very strong words as they do not just generally imply the necessity of moral reckoning but point to very concrete facts on the ground and conclude with an explicit call for the investigation of Israeli responsibility—all this, remember, in *The Times* which is in general sympathetic to the Israeli predicament and

---

[4]White phosphorous is a highly incendiary chemical material. It was used during the war by the Israeli forces as a smokescreen and as such not automatically illegally. However, its use in heavily built-up areas is very problematic even as an obscurant, for its incendiary nature will almost inevitably cause serious side-effects. It is for this reason that all the human rights investigations condemned the manner in which Israel deployed white phosphorous, with Human Rights Watch (2009, p. 65) concluding that it was "indiscriminate or disproportionate, and indicate[d] the commission of war crimes". Although at the time Israel heavily contested these positions, in 2013 it announced that it would completely stop using the material in built-up areas.

which in particular accepted the Israeli justification for launching Operation Cast Lead.

So what happens next? How does the newspaper continue its moral accounting? How does it continue its *critical* engagement with the agent it is known as *sympathetic* towards? Here is how the editorial continues:

Extract 7

It is time to clear the air. Israel has a right to defend itself, and the nature of its enemy makes that task extraordinarily hard. *Hamas, like Hezbollah in southern Lebanon, regards the use of civilians as human shields* as a central plank of its strategy for tormenting Israel. Like its principal state sponsor, Iran, *Hamas's rallying cry is not the creation of a Palestinian state but the destruction of the Jewish one.* This is why, when a ceasefire ended last month with an onslaught of Hamas rockets aimed at civilian Israeli targets, *Israel had no choice but to prosecute this war.* But the need to strike back does not excuse the mistakes that Israel has made in doing so. (The Times, 16 January—italics added)

The first thing to note here is that the newspaper immediately shifts its focus. The direct inquiry into Israeli responsibility is dropped; instead, we read about Hamas. The second thing to note is that even an inquiry into *jus in bello* (law *in* war) is dropped as the newspaper rehearses arguments into *jus ad bellum* (law *to* war). Of course, these could be fairly typical strategies in and of themselves as inquiry into Israeli responsibility would necessitate inquiry into the context in which Israeli choices take place. However, the context constructed here differs, and differs significantly from how *The Times'* occasioned Hamas, Israel and law to war *in the beginning of the war.*

Namely, the "Hamas" we encounter here is rather different from the "Hamas" we encountered earlier. More precisely, it resembles not the "Hamas" we encountered in *The Times* but the one we encountered in the *Daily Telegraph*. It is not any more an agent that acts partly in response to Israeli action but one that is acquiring the attributes of pure evil: one that uses its own civilians to torment Israel; and one whose goal is not constructive (i.e. the "creation of a Palestinian state") but purely destructive (i.e. "the destruction of the Jewish one"). And similarly, not only is Israel's launching the war seen as unequivocally justified here, but Israel is presented as having had "no choice"—once again in line with how the *Telegraph* argued about *jus ad bellum* but in contrast with how *The Times* itself did.

The editorial continues:

Extract 8

Israelis grieve as all humans do for the children cut down in Gaza's maelstrom, and their leaders know full well the damage that this conflict is doing to the country's reputation, especially where images of Palestinian suffering are broadcast more as propaganda than news. (The Times, 16 January)

Once again, the explicit call for examining Israel's responsibility that we encountered in Extract 6 is not followed up but leads to a contextual declaration, this time of Israeli humanity. Further complementing the emerging picture of a demonic Hamas, we have what we could call a humanising perspective on Israel. Both affectively and cognitively speaking, Israelis are becoming just like "us", like "all humans". The moral account that *The Times'* rendering of Israeli deployment of white phosphorous foreshadowed has, we can ascertain, not materialised yet. What we have instead is a Hamas that is acquiring demonic characteristics, an Israel that is represented, paradoxically, with no moral responsibility ("no choice") and with a very human face ("as all humans do").

In what follows, we will see how *The Times'* moral account of the Israeli Defense Forces' (IDF) use of white phosphorous concludes.

Extract 9

White phosphorus is illegal under international law when used in built-up areas, but a legitimate weapon of war when used to provide cover for troops in open country. There is scant evidence of the IDF using it deliberately against civilians, but northern Gaza, where the fighting is concentrated, is one of the most densely populated places in the world. Civilian casualties were inevitable, and the deep burns that white phosphorus can cause are virtually untreatable. The longer that the IDF equivocate about its use, the more ammunition they hand to those who would accuse them of war crimes. (The Times, 16 January)

What we may conclude having read this curious paragraph is that *The Times'* moral account is in fact a pseudo-moral account. Despite stating that white phosphorous is "illegal under international law when used in built-up areas" and that "northern Gaza, where the fighting is concentrated, is one of the most densely populated places in the world", the newspaper does not conclude its argumentation with, say, a call for an independent inquiry into the conduct of the Israeli armed forces. Instead, it concludes by simply pointing out that the IDF's "equivocating about its [i.e. white phosphorous] use" is counterproductive. That is to say, *The Times* not only refrains from critiquing Israel but also neglects even to call on Israel to stop using white phosphorous. All that is required from Israel at this point is to stop equivocating about its use of white phosphorous before Israel's enemies are handed further "ammunition". This makes clear that *The Times* itself is not an enemy of Israel; the IDF is not, therefore, criticised for the use of white prosperous per se, but rather it is criticised for continuing a practice which can be used against it by its opponents. *The Times'* criticism is thus not predicated on a moral failure on the part of Israel, but on a strategic failure.

To sum up, both in the *Daily Telegraph* and eventually in *The Times*, a possible critical perspective on Israeli action and responsibility was narrowed down and then closed. In fact, in the case of *The Times*, the more inevitable such a perspective appeared, the more concerted were the arguments for its closure. This went hand in hand with the newspapers' demonization of Hamas: in the *Telegraph*'s case the Palestinian organisation's image was that of total nihilistic destruction from the beginning; for *The Times* a more nuanced and relational image was suddenly replaced with a demonic one *just as Israel*'s conduct of the war became problematised.

Non–Conservative Critical Perspectives: Listening to the "Other"

Yet there clearly is more to this story than the ever more demonic image of Hamas and the ever more innocent Israel. Namely, there is another "other" to reckon with and just as stakes are getting higher, this other "other" seems to gain more and more relevance in the conservative account.

For instance, examining once again the conclusion of Extract 9, *The Times'* call for the end of Israeli equivocation around white phosphorous is presented for no legal or moral reason, but because failing to do so would hand "more ammunition... to those who would accuse them of war crimes". It is with regard to *this* eventuality that Israeli leaders are called upon (or advised?) not to equivocate about the IDF's use of white phosphorous. Needless to say, it is a curious state of affairs that from a fact to be confirmed, Israeli use of white phosphorous has thereby become implied to be either non-problematic or even downright non-existent. Yet, it is equally important that there *is* actually an eventuality which the Israeli leader's desired lack of equivocation would attend to: and this is, precisely, the sudden presence of someone else, another agent whose conduct has suddenly become relevant, another "other": "those" who would use the Israeli equivocation as "ammunition" against Israel.

Who are "those"? What else do we learn about them beyond the suspicion of some alternative or metaphorical form of belligerence (i.e. "ammunition")? Some shadowy and suspicious figures in fact have already made their appearance by this point. Looking at Extract 8, we find not only Hamas cropping up as essentially evil, but that Israeli action is once again imagined against the background of another "other" that uses Israeli action to certain ends: "where images of Palestinian suffering are broadcast more as propaganda than news". That is to say, an alternative critical perspective is once again present in the moral argumentation of *The Times*. We still do not quite learn who the people are that would "broadcast [Palestinian suffering] more as propaganda than news". Yet it is clear that their interest is not in Palestinian suffering as such and for this reason they cannot be simply pro-Palestinian. It is instead that they would, rather cynically, *(ab)use* Palestinian suffering for propaganda purposes.

To find out more about this other "other", let us perhaps also consult Extract 1 and the *Daily Telegraph*'s first paragraphs on the war. Once again, the point reached by *The Times* at the end of its argumentation was already present in the *Telegraph* in the beginning. As we can see in Extract 1, the *Telegraph* not only presents its own position on the war but is explicitly arguing against other perspectives. As regards these alternative perspectives, the problem is not merely that alternative, critical perspectives on Israel would be mere "first reactions" or represent an impulsive "jumping to a conclusion". We also read: "Israel's enemies in the liberal West are already pinning the blame squarely on 'Zionists'. So are most Muslims" (*Daily Telegraph*, 29 December). To blame Zionists for the war certainly seems unreasonable as Zionism as a political ideology would offer no straightforward prescriptions for or against the invasion. Yet the editorial's point is arguably not this. For why would the to-be-blamed-Zionists (but not liberals or Muslims) appear here within *scare quotes* for any reason other than indicating that, actually, those being blamed are not quite Zionists but *the Jews*. That is, that the alternative political-moral arguments offered are mere facades and only cover up what essentially are, intentionally or not, *antisemitic perspectives*.

Likewise, we learn unexpected things about Israel's critics from *The Times*.

Extract 10
Israel has a powerful ally in the United States.

>   Its critics are wont to condemn this alliance as a Jewish axis blind to heart-rending reali-
>   ties in Gaza and to the sacrifices necessary for peace.
>   No one can be unmoved by the suffering witnessed by the Norwegian surgeon who
>   texted friends to tell them "we're wading in death, blood [and] amputees". But the way to
>   end it is not to abandon Israel. It is to defeat Hamas. (The Times, 10 January)

The "Jewish axis" that is "blind to heart-rending realities in Gaza" is a clear antisemitic topos, and it certainly makes the political proposal of "abandoning Israel" in
the face of Palestinian suffering as yet another antisemitic position. This way, *The
Times* too joins ranks with the *Daily Telegraph* in suggesting that what, on appearance, presents as criticism of Israel (cf., "its critics") is actually an antisemitic perspective: apparently legitimate political and moral arguments, purporting to display
mere criticism of a political entity (i.e. the State of Israel) are in fact cover-ups for
murderous and racist ideologies.

Conclusion

This chapter sought to examine the British conservative broadsheets' editorial
arguments about the First Gaza War. Standing opposed to the efforts of the State
of Israel and the Israeli Defense Forces were two "others": Hamas, and a critical
perspective varyingly ascribed to "liberals"/"Muslims" (*Telegraph*), or
"propagandists"/"Israel's critics"/"those who would accuse [Israel] of war
crimes" (*The Times*).

Hamas was depicted as essentially different and essentially destructive, and
therefore an agent with which dialogue is impossible. It was from the outset
depicted in the *Daily Telegraph* in terms which made Israel's launching a war not
so much a justified choice but a sacred necessity. *The Times,* intriguingly, started
its account with an image of Hamas which allowed, in theory at least, for non-
violent relationships and therefore negotiations with Hamas. Yet, at the very point
at which the spectre of Israeli responsibility was raised, and Israeli actions which
may have constituted war crimes were reported, its construction of *Hamas* radically changed: it was *then* that the Palestinian organisation turned into the agent
of nihilistic total destruction that it had always been in the *Telegraph*.

As for the figure representing an alternative political-moral perspective to that of
the conservative newspapers, these were again present from the start of the war in the
Telegraph, and subsequent to the Israel's use of phosphorous in *The Times*. Neither
of the newspapers explicitly tackled the question of *who* exactly this other "other" is,
and *what* it is like. Yet what could be gathered from their implicit rhetoric was that
these people are not simply supportive of Palestinian efforts or critical of Israeli
ones. In fact, they might not even be found on a political-moral landscape where one
can support Palestinians and criticise Israelis. They are instead antisemitic and as
such play no legitimate part in discussions over Palestine and the State of Israel.

Thus, regarding both Hamas and the "critics", the identity constructed was not
just one descriptively differing from the political-moral perspective the newspapers
adopted, but *categorically different* to the extent that it was impossible to engage

with them. These constructions therefore reflexively constituted the rhetoric of the *Telegraph* and *The Times* alike: being destructive and nihilistic, Hamas *could only be* fought violently; being antisemitic, the alternative political-moral perspective *could only be* fought and hopefully eradicated.

Having come to this conclusion, where now for the discourse analyst? Going back to the dilemmas of discourse-and-truth and discourse-and-morality as touched on in the Introduction, which direction should/can we take our analysis from here?

It will surely not come as a shock that, for one thing, the perspective that governed this chapter is that its analysis was already seeped in a political-moral perspective. A certain topic was chosen; certain representations were chosen; certain analytic materials were chosen; certain media were chosen; certain parts of the media (and then parts within those parts) were chosen, etc. All of these choices constitute and are constitutive of political-moral discourses. For another thing, there is equally nothing natural or scientific about stopping analysis at just the point where this chapter has done (cf., Kaposi, 2012). Constructions identified in the newspapers can be contrasted with constructions identifiable elsewhere. And whilst we can really *not say* which construction will be the true one or the right one in any absolute sense, we can in fact enquire, first, on what conditions, on what premises a certain construction may prove to be true/right; and second, what consequences a certain condition may lead to.

To summarise, the analysis of this chapter certainly leaves us with the intriguing question of how the description conservative newspapers offered of Hamas and "Israel's critics"/"liberals" compares to alternative descriptions, and how and on what basis we might judge these various descriptions. Claiming to do discourse analysis should not prevent us from such vital future inquiries.

Yet the chapter has, hopefully, already left us with something more immediate. That is to say, if the analysis presented here is acceptable, then (positing an absolute distinction between the innocent and the blameworthy, between the pure and the impure, between the good and the bad) the perspective the *Telegraph* and ultimately *The Times* too offered was a characteristically *metaphysical* one. And a metaphysical perspective cannot in fact be acceptable: not for the conservative newspapers *themselves* as they claim to offer secular political-moral criticism and as they argue for a two-state (i.e. negotiated) solution to the conflict between Israelis and Palestinians; and not for anyone else who thinks that whilst war and violence might temporarily be inevitable or even the right thing to do, it is only humans' capacity to converse, argue, disagree, and agree that helps them to settle their differences. War and violence may happen on the route, but it is only dialogue and politics which is the *sine qua non* of peace.

References

Amnesty International. (2009). *Israel/Gaza: Operation "Cast Lead": 22 days of death and destruction* (Index: MDE 15/015/2009).

Billig, M. (1999). Whose terms? Whose ordinariness? Rhetoric and ideology in conversation analysis. *Discourse and Society, 10*, 543–558.

Conway, M. (Ed.). (1992). Memory and discourse: Special edition. *The Psychologist, 5*, 439–455.
Corcoran, T. (2009). Second nature. *British Journal of Social Psychology, 48*, 375–388.
Corcoran, T. (2010). What else life if not awkward? *British Journal of Social Psychology, 49*, 679–684.
Edwards, D., Ashmore, M., & Potter, J. (1995). Death and furniture: The rhetoric, politics and theology of bottom line arguments against relativism. *History of the Human Sciences, 8*, 25–49.
Edwards, D., Middleton, D., & Potter, J. (1992). Remembering, reconstruction and rhetoric: A rejoinder. *The Psychologist, 5*, 453–455.
Edwards, D., & Potter, J. (1992a). *Discursive psychology*. London: Sage.
Edwards, D., & Potter, J. (1992b). The chancellor's memory: Rhetoric and truth in discursive remembering. *Applied Cognitive Psychology, 6*, 187–215.
Edwards, D., Potter, J., & Middleton, D. (1992). Toward a discursive psychology of remembering. *The Psychologist, 5*, 441–446.
Howoritz, A., Ratner, L., & Weiss, P. (Eds.). (2011). *The goldstone report: The legacy of the landmark investigation of the Gaza conflict*. New York: Nation Books.
Human Rights Watch. (2009). *Rain of fire: Israel's unlawful use of white phosphorous in Gaza*. New York: Human Rights Watch.
Kaposi, D. (2012). Truth and rhetoric: The promise of John Dean's memory to the discipline of psychology. *Journal for the Theory of Social Behaviour, 42*, 1–19.
Kaposi, D. (2014). *Violence and understanding in Gaza: The British broadsheets' coverage of the war*. London: Palgrave Macmillan.
Kaposi, D. (2016). On the possibility of critiquing Israel: *The Times*' engagement with the Israeli use of white phosphorous during the first Gaza war. *Media, Conflict & War, 9*, 272–289.
Kaposi, D. (2017). A proper study of Gaza? Methodological implications of a large-scale study. *British Journal of Middle East Studies, 44*, 393–407.
Morris, B. (1999). *Righteous victims: A history of the Zionist-Arab conflict, 1881–1998*. London: Knopf Doubleday.
Neisser, U. (1981). John Dean's memory: A case study. *Cognition, 9*, 1–22.
Neisser, U. (1992). The psychology of memory and the sociolinguistics of remembering. *The Psychologist, 5*, 451–452.
Philo, G., & Berry, M. (2011). *More bad news from Israel*. London: Pluto Press.
Potter, J. (2010). Contemporary discursive psychology: Issues, prospects and Corcoran's awkward ontology. *British Journal of Social Psychology, 49*, 657–678.
Schegloff, E. (1998). Reply to Wetherell. *Discourse and Society, 9*, 413–416.
Schegloff, E. (1999a). 'Schegloff's text' as 'Billig's data': A critical reply. *Discourse and Society, 10*, 558–572.
Schegloff, E. (1999b). Naivety vs sophistication or discipline vs self-indulgence: A rejoinder to Billig. *Discourse and Society, 10*, 577–582.
The Goldstone Report (2011). Howoritz, A., Ratner, L. & Weiss, P. (eds). New York: Nation Books.
Walzer, M. (2000). *Just and unjust wars: A moral argument with historical illustrations* (3rd ed.). New York: Basic Books.
Walzer, M. (2006). *Arguing about war*. New York: Yale University Press.
Wetherell, M. (1998). Positioning and interpretative repertoires: Conversation analysis and post-structuralism in dialogue. *Discourse and Society, 9*, 387–412.

Chapter 8
The Dynamics of 'Pacifism' and 'Warmongering': The Denial of Stake in Debates Preceding the 2003 Invasion of Iraq

Joseph Burridge

Introduction

On 18th March 2003, following a long debate, both Houses of the UK Parliament voted to support the bombing and invasion of Iraq by a 'Coalition' of the US and UK military, with support from others.

The decision and voting represented a climactic moment preceded by over 12 months of political manoeuvring by the UK government (then led by Prime Minister Tony Blair), with controversy over the perceived motivations for military action, and unprecedented anti-war protests in the form of a march on 16th February 2003 estimated to have featured between three quarters of a million and two million participants (BBC, 2003). The conflict toppled Saddam Hussein's regime and is estimated to have led directly or indirectly to the death of over a quarter of a million people, combatants included (Iraq Body Count, 2017). The impact of this is ongoing for the surviving people of Iraq and is still felt in UK politics, where the publication of the report of the public inquiry into the build up to war came as recently as 2016 (Chilcot, 2016).

One significant feature of the widespread public debate that preceded the invasion was the prominence of processes of categorization as each 'side' in the debate attempted to explain and undermine their opponents. For instance, opponents of military action were often categorized as 'anti-American' (Burridge, 2007), or as appeasers of Saddam Hussein—with the attendant implication of failing to learn appropriate lessons from history (Burridge, 2013; Gibson, 2012a).

This chapter synthesises and develops two chapters from my ESRC-funded PhD thesis (Burridge, 2005) and was greatly enhanced by time spent at Loughborough University as part of my ESRC-funded postdoctoral fellowship (Reference: R4220134082 and PTA-026-27-0591, respectively).

J. Burridge (✉)
University of Portsmouth, Portsmouth, UK
e-mail: joseph.burridge@port.ac.uk

© Springer Nature Switzerland AG 2018   133
S. Gibson (ed.), *Discourse, Peace, and Conflict*, Peace Psychology Book Series,
https://doi.org/10.1007/978-3-319-99094-1_8

Categorization, identity ascription, reference to -isms, and their denial and particularization, are processes which have been studied with regularity by forms of discursive psychology (e.g. Antaki & Horowitz, 2000; Augoustinos & Every, 2007, 2010; Rapley, 1998; Stokoe, 2015; Wetherell & Potter, 1992). This is in part because they relate directly to a range of conceptual concerns connected to the dilemma of stake (Edwards & Potter, 1992). This concept captures the problem involved for speakers in relation to them providing an account for some sort of interest—whether a political position, or something more mundane—when it could be held to account, and undermined, as interested (see Edwards & Potter, 1992, p. 158).

Categories, and especially those associated with -isms (or possible -isms; Whitehead & Stokoe, 2015) carry potentially problematical consequences as they can be used to suggest that those categorized have a stake in the matter at hand— some form of self-interest, relevant ideology or other 'prejudice'—which means that their words should be taken less seriously, or, indeed, disqualified (Antaki & Horowitz, 2000). Associated with this can be a phenomenon which Potter (1996, p. 125) labels 'stake inoculation' whereby speakers attempt to forestall such potential categorizations often by mentioning and denying in various ways their applicability to them—something also captured in sociology by the term *disclaiming* (Hewitt & Stokes, 1975).

This chapter engages with these issues as evident in contributions to the public debates, including newspaper content, but primarily focusing upon contributions to UK Parliamentary debates preceding the 2003 invasion of Iraq. It examines denials of stake by focusing upon contributions on both sides of the debate which resisted available categorizations that threatened the extent to which the speakers might be taken seriously. It does so with a view to exemplifying some ways in which discursive concepts and methods can illuminate issues relevant to peace psychology.

Of specific interest to peace psychology in this specific discursive context should be the contestation of two specific sets of categorizations—those of the 'pacifist' and the 'warmonger'.[1] In the context of proposed wars in general, and therefore in the debates that preceded the invasion of Iraq, both of these categories carry the implications that those to whom the labels are applied are entrenched in their position—afflicted by pacifism or warmongering—such that they are either intransigently against war regardless of the circumstances, or petitioning for it eagerly, in ways that ought to be considered irrational.

Pacifism, Warmongering, and Discursive Psychology

Issues around the categories and categorization processes of interest here have been explored previously in social science and humanities research. For instance, there are examples of sociological studies of pacifism as a phenomenon (Martin, 1965),

---

[1]An important point of clarification is that these two categories—pacifist and warmonger—are not entirely congruent with the binary avian metaphors often used to make sense of positions on foreign policy—the hawk and the dove. For more on 'Avian Metaphors' see Burridge (2005, pp. 211–214).

and attempts to differentiate between different types (e.g. Wanner, 2016, p. 178). One can also locate philosophical attempts to undermine it as incoherent (Narveson, 1965), as well as attempts to fix its position vis-a-vis both 'warmongering' and 'appeasement' (Harold, 2013).

While pacifism may have tended to have been back-grounded in scholarship in areas like International Relations (Jackson, 2014, 2016), it has been explored explicitly by the wider humanities and social sciences much more commonly than has 'warmongering'—something that surely reflects pacifism's problematic, deviant, and non-normative status, as well as the extent to which, at the very least, acknowledging the possible legitimacy of war is normative, or, indeed, hegemonic in the global North/West.

A particularly significant theoretical contribution relevant to both categories comes from Cady (2010, p. 106), who advanced an argument about the need to understand pacifism and what he refers to as 'warism' as existing on a continuum with one another. For Cady (2010, p. *xvii*), warism is 'an uncritical presumption in modern society that war is morally justifiable, even morally required', and, as such, it constitutes 'the primary cultural obstacle to taking pacifism seriously' (Cady, 2010, p. 17).

Importantly, when it comes to how pacifism is treated, Cady notes that it 'rarely gets taken seriously' and is 'flippantly rejected as naïve and misguided' (Cady, 2010, p. *xv*), or as impractical and unrealistic (Cady, 2010, p. 94; also see Martin, 1965, p. 133 and p. 203 on its alleged 'political impotence' and 'impossibility'). It is viewed as a marginal position in both quantitative and qualitative terms (see Narveson, 1999, p. 120), and is thus a perpetual minority position. In more ambivalent terms, it is 'at once respected for its moral strength and disregarded as utopian fantasy' (Cady, 2010, p. 29).

Arguing for greater attention to pacifism in order to expand the 'ethical horizon' of International Relations (IR) as a discipline, Jackson (2016, p. 1) nevertheless agrees with the diagnostic thrust of many of these observations, arguing that in the Global North/West, pacifism is 'widely viewed as intellectually inferior, politically unrealistic, or even morally dangerous'. Jackson undertook interviews with 40 IR scholars and noted that significant numbers associate pacifism with 'radicalism, impracticality, or political naivety' (Jackson, 2016, p. 5), with those who self-identified as pacifist tending to qualify that with labels such as 'pragmatic pacifist', 'practical pacifist', or 'ethical pacifist' (Jackson, 2016, p. 5). We will see below that somewhat similar 'clarification' and complex positioning activity is evident in the data upon which this chapter is based.

Notwithstanding the growing volume of research on 'militarization' or 'militarism' (e.g. Burridge & McSorley, 2013; Geyer, 1989; Lutz, 2009), when it comes to the issue of 'warmongering' specifically there is much less existing research. A key contribution comes from Gibson's work on the same discursive context as this chapter—the accusation of 'warmongering' in the debate preceding the invasion of Iraq (Gibson, 2011, 2012a, 2012b). Through a close discursive psychological analysis of a small number of examples from televized debates, Gibson identifies a range of processes related to the category 'warmonger'. In particular, he focuses upon the disclaiming of warmongering as a category (Gibson, 2012b, p. 163), and therefore the ways in which the category is associated with a 'dispositional predilection' for war (Gibson, 2011, p. 246), which those speaking in favour of war had to deny. For Gibson (2012b, p. 167), as a category, 'warmonger' carries with it implications of a 'premature, unrestrained, unthinking thirst for conflict' (Gibson, 2012b, p. 167). While the dispositional implications of this can root the explanation for someone's position on war internally—as a matter of their psychology—a metaphor such as 'thirst' also implies a bodily and therefore implicitly irrational, rather than well considered, basis for this.

As Gibson (2012b, p. 167) also puts it:

> A pro-war position is treated as accountable (by both advocates and opponents) to the extent to which it appears to betray an unthinking and unseemly haste to engage in conflict

A warmonger's positive disposition towards war (if not *eagerness* for it) calls their position on a specific case into disrepute as merely another example of that wider pattern. So, Gibson (2012b, p. 165) argues that denial and disclaiming of 'warmongering' is fundamentally tied up with pursuit of a 'category entitlement to claim […] non-pro-war identity' (Gibson, 2012b, p. 165)—which is itself a necessary component of being taken seriously.

It is well established through methods associated with discursive psychology that because of a 'general cultural norm against prejudice' (Billig, 1991, p. 125), successful prejudice-avoidance can be an important component of a 'rational and reasonable self-presentation' (Stapleton, 2015, p. 494). As Augoustinos and Every (2007, p. 125) argue, it is important to construct one's views: 'as reflecting the external world rather than one's psychology'—so that they are seen as 'reasonable, rational, and thoughtfully arrived at' (Augoustinos & Every, 2007, p. 127). Reasons are therefore frequently externalized, amounting to the claim that 'it is the empirical nature of the world, rather than the prejudices of the self, which has led to the conclusion' (Billig, 1991, p. 131)—the views are the product of a situation rather than a disposition (also see Gilbert & Mulkay, 1984).

So, categorization as a 'pacifist' or 'warmonger' has associated with it the implication that the person so categorized possesses a disposition that explains their avowed position on the invasion. They are portrayed as the sort of person who would say that (Edwards & Potter, 1992, p. 117–118)—something designed to undermine their argument, and de-legitimate their continued contribution to debate. As a result of what are constructed as internal, dispositional issues, they are likely to be treated as non-responsive to the external world, and therefore should not be taken seriously. The tendency then, when faced with such potential categorizations that imply dispositions that are prejudiced, is likely to be a denial of the disposition, and an affirmation of a more situational reason for the position adopted—one located not in one's psychology, in dispositions, but in situations—the external world of facts. We can see many examples of this in the data below.

Some Methodological Reflections[2]

The data upon which this chapter is based are drawn from a larger corpus of over 15,000 documents relevant to the invasion of Iraq. Examples here are drawn from newspaper articles and editorials published in the months prior to the start of military action, and from *Hansard*—the official records of parliamentary debates, and specifically from five debates in late 2002 and early 2003. In the latter case—*Hansard*—the data therefore consist of cleaned up versions of what was actually uttered in the UK parliament. They therefore lack the prosodic features of the debate—intonation, hesitation, and the guffawing that often run alongside the speeches being made. As Chilton (2004, p. 94) puts it, they are therefore an 'idealized' version of what actually took place. Nevertheless, they are more than adequate for the purposes at hand.

It is one of the great strengths of discursive psychology that it treats as an analytical matter questions regarding categorization and motivation—part of its move to focusing upon action rather than cognition (Edwards, 1991, p. 517; Edwards & Potter, 1992, p. 154). That is, in the activity that analysts undertake, categorization and mobilization of psychological concepts are understood as ongoing performative features of the interactions of people and situations who are being analysed (Wetherell & Potter, 1992). As Potter (2005, p. 740) puts it: 'The psychosocial categories that make up the mental thesaurus can be studied as a kitbag of resources for doing things'.

As such, its approach resonates to an extent with Giddens' (1984, pp. 281–284) conceptualization of the 'double hermeneutic' to which the social sciences can be subject. Giddens suggests that there is potentially a back and forth relationship between social science concepts and 'lay' concepts that cannot be transcended completely. Psychology and its concepts are perhaps rather more subject to this than the Sociology upon which Giddens focused, because, as Rose (1998) and others have noted, terms and techniques from the 'psy-disciplines' have been especially successful at working their way into the ways that humans make sense of their lives—becoming part of Potter's (2005) kitbag.

The analysis below attempts to make sense of some of the dynamics of the public debate that preceded the invasion of Iraq in 2003. Specifically, it mobilizes insights from discursive psychology, and elsewhere, to look at the significance of categorization processes relating to 'pacifism' and 'warmongering'. It does so by highlighting contributions from those arguing against war which are orientated towards resisting categorization as 'pacifists', and arguments from those in favour of it which resist their categorization as 'warmongers'.

So, in a context concerned with questions of peace and war, the chapter examines some aspects of the dynamics of the debate in terms of processes of categorization

---

[2] A personal 'stake confession' (Potter, 1996, p. 130) is necessary here. As well as not being a peace psychologist, I could not even really be described as any sort of psychologist. I am a *sociologist* who is interdisciplinary enough to use discursive psychology in his work. Alternatively, I am not a charlatan, but…

in relation to issues of entitlement and stake (Potter, 1996) as well as 'prejudice' and reason (Billig, 1991)—especially as demonstrated through well-known processes of disclaiming (Hewitt & Stokes, 1975)—understood as actions of attempted stake inoculation.

In line with the approach of much discursive psychology, the accounts and versions are viewed as a topic rather than a resource—as the objects of investigation rather than as a source of information (Wetherell & Potter, 1992). As such, analytically, I have no real interest in adjudicating whether any of these categorizations or the resistance to them upon which I focus is 'correct'. Instead, although I am not ignoring semantics completely, I am primarily interested in the pragmatic and rhetorical significance of their denial in the doing of things (or in the attempted doing of things). I am also not interested in evaluating whether the categorizations themselves involve fallacies or violations of normative argumentative rules—as a form of *argumentum ad hominem* in pragma-dialectics (van Eemeren, Meuffels, & Verburg, 2000).

It is important to acknowledge that the work of categorization and denial is of course situated action. It is also important to note that speakers orientate themselves towards 'the debate' as an ongoing, *sui generis* entity that also takes place elsewhere. As Billig (1991, p. 43) puts it, speakers: 'locate [themselves] within a public controversy', thereby acknowledging a 'wider argumentative context of criticism and challenge' (Billig, 1991, p. 42). As such, their disclaimers, denials, and other stake inoculation actions are not simply orientated to immediately sequentially prior discourse, but to their versions of tendencies in the debate in specific institutional contexts like the UK parliament, as well as to public debate more widely.

The analysis begins with three excerpts from editorials in each of the three UK national newspapers which were most consistently hostile to the invasion—the *Mirror*, *Guardian*, and *Independent*—all of which are from early 2003. These editorials all deny, with varying degrees of directness, pacifism as a motivation for their opposition to military action. The chapter then explores some parliamentary denials of pacifism on the part of those arguing against invading Iraq. It then moves on to discuss several different but interconnected examples of the denial of warmongering on the part of those who were arguing for a military solution.[3]

Analysis

The Denial of Pacifism

The arguments of those endorsing war often attempted to locate pacifism outside of the legitimate parameters of debate. One of the most straightforward examples of this comes from the Member of the House of Lords and writer for *The Times*

---

[3] Space permits the inclusion of only a limited number of examples. More can be found in Burridge (2005), and many others are spread throughout the UK parliamentary record.

newspaper, William Rees-Mogg, who in an opinion piece mobilized the question of pacifism, identified its significance, and asserted that: 'A small minority take the isolationist, or pacifist, view: no war in any circumstances. They are outside the mainstream of the debate' (*The Times*, 21/10/02, p. 18).

Those arguing against war often deny pacifism since its influence would compromise the legitimacy of their contribution, amounting to an admission that they were incapable of being persuaded that violence and war are ever acceptable. As Rees-Mogg identifies, remaining open to such persuasion seems to be an important qualification for being inside the mainstream of the debate.

Three examples of discursive work denying the influence of pacifism can be seen below, one drawn from the editorial of each of the British daily newspapers which consistently opposed the military action. Each is from early 2003—as the debate began to intensify and sharpen on the possibility of military action:

> The Mirror is not a pacifist newspaper. We reluctantly support military action where there is no alternative
> *But we prefer peace to war. And we do not believe this war is justified*.
> (Voice of the Daily Mirror, *Daily Mirror*, 28/1/03, p. 6, emphasis in original).

> War cannot and should not always be avoided. Here is no argument for a blanket pacifism; this newspaper supported the Kosovo intervention and the 1991 Gulf conflict. But war must be a means of last resort, when all else fails. That moment has not yet come. It may never do so
> (Editorial, *The Guardian*, 30/1/03, p. 23).

> [W]e remain to be convinced.
> That is not because we are opposed to the use of force to uphold international law. We supported the war in Kosovo, conducted by a US-led coalition but not endorsed by the UN, because it averted imminent genocide and the negative consequences were limited. We supported the war against the Taliban in Afghanistan because that regime harboured people who posed a pressing threat to citizens of the West.
> (Editorial, *The Independent*, 7/2/03, p. 16).

In the first of these examples, a stance informed by an implicitly prejudiced pacifism is denied directly by the *Daily Mirror* ('The Mirror is not a pacifist newspaper') and then the paper's openness to war in some circumstances is affirmed ('where there is no alternative'). Support for any war is constructed as reluctant, and a distinction is drawn between this position on potential wars that could be justified, and the specific situation at hand which is asserted as not justified. The denial of stake is part of some complex triangulating positioning work which contrasts the position of the newspaper with *both* the case for war, *and* from what are to be taken as less legitimate reasons for opposition to it. As such, it is arguably a construction of the newspaper as 'moderate'—as contrasted with alternative extreme positions (Wetherell & Potter, 1992, p. 168).

The *Guardian* editorial offers an attempt at stake inoculation in relation to potential accusations of pacifism by denying that it is not proposing a 'blanket pacifism', asserting clearly that there are circumstances in which war is justified, and then giving specific examples (in Kosovo and the Gulf War of 1991) in which the newspaper previously has endorsed military action—offered as evidence for an openness to war. The editorial then contrasts that general position of openness to the specific situation at hand—opposition is therefore not categorical but particularized (Billig, 1996). Having set up a specific threshold located in the external world rather than attributed to any sort of disposition—that war is legitimate as a 'last resort, when all else fails'—it is then asserted that this is not the situation at hand: all else has not (yet) failed. The situations in which the paper's support for war has been offered are contrasted with Iraq in 2003.

The extract from *The Independent* editorial does not explicitly deny a pacifist stance, but is nevertheless orientated to the same concerns—the extent to which its position could be interpreted as originating in a disposition. It begins with a sentence that constructs the newspaper as being open to persuasion regarding the possibility of military action in the prevailing situation. Stating that one remains to be convinced implies that conditions exist in which being convinced is a possibility—that a theoretical situation that met the criteria for military action is plausible, but that the evidence is not sufficient to make this the case here and now. The editorial distances the paper from a position of hostility to the use of force, and, like the *Guardian* editorial, offers examples in which it supported military action—again Kosovo is invoked as such a context—even when the legality of that operation was questioned ('not endorsed by the UN'), as well as the war in Afghanistan. Again, the opposition is particular rather than categorical and is constructed as orientated to the situation, with dispositional explanations disavowed.

In all three instances, openness to military action in some circumstances is acknowledged, even as its legitimacy in this specific instance is denied. As such, all three would be viewed as instances of 'contingent pacifism', in Fiala's (2014, p. 467) sense, since a pacific conclusion is asserted as having been drawn here and now, but all three construct versions of the world in which they are 'open to other conclusions given different circumstances'. This openness to war in other circumstances is used to construct reasonableness and moderation here. The explanation is to be found in the situation and not in a disposition (be that a psychological or ideological prejudice).

Similar discursive work, orientated towards the dilemma of stake, and the prospect of being categorized as pacifist, and therefore as predisposed to reject military action (and not to be taken seriously), was evident in a UK parliamentary context. Speaking in the House of Commons on the day of publication of the government's infamous 'dossier' on Iraq's Weapons of Mass Destruction (UK Government, 2002), David Heath (Liberal Democrat) spoke of the wider debate, and his own position, as follows:

> [S]ome portray those with doubts about military action as either wishing to support the Iraqi regime or being involved in a pacifism that does not take account of circumstances. I think a great deal of respect is owed to those who have deeply held pacifist views, but many, myself included, do not have such views, and are quite prepared to see British military forces used in the right circumstances. We would argue, however, that these are not the right circumstances.
>
> (Hansard, 2002a, column 106).

Heath here professes respect for pacifism, while nevertheless distancing himself from it (an apparent ambivalence that has been noted elsewhere—see Burridge, 2005). He claims that he is prepared to support military action in some (hypothetical) circumstances, but claims that the context in question differs from those circumstances—it is particularized and not dispositional. As such, his contribution is very similar in strategy to that of the *Daily Mirror* above—located in the situation rather than a disposition. Also important for our purposes here is that pacifism's presence is constructed as disqualifying in a context where a decision about war is at stake—and specifically because it 'does not take account of circumstances'. It is dispositional, not situational, and therefore prejudiced and unreasonable.

In the corresponding debate in the House of Lords, the then Lord Bishop of Oxford, Richard Harries, similarly asserted the following:

> I hope that your Lordships will forgive me if I stress that *not only am I not a pacifist but I am a long-standing opponent of the crypto-pacifism which has infiltrated too many Church statements* [...] I found that with much moral fear and spiritual trembling I supported a policy of nuclear deterrence in the bad days of the Cold War. I supported military action in the Falklands, against Iraq in 1990 and in Afghanistan last year. I believe that we should have intervened much earlier than we did in the aftermath of the break up of Yugoslavia. I took such positions because I believed that the conditions for force to be used in a morally licit way were met. I do not believe that on present evidence the criteria are met for military action against Iraq.
>
> (Hansard, 2002b, col. 898, emphasis added).

Here Harries also stresses that he is not a pacifist, supporting this with a claim about a 'long-standing' opposition to pacifism. He claims a history of behaving in a particular way—supporting previous military action—to provide evidence that his opposition to this proposed war is particular rather than categorical. To bolster this, like the other examples seen already, Harries also gives examples of situations in the past when, despite 'moral fear and spiritual trembling', he supported particular uses of military action. The 'criteria' and 'conditions' that justified these wars are contrasted with the situation of Iraq, and the criteria are constructed as not being met on the present evidence. This, of course, leaves open the possibility that the evidence could change, and that Harries could be persuaded, thereby confirming him as open to persuasion and therefore as 'reasonable'. His position is therefore situational and not dispositional.

Perhaps interestingly Harries' contribution contrasts with Heath in its rather more negative portrayal of pacifism—as something that has 'infiltrated' the position of the church of which he is a member. Here, we do not therefore encounter the pattern of praise for pacifism followed by its dismissal as legitimate in relation to a real decision about military action.

Jackson (2016, p. 6) writes of the silencing of pacifism in IR scholarship. I would suggest that an important mechanism for its marginalization more generally—in debates about war—might be the extent to which those drawing contingently pacific conclusions nevertheless distance themselves from pacifism and thereby reinforce the notion that it is illegitimate or disqualified in discussions of potential military action. The continued denial of pacifism may be highly useful to the continued purchase of warism in Cady's (2010) sense.

The Denial of Warmongering

The figure of the pacifist is one who, regardless of the evidence, cannot be convinced that war is legitimate and necessary. Similarly, in ways very resonant with Gibson's (2011, 2012a, 2012b) analysis, the warmonger is constructed as possessing a disposition to favour military action in a manner insufficiently open to the evidence to be found in the situation.

An example of this categorization, which is indirect in that it does not use the term warmongering explicitly, comes from the journalist and political commentator Gerard Baker, who referred to the 'war-now brigade' which he argued:

> [...] thinks its case is so overwhelming that only an apologist for Saddam Hussein could oppose it. The war-never crowd thinks the whole thing has been got up by the US in a fit of evil madness. [...] Mr Hussein is an evil man and I have not a shred of doubt that the world would be a far safer place without him. But a preventive war is an extraordinary step that requires an extraordinary level of confidence that it is really the only means to avert a greater tragedy.
> (*Financial Times*, 27/1/03, p. 21).

Here, Baker's construction of these two groups—the 'war-now brigade' and 'war-never crowd'—is a clear example of a process of someone constructing themselves as moderate (Wetherell & Potter, 1992). Baker invokes these two alternative positions to his own in order to locate himself somewhere other than where these two extremes are located. He claims that he is currently against war, but not eternally so—if the 'extraordinary level of confidence' required for justification can be achieved. Aside from positioning himself as open to persuasion, what is most significant about Baker's contribution is the importance attributed to the twin issues of time and patience. If you want war 'now' you are impatient for it, regardless of the evidence, whereas if you want it 'never' then it does not matter how much time and effort go unsuccessfully into achieving a diplomatic solution, you are unwilling to countenance war—your patience is infinite, and you are not responsive to the evidence.

In assertions like this, there is an interesting implication regarding evidence, but also time, or sequence. It is important how the relationship between the evidence and the decision is configured. The evidence—the situation, or the world of external facts—is constructed as prior to the position on war. An implicit condition of legitimacy is that contributors to debate have no prejudice and are open to changes in the evidence.

The positions of people categorized in ways that suggest that their position is entrenched are often constructed as 'merely' a product of their presence in these asserted categories, and the bases of the views espoused are open to being seen as 'mere rationalisations' (van Eemeren et al., 2000, p. 420). Such rationalizations come after the conclusion rather than before it—so evidence features insufficiently.

One significant distinction here is that between a *casus belli*—a valid reason, something discovered rather than created, and which is argued to make military action *necessary*—and an illegitimate *pretext* which is more in the realms of a retrospective or post hoc excuse for a course of action that had already been determined (see Bamford, 2004).

Returning to the category of 'warmonger', speaking in support of military action, Lord Maginnis of Drumglass (Crossbench[4]) disavowed directly his membership of the category:

> I am no warmonger. War is and should be the last resort. But I believe in moral obligations and that war may be the only way to avert greater wars, greater aggression and greater oppression.
> (Hansard, 2003c, col. 176).

Here, Lord Maginnis denies directly that he is a warmonger and claims that war should be a matter of 'last resort'—a phrase that was a frequently occurring and important part of the debate, and has taken on even greater significance more contemporarily, as the public inquiry into the decision to go to war asserted strongly that when the invasion began, 'The point had not been reached where military action was the last resort' (Chilcot, 2016, p. 47).

Lord Maginnis makes reference to moral obligations, and the possibility that a war can be justified if it averts a greater and more serious war later. The logic of this sort of claim relates very closely to the role and functioning of a 'discourse of peace' in relation to the proposed war (see Gibson, 2011, p. 247), and the seemingly paradoxical but regular 'framing of war as a route to peace' (Gibson, 2012a, p. 13). According to Maginnis' contribution, war can be justified—and justified on somewhat utilitarian grounds via reference to peace—if it can be constructed as contributing to less war later on.

The theme of a positive portrayal of peace, and a negative portrayal of war, is also observable in other contributions nevertheless made in favour of military action, although not always addressing directly the notion of 'warmongering'. In such cases, it is the contributor's *general orientation* towards war which is invoked—they dislike it, and are generally opposed to it. If they are to be believed, they are most definitely *not* in favour of war per se. For example, here is an extract from a speech by Sir Nicholas Winterton (Conservative):

> I am not in favour of war. In fact, I am *positively opposed* to it. War is brutal, cruel and indiscriminate. Innocent people will undoubtedly die in any conflict that takes place, but there are occasions on which war is inevitable if the civilised world is to defend its civilisation against a despotic tyrant such as Saddam Hussein.
> (Hansard, 2003b, col. 800, emphasis added).

---

[4] Members of the UK House of Lords who are independent of the major political parties, which includes many clergy, are described as crossbench—and sit on benches which cross the sides of the chamber.

Here, several highly negative adjectives are applied to war—it is generally 'brutal, cruel and indiscriminate'. This description is followed by a 'but'—that war can be 'inevitable' if the 'civilised world' needs to defend itself, in this case against the specific threat of a 'despotic tyrant'. Although portrayed as generally 'bad', it is not the general moral evaluation of war that is therefore at stake; rather, it is its alleged necessity in this specific situation that matters.

Another way of disclaiming a generally positive orientation toward war involves people stressing their membership of a wider community disliking war—something dispositional, but that can be overcome by the situational. As ever, a declaration of membership of this 'we' is often followed by a 'but' with specific situational (rather than dispositional) reasons for being in favour of it in the specific case under consideration.

Often such contributions claimed a universal consensus against war, also allocating firmly the responsibility for any necessary action to a specific individual (Saddam Hussein), a practice also more widely present in the debates. For example:

> None of us wants to see that; none of us wants to see military conflict. We do not want war. It is indeed terrible to contemplate. But the time may soon be upon us all when Saddam Hussein makes his choice, when he rejects the wishes of the international community and instead chooses fear, violence, terrorism and dictatorship.
> (Baroness Symons of Vernham Dean [Labour], Hansard, 2003a, col. 251).

This constructs a version of what 'none of us' wants, and war is described as 'terrible to contemplate'. The significance of the contrastive 'but' is entirely familiar, and Baroness Symons follows this with a version of Saddam Hussein's likely course of action. The situation described is one in which Hussein's decision is determinant. If there is war, it will ultimately be his agency that caused it. He has the power to avoid war by complying with the wishes of the international community. Therefore, the argument is that any war will be due to his failure to act in the manner available to him which would avoid it. It will be a reaction on the part of the US/UK to the particular situation he creates.

Connected to this is the associated view that a peaceful solution—in which Saddam Hussein did what was required by him to avoid war—was only possible with the looming threat of violence. Diplomacy had to be underpinned by the threat of war, and the level and extent of that diplomacy was often portrayed positively—and as evidence of the absence of warmongering.

For an example, we can again refer to Baroness Symons of Vernham Dean (Labour):

> [T]his is a moment that we hoped we would not reach; a moment that my right honourable friends the Prime Minister and the Foreign Secretary, and many others, have worked immensely hard to avoid through our huge diplomatic efforts.
> (Hansard, 2003c, col. 223).

The moment of decision is portrayed as unwanted, and this is evinced by the fact that the government have worked 'immensely hard' with 'huge diplomatic efforts' to avoid it. Also, since 'we' have tried so hard to avoid war, responsibility for the present situation is again deflected onto Saddam Hussein, who has failed to comply.

The importance variously placed upon the effort put into the avoidance of war implies that a lack of eagerness (a patience) is a key component in pursuit of demonstrating that you are not systematically in favour of war—that your advocacy is situational not dispositional, and that you are reasonable, moderate, legitimate.

A possible implication of this is that talk about 'warmongering' can actually work to your advantage if you are one of those so accused. A shrill and intense caricature of warmongering, if it fosters extreme expectations of the behaviour of those so categorized, can make it easier to provide evidence violating such a portrayal. Based upon such an understanding it might be possible to claim that the extreme portrayals of the US administration made by those against the war—as crazed, hawkish, warmongers desperate to go to unilateral war as soon as possible—were ultimately self-defeating in the sense that they were fairly easily violated. In such a climate, evidence of a contrastive moderation can be assembled. If your opponents are vocal about how rushed and unthinking your actions will be, it can be relatively easy to evade such characterizations by not acting in such a manner; not acting according to the script already written.

Of course, all categorization and denials thereof are potentially defeasible, but this is perhaps one way in which the affordances of the category of warmonger are significantly different from those of the pacifist. There is already this notion that the pacifist might be viewed positively in some way—as worthy of respect. The same cannot really be said for the warmonger. More interestingly, those accused of being a warmonger—by demonstrating any efforts towards diplomacy, and interruptions to a direct procession to war—can start to build evidence against their level of rabidity. Those accused of being pacifist on the other hand, seemingly need to mobilize evidence that involves support for a war—which is perhaps not always quite as easy to produce.

Conclusion

This chapter has drawn upon examples of people resisting categorization as a 'pacifist' or 'warmonger' in the context of the UK public debate that preceded the 2003 invasion of Iraq. It has highlighted the ways in which such categorizations are problematic for contributors to debate in terms of their legitimacy and has looked at various forms that the work of denial and attempts at stake inoculation can take.

I have shown some of the ways in which the potential of being categorized as pacifist or warmonger results in contributors to debate taking trouble to provide evidence that they should not be so categorized. In relation to 'pacifism' in particular I have suggested that the regularity with which it is denied might play a role in reinforcing its perceived illegitimacy. Peace psychology might benefit from taking seriously the cultural (and discursive) violence that can be involved in such processes of categorization (albeit as a by-product of pragmatic and rhetorical manoeuvres).

Cady (2010, p. 54) suggests that warist discourse often 'precludes consideration of peaceful options by defining them out of existence' (Cady, 2010, p. 54). In the data considered here, in a much less final fashion, we see some consequences of proponents of war attempting to undermine the arguments of those opposing it by attempting to categorize them out of relevance. The same goes for the reverse, of course, in that we can also see evidence of the impact of those arguing against war trying to define out of relevance those who seem excessively eager for it. The boundaries of what is legitimate are contested and the dynamics of what is disposi- tional and what is situational are invoked and denied.

These issues should be of interest to peace psychology because of the topic itself, and because we need to attend to the ways in which peace and war are justified and mediated by language (see Gibson, 2011). The sense in which when war is dis- cussed there is a conflict over conflict—and an adversarial approach adopted—itself is also amendable to exploration by a discursive orientated peace psychology in pursuit of more effective, productive, and empathetic intergroup dialogue (see Christie & Montiel, 2013, p. 508).

This should also be of interest in terms of the important role that categorization plays in academic contexts. Peace psychology involves taking a fundamentally nor- mative stance in favour of peace (Vollhardt & Bilali, 2008, p. 13). Indeed, based upon the framework and arguments of Galtung (1969, 1990), Christie (2006), and Christie, Wagner, and Winter (2001), the conception of peace involved extends far beyond the mere absence of direct or episodic military violence. It also orientates itself to persistent structural, cultural, and symbolic violence, and inequality and injustice more generally. Overtly mobilizing such a package of normative concerns raises the question of the extent to which practitioners of peace psychology can insert themselves into discussions about violence in ways that deal with that interest without being undermined as interested (to return to Edwards & Potter, 1992).

In relation to violence and war, those who fairly systematically reject military action, need to deal with the constitutive exclusion of pacifism from legitimate dis- cussion. On the basis of my suggestion that the denial of pacifism in pursuit of legitimacy itself helps to reinforce the illegitimacy of pacifism, this also raises ques- tions about the extent to which that approach to seeking legitimacy might not be practically useful, or desirable, in pursuit of 'Positive peace' (see Christie, Tint, Wagner, & Winter, 2008, p. 547).

On a rhetorical level, if not in practice, peace is a normative value. As we have seen, and as Gibson (2011) has suggested, a discourse of peace is often observable working in the arguments of those advocating war. As Galtung (1969, p. 167) put it some time ago: 'it is hard to be all-out against peace'. However, it is also hard to be all-out for peace if that is considered to be a disqualification from certain relevant discursive contexts. Given some of the dynamics observable in the data explored here, and within the literature on pacifism, this raises the question of how peace psychologists can best frame their interventions in relation to pacifism. Can we develop alternative ways of relating to these practical problems of self-presentation in relation to legitimacy?

References

Antaki, C., & Horowitz, A. (2000). Using identity ascription to disqualify a rival version of events as 'interested'. *Research on Language and Social Interaction, 33*, 155–177.

Augoustinos, M., & Every, D. (2007). The language of 'race' and prejudice: A discourse of denial, reason, and liberal-practical politics. *Journal of Language and Social Psychology, 26*, 123–141.

Augoustinos, M., & Every, D. (2010). Accusations and denials of racism: Managing moral accountability in public discourse. *Discourse and Society, 21*, 251–256.

Bamford, J. (2004). *A pretext for war: 9–11, Iraq and the abuse of America's intelligence agencies*. London: Doubleday.

Billig, M. (1991). *Ideology and opinions: Studies in rhetorical psychology*. London: Sage.

Billig, M. (1996). *Arguing and thinking: A rhetorical approach to social psychology*. Cambridge: Cambridge University Press.

British Broadcasting Corporation (BBC). (2003). 'Million' march against Iraq war. *BBC Online*. Retrieved from http://news.bbc.co.uk/1/hi/uk/2765041.stm

Burridge, J. D. (2005). The construction of discursive difficulty: The circulation of, and resistance to, moral asymmetries in the public debate over the invasion of Iraq in 2003 (Doctoral thesis, University of Nottingham).

Burridge, J. D. (2007). The 'spectre of anti-Americanism' in the British public debate over the 2003 invasion of Iraq. *The Journal of Language and Politics, 6*, 201–221.

Burridge, J. D. (2013). Appeasement analogies in British parliamentary debates preceding the 2003 invasion of Iraq. In C. Karner & B. Mertens (Eds.), *The use and abuse of memory: Interpreting WWII in contemporary European politics* (pp. 42–58). New Brunswick, NJ: Transaction.

Burridge, J. D., & McSorley, K. (2013). Too fat to fight? Obesity, bio-politics and the militarisation of children's bodies. In K. McSorley (Ed.), *War and the body: Militarisation, practice and experience* (pp. 62–77). London: Routledge.

Cady, D. L. (2010). *From warism to pacifism: A moral continuum* (2nd ed.). Philadelphia, PA: Temple University Press.

Chilcot, J. (2016). *The report of the Iraq inquiry, Executive summary*. Retrieved from http://www.iraqinquiry.org.uk/the-report/

Chilton, P. (2004). *Analysing political discourse: Theory and practice*. London: Routledge.

Christie, D. J. (2006). What is peace psychology the psychology of? *Journal of Social Issues, 62*, 1–17.

Christie, D. J., & Montiel, C. J. (2013). Contributions of psychology to war and peace. *American Psychologist, 68*, 502–513.

Christie, D. J., Tint, B. S., Wagner, R. V., & Winter, D. D. (2008). Peace psychology for a peaceful world. *American Psychologist, 63*, 540–552.

Christie, D. J., Wagner, R. V., & Winter, D. D. (2001). Introduction to peace psychology. In D. J. Christie, R. V. Wagner, & D. D. Winter (Eds.), *Peace, conflict, and violence: Peace psychology for the 21st century*. Englewood Cliffs, NJ: Prentice-Hall.

Edwards, D. (1991). Categories are for talking: On the cognitive and discursive bases of categorization. *Theory and Psychology, 1*, 515–542.

Edwards, D., & Potter, J. (1992). *Discursive psychology*. London: Sage.

Fiala, A. (2014). Contingent pacifism and contingently pacifist conclusions. *Journal of Social Philosophy, 45*, 463–477.

Galtung, J. (1969). Violence, peace, and peace research. *Journal of Peace Research, 6*, 167–191.

Galtung, J. (1990). Cultural violence. *Journal of Peace Research, 27*, 291–305.

Geyer, M. (1989). The militarization of Europe, 1914-1945. In J. Gillis (Ed.), *The militarization of the western world* (pp. 65–102). New Brunswick, NJ: Rutgers University Press.

Gibson, S. (2011). Social psychology, war and peace: Towards a critical discursive peace psychology. *Social and Personality Psychology Compass, 5*, 239–250.

Gibson, S. (2012a). History in action: The construction of historical analogies in televised debates concerning the Iraq war. *Papers on Social Representation, 21*, 13.1–13.35.

Gibson, S. (2012b). 'I'm not a warmonger but…' discourse analysis and social psychological peace research. *Journal of Community and Applied Social Psychology, 22*, 159–173.

Giddens, A. (1984). *The constitution of society: Outline of the theory of structuration.* Cambridge: Polity.

Gilbert, G., & Mulkay, M. (1984). *Opening Pandora's box: A sociological analysis of scientists' discourse.* Cambridge: Cambridge University Press.

Hansard. (2002a, September 24). *Official report of the House of Commons, 390*(187), 1–155.

Hansard. (2002b, September 24). *Official report of the House of Lords, 638*(180), 857–1026.

Hansard. (2003a, February 26). *Official report of the House of Lords, 645*(52), 244–379.

Hansard. (2003b, March 18). *Official report of the House of Commons, 401*(65), 760–911.

Hansard. (2003c, March 18). *Official report of the House of Lords, 646*(66), 138–232.

Harold, J. A. (2013). Distinguishing the lover of peace from the pacifist, the appeaser, and the warmonger. *Forum Philosophicum, 18*, 5–17.

Hewitt, J. P., & Stokes, R. (1975). Disclaimers. *American Sociological Review, 40*, 1–11.

Iraq Body Count. (2017). Retrieved from https://www.iraqbodycount.org/

Jackson, R. (2014). Bringing pacifism back into international relations. *Social Alternatives, 33*, 63–66.

Jackson, R. (2016). *Pacifism and the ethical imagination in IR.* Paper presented at the Sie Cheou-Kang Center for International Security and Diplomacy, Josef Korbel School of International Studies, University of Denver.

Lutz, C. (2009). The military normal: Feeling at home with counter-insurgency in the United States. In Network of Concerned Anthropologists (Ed.), *The counter-counterinsurgency manual* (pp. 22–37). Chicago, IL: Prickly Paradigm Press.

Martin, D. A. (1965). *Pacifism: An historical and sociological study.* London: Routledge & Kegan Paul.

Narveson, J. (1965). Pacifism: A philosophical analysis. *Ethics, 75*, 259–271.

Narveson, J. (1999). *Moral matters.* Letchworth: Broadview.

Potter, J. (1996). *Representing reality: Discourse, rhetoric and social construction.* London: Sage.

Potter, J. (2005). Making psychology relevant. *Discourse and Society, 16*, 739–747.

Rapley, M. (1998). 'Just an ordinary Australian': Self-categorization and the discursive construction of facticity in 'new racist' political rhetoric. *British Journal of Social Psychology, 37*, 325–344.

Rose, N. (1998). *Inventing ourselves: Psychology, power, and personhood.* Cambridge: Cambridge University Press.

Stapleton, K. (2015). Accountable preferences? Discourse, identity, and the anti-prejudice norm. *Journal of Language and Social Psychology, 35*, 491–514.

Stokoe, E. (2015). Identifying and responding to possible *-isms* in institutional encounters: Alignment, impartiality, and the implications for communication training. *Journal of Language and Social Psychology, 34*, 427–445.

UK Government. (2002). *Iraq's weapons of mass destruction: The assessment of the British government.* Retrieved from https://archive.org/stream/IraqsWeaponsOfMassDestruction/IraqsWeaponsOfMassDestructionByTonyBlairBritishPrimeMinister#page/n0/mode/2up

van Eemeren, F. H., Meuffels, B., & Verburg, M. (2000). The (un)reasonableness of ad hominem fallacies. *Journal of Language and Social Psychology, 19*, 416–435.

Vollhardt, J. K., & Bilali, R. (2008). Social psychology's contribution to the psychological study of peace: A review. *Social Psychology, 39*, 12–25.

Wanner, K. J. (2016). In a world of super-violence, can pacifism pack a punch?: Nonviolent superheroes and their implications. *The Journal of American Culture, 39*, 177–192.

Wetherell, M., & Potter, J. (1992). *Mapping the language of racism: Discourse and the legitimation of exploitation.* London: Harvester Wheatsheaf.

Whitehead, K. A., & Stokoe, E. (2015). Producing and responding to *-isms* in interaction. *Journal of Language and Social Psychology, 34*, 368–373.

Chapter 9
Revisiting the Past: A Discursive Psychological Approach to Anglo-Japanese Reconciliation Over the Second World War

Kyoko Murakami

Introduction

Reconciliation is an important process for peace-making in the aftermath of conflict. This chapter is focused on examining reconciliation as a discursive accomplishment and is aimed at elucidating a possible contribution of discursive psychology to studies of reconciliation within peace psychology and the broader domain of peace and conflict studies. In doing so, the chapter explores the narrative of memory—a research focus that is familiar from studies of remembering and memory work in peace studies and related disciplines (e.g. Young, 2012), but which has also been the focus of considerable attention in discursive psychology (e.g. Middleton & Edwards, 1990) and in the wider critical psychology of memory which has drawn on it (e.g. Middleton & Brown, 2005).

The literature regarding remembering and reconciliation embraces many social sciences disciplines, including philosophy, psychology, sociology, anthropology, political science, and cultural studies. The psychology of memory has largely been preoccupied with the representation of reality at the level of the individual mind, and in so doing has tended to reproduce a dualism between the individual and the social. Where the psychology of memory has taken the individual to be its proper focus, the social nature of memory and remembering has tended to be left to other disciplines. This dualism has characterized our understanding of memory and remembering for many centuries since the classical period of Greek scholarship. However, it arguably constrains our understanding in two important ways: First, it has led to a tendency to avoid studying actual social practices of remembering in psychology. Second, it leads to a conception of memory as a fixed, static mental state, as an outcome of information processing. By contrast, here I address how remembering and reconciliation are conceived in terms of the social organization of

K. Murakami (✉)
University of Copenhagen, Copenhagen, Denmark
e-mail: kyoko.murakami@psy.ku.dk

S. Gibson (ed.), *Discourse, Peace, and Conflict*, Peace Psychology Book Series,
https://doi.org/10.1007/978-3-319-99094-1_9

the past, how the past is socially constructed and organized (Shotter, 1991). Remembering and discursive reconciliation are considered as a dynamic human 'activity' in which sense-making is performed and shared meanings are achieved with the use of language.

Likewise, inspired by the critical position of discursive psychology toward the conventional psychology of memory, I approach the concept of reconciliation as a discursive practice, within which a communicative action of remembering elucidates the social organization of the past and constitutes the very act of reconciliation. Moreover, as a process that inevitably orients to past (conflictual) events, reconciliation is necessarily imbued with memory and remembering. Thus, as a starting point for discursive reconciliation, I suggest we should consider 'memory as a socioculturally constituted process in which the individual and the social are united in cultural artefacts' (Cole, 1990, pp. viii–ix).

In this chapter, I will briefly review work that treats reconciliation—whether explicitly or implicitly—as an internal mental process. I will then outline a discursive approach to reconciliation, and illustrate this through an analysis of an extract from an interview with a British former prisoner of war who was held captive by Japan in the Second World War.

Reconciliation as Mental Process

Reconciliation is a ubiquitous social phenomenon, woven into the fabric of social lives, and is integral to peace and the resolution of conflict. It ranges from interpersonal relationships observed in the everyday life of families, schools, and local communities to a wider social context of institutions concerned with education, health, business, politics, government, international relations, and philanthropy. Reconciliation is analogous, for many, to conflict resolution, in which the chief aim is to restore and maintain peace between states through diplomatic talks and negotiation as well as ongoing social and international debates on apology, compensation, and restitution (Abado, 1990; Gibney, 2008; Ide, 1998; Murata, 1998; Tavuchis, 1991).

Examination of literature on social practices of reconciliation, conflict resolution, international relations, and peace studies informs a popular view of reconciliation that has been developed by adopting a broadly psychological model of reconciliation processes and states (Asmal, Asmal et al., 1997; Brecke & Long, 1999; Coleman, 1999; Green and Ahmed, 1999; Krondorfer, 1995; Norval, 1998; Retzinger, 1991; Swartz & Drennan, 2000; Tavuchis, 1991; Tutu, 1999; Vangelisti, 1992). These studies are commonly concerned with identifying causal psychological mechanisms of reconciliation by looking at what psychological factors lead to conflict and how such conflict can be resolved. In other words, they seem to assume that there is an inner model at work—the causal mechanisms are theorized at the level of the human mind. For example, Brecke and Long (1999) articulate this individual view of reconciliation, suggesting that 'Reconciliation events … are evidence of "forgiveness"—the process of overcoming certain psychological attitudes (mainly the overcoming of various forms of anger or resentment)' (Brecke & Long, 1999, p. 100). It is in this spirit that they recommend conducting 'a theoretically-informed search for the mechanism by which reconciliation leads to a subsequent improvement in bilateral relations' (Brecke & Long, 1999, p. 113).

Storytelling as Discursive Reconciliation

Approaches which focus on the internal mechanisms of change and reconciliation can be contrasted with those that emphasize the social, publically available nature of reconciliation processes. Central to many such approaches is a concern with storytelling. For example, Norval (1998) argues that storytelling seems to be a principal human activity that engages people in reconciliation activities. Discussing the South African Truth and Reconciliation Commission (TRC), Norval argues that 'one of the most important effects of the memory work of the TRC is the way in which it has offered an occasion for survivors to gain recognition of their plight in full public view' (Norval, 1998, p. 258). The TRC hearings brought injustices perpetrated against ordinary citizens into the public domain and made the search for justice visible. Norval argues that the TRC has allowed moral sanctioning of the past wrongdoing and gives a voice to ordinary people. In this sense, their participation in a public memorial exercise has different consequences from the standard nationalist use of memory and monuments. If the social practice of telling one's story is at the heart of reconciliation activity, what does it lead to? Does it simply create a profusion of memories and versions of the past including unpleasant details of violence and other events? And what then is the role of storytelling in reconciliation and memory work in dealing with the troubling past caused by conflict and oppression?

To address these questions, I now turn to Bruner's (1990, p. 95) notion of narrative as 'a means of cultural peace keeping'. Bruner states that narrative is 'the human gift for presenting, dramatizing, and explicating the mitigating circumstances surrounding conflict-threatening breaches in the ordinariness of life'. He goes on to say:

> The objective of such narrative is not to reconcile, not to legitimize, not even to excuse, but rather to explicate. And the explications offered in the ordinary telling of such narratives are not always forgiving of the protagonist depicted. Rather, it is the narrator who usually comes off best... Our sense of the normative is nourished in narrative, but so is our sense of breach and exception. Stories make "reality" a mitigated reality... Without those narrative skills, we could never endure the conflicts and contradictions that social life generates. We would become unfit for the life of culture. (Bruner, 1990, pp. 95–7)

To take this argument further, I take an approach inspired by discourse analysis and discursive psychology (Antaki, Billig, Edwards, & Potter, 2003; Benwell & Stokoe, 2006; Edwards & Potter, 2001; Potter, 2003; Potter & Wetherell, 1987; Schiffrin, Tannen, & Hamilton, 2003; Wetherell, Taylor, & Yates, 2001), and in particular by discursive work on social remembering (Middleton & Edwards, 1990). In this approach, I argue that reconciliation is a continual process—situated in the local interactional communicative practice and discursively managed and accomplished as a temporary settlement of meaning-making. The discursive approach to reconciliation works toward unpacking how the singular voice of nationhood emerges, how different voices and views are held together and translated into the monolithic discourse of reconciliation.

I put forward this alternative view of discursive reconciliation, in which people's differences and multiplicity of opinions, views, and attitudes are not 'resolved' to produce a single voice. I propose an argument that reconciliation is an 'unfinished' process, in which people constantly reflect upon past events and experiences and continually evaluate them in terms of the current circumstances and a projected future. Central to discursive reconciliation is the role of narrative and storytelling as a tool that people use in order to settle with a meaning of a particular experience or event and the constitution of situated identities within social relations.

The Discursive Psychological Approach to Reconciliation Practices

As Pratt, Elder, and Ellis (2001) observed, reconciliation practices can produce a harmonious social order that masks other, defiant, multiple voices. In studying the discursive organization of reconciliation, analytical categories are not predetermined. I do not set out to identify an underlying mechanism with an assumption that people's voices were repressed by some institutional power generated by social relations. Instead, my analysis of talk-in-interaction focuses on language use. I therefore examine the consequences of discursive action without mobilizing a social theory of power and ideological argument that exists beyond what is made relevant in the participants' talk-in-interaction. In other words, my analysis is primarily concerned with how varying voices and positions regarding reconciliation are made available and how they are made relevant (Thomas & Seely, 2011).

One discursive device that exemplifies discursive reconciliation is the way in which interview participants use various positions to claim a change of identity—as someone who has changed, who is no longer the same person, or sees themselves differently. For instance, without speculating on the emotional state of a person, I can treat an utterance such as 'I feel like a better man' as a moral claim of his conciliatory position. I look at how moral accountability is used to warrant participants' position of reconciliation. Such a claim about one's change of position and worldview would entail a concept of identities that are interactionally constituted and situated within social contexts and cultural practices, dismissing the idea of a single coherent identity throughout the life course. Instead of simply reporting the participants' declaration of reconciliation, I discuss how these identity claims would afford reconciliation. In other words, I show how reconciliation is both claimed and demonstrated. The participants' narratives and talk produced in the interviews are our analytical resource and enable us to explore the ways in which one's redemption of self is a storied feature of moral accountability involving identity change.

My analysis draws upon the discursive psychological perspective (Edwards, 1997; Edwards & Potter, 1992; Edwards, Potter, & Middleton, 1992). In discursive psychology, accounts are not treated as definite facts about people's lives and past events, but are occasioned in the context of their telling and address the current concerns of the participants who are engaged in the interview. In addition, the interview participants and interviewer can be seen to handle alternative versions of their experiences of life. The project reported in this chapter was focused not on gathering participants' accounts of war and associated atrocities and violence per se, but rather on the consequence of their participation in a 'reconciliation trip' back to Japan. This trip to Japan was organized some 40 years after their wartime experience. I am interested in what the participants did with the event and their experience of having participated in such reconciliation activities. The issue here is not to judge whether they have become reconciled in any absolute sense, or to identify the causal factors that led them to reconciliation as an outcome of the trip. Rather, the interview talk was looked at in terms of the following questions: (1) What do the participants say about their current position in relation to the wartime experience of captivity in POW camps? (2) What has been constituted as the impact of the war experience on their post-war life? (3) What identities are invoked which work in the participants' telling of the narratives? (4) How do they establish a particular version of the past as relevant to demonstrate their current position?

Narratives of Redemption

In emphasizing accountability in my analysis of the veterans' narratives of reconciliation, I draw on the following definition of narrative:

> Narratives can function as an account by verbally reconstructing a temporal sequence of particular events and the actor's part in them so as to justify actions. … Narratives as a discourse genre work as accounts when tellers represent past events in such a way to defend their conduct. (Buttny, 1993, p. 18)

I use the term 'redemption' to describe the narrative being told by the veterans as their way of claiming reconciliation. Whilst it might not be immediately obvious what it is that the veterans are being redeemed *from*, it is notable that journalistic interviews and accounts have, over the years, reported that former British POWs held prisoner by Japan have shown antipathy to Japanese people. It is the redemption from these antipathetic feelings that are constructed in the interview narratives.

Moreover, the reality of the reconciliation captured in the interviews can be challenged. Across the corpus as a whole, no categorical statements such as 'I have been reconciled' were made. Reconciliation as a conversational topic was mentioned and attended to by the ex-POW participants as well as by the interviewer, yet there was neither an exposition nor an explicit claim of reconciliation. To some, this may pose a question of whether the ex-POW participants had 'really' been reconciled. What, then, are the criteria in judging whether these participants have been reconciled? The discursive perspective treats such problems of facticity and veracity as a participant's concern, and examines the way in which the facticity and veracity of reconciliation is discursively accomplished in talk. The analyst is thus not concerned with coming to a conclusion of whether 'real' or 'genuine' reconciliation has occurred. In other words, the participants 'do' facticity and veracity as social accountability, and these issues are oriented to and managed in the interview talk by both participants and researcher.

Accounting for Change: Positioning

In the analysis of redemption narratives, I examine the mobilization of identities and their rhetorical effects—the ways in which positions are made legitimate and stories become persuasive (Antaki & Widdicombe, 1998). My analysis was informed by using positioning theory as a guiding concept, illustrating the flexible, dynamic discursive moves located in time and place and the attribution (and non-attribution) of agency. Positioning theory is a name given to a range of related attempts to articulate an alternative way of reading and understanding the dynamic of human relationships within a social constructionist paradigm.

Drawing on the pioneering work of Henriques, Hollway, Urwin, Venn, and Walkerdine (1984), especially Hollway's (1984) chapter, positioning theory was developed by Davies and Harré (1990, see also Harré, 2012, Harré & Moghaddam, 2003, Harré & van Langenhove, 1998, Harré & Van Langenhove, 1999). The concept of positioning is introduced as a metaphor to enable an investigator to grasp how persons are 'located' within conversations as observably and subjectively coherent participants in jointly produced storylines. The act of positioning refers to the assignment of 'parts' or 'roles' (positions) to speakers in the discursive construction of personal stories.

I apply positioning theory to my analysis in order to understand the nature of the experience of reconciliation—what it is to remember the problematic past and what it is to be reconciled with it. Harré and Van Langenhove (1991; Van Langenhove & Harré, 1993) note that there are three ways of expressing and experiencing one's personal identity or unique selfhood: by stressing one's agency in claiming responsibility for an action; by indexing one's statements with the point of view one has on some relevant aspect of the world; or by presenting a description/evaluation of some past event or episode as a contribution to one's biography. I will show in the following analysis how such indexing and marking of one's agency are empirically observed in the redemption narrative.

Furthermore, Harré and van Langenhove argue that positioning has larger theoretical implications for the moral sensibility of a person in taking a particular position in a given conversational setting. Any utterance is indexed with a person's spatial and temporal location, and as a claim about a state of affairs it can be seen to index a speaker's moral standing (Harré & van Langenhove, 1991; Harré & Van Langenhove, 1999). Such indexing allows us to look at the ways in which a speaker takes responsibility for the reliability of his or her claim. Discourse produced in the interview is thus not treated as straightforwardly representing the truth, but is instead treated as the speaker's version of truth that is produced as relevant to a particular set of social relations. The discursive act of positioning thus involves a reconstructive element: the biographies of the one being positioned and the 'positions' may be subject to rhetorical re-descriptions (van Langenhove & Harré, 1993). The question, then, is to examine how this 'rewriting' is understood with regard to personal identity and selfhood (van Langenhove & Harré, 1993, p. 85). The analysis below will provide an illustrative example of this process of rhetorical description (and re-description).

Thus, as with a range of work in critical and discursive psychology, positioning does not assume a stable, fixed identity or individual state of mind, but instead conceives of the self as situated in, and reproduced by, discursive practices. However, van Langenhove and Harré note that '[t]here seems to be a tension between the multiplicity of selves as expressed in discursive practices and the fact that across these discursive practices a relatively stable self-hood exists as well' (p. 82). In acknowledging this tension, they do not seek to resolve these apparently contradictory positions, but instead hold both positions together:

> [T]he singularity of selfhood … is equally a product of discursive practices as the multiplicity of selfhood … . Moreover, in order to make it possible for a person to understand him- or herself as a historically continuous unity, he or she will have to engage in very different— possible contradictory—forms of biographical talk. (p. 82)

I see this argument working in tandem with my own view of reconciliation. Using positioning theory, reconciliation can be construed as a move not only to resolve this tension, but also to hold the two positions together as a way of understanding the multiplicity of selves, voices, and identities in analysing narrative. What the particular experience means to an individual is up for grabs for re-description and reformulation in the activity of telling stories. Flexibility and variability are key features in positioning theory, and these can typically be observed in the course of a conversation, during which we explain our positions, defend them and alter them. Furthermore, we often try to position others, as, for example, wrong, incompetent, misinformed, or right, competent, knowledgeable. Finally, these positions tend to be taken up according to an unfolding narrative. The positions will be tried out and abandoned or maintained, depending upon the outcome they generate. In the following, I demonstrate how accounting for change in the narrative is performed discursively. Rather than stating, 'I have changed', the speaker claims change by discursively producing two different ways of being at two different occasions.

I use the term 'narrative of redemption' to describe those narratives in which the participants address the moral sensibility of the problematic status of their wartime past and reconfigure and reformulate the significance of the past in relation to their present position of reconciliation. Adopting positioning theory as a guiding analytic concept, my analysis demonstrates how such talk shapes experiences of reconciliation with a problematic past. I focus on the redemption narrative to uncover the interactional work of positioning, with special attention to similar concepts such as footing and reported speech. I will then briefly discuss the implications of applying positioning theory to the work of reconciliation studies.

Illustrative Example

I will illustrate these conceptual points through an analytic example drawn from a project exploring reconciliation narratives amongst British former prisoners of war who had been held captive by Japan during the Second World War (Murakami, 2001, 2012). The research is based on interviews with surviving former British POWs—their recollection of experiences of post-war reconciliation as well as their captivity in the 'Far East' during World War II. The interviewees had all taken part in a reconciliation project involving former POWs who had been imprisoned at a labour camp in Iruka, Japan. These POWs had initially being amongst nearly 100,000 British soldiers who were captured by the Japanese army at the fall of Singapore in 1942 and were taken to Thailand to work on the Thai–Burma Railway. Later, 300 of the soldiers were transferred to a labour camp in Japan to work in a copper mine with local villagers and student workers. Whilst they were interned in the camp, 13 of them died due to malnutrition and tropical diseases, which they contracted from the prison camps in Thailand prior to arriving in Japan. A small grave for the dead soldiers was built near the camp by fellow soldiers. At the end of the war in 1945, the remaining POWs were released and returned to Britain. After their departure, local villagers in Japan carried on with the maintenance of this grave, which they called 'Little Britain', and a senior citizens' group took on the responsibility of looking after it. In late 1980, a refurbishment of the grave was proposed and it was completed as a village-wide project. For all these years, there was no contact between the surviving former POWs and the Japanese villagers. Around the same time, a newspaper article with a photo of the refurbished grave/cemetery, written by a British expatriate Catholic priest, was read by a former POW in Northumberland. Correspondence between the Japanese and the ex-British POWs began. In 1992, nearly 50 years after the war, the 28 surviving members of the POWs who worked in the camp and their family members were invited to take part in a reconciliation trip to Japan. They visited the former campsite and the refurbished cemetery and attended the joint memorial for the 13 dead soldiers. The 1992 reconciliation trip to Japan was a pivotal event that put Anglo-Japanese reconciliation back on the table. The current research set out to examine the discursive practices of reconciliation amongst those British veterans who participated in the trip, asking them to speak about their wartime captivity by the Japanese and the post-war experience of reconciliation (see Murakami, 2012, for further details).

The project as a whole featured three group interviews and two individual inter-views with a total of eight surviving former POWs and five of their family mem-bers. The interviews were held in their homes in five English towns and cities. The specific example used here is an extract from a group interview with four interview participants: Freddie and Bill, two veterans who took part in the reconciliation trip; Bill's wife, Eileen, and Maki, a Japanese woman who accompanied the group as an interpreter during the first reconciliation trip to Japan in 1992. The interview was conducted at Bill's home in Greater London in Spring 1998. It lasted nearly four hours, including afternoon tea served by Eileen halfway through the interview. Freddie, Bill, and Eileen were in their late 70s at the time of the interview. The extract features a story told by Freddie. This particular story follows from Freddie's recollection of a 'little reunion' with his old mates at Heathrow Airport whilst departing for Japan on their reconciliation trip. He said that the reunion put him on the road to reconciliation after having experienced old camaraderie at the airport. I will now examine how the story is told and is made relevant to the issue of reconciliation.

The photograph story

1	Freddie:	I was in Battersea Par:k some years ago
2		after the war, ten years after the war (1.0)
3		and I'm sitting out in the open air a cup
4		of tea at the table and two little (0.8)
5		children running around in front of me (2.0)
6		and I thought to myself, 'oh my god, >is
7		that< Japanese↓.' because they could be
8		Chinese or (0.8) [Thai, or any=
9	Interviewer	[°hum° °hum°
10	Freddie =	>you know what I mean< but to me they
11		were Japanese (1.0) I thought (0.8)
12		and I didn't have to wo-wonder very long
13		because It's just behind me (.)
14		somebody called out
15		'*Oi, koi.*' (1.8) right?
16		(.)
17	Freddie	come here or
18	Interviewer	[°hum°
19	Freddie	[yeah, I thought (.)
20		I know that↓((hushed dramatic voice))(.)
21		that means come here (.) or means
22		of course come back (.) and
23		I half reluctantly turned around and the
24		next table behind me was a Japanese man and
25		woman (.) they was (.) and
26		they all got up and they went down (.)
27		stood by the lake (.) and this is the story (.)
28		He:h took (.) a picture (.)
29		of his wife and two children
30		°assume it's his wife° and two children (.)
31		she:h came (.) and took a picture
32		of him and the two children (.)
33		and me being (.) Having

34		used a camera and all that,
35		>I thought to myself<
36		oh↑ what I would,
37		what I would nor:mally do in
38		A case like that (.) °and I have done it (.)
39		many times° (.) I would go out and say and
40		'excuse me >do you mind if< (.) would you like
41		me to take a photograph of all of you?'
42	Interviewer	yes (.)
43	Freddie	I-I half got up and I thought (.)
44		'°no why should I↓°' ((dramatic voice)) (.)
45		And I've regretted that.
46		I didn't. °I regret it.°
47		but some years later, when I was over at
48		Haruko's place in Croydon, a Japanese (.)
49		man, lady, doctor?
50	Interviewer	Hum
51		Maki Hiro?
52	Freddie	and the two children they came and they
53		stood (.).hh on the (.) by the stairs
54		in Haruko's room there and I took a
55		photograph with my camera then. I thought
56		(.) perhaps I've been redeemed at last.
57		–ha hh You know.h [That's a little thing.
58	Maki	[hh [hh
59	Interviewer	Yes

At first glance, this story appears to be a straightforward description of events that the speaker, Freddie, experienced. Ostensibly, there is a contrast between his actions in a sequence of two events, in which we see Freddie's photo-taking experience on two different occasions— presumably before ('some years ago after the war') and after the reconciliation trip ('some years later' after seeing the family in the park). The story invokes a notion of change in the brief biography of the speaker. What is implied here is that this trip afforded him the opportunity to see himself differently. The story features the speaker's change by recounting two different ways of behaving in the presence of Japanese people. It discursively marks the point when Freddie realizes that all these years of being an ex-POW had prohibited him from being the person that he normally is, in this case, an agreeable person who would offer to take a photo for someone in a public place.

This narrative was produced following the speaker's comment pertaining to reconciliation: 'the little reunion' at Heathrow Airport that put him on the road to reconciliation. How, then, does the narrative work as a stronger claim of reconciliation rather than simply claiming 'I have reconciled'? In arguing that storytelling is an act of remembering, Edwards (1997) points out that not only analysts of 'narrative structures', but also participants themselves, display sensitivity to what might count as a proper, 'well-formed' instance of a story. Accountability is being managed, on two levels, both in the story itself, and in the current interaction (Edwards & Potter, 1992, 1993) with regard to culpability, reasons for actions and the reasons for describing them one way or another (Edwards, 1997).

I therefore suggest that this narrative attends to accountability in that the consequences of, and reasons for, participating in the reconciliation trip to Japan are made available to participants in this setting. The narrative serves not only to claim the speaker's reconciliation, but also to show how it happened as part of reconstructing two contrasting ways of being. The speaker's narrative does not 'explain' the meaning of reconciliation per se, but by describing two events, the sense of Freddie being different from whom he was in the first instance is generated.

The story begins with a detailed description of where and when the event took place (ll. 1–2) and who the protagonist is (l. 1). The first few lines (ll. 2–5) consist of 'scene-setting' talk (Buchanan & Middleton, 1995), providing rich and vivid descriptions of a seemingly ordinary setting—Freddie (i.e. the speaker) sitting in the open air and drinking tea in a park. Buchanan and Middleton (1995), drawing on the work of Sacks (1984, 1992) and Schrager (1983), point to the way in which talking about the past works to locate us in this event, setting up a context for an extraordinary experience to happen (for an extended application, see Wooffitt, 1992).

Using the concept of 'experience narrative', Schrager (1983) explains the complicated relationship between the narrator and the events described. This involves not only the narrator's own position with respect to what happened, but also the stances he or she takes toward other participants in the events. In pointing out the social nature of narratives, he says: 'When we tell about the past, we incorporate the experiences of a multitude of others along with our own; they appear in what we say through our marvellous capacity to express other perspectives' (Schrager, 1983, p. 80). One of the ways in which these multiple experience can be incorporated into narrative is through the use of reported speech (e.g. Buchanan & Middleton, 1993; Buttny & Williams, 2000; Holt, 1996; Leudar & Antaki, 1996). By focusing on Freddie's use of reported speech, we can see how he incorporates multiple perspectives that are both his, at different times, and those of others.

Freddie adopts two different positions in terms of his attitude toward Japanese people in this narrative, and his identity as an ex-POW is clearly relevant. In other words, in this two-part narrative of the past, the speaker's two different positions are made available, which serve to account for a re-alignment of his position toward Japanese people. The speaker's different positions are situated in two different occasions in past encounters with Japanese families—'ten years after the war' (l. 2) and 'some years later' (l. 47). The multiple positions (or voices) converge in this narrative by way of reported speech, warranting his claim about change and generating a sense of his redemption from the troubling past.

Using reported inner speech, this narrative shows that the speaker's identities are situated in two different moments of the past in his post-war life. The utterance 'oh my god, is that Japanese' (ll. 6–7), signalling Freddie's perturbation with the presence of the Japanese in the park, formulates his recognition that what he was seeing in the park might present trouble. This is made available from the position of Freddie-in-the-past. The speaker however immediately undermines this first-hand judgement made during the encounter in the park. Why? Because the recipients of the story (others present in the interview) could come back and point out that his judgement was hastily formed, mistaken, or biased without having a valid way of confirmation. Therefore, he manages such a possibility precisely (ll. 7–9: 'because they could be Chinese or Thai or any').

This is an example of 'stake inoculation'—the way interests (in this case the speaker's) are oriented to in the production of versions of events (Potter, 1996). This utterance is designed for those hearing the story, the recipients, and enables Freddie to establish the rationality of his initial judgement. His use of reported inner speech, and his subsequent gloss on it, shows the recipients that at the time of the encounter he was predisposed to see people as Japanese even when there were other possibilities ('but to me they were Japanese'), but also demonstrates that he is now aware of the irrationality of this predisposition. Freddie thus not only positions his former self as having being wary of Japanese people ('Oh my God'), but positions his current self as being reflexively able to see the problematic status of this wariness.

On line 15 Freddie relates how he then overheard an utterance, 'Oi, koi', and this utterance assured him that the family he saw at the park was indeed Japanese. 'Oi koi' has a heavy interactional currency. It is a form of imperative, the English equivalent of '[Hey] you! Come [here]!' as the speaker provides his gloss on the utterance and checks with the Japanese participants in the interview (i.e. Maki and the interviewer). In l. 20, his acknowledgement of 'Oi, koi' ('I know that') constitutes Freddie as someone who knows this language, but for him it is also the language of the POW camp, making his identity as a former POW relevant. There is audibly a sense of 'then-ness' or 'there-ness' in the way that this Japanese expression is used in the story and how Freddie constructs his hearing of it in the park. 'Oi koi' opens up an array of experiences in the camp—characterized by captivity, austerity, and work under surveillance, in which language of this kind was routinely used.

The use of 'Oi koi' provides an interesting juxtaposition of two events in two different times, in both of which he is faced with the Japanese people. With his 'half' reluctance in turning around (l. 23), Freddie signals a delicate issue of him facing the Japanese in his post-war life. The description from l. 23 onward, which details the sequence of actions of the Japanese couple's photo-taking, constructs the situation as one in which he could offer to take photos for this family. This action of offering to take photos is formulated as a normative action for him (ll. 33–41). It is indicated that he even thought about offering to take a photo then. Using an internal dialogue (thinking to himself), two different Freddies in two different times—what he normally is and the exception to it—are described in ll. 43–45. The speaker formulates this action as a missed opportunity, as a morally problematic 'regret' (ll. 45–46). Here, what he considers normative is made questionable. The voice of aversion and resistance to the possible action of kindness (i.e. to offer to take a photo) in line 44, 'no, why should I', is dramatically presented in a hushed voice. This creates a conflict between two voices (Freddie-in-the-park and Freddie-as-a-moral-being) in which the troubling experience with the wartime past warrants Freddie's failure of action. In other words, hearing the language of the camp reveals a discrepancy between who he normally is and the way he acted at that particular post-war time.

Reported speech in this story mobilizes his own inner voice and the voices of others linked to the troubling war-related past, rhetorically formulating the conflict Freddie had within himself about the Japanese family at the park—whether he should offer to take a photo or not. The rest of the story recounts a second occasion on which this photo-taking action became relevant, and on this occasion Freddie was redeemed from the regret.

Reconfiguring the Past in Storytelling

For some narrative researchers, this story might be analysed rather differently from the discursive analysis produced here. For example, they might examine formal structural properties of narratives in relation to their social functions (e.g. Labov, 1972; Labov & Waletzky, 1967). Labov (1972) suggests that a fully formed oral narrative of personal experiences has a six-part structure—abstract, orientation, complicating action, evaluation, resolution, and coda. Indeed, the narrative analysed here has this very structure, yet the application of the structure prevents us from looking at a relational aspect of storytelling. In taking a discursive approach, Edwards's (1997) criticism of the structural approach to narrative is relevant here:

> The analysis of narratives in the human and social sciences has mostly ignored the interactional business that people might be doing in telling them … and studies of narrative have tended to pursue generalized types and categories of narrative structure, rather than dealing with how the specific story content, produced on and for occasions of talk, may perform social actions in-the-telling. (Edwards, 1997, pp. 265–266)

Edwards views narrative as an outcome of social interaction. Thus, we look not only at the story content, but also at the place of narrative in the social organization of conversation in which multiple positions are identified and a particular kind of person is developed and constructed within a particular storyline, in a particular interactional setting. The first episode, when Freddie did not go to the family to offer to take a picture, is a missed opportunity for Freddie. The speaker formulated it as a regret, moralizing his past failure of action in two relational ways. One way is that Freddie-now acknowledges Freddie-then as failing to act to his own standards of conduct. This is a reflexive evaluation of self, marking himself as a different kind of person from the one he was in the past. The other is by way of talking to the others present at the interview. The telling of this narrative makes this missed opportunity both personally and publicly significant for Freddie-now and the interview participants, and sets up the need for redemption.

The telling of narrative allows the participants, including the speaker, to re-evaluate his actions and interpret the story. Moral sensibility—the right way to act—was not just a matter for Freddie then, but it was made a matter for the other participants in the interview talk. The telling of narrative is what might be termed an accomplishment of moral accountability, in which the speaker accounts for a moral failure of his past conduct and his overcoming this failure located in a different time and place. The past events told are not fixed in time and place, but rather are made available for the discursive practice of moral accountability.

It is important to note that this analysis is concerned with the way in which the narrative was told in relation to who was hearing the story and how it was construed.

Therefore, the trajectory of the told events was not a fixed inbuilt feature of the story; it is a constructed element in the social organization of the past. Although seemingly minimal, what the listeners are doing (even though they say very little) can be understood as interactionally significant. The narrative unfolds, utterance by utterance, turn by turn, to the participants. Freddie's formulation of redemption affords his claim for reconciliation in the narrative form of accountability. We view the speaker's redemption not as an inherent, pre-designed element of the story. The analysis highlights the social nature of the storytelling as it positions morality and remembering of the past as things that transcend the conventional notion of the past as fixated in time and place. Morality and remembering thus are to be considered social activities, rather than mental activities that take place in the individual mind. In identifying the way in which Freddie constructs his narrative through a delicate choreography of positions—of both himself and others—a moral sensibility *emerges* in the unfolding of the narrative, rather than being represented in the story in an *a priori* fashion.

We may see a culturally appropriate moral principle at work here, but such a principle is not based on a single universally reduced logic of morality. For instance, Freddie did not have to get up and take a photo for the family in the park (it may be perfectly appropriate not to interfere in the family affair there). This was not expected of him in the first place. His action in the park was turned into a failure and regret in the way he told the story, making relevant his identity as an ex-POW and his knowledge of some basic Japanese that he learned in the POW camp. By way of telling the narrative, managing potential critiques and comebacks from the listeners, the speaker-Freddie achieved reconciliation, illustrating what it means for him to relate to Japanese people in the post-war era.

In this chapter, I have approached an examination of reconciliation in terms of positioning. Analysing the use of positioning, I have suggested that reconciliation is not a once-and-for-all settlement of the problematic past. Rather, it is a dynamic process in which participants discursively achieve reconciliation, whilst constituting moral accountability and mobilizing relevant identities and formulating (and reformulating) the past. I have illustrated the use of reported speech as a specific device for constructing a vivid representation of past events, and as a way of constructing emotions and moral dilemmas, and—ultimately—for narrating a redemptive change. This change is, however, a rhetorical effect emerging from discursive practice. The approach to studying reconciliation outlined here does not therefore involve merely the task of defining and evaluating who has reconciled, and with what. Instead, the discursive analysis illustrated here has detailed the delicately negotiated positions emerging from the interview talk, and the resolution of a moral quandary constructed for himself by the speaker which, ultimately, allows him to warrant his claim of having been redeemed.

Taking a discourse-analytic approach to the work of positioning, it has been shown that the narrative is a place where the discursive accomplishment of reconciliation takes place in social interaction, rather than in the mind of an individual. We can free ourselves from the structural treatment of narratives by considering that this narrative itself does not have a particular a priori moral principle. The moral sensibility of the story was up for grabs by the participants, both the speaker and the listeners. The analysis examined this dynamic, flexible, interactional process—the joint construction and sense-making of events and experiences. The discursive approach to reconciliation provides a way to empirically examine the reconciliation process by focusing on language use and positioning, identifying participants' discursive reconfiguring of the world, and seeking possibilities of being otherwise.

Appendix: Transcription notation (A)

The transcription convention used in the chapter has been developed by Gail Jefferson for the purposes of conversation analysis (see Atkinson & Heritage, 1984).

[ ]	Speech overlap
[	Overlap begins
↑↓	Vertical arrows precede marked pitch movement, over and above normal rhythm of speech.
<u>Underlining</u>	Signals vocal emphasis
CAPITALS	Mark speech that is obviously louder than surrounding speech
°I know it°	'degree' signs enclose obviously quieter speech
( )	Inaudible, indecipherable utterance, uncertain hearing
(0.4)	Pause (in seconds and/or tenths of a second)
(.)	A micropause, hearable but too short to measure.
((text))	Additional comments from the transcriber, e.g., gesture, context or intonation comments by the transcriber
she wa::nted	Prolonged syllable or sound stretch
hhh	Audible aspiration or laughter
.hhh	Audible inhalation

Yeh, Commas indicate that the speaker has not finished; marked by fall-rise or weak rising intonation,
as when enunciating lists.

y'know?	Question marks signal stronger, 'questioning' intonation, irrespective of grammar.
Yeh.	Periods (full stops) mark falling, stopping intonation ('final contour'), irrespective of grammar, and not

necessarily followed by a pause.

bu-u-	Hyphens mark a cut-off of the preceding sound
>he said<	'greater than' and 'lesser than' signs enclose speeded-up talk.
<he said>	'lesser than' and 'greater than' signs enclose slower talk.
solid.= =We said	Latched utterance (no interval between them)
Sto(h)p i(h)t.	Laughter within speech is signalled by h's in parentheses.
heh heh	Voiced laughter. Alternatively, some laughter of Japanese speakers were transcribed as haha, hehehe.
uh um	Filler between words. Alternatively 'er,' 'erm', and 'ah' 'ehh' are used.
Oi koi	Italicised words are of Japanese origin.

References

Abado, A. (1990). The speech act of apology in political life. *Journal of Pragmatics, 14*, 467–487.
Antaki, C., Billig, M., Edwards, D., & Potter, P. (2003). Discourse analysis means doing analysis: A critique of six analytic shortcomings. *Discourse Analysis Online, 1*(1). Retrived from https://extra.shu.ac.uk/daol/articles/open/2002/002/antaki2002002-paper.html
Antaki, C., & Widdicombe, S. (Eds.). (1998). *Identities in talk*. London: Sage.
Asmal, K., Asmal, L., & Suresh, R. R. (1997). *Reconciliation through truth: A reckoning of apartheid's criminal governance* (2nd ed.). Cape Town: David Philip Publishers.
Benwell, B., & Stokoe, E. (2006). *Discourse and identity*. Edinburgh: Edinburgh University Press.
Brecke, P., & Long, W. J. (1999). War and reconciliation. *International Interactions, 25*, 95–117.
Bruner, J. S. (1990). *Acts of meaning*. Cambridge, MA: Harvard University Press.
Buchanan, K., & Middleton, D. J. (1993). Discursively formulating the significance of reminiscence in later life. In N. Coupland & J. F. Nussbaum (Eds.), *Discourse and lifespan identity* (Vol. 4, pp. 55–80). Newbury Park: Sage.
Buchanan, K., & Middleton, D. (1995). Voices of experience: Talk, identity and membership in Reminiscence groups. *Aging and Society, 15*, 457–491.
Buttny, R. (1993). *Social accountability in communication*. London: Sage.
Buttny, R., & Williams, P. L. (2000). Demanding respect: The use of reported speech in discursive constructions of interracial contact. *Discourse & Society, 11*, 109–133.
Cole, M. (1990). Preface. In D. Middleton & D. Edwards (Eds.), *Collective remembering* (pp. vii–vix). London: Sage.
Coleman, P. G. (1999). Creating a life story: The task of reconciliation. *The Gerontologist, 39*, 133–139.
Davies, B., & Harré, R. (1990). Positioning: The discursive production of selves. *Journal for the Theory of Social Behavior, 20*, 43–63.
Edwards, D. (1997). *Discourse and cognition*. London: Sage.
Edwards, D., & Potter, J. (1992). *Discursive psychology*. London: Sage.
Edwards, D., Potter, J., & Middleton, D. (1992). Toward a discursive psychology of remembering. *The Psychologist, 5*, 441–455.
Edwards, D., & Potter, J. (1993). Language and causation: A discursive action model of description and attribution. *Psychological Review, 100*, 23–41.
Edwards, D., & Potter, J. (2001). Introduction to discursive psychology. In A. M. McHoul & M. Rapley (Eds.), *How to analyse talk in institutional settings: A casebook of methods* (pp. 12–24). London: Continuum International.
Gibney, M. (2008). *The age of apology: Facing up to the past*. Philadelphia, PA: University of Pennsylvania Press.
Green, R. H., & Ahmed, I. I. (1999). Rehabilitation, sustainable peace and development: Towards reconceptualisation. *Third World Quarterly, 20*, 189–206.
Harré, R. (2012). *Positioning theory: Moral dimensions of social-cultural psychology*. In J. Valsiner (Ed.), The Oxford handbook of culture and psychology. Oxford: Oxford University Press.
Harre, R., & Moghaddam, F. M. (Eds.). (2003). The self and others: Positioning individuals and groups in personal, political, and cultural contexts. Westport, CT: Greenwood Publishing Group..
Harré, R., & van Langenhove, L. (1991). Varieties of positioning. *Journal for the Theory of Social Behaviour, 21*, 393–407.
Harré, R., & van Langenhove, L. (Eds.). (1998). *Positioning theory: Moral contexts of international action*. Oxford: Blackwell Publishers.
Harré, R., & Van Langenhove, L. (1999). Reflexive positioning: Autobiography. In R. Harré & L. Van Langenhove (Eds.), *Positioning theory: Moral contexts of intentional action* (pp. 60–73). Oxford: Blackwell.
Henriques, J., Hollway, W., Urwin, C., Venn, C., & Walkerdine, V. (Eds.). (1984). *Changing the subject: Psychology, social regulation and subjectivity*. London: Methuen.

Hollway, W. (1984). Gender difference and the production of subjectivity. In J. Henriques, W. Hollway, C. Urwin, L. Venn, & V. Walkerdine (Eds.), *Changing the subject: Psychology, social regulation and subjectivity* (pp. 227–263). London: Methuen.

Holt, E. (1996). Reporting on talk: Direct reported speech in conversation. *Research on Language and Social Interaction, 29*, 219–245.

Ide, R. (1998). 'Sorry for your kindness': Japanese interactional ritual in public discourse. *Journal of Pragmatics, 29*, 509–529.

Krondorfer, B. (1995). *Remembrance and reconciliation: Encounters between young Jews and Germans*. New Haven, CT: Yale University Press.

Labov, W. (1972). *Language in the inner city: Studies in the Black English vernacular*. Philadelphia, PA: University of Pennsylvania Press.

Labov, W., & Waletzky, J. (1967). Narrative analysis. In J. Helm (Ed.), *Essays on the verbal and visual arts* (pp. 12–44). Seattle: Washington University Press.

Leudar, I., & Antaki, C. (1996). Discourse participation, reported speech and research practices in social psychology. *Theory & Psychology, 6*, 5–29.

Middleton, D., & Brown, S. D. (2005). *The social psychology of experience: Studies in remembering and forgetting*. London: Sage.

Middleton, D. J., & Edwards, D. (Eds.). (1990). *Collective remembering*. London: Sage.

Murakami, K. (2001). *Revisiting the past: Social organisation of remembering and reconciliation*. Unpublished PhD thesis. Loughborough University, UK.

Murakami, K. (2012). *Discursive psychology of remembering and reconciliation*. Hauppauge, NY: Nova Science Publishers.

Murata, K. (1998). Has he apologized or not?: A cross-cultural misunderstanding between the UK and Japan on the occasion of the 50th anniversary of VJ day in Britain. *Pragmatics, 8*, 501–513.

Norval, A. J. (1998). Memory, identity and the (im)possibility of reconciliation: The work of the Truth and Reconciliation Commission in South Africa. *Constellations, 5*, 250–265.

Potter, J. (1996). *Representing reality*. London: Sage.

Potter, J. (2003). Discourse analysis and discursive psychology. In P. M. Camic, J. E. Rhodes, & L. Yardley (Eds.), *Qualitative research in psychology: Expanding perspectives in methodology and design* (pp. 73–94). Washington, DC: American Psychological Association.

Potter, J., & Wetherell, M. (1987). *Discourse and social psychology: Beyond attitudes and behaviour*. London: Sage Publications.

Pratt, A., Elder, C., & Ellis, C. (2001). 'Papering over the differences': Australian nationhood and the normative discourse of reconciliation. In M. Kalantzis & B. Cope (Eds.), *Reconciliation, multiculturalism, identities: Difficult dialogues, sensible solutions* (pp. 135–147). Altona, VIC: Common Ground Publishing.

Retzinger, S. M. (1991). *Violent emotions: Shame and rage in marital quarrels*. Newbury Park: Sage Publications.

Sacks, H. (1984). On doing "being ordinary". In J. M. Atkinson & J. Heritage (Eds.), *Structures of social action: Studies in conversation analysis* (pp. 413–429). Cambridge: Cambridge University Press.

Sacks, H. (1992). *Lectures on conversation*. Oxford: Blackwell.

Schiffrin, D., Tannen, D., & Hamilton, H. E. (Eds.). (2003). *The handbook of discourse analysis*. Oxford: Wiley-Blackwell.

Schrager, S. (1983). What is social in oral history? *International Journal of Oral History, 4*, 76–98.

Shotter, J. (1991). The social construction of remembering: A rhetorical-responsive account. *Activity Theory, 9*, 26–31.

Swartz, L., & Drennan, G. (2000). The cultural construction of healing in the Truth and Reconciliation Commission: Implications for mental health practice. *Ethnicity & Health, 5*, 205–213.

Tavuchis, N. (1991). *Mea culpa: Sociology of apology and reconciliation*. Stanford, CA: Stanford University Press.

Thomas, D., & Seely, J. B. (2011). *A new culture of learning: Cultivating the imagination for a world of constant change*. Charleston, SC: Createspace.

Tutu, D. (1999). *No future without forgiveness*. London: Rider.

van Langenhove, L., & Harré, R. (1993). Positioning and autobiography: Telling your life. In N. Coupland & J. F. Nussbaum (Eds.), *Discourse and lifespan identity* (pp. 81-99). Newbury Park: Sage.

Vangelisti, A. L. (1992). My fault or yours? (Book review). *Contemporary Psychology, 37,* 1314.

Wetherell, M., Taylor, S., & Yates, S. J. (Eds.). (2001). *Discourse as data: A guide for analysis*. London: Sage.

Wooffitt, R. (1992). *Telling tales of the unexpected: The organisation of factual discourse*. Hemel Hempstead: Harvester Wheatleaf.

Young, N. (2012). The representation of conflict in modern memory work. In S. Gibson & S. Mollan (Eds.), *Representations of peace and conflict* (pp. 245–262). Basingstoke: Palgrave Macmillan.

Part III
Refuge and Migration

Chapter 10
Discursive Psychological Research on Refugees

Steve Kirkwood and Simon Goodman

Introduction

Peace and violence are at the core of understanding the topic of refugees. In this chapter, we will explore discursive psychological research relating to refugees and asylum seekers, including the relationships between notions of place, identity, danger, and safety, the construction of asylum seekers and refugees as 'threats', refugees' and asylum seekers' accounts of racism and violence, and the way in which harsh aspects of the asylum system are justified or criticised. We will end by examining how discursive psychology can contribute to understanding present-day issues in the form of the European refugee 'crisis'. Most of the examples we draw on are based in the UK, although some are from other countries, such as Australia and France. Data extracts are reproduced with their original transcription conventions, usually Jeffersonian notation (Jefferson, 2004). Our overall argument is that the topic of refugees has inherent relevance to peace psychology, and discursive psychology offers a way of understanding how refugees and asylum seekers are constructed through discourse, the consequences of which are a matter of life or death. As we will show, one ironic aspect of this subject is that arguments in favour of peace may be used in ways that prevent refugees from finding the peace they seek.

By definition, refugees are people who have fled danger in search of safety; and definitions are important, for only by demonstrating that they were forced to flee can refugees avail themselves of the legal protections afforded by asylum systems. More

S. Kirkwood (✉)
The University of Edinburgh, Edinburgh, UK
e-mail: s.kirkwood@ed.ac.uk

S. Goodman
Coventry University, Coventry, UK

© Springer Nature Switzerland AG 2018
S. Gibson (ed.), *Discourse, Peace, and Conflict*, Peace Psychology Book Series,
https://doi.org/10.1007/978-3-319-99094-1_10

specifically, the United Nations 1951 Convention Relating to the Status of Refugees defines a refugee as someone who:

> owing to well-founded fear of being persecuted for reasons of race, religion, nationality, membership of a particular social group or political opinion, is outside the country of his [*sic*] nationality and is unable or, owing to such fear, is unwilling to avail himself of the protection of that country; or who, not having a nationality and being outside the country of his former habitual residence as a result of such events, is unable or, owing to such fear, is unwilling to return to it.
> (UNHCR, 2010)

This means that only certain *people*, with certain *motivations*, who have moved between certain *places*, are able to gain such protection. 'Asylum seeker' is the term often applied to those who have submitted an application for asylum and have yet to have a determination of their case, whereas the term 'refugee' is often (although not exclusively) applied to those who have received formal recognition of their refugee status.

Contemporary Western discourse on refugees is characterised by ambivalence and hostility towards refugees, with moments of compassion (Kushner, 2006). In particular, public and political discourse on refugees tends to question the motivations of refugees, often defining them as economic migrants who are moving between countries on a voluntary basis, rather than because they have been forced to flee (Every & Augoustinos, 2008; Goodman & Speer, 2007). Such characterisations work to question the validity of their status as refugees, presenting them as not needing protection and as having questionable moral attributes, including allegedly entering potential host countries to take advantage of welfare provision, support services, healthcare, and job opportunities, while abusing the asylum system and the generosity of the host society (Every & Augoustinos, 2008). These discourses work to limit the obligations of host societies towards refugees while maintaining the moral status of the people and nations that support such views. They do this through removing the people under discussion from the group of 'genuine refugees', instead portraying them in other ways, such as 'economic migrants', 'bogus asylum seekers', 'criminals', and 'terrorists' (Lynn & Lea, 2003; Malloch & Stanley, 2005; Zetter, 2007).

Notions of peace and violence feature in multiple ways in relation to discourse regarding refugees. In particular, refugees are defined by having fled certain places, and those places are defined by violence. In this way, the discursive constructions of people and place can be seen as mutually constitutive (Kirkwood, McKinlay, & McVittie, 2013a). Defining someone's country of origin as a place of violence, death, persecution, and threat constitutes the individual as a person who has been forced to flee and is therefore in need of protection. Similarly, defining oneself as an individual who has been forced to flee renders the country of origin as a place of threat. In this regard, the official definitions of refugees are extremely important: only certain types of violence and danger count when it comes to being treated as a refugee. For instance, economic hardship, no matter how great, tends not to be accepted as a legitimate reason for leaving a country, and indeed drawing on such accounts—what is presented as 'seeking a better life'—can be treated as rendering the individuals concerned as morally dubious (Kirkwood & McNeill, 2015; Long, 2013).

These discourses are important for understanding the structural violence relating to immigration systems. That is, discourses that delegitimise refugees and reinforce the need for tighter borders, greater security, increased use of detention and forced removal, and other punitive responses to asylum seekers, such as enforced destitution, work to create and reinforce structural violence against those seeking to move between nations. These effects include keeping people in, or returning people to, countries where their lives, rights, and well-being are harmed, through war, harassment, torture, persecution, and other forms of hardship. It also makes things more dangerous for those attempting to move between countries, particularly when forced to use illicit and unsafe means, risking harm, abuse, and death, such as is clear in the increasing number of deaths in the Mediterranean in recent years and people who die when stowing away on transport (Kassar & Dourgnon, 2014; Perkowski, 2016; Spijkerboer, 2007). Moreover, even those who cross borders to a supposed safe country may find their experiences are far from safe. They may experience abuse, destitution, detention, and intrusive surveillance in the host countries (Spicer, 2008; Stewart & Mulvey, 2014), all of which demonstrates the extent to which immigration systems constitute forms of institutionalised violence and perpetuate social injustice.

Notions of violence and peace feature heavily in political discourse regarding refugees. Those who support the plight of refugees may make reference to the violence that is present in particular countries that produce refugees, highlighting the need of certain nations to recognise that violence, support refugees, and potentially consider other types of intervention—whether diplomatic or military—to address underlying causes (Every & Augoustinos, 2008; Kirkwood, 2017). In political and lay discourse, as well as the accounts from refugees themselves, references to racism are important for understanding how these notions are advanced, justified, or challenged. For instance, politicians may present others as racist in order to justify greater support for refugees; equally, those arguing for less support for refugees, or indeed arguing that supposed refugees are in fact not refugees, will present themselves as not racist (Every & Augoustinos, 2007). This is also evident in lay discourse. People discussing refugees may debate the extent to which certain responses to refugees do or do not constitute racism (Goodman, 2010; Goodman & Burke, 2010). In their own accounts of racism, refugees carefully manage the implications of whether their experiences do or do not constitute racism, given that making accusations of racism is generally treated as 'taboo', and may be particularly sensitive for those reliant on protection in the host society (Kirkwood, McKinlay, & McVittie, 2013b). Accounts of violence and racism therefore function to justify particular responses to refugees as well as supporting or challenging certain forms of social relations.

Constructions of Place, Identity, Safety, and Danger

Given that refugees are defined as having crossed borders fleeing persecution, the notion of place is central to their identities and therefore their recognition as refugees (and the rights that this involves). In this regard, the notion of 'place-identity' is helpful for understanding this topic. Place-identity was developed as a concept by Proshansky, Fabian, and Kaminoff (1983, p. 59) and defined as a 'sub-structure of the self-identity of the person consisting of, broadly conceived, cognitions about the physical world in which the individual lives'. Their definition treated place identity as a cognitive and affective concept. Dixon and Durrheim (2000) reworked the concept in terms of discursive social psychology, treating it in terms of the way that notions of place are discursively constructed and how relations between places and people are constituted through language. Applying this concept is a helpful way of examining issues relevant to refugees from a discursive psychological perspective.

Fleeing persecution and violence is seen as an essential aspect of being treated as a 'genuine' refugee. This means that comparisons between places based on their levels of danger or safety can function to treat people in these terms, such that people are considered in relation to their need to flee and be provided with asylum. For instance, Kirkwood et al. (2013a) illustrated that the extent to which people discuss countries in economic terms (i.e., European countries such as the UK as being wealthy and asylum seekers' countries of origin as being poor) similarly positions people as being motivated by economic concerns. In this way, refugees are repositioned as 'economic migrants' given the logic of an argument that emphasises economic issues and assumes that people are motivated by these considerations. Conversely, framing the discussion in terms of danger and safety can work to construct asylum seekers' countries of origin as dangerous places, whereas host societies are presented as relatively safe, which positions asylum seekers in terms of their need to find safety and constitutes their identity as refugees (Kirkwood, Goodman, McVittie, & McKinlay, 2015).

Clearly, the extent to which a refugee's country of origin is presented as sufficiently dangerous as to justify fleeing is a core consideration in terms of their legitimacy as a refugee. Constructing a country as extremely dangerous works to construe someone from that country as a 'genuine refugee'. It is worth noting that the Convention definition of a refugee makes reference to a 'well-founded fear of being persecuted' (UNHCR, 2010), which contains both 'subjective' aspects (the 'fear') and 'objective' aspects (the fear being 'well-founded'). Edwards (2005) refers to these as the 'subject side' and 'object side' of accounts. Both of these aspects are identifiable in refugees' accounts of their countries of origin. In terms of the 'object side' of such accounts, these may focus on details of extreme violence and death, particularly among those close to the refugee, such as family members, as a way to work up such accounts as 'real' and such dangers as potentially affecting the speaker (Kirkwood et al., 2015). Constructing countries of origin as places where killing is commonplace and death is inevitable works to constitute asylum seekers as needing to flee in order to survive, as being in need of protection, and as being justified in leaving their homes in search of safety. In terms of the 'subject side' of such accounts, these may make reference to what may happen to them if they return to their countries of origin as well as including displays of emotion, as shown in the following extract from an interview with an asylum seeker:

> It was very very cold I feel so many difficulties because of all those

experiences but I can't go back because I can go back and I would die. I
can't go back because if I go back I would die I do not have a good life
here ((crying)) as I struggle a lot
(Goodman, Burke, Liebling, & Zasada, 2015, p. 333)

This account draws on notions of place in a way that not only justifies the need for
the speaker to leave their country of origin but also works to legitimise her reasons
for being in the host country. More specifically, stating 'I can't go back because I
can go back and I would die' emphasises the imminent danger related to the country
of origin, thereby implying that fleeing was necessary. Moreover, stating 'I do not
have a good life here' implicitly argues against the suggestion that she has come to
the UK 'merely' to improve her life or for economic benefits. Crying during the
interview reinforces the emotional dimensions of the account, providing a bodily
demonstration of the suffering that she experiences, as well as potentially the real
fear she feels in relation to the idea of returning home and perhaps the loss of this
possibility (see Ladegaard, 2014). The way that places are presented—particularly
refugees' countries of origin, but also potential host societies—are clearly tied up
with refugees' identities, and both connect with the legitimacy of their need for
asylum (Kirkwood et al., 2013a).

Constructing Refugees as an Economic Threat to the Host Nation

It has been demonstrated that people construct themselves as refugees by working
up descriptions of conflict, and that they seek refuge in other countries because they
claim this move offers peace (e.g. Goodman et al., 2015). However, there are a
number of ways in which refugees are presented as being threatening to host
countries, including being economically threatening, culturally threatening and
representing a risk of violence and further danger in the form of terrorism and
criminality. All of these representations work together to construct refugees as
either in potential, or real, conflict with host nations, which in turn all work as
arguments against hosting refugees.

The suggestion that refugees represent an economic threat is one of the most
commonly used arguments against supporting refugees and there are several ways
that this economic threat is constructed. As mentioned above, the most common of
these is to suggest that refugees aren't really refugees at all and that instead they are
economic migrants. Van Dijk (1997) demonstrated how the term 'economic refugee'
was first used in the 1980s to refer to Tamil refugees arriving in Europe. This term
works to blur the distinction between refugees (this category would certainly apply
to Tamils who were fleeing Sri Lanka's civil war) and those who are travelling for
purely financial reasons (who would not be refugees).

Lynn and Lea (2003, p. 432) referred to a strategy of 'differentiating the other' in
which refugees are split into either 'genuine' or 'bogus' asylum seekers where only

'genuine' ones are deemed worthy of support. They present an example of a letter written to the editor of the British *Daily Express* newspaper:

> No-one begrudges genuine refugees a home, but when bogus ones are housed within weeks and UK citizens, black and white, are left to rot in hostels, it does seem unfair?
> (Lynn & Lea, 2003, p. 433)

Central to this strategy of distinguishing 'genuine' from 'bogus ones' is the suggestion that there is no animosity towards 'real' refugees, and only towards those who are cheating. This means that speakers can protect themselves against potential accusations of being uncaring towards refugees. Instead, it is only those who are presented as cheats, and therefore who have no right to be in the host country, that are presented as problematic. These 'bogus' refugees are positioned as being a threat to the existing community because they are taking away valuable resources from needy people in the host nations (here those 'rotting' without a home) rather than because of any hatred or ill-will towards refugees. In Lynn and Lea's example, using a common strategy for defending against claims of racism (Augoustinos & Reynolds, 2001; Augoustinos, Tuffin, & Rapley, 1999; Kirkwood, Liu, & Weatherall, 2005), the writer refers explicitly to 'UK citizens, black and white' in an attempt to demonstrate that this is a general threat for the entire population and that this opposition is nothing to do with racial conflict (as it is equally problematic for black and white citizens). The nature of this conflict is therefore presented as an economic one about finite resources and as about fairness.

There are many further examples of refugees being presented as economic migrants rather than people seeking safety. Goodman and Speer (2007) developed van Dijk's (1997) and Lynn and Lea's (2003) work on categories by showing that participants in debates about refugees topicalize and argue about which categories should be applied, with critics of supporting refugees claiming that refugees are really migrants while supporters of refugees claim that these opponents wrongly call refugees economic migrants. Goodman and Speer also demonstrated that speakers often mix up talk about economic migration and refugees so that the distinction between the two comes to be blurred. This means that on top of 'distinguishing the other' where refugees are split into two types, there is also a blurring of the other so that all refugees can come to be viewed as, at least potentially, economic migrants. This means that all refugees come to be presented as a potential threat to the host nation's economy.

The idea that refugees represent an economic threat was also prominent in the work of Goodman and Burke (2011) who showed that economic arguments were presented as a key reason for people to oppose asylum seekers. They present the following example, where there was a discussion of whether or not opposing asylum seeking constitutes racism:

> if you just h- (0.4) oppose the who:l:e (0.6) asylum seeking system >s- in the (sense) that< (0.5) oh:: (.) they're living off us >in the sense that< it's all basic- (.) on (0.4) based around (0.8) the whole financial bit of it then I suppose that's not really being raci:st you're just saying y'know (.) they're living off us
> (adapted from Goodman & Burke, 2011, p. 114)

This explanation is presented as a legitimate reason for people to oppose asylum seeking, and this is especially favoured over racism as an explanation for opposing asylum seeking. This tells us two important things about refugees and conflict. First, it is accepted that there *is* a conflict between refugees and settled communities. This conflict takes the form of an economic one, where refugees are viewed as a potential financial drain on the established population. Second, it is also widely accepted by most that the conflict with refugees is nothing to do with racial conflict, but is an economic one. Central to this argument is the idea of an 'us and them distinction' (Goodman, 2005; Lynn & Lea, 2003; Mehan, 1997; Van Der Valk, 2003; van Dijk, 1997; Verkuyten, 2005) which is a well-documented strategy in the presentation of refugees. This works to present refuges as unlike, and different from, 'us', citizens of the host nation. This construction of difference, when coupled with the idea that an outside 'they' are living off 'us', frames the relationship between the two (constructed) groups as very much one of economic conflict: people will oppose 'them' because of the cost they will have for 'us'.

Constructing Refugees as Criminals and Terrorists

It has therefore been demonstrated that refugees, who are regularly presented as falsely claiming to be refugees, are presented as being in economic conflict with citizens of host nations. Their acceptance into host nations is therefore challenged because it represents a financial threat to settled communities. There are, however, other ways in which refugees are presented as threatening to host nations, in which they are presented as criminal and potential terrorists.

The suggestion that many refugees are in fact 'bogus', already implies that refugees may be of poor moral character and gives credibility to the category 'illegal immigrant', which is a term that some opponents of asylum seeking attempt to impose onto refugees (see Goodman & Speer, 2007 for examples of this). However, other representations of refugees go further by suggesting that they are likely to be criminals, and in some cases even terrorists.

Leudar et al. (2008, p. 198) show how crime and asylum seekers are often spoken about together to create what they describe as a 'salient category-bound activity applicable to both'. This means that the category of asylum seeker comes to contain an element of criminality. They provide two examples that support this, the first from the newspaper the *Daily Mail*:

> Blunkett: Asylum seekers may be tagged
>   Asylum seekers could be electronically tagged rather than locked up in detention cen-
> tres, Home Secretary David Blunkett said. A new Asylum Bill will bring in powers which
> would largely be used to tag asylum seekers whose applications have been rejected.
>   (adapted from Leudar et al., 2008, p. 198).

This first example is a report of the then UK Home Secretary announcing a new policy that failed asylum seekers should have electronic tags, rather than be detained.

While the policy is presented as a relatively lenient one, it nevertheless suggests that asylum seekers may well be criminals and criminalises asylum seekers whose claims are not approved. In UK law, it is unusual to detain any innocent person (refugees are the exception, see Kirkwood et al., 2015 for more on detention), so references to detention already imply some level of criminality. This means that even the downgraded reference to 'tags' (which are often associated with punishment for anti-social behaviour) still implies that these rejected asylum seekers are somehow criminal. Indeed, the whole notion of a 'failed' or 'rejected' asylum seeker supports the idea of the 'bogus' or 'illegal' asylum seeker, even though this may say more about the way asylum claims are decided. Leudar et al. (2008) show how this idea of criminality also permeates the talk of citizens of host countries as well as the media, as can be seen in this next example:

> if they're true and they are really going to get persecuted in their own country (.) by all means yes (.) come here but if they're just here so they can get their their (.) they get this they get that money, housing, blah blah, send them back (2.0) er: when they do come
> (adapted from Leudar et al., 2008, p. 201)

This example contains a number of the anti-refugee arguments that have been presented so far, including that refugees are split into 'genuine' and 'bogus' types, who all present a potential economic threat to the host country. In addition to this is the suggestion that refugees have criminal characteristics, and so may be claiming asylum purely to defraud the country they are claiming in.

While the threat of crime is a serious one that can be used to justify the exclusion of refugees, the threat of terrorism is potentially even more serious and worrying for a host nation. Presenting refugees as constituting this type of threat can therefore work to effectively construct refugees as undesirable, thereby positioning them as problematic and dangerous. The following example, a *Mail Online* headline, shows how refugees come to be associated with a threat of terrorism:

> Paris terrorist ringleader bragged he entered France among a group of 90 jihadis and claimed the migrant crisis had made it easy for them to travel freely across Europe
> (Goodman, Sirriyeh, & McMahon, 2017, p. 110)

This headline followed a major terrorist attack in Paris, which represents a serious point of conflict which is constructed here as being between Jihadis and Europeans (and Paris in particular, where many people were killed and injured in the attack). While this particular headline doesn't refer to refugees (or asylum seekers), the reference to 'migrant crisis' nevertheless makes refugees salient, as the 'crisis' (which as Goodman et al., 2017, demonstrate was called different things at different points) implies refugees (especially those fleeing the Syrian civil war). Therefore refugees (and migrants more generally) come to be associated with the ongoing threat of terrorism to Europe. This is yet another way in which refugees come to be presented as in conflict with host nations and as a threat to their safety. When refugees are presented as a threat, this justifies attempts to prevent their right to asylum.

Constructing Refugees as a Threat to Community Cohesion

Refugees can also be presented as a threat to community cohesion within a host country, which means that opposing refugees can be viewed as being in the interests of cohesion, and therefore supportive of peace and to prevent conflict. Goodman (2008) showed how political figures argued over the extent to which harsh government policy on refugees protected social cohesion. The following example, which comes from a televised debate programme about asylum laws, contains an exchange between the (then) incumbent government minister, Beverley Hughes, the chair and Andrew Green, the head of an anti-immigration pressure group:

Hughes: I think we are radically transforming the system and generating public confi-
          dence in er in the asylum system .hhh it's a fundamental prerequisite for us its
          fundamental for community relations in this country [lines omitted]
Chair: Well Andrew Green I saw you waving there er er they're talking tough (.) are
          they getting tough enough?
Green: [lines omitted] I think there's a real risk (.) that people are going to feel that (.)
          er immigration and asylum is not under control (.) and this is what is undermin-
          ing confidence in the system (.) and doing great damage I think to community
          relations

(adapted from Goodman, 2008, pp. 113–114)

It can be seen how the government minister claimed that policy (described by the chair as 'talking tough') works to support community cohesion, and then that the policy is criticised by the opponent of asylum for failing cohesion. While there is clearly disagreement between Hughes and Green, they are both in agreement that community cohesion is a positive thing that should be protected, and that perceptions of the asylum system can have a negative impact on them. The outcome is that community cohesion, a lack of conflict, comes to be the stated aim of policy makers, and the suggestion that asylum seekers (or migrants) may damage this comes to be established as factual and goes unchallenged. This means that the positive benefits of community cohesion come to be placed above offering safety to refugees (see Mulvey, 2010).

Connected to the idea that community cohesion is a positive thing that can be damaged by asylum seekers is the threat of far right extremists gaining support. This argument can be seen in the following example from a BBC news report on a speech by the (then) Conservative leader, Michael Howard:

but if you look at the opinion po:lls (.) asylum and immigration is right up there now as one
of the issues people are most concerned about (.) and if the Tories don't talk about it (.)
there's a whole lot of people to their right (.) who will and are talking about it (.) so I think
(.) they're (.) they may be concluding (.) that the bigger risk (.) er is not raising it

(Goodman, 2008, pp. 117–118).

In this example, asylum is presented as a matter of concern for the public, so much so that failure for the UK's centre right Conservative party ('Tories') to deal with these concerns may allow the extreme right to garner support. This argument is therefore very similar to the one about community cohesion: if political parties do not address legitimate concerns about asylum seekers coming to the UK, then far right parties (who represent a threat to community cohesion) may come to power. These are circular arguments, because they suggest that mainstream parties need to act like extremist parties, to prevent extremists from coming to power and therefore protecting community cohesion. However, despite this, they nevertheless give credibility to harsh anti-asylum policies, which harm refugees, on the grounds of preventing conflict and maintaining peace.

Accounts of Racism and Violence Towards Refugees

Once asylum seekers and refugees reach a potential host society, this does not mean that they now find themselves to be safe. Unfortunately, experiences of racism, violence, and abuse can occur even once refugees have found asylum (Kirkwood et al., 2013b; O'Nions, 2010; Spicer, 2008; Stewart & Mulvey, 2014). This challenges the notion that host societies do in fact constitute places of safety. So how are such issues accounted for? Members of the general public may talk about racism in ways that suggest: (1) that such negative views are generally limited to a minority of people; (2) that such views are due to ignorance; and (3) that if they only knew the truth about asylum seekers and refugees they would not hold such negative views (Kirkwood et al., 2015). This is illustrated in the following extract:

P5   […] as I say you still have your minority (.) that em
       (1.5) don't agree wi' people being here
SK   mm-hmm
P5   (0.8) but not even that, I think it's just that they're ignorant (.)
SK   right=
P5   =and don't know the facts

(Kirkwood et al., 2015, p. 123)

Suggesting that such views are only held by a minority of people works to discredit the views through implying that they are not widely held. It also works to protect against the suggestion that the host society is generally racist. Suggesting that the views are due to ignorance works to reduce the culpability of the people who hold such views. Stating that people would have more favourable views if they knew the truth suggests that positive change is possible while also working to legitimise the presence of refugees and asylum seekers (i.e., the true reasons are reasonable and would not provoke negative reactions if people only knew them). In this way, such accounts of racism manage the troubling existence of antagonism in the host society while working to portray it as a place where asylum seekers and refugees can belong.

As well as considering how local people talk about racism in the host society, it is important to consider how asylum seekers and refugees produce accounts of this antagonism, as shown in the following extract:

R10   asylum-seekers (1.2) mm (1.0) I know most of it's it's not- it's got nothing to do with
       your (0.8) colour or y-
SK   °oh okay°

```
R10   mm
SK    °right°
R10   it's just a minority those who just think that (1.6) you just coming in to get a job or
      things like that heh
```
(Kirkwood et al., 2015, p. 131)

As shown in this extract, as with accounts from people who are not refugees, asylum seekers and refugees may also produce accounts that portray racism as due to ignorance. Moreover, racism may be presented in a way that minimises its nature and extent and reduces the culpability of those who display it. For instance, accounts of verbal abuse and physical violence may present these as unintentional, as not directly targeted at the asylum seekers and refugees themselves, or as not being racially motivated. This is shown in the above extract, as the speaker states 'it's got nothing to do with your (0.8) colour', where the racist motivation is directly negated. Moreover, those who express the antagonism are portrayed as a 'minority' and under a potentially mistaken apprehension: 'those who just think that (1.6) you just coming in to get a job'.

As shown by Kirkwood et al. (2013b), where the potentially racially motivated aspects of violence are referred to, the account can be presented in a way that refers to the racist aspects only indirectly ('my skin'), presents it in a tentative way ('maybe'), embeds it in a narrative that portrays the racist explanation as a 'last resort', and overall presents the speaker as reluctant to interpret the violence as racially motivated:

```
R9    yeah certainly so and I say I did nothing to nobody [as far as I know
INT                                                        [mmm yeah
R9    you know and I will say maybe (.) this thing is is my skin (1.0) yeah and I hate to say
      that
```
(Kirkwood et al., 2013b, p. 756)

Providing accounts in this way works to minimise the interpretation of the host society as being a racist place and also works to emphasise the potential for asylum seekers and refugees to belong. It also sensitively manages the 'taboo' on making accusations of racism (Goodman & Burke, 2010), in this case about a society that has provided protection from persecution, albeit not providing an environment that was free from harm. However, it also raises questions about how racism is to be identified and addressed, as both general members of the public and asylum seekers and refugees may talk about racism in ways that make it seem to disappear.

Justifying and Criticising Harsh Responses to Asylum Seekers

Some responses to asylum seekers are very harsh, particularly detention, destitution, and forced return. The use of such measures risks portraying the host society as uncaring towards refugees and undermining the values of protection. For this reason, justification for these responses depends on presenting them as reasonable and portraying asylum seekers as people who are deserving of such responses. At one level, this can be done through distinguishing between 'genuine refugees' and others who neither need nor deserve asylum; this avoids the portrayal of treating 'refugees' harshly. Going further, as illustrated above, those who are on the receiving end of such processes can be portrayed as 'criminals' and as presenting a danger to the host society, which justifies the use of such practices in order to 'protect' the host society, while depoliticising the response (Malloch & Stanley, 2005). That is, by being 'illegal' these people are deemed deserving of any harsh punishment they receive.

Equally, these responses can be challenged or resisted, particularly through construing these responses as immoral by the host society's standards or as inappropriate given refugees' nature. For instance, Lynn and Lea (2003) demonstrated that detention centres could be portrayed in ways that emphasised their harsh nature and thereby troubled their existence in the host society, as shown in the following extract from a letter to the editor of the *Daily Mail*:

> While awaiting classification by the authorities, suspicious foreigners are to be 'concentrated' into 'reception centres', many of them isolated camps with high-security perimeter fences. For now we are told that this is for their own protection – but barbed wire works both ways, and what might happen in these camps under an even more Right-wing government?
>
> (Lynn & Lea, 2003, p. 442)

In this extract, references to 'isolated camps', 'high-security perimeter fences', and 'barbed wire' works to present the 'reception centres' in ways that emphasise their harsh nature. Moreover, reference to 'concentrated' and 'camps' and 'even more Right-wing government' make implicit connections with Nazi concentration camps (Lynn & Lea, 2003), further reinforcing the severity of this response to asylum seekers and presenting it as morally questionable. Relatedly, Lynn and Lea (2003, p. 442) presented materials in which asylum seekers were portrayed as 'children, pregnant women, the elderly, the ill and survivors of torture'. In this way, asylum seekers were constituted as those who are innocent, vulnerable, or otherwise in need of care. Similarly, Bates and Kirkwood (2013) showed how local activists who worked to stop dawn raids on asylum seekers in Scotland presented their accounts in ways that emphasised the harshness of the raids and the innocence of the asylum seekers. This included describing the dawn raids as involving 'armoured gear', 'helmets', 'handcuffs', and 'cages' whereas the asylum seekers were referred to as 'families' and 'little boys' in 'pyjamas' (Bates & Kirkwood, 2013, p. 25). Likewise, Kirkwood et al. (2015, p. 168) illustrated how practitioners who support asylum seekers could present detention centres as 'prison' and asylum seekers as 'families', 'children', and 'babies'. Overall, this works to present the response to asylum seekers as incompatible with their nature, in the sense that asylum seekers are construed as those who are innocent or vulnerable, whereas the responses are portrayed in ways that emphasise their harsh nature. In this way, such accounts do moral work (Drew, 1998), criticising the use of detention and other punitive responses through highlighting their immoral nature. By humanising refugees and asylum seekers, such accounts work to challenge and resist existing policies towards refugees, particularly those that are likely to have negative effects on those subject to them (Kirkwood, 2017).

A Present-Day Example: Peace, Conflict, and the European Refugee 'Crisis'

As the examples above demonstrate, issues around refugees have been topical throughout the twenty-first century. However, since the start of the 'refugee/migrant crisis' in April 2015 it has become more topical than ever, dominating much of the news in the UK and Europe in the summer of 2015 and beyond. The 'crisis' itself was partly the result of the civil war in Syria and the destabilisation of Libya, so the causes of this event are deeply rooted in conflict, where people affected by the conflicts searched for peace and safety. Goodman et al. (2017) demonstrated how the naming of this 'crisis' in UK media fluctuated over time. It began as a 'Mediterranean Migrant crisis', which presented the problem as far away, and notably one involving migrants, rather than refugees. Next it became a 'Calais Migrant crisis', which suggested more of a threat to the UK. At this point, threatening imagery of 'migrants' was used which implied a risk of conflict. A major event that occurred during the 'crisis' was the publication of photographs of a 3-year-old Syrian boy, Alan Kurdi, who died attempting to reach the safety of Europe (see Byford, this volume). This event had a great impact on the representation of the 'crisis', resulting in the renaming of the 'crisis' from a 'migrant crisis' to a 'refugee crisis' in different countries (Goodman et al., 2017; Parker et al., 2018). This change, however, was short lived, as the 'crisis' came to be associated with terrorism, and soon reverted back to a 'migrant crisis'. The 'crisis' was always presented as one for Europe (or the UK) and never for the refugees themselves (Goodman et al., 2017).

Throughout the 'crisis' many of the previously established findings on the representations of refugees could be seen, alongside other representations that were new. First, the threat posed to host nations by refugees remained, so that opposition to supporting refugees continued. The following is an example of how the 'European migrant crisis' was presented by the BBC in August 2015:

> Thousands of migrants have died and many thousands more have been rescued after setting sail from Libya recently. Wednesday's rescue operation was one of 10 such missions currently taking place in the waters off Libya, the Italian coastguard said. … Ahead of the summit, Austrian Foreign Minister Sebastian Kurz told the BBC that current EU asylum regulations were not working. Earlier in the week, Macedonian police had to use stun grenades after thousands of migrants broke through police lines at the Greek border.
>
> (Parker et al., 2018)

From this example, it is clear that while refugees (referred to here as migrants, which works to delegitimise them) are in serious danger and are risking their lives, they nevertheless present a security concern for Europeans because they are being controlled with force in a situation that is presented as a violent conflict (indeed war analogies have been shown to present refugees negatively; Van Der Valk, 2003). Goodman et al. (2017, p. 108) also show how talk of conflict and violence can be used to describe the 'crisis', with an example from Channel 4 news: 'Plans to force European Union member states to receive a "fair" share of refugees seeking asylum in Europe are to be fought by the UK, in favour of deploying gunships to tackle trafficking gangs'.

During the brief period when the 'crisis' was referred to as a 'refugee crisis' there were generally more positive representations of refugees, who were humanised and more widely viewed as legitimate. This period coincided with an outpouring of public support for refugees. Kirkwood (2017) showed how the phrase 'human beings' was used by members of the UK parliaments to refer to refugees. This term works to remove the potential conflict between refugees and host communities and provides a more peaceful construction, where the 'us and them' distinction, so commonly used in anti-refugee talk, can be minimised, therefore constructing a superordinate category.

Nevertheless, there remained ways to challenge, and delegitimise refugees. As the 'crisis', and the reporting of Alan Kurdi's death demonstrated, the people affected by the 'crisis' were refugees fleeing conflict in search of safety. This meant that the common strategy of presenting refugees as illegitimate (i.e. economic migrants or 'bogus asylum seekers') was less readily available (although for some, including the UKIP leader Nigel Farage, this idea persisted; Nightingale & Goodman, 2016). Nevertheless, there was still scope to challenge the legitimacy of refugees when the UK government decided to allow a limited number of child refugees into the UK. Goodman and Narang's (under review) analysis of a discussion forum about this policy demonstrated that refugee children were presented as adults posing as children, and these adults were deemed to threaten peace in the UK, as can be seen in the following example:

> That poor young woman who was murdered in Sweden in January was working in a 'child migrant centre'. Her killer claimed to be 15 but has been deemed by the courts to be 'at least 18'. Her family say many of the 'children' are in their 20s.
>   (Goodman & Narang, under review)

This comment, like many others, works to challenge the claim that child refugees are really children and also presents these refugees as particularly dangerous and threatening. The debate about child refugees briefly became a major news story itself in 2016, when the tabloids ran headlines claiming that adults were getting into the UK posing as children, which demonstrates that even when it is clear that refugees are fleeing conflict, and even when debates turn to supporting children, who were shown to be vulnerable in the 'crisis', they can still be presented as a threat to the host nation, but in this case by shifting categorical boundaries from children to adults.

Conclusion

This chapter has demonstrated the important contribution that discursive psychology has made to understanding arguments about asylum seekers and refugees. It has been shown that discursive psychology allows for a detailed understanding of the ways in which refugees' countries of origin are debated so as to be either presented by refugees and their supporters as places of danger and war, or as places of safety but poverty by those arguing against them. Such constructions of place determine the identity of refugees, so they come to be seen as legitimate only when their countries of origin are accepted as places of conflict. Discursive psychology also illustrates how arguments over whether or not refugees should be accepted are grounded in the idea that refugees are a potential threat, in conflict with settled communities. This threat is presented as coming in the form of economic conflict, where refugees are presented as taking away resources from those already in the country. Refugees can be presented as even more threatening, in the form of being potential criminals or terrorists, and as constituting a threat to community cohesion, and therefore peace itself. What this means is that arguments about peace, conflict, threats, and safety are central to debates about whether or not refugees should be allowed access to host countries. Arguments that are based on the idea of protecting peace, can therefore be used to prevent people fleeing conflicts from accessing peace. Put simply, peace is used as an argument to prevent victims of wars from finding peace. By better understanding these arguments, discursive psychology offers the important potential to challenge these strategies for denying people peace.

References

Augoustinos, M., & Reynolds, K. J. (2001). Prejudice, racism, and social psychology. In M. Augoustinos & K. J. Reynolds (Eds.), *Understanding prejudice, racism and social conflict* (pp. 1–23). London: Sage.

Augoustinos, M., Tuffin, K., & Rapley, M. (1999). Genocide or a failure to gel? racism, history and nationalism in Australian talk. *Discourse & Society, 10*, 351–378. https://doi.org/10.1177/0957926599010003004

Bates, D., & Kirkwood, S. (2013). "We Didnae Do Anything Great…" discursive strategies for resisting detention and deportation in Scotland and the North East of England. *Refugee Review, 1*, 21–31. Retrieved from https://refugeereview.wordpress.com/2013/07/21/deportation/

Dixon, J., & Durrheim, K. (2000). Displacing place-identity: A discursive approach to locating self and other. *British Journal of Social Psychology, 39*, 27–44. https://doi.org/10.1348/014466600164318

Drew, P. (1998). Complaints about transgressions and misconduct. *Research on Language and Social Interaction, 31*, 295–325. https://doi.org/10.1207/s15327973rlsi3103&4_2

Edwards, D. (2005). Moaning, whinging and laughing: the subjective side of complaints. *Discourse Studies, 7*, 5–29. https://doi.org/10.1177/1461445605048765

Every, D., & Augoustinos, M. (2007). Constructions of racism in the Australian parliamentary debates on asylum seekers. *Discourse & Society, 18*, 411–436. https://doi.org/10.1177/0957926507077427

Every, D., & Augoustinos, M. (2008). "Taking advantage"or fleeing persecution? Opposing accounts of asylum seeking. *Journal of SocioLinguistics, 12*, 648–667. https://doi.org/10.1111/j.1467-9841.2008.00386.x

Goodman, S. (2005). Constructing asylum seeking families. *Critical Approaches to Discourse Analysis Across Disciplines, 1*, 36–50. Retrieved from http://cadaad.net/files/journal/CADAAD1-1-Goodman-2007-Constructing_Asylum_Seeking_Families.pdf

Goodman, S. (2008). Justifying harsh treatment of asylum seekers through the support of social cohesion. *Annual Review of Critical Psychology, 6*, 110–124. Retrieved from http://www.discourseunit.com/arcp/arcp6/goodman.pdf

Goodman, S. (2010). "It's not racist to impose limits on immigration": Constructing the boundaries of racism in the asylum and immigration debate. *Critical Approaches to Discourse Analysis, 4*, 1–17.

Goodman, S., & Burke, S. (2010). "Oh you don"t want asylum seekers, oh you're just racist': A discursive analysis of discussions about whether it's racist to oppose asylum seeking. *Discourse & Society, 21*, 325–340 https://doi.org/10.1177/0957926509360743

Goodman, S., & Burke, S. (2011). Discursive deracialization in talk about asylum seeking. *Journal of Community and Applied Social Psychology, 21*, 111–123. https://doi.org/10.1002/casp

Goodman, S., Burke, S., Liebling, H., & Zasada, D. (2015). "I can't go back because if I go back I would die": How asylum seekers manage talk about returning home by highlighting the importance of safety. *Journal of Community and Applied Social Psychology, 25*, 327–339. https://doi.org/10.1002/casp

Goodman, S., & Narang, A. (under review). "Sad day for the UK": The linking of debates about settling refugee children in the UK with Brexit.

Goodman, S., Sirriyeh, A., & McMahon, S. (2017). The evolving (re)categorisations of refugees throughout the "refugee/migrant crisis". *Journal of Community and Applied Social Psychology, 27*, 105–114. https://doi.org/10.1002/casp.2302

Goodman, S., & Speer, S. A. (2007). Category use in the construction of asylum seekers. *Critical Discourse Studies, 4*, 165–185. https://doi.org/10.1080/17405900701464832

Jefferson, G. (2004). Glossary of transcript symbols with an introduction. In G. H. Lerner (Ed.), *Conversation analysis: Studies from the first generation* (pp. 13–31). Amsterdam: John Benjamins Publishing Company.

Kassar, H., & Dourgnon, P. (2014). The big crossing: Illegal boat migrants in the Mediterranean. *European Journal of Public Health, 24*(Suppl. 1), 11–15. https://doi.org/10.1093/eurpub/cku099

Kirkwood, S. (2017). The humanisation of refugees: a discourse analysis of UK parliamentary debates on the European refugee "crisis.". *Journal of Community and Applied Social Psychology, 27*, 115–125. https://doi.org/10.1002/casp.2298

Kirkwood, S., Goodman, S., McVittie, C., & McKinlay, A. (2015). *The language of asylum: Refugees and discourse*. Basingstoke, UK: Palgrave Macmillan.

Kirkwood, S., Liu, J. H., & Weatherall, A. (2005). Challenging the standard story of indigenous rights in Aotearoa/New Zealand. *Journal of Community and Applied Social Psychology, 15*, 493–505.

Kirkwood, S., McKinlay, A., & McVittie, C. (2013a). The mutually constitutive relationship between place and identity: The role of place-identity in discourse on asylum seekers and refugees. *Journal of Community and Applied Social Psychology, 23*, 453–465. https://doi.org/10.1002/casp

Kirkwood, S., McKinlay, A., & McVittie, C. (2013b). "They"re more than animals': Refugees' accounts of racially motivated violence. *The British Journal of Social Psychology, 52*, 747–762. https://doi.org/10.1111/bjso.12007

Kirkwood, S., & McNeill, F. (2015). Integration and reintegration: Comparing pathways to citizenship through asylum and criminal justice. *Criminology and Criminal Justice, 15*, 511–526. Retrieved from http://crj.sagepub.com/content/15/5/511

Kushner, T. (2006). *Remembering refugees: Then and now*. Manchester: Manchester University Press.

Ladegaard, H. J. (2014). Crying as communication in domestic helper narratives: Towards a social psychology of crying in discourse. *Journal of Language and Social Psychology, 33*, 579–605. https://doi.org/10.1177/0261927X14538823

Leudar, I., Hayes, J., Nekvapil, J., & Turner Baker, J. (2008). Hostility themes in media, community and refugee narratives. *Discourse & Society, 19*, 187–221 https://doi.org/10.1177/0957926507085952

Long, K. (2013). When refugees stopped being migrants: Movement, labour and humanitarian protection. *Migration Studies, 1*, 4–26. https://doi.org/10.1093/migration/mns001

Lynn, N., & Lea, S. (2003). 'A phantom menace and the new apartheid': The social construction of asylum-seekers in the United Kingdom. *Discourse & Society, 14*, 425–452. https://doi.org/10.1177/0957926503014004002

Malloch, M. S., & Stanley, E. (2005). The detention of asylum seekers in the UK: Representing risk, managing the dangerous. *Punishment & Society, 7*, 53–71. https://doi.org/10.1177/1462474505048133

Mehan, H. (1997). The discourse of the illegal immigration debate: A case study in the politics of representation. *Discourse & Society, 8*, 249–270.

Mulvey, G. (2010). When policy creates politics: The problematizing of immigration and the consequences for refugee integration in the UK. *Journal of Refugee Studies, 23*, 437–462. https://doi.org/10.1093/jrs/feq045

Nightingale, A., & Goodman, S. (2016). Building the barricade: Public and media debates of the refugee crisis. *The Psychologist* Retrieved from https://thepsychologist.bps.org.uk/migration-crisis-psychological-perspectives

O'Nions, H. (2010). What lies beneath: Exploring links between asylum policy and hate crime in the UK. *Liverpool Law Review, 31*, 233–257. https://doi.org/10.1007/s10991-010-9080-y

Parker, S., Naper, A., & Goodman, S. (2018). How a photograph of a drowned refugee child turned a migrant crisis into a refugee crisis: A comparative discourse analysis. *For(E)Dialogue, 2*(1), 12–28.

Perkowski, N. (2016, March). Deaths, interventions, humanitarianism and human rights in the Mediterranean "migration crisis.". *Mediterranean Politics, 9395*, 1–5. https://doi.org/10.1080/13629395.2016.1145827

Proshansky, H. M., Fabian, A. K., & Kaminoff, R. (1983). Place-identity: Physical world socialization of the self. *Journal of Environmental Psychology, 3*, 57–83 https://doi.org/10.1016/S0272-4944(83)80021-8

Spicer, N. (2008). Places of exclusion and inclusion: Asylum-seeker and refugee experiences of neighbourhoods in the UK. *Journal of Ethnic and Migration Studies, 34*, 491–510. https://doi.org/10.1080/13691830701880350

Spijkerboer, T. (2007). The human costs of border control. *European Journal of Migration and Law, 9*, 127–139. https://doi.org/10.1163/138836407X179337

Stewart, E., & Mulvey, G. (2014). Seeking safety beyond refuge: The impact of immigration and citizenship policy upon refugees in the UK. *Journal of Ethnic and Migration Studies, 40*, 1023–1039. https://doi.org/10.1080/1369183X.2013.836960

UNHCR. (2010). *Convention and protocol relating to the status of refugees*. Retrieved from http://www.unhcr.org/uk/3b66c2aa10

Van Der Valk, I. (2003). Right-wing parliamentary discourse on immigration in France. *Discourse & Society, 14*, 309–348. https://doi.org/10.1177/09579265030143004

van Dijk, T. A. (1997). Political discourse and racism: Describing others in Western parliaments. In S. H. Riggins (Ed.), *Language and politics of exclusion* (pp. 31–64). London: Sage. https://doi.org/10.2307/1961773

Verkuyten, M. (2005). Accounting for ethnic discrimination: A discursive study among minority and majority group members. *Journal of Language and Social Psychology, 24*, 66–92. https://doi.org/10.1177/0261927X04273037

Zetter, R. (2007). More labels, fewer refugees: Remaking the refugee label in an era of globalization. *Journal of Refugee Studies, 20*, 172–192. https://doi.org/10.1093/jrs/fem011

Chapter 11
Unlawful, Un-cooperative and Unwanted: The Dehumanization of Asylum Seekers in the Australian Newsprint Media

Martha Augoustinos, Clemence Due, and Peta Callaghan

Introduction

Recent international crises such as the war in Syria have led to the displacement of unprecedented numbers of people seeking refuge in western liberal democratic nations in Europe and elsewhere. The response by western governments and their citizens to those seeking asylum and refuge has been polarized, making their resettlement a highly politicized issue that has divided host communities. The politics of border control and the treatment of asylum seekers has dominated Australian domestic politics and public discourse since 2001. During this period, asylum seekers arriving by boat have been represented in the public domain as threatening to Australia's sovereignty, security, and culture in ways that have recently been evidenced in Europe by the Syrian crisis. We draw on notions of border security, the state of exception and *homo sacer*, to demonstrate how a discursive psychological approach to peace psychology can contribute to understanding how dehumanizing representations of asylum seekers serve to maintain intergroup conflict by turning debates about how to respond to displaced persons seeking refuge—an issue that is essentially about humanitarian responsibilities in a globalized world—into national and international anxieties about border security and control that function to position asylum seekers as 'enemies' of the nation state.

M. Augoustinos (✉) · C. Due · P. Callaghan
University of Adelaide, Adelaide, SA, Australia
e-mail: martha.augoustinos@adelaide.edu.au

© Springer Nature Switzerland AG 2018
S. Gibson (ed.), *Discourse, Peace, and Conflict*, Peace Psychology Book Series,
https://doi.org/10.1007/978-3-319-99094-1_11

Border Security: Homo Sacer and the State of Exception

Given increasing concerns over mobility and growing numbers of people seeking asylum in western nations, a growing body of academic work has focused on the ongoing, and escalating focus on 'security' within countries such as Australia (McMaster, 2002; Pugh, 2004). Andreas (2003) argues that the nature of border control is changing from militarization and economic regulation to policing to ensure that 'undesirable' migrant groups are excluded from the nation-state, while simultaneously ensuring that access to the state is provided to those identified as 'desirable'. Thus borders function to define sovereign spaces according to supposed cultural similarities and norms, through which it becomes possible to segregate those who do not 'belong' from those who do (Carrington, 2006). Andreas (2003) further argues that this focus on 'security', involving rising budgets for border control, the use of military personnel, increased surveillance technologies, and punitive legislation surrounding unauthorized entries, represents a 'rebordering' of the state. This 'rebordering' involves a move towards policing, legitimated by discourses of 'dangerous mobilities' which functions to sort the unwanted from the wanted (Walters, 2006). Indeed, it has been argued that it is the ability to 'reborder the state' and to segregate people in this way that ensures that a state has sovereignty over its territory (Andreas, 2003; Carrington, 2006). As Fernandez, Gill, Szeman, and Whyte (2006) argue: 'Borders seem to be the clearest example of a social construction…in which open fields are suddenly turned into closed spaces. From the border I can define myself and the Other—a code of ownership and belonging' (p. 468). In relation to asylum seekers, such exclusion results in increasingly strict border security and protection methods and surveillance techniques to ensure that they cannot enter the state (Pickering, 2004). Borders, then, are intimately bound to the ability to maintain sovereign control of the State by virtue of their ability to be used to control who is able to enter.

Agamben (1998, 2005) argues that this process of inclusion and exclusion is critical in that it allows the sovereign to maintain their sovereignty. Forms of life not protected are referred to as depoliticized (as opposed to political life—most evidently citizens), and termed *homo sacer*, or 'bare life' (Agamben, 1998, 2005). Those who are considered *homo sacer* and are exempt from the law are frequently deferred to states of exception (Agamben, 1998). The state of exception is implicit in the idea of the nation-state, in that a sovereign power can employ or defer to a 'state of exception' in time of supposed crisis, in which the normal rule of law is suspended. In Australia, the state of exception has become refugee detention camps or 'centres' established for the containment of human beings considered *homo sacer*. The detention centre, as a state of exception, operates both externally to the sovereign law (in that it is exempt from the rule of law), while simultaneously perpetuating it by enabling the sovereign to control those who are excluded (Agamben, 1998). The detention center represents a space, both inside and outside the law (but in which the normal order is suspended), in which those deemed external or offending to the sovereignty of the nation-state can be contained (Perera, 2002).

The state of exception operates in reaction to both appeals to an emergency and a fictionalized notion of the enemy. In many instances, as Agamben argues, the state of exception is justified through recourse to *unlawfulness*. However, it is also through 'othering' of out-group members that exclusionary policies and the legitimization of detention can be justified. One such way in which asylum seekers are 'othered' is through practices of dehumanization.

Dehumanization

Dehumanization occurs when particular characteristics are either denied or attributed to a group of people based on their group membership, which allows others to perceive them as not fully human (Kelman, 1973). Dehumanization does not only occur on an individual level: institutions, the government, and the state can engage in systematic practices of dehumanization, treating non-citizens such as asylum seekers as less than human so that citizens will be more likely to support their detention, deportation, and the use of violence against them (Browning, 1992; Haslam, Bain, Douge, Lee, & Bastian, 2005; Livingstone-Smith, 2014). State-sanctioned enactments of systematic dehumanization such as the Genocide in Rwanda in 1994 and the Holocaust in Nazi Germany (1933–1945) are both cases in point (Alverez, 1997; Browning, 1992; Hagan & Rymond-Richmond, 2008; Kelman & Hamilton, 1989).

Dehumanization has been identified as stemming from essentialist thinking, whereby members of an out-group are depersonalized, deindividuated, delegitimized, made to look like children or animals, excluded from moral sensibilities, or denied essential human characteristics such as explicitly human emotions and shared values (Haslam, 2006; Haslam et al., 2005; Haslam, Rothschild, & Ernst, 2000, 2002; Rothbart & Taylor, 1992). While intergroup conflict can create the conditions for the dehumanization of out groups, it is not a necessary precursor for dehumanization (Kelman & Hamilton, 1989). Below we describe some of the ways in which dehumanization can occur.

Delegitimization usually comes from inter-ethnic conflict and is used to explain and justify the conflict and provides one's group with a sense of superiority (Haslam, 2006). *Moral exclusions and disengagement* refer to the ways in which out-group members' identities are deindividuated and any sense of their moral character is denied, thereby allowing for the justification of negative treatment, including violence or exclusion. This can also involve psychological processes like distancing, condescension, and technical orientation (Haslam, 2006). When out-groups are perceived to hold different *values*, they are subsequently perceived to lack humanity. This is particularly so for pro-social values, where dehumanized out-groups are perceived to lack what may be deemed more 'uniquely human' values, such as community or justice (Haslam, 2006).

Infra-humanization is a subtle form of dehumanization, whereby out-groups are denied an identity as *fully* human (Haslam & Loughnan, 2014). Specifically, infra-humanization focuses on the characteristics of intelligence, language, and 'secondary emotions' or 'sentiments'. Both positive and negative secondary emotions (such as joy or embarassment) are denied to out-groups, and this subtle form of dehumanization can occur independently of a negative evaluation of the out-group (Haslam & Loughnan, 2014). As such, out-groups may not be considered bad, or immoral, they are simply denied a full human identity. In addition, dehumanization occurs as a form of *objectification* of the other. Nussbaum (1999) proposed seven aspects of objectification: *Ownership and instrumentality*, which is expressed through treating others as commodities; *violability*, which allows for the violation of members of specific groups; *fungibility*, which involves viewing people as interchangeable; *inertness and rejection of autonomy*, reflected in a lack of agency and self-determination; and *denial of subjectivity*, which is similar to the concept of infra-humanization, and which allows particular emotions and experiences of others to be neglected. These mechanisms of dehumanization help to justify the denial of obligations for protection and rights (Alverez, 1997; Browning, 1992; Kelman & Hamilton, 1989; Nussbaum, 1999).

Dehumanization can arise out of both physical and symbolic acts of violence. According to Galtung (1990), violence is both a physical/psychological act of aggression, and simultaneously the legitimization of such acts. The legitimization of violence is constituted by aspects of a culture—such as religion, language, ideology, and knowledge systems—and is referred to by Galtung as *cultural violence* (Galtung, 1969, 1990). Moreover, cultural violence involves both *direct violence*, which includes the use of physical acts which result in physical and psychological harm; and *structural violence*, which is described as those acts embedded within cultural systems which result in exploitation, marginalization, and segregation (amongst others). Moreover, Bourdieu (1991) argued that the dehumanization of groups of people through acts of violence can impose a state of legitimacy of a given policy or social order, which includes discriminatory enactments such as dominance, unequal racial and ethnic hierarchies, and the lack of rights.

Tileagă (2007) demonstrated the ways in which dehumanization, delegitimization, and depersonalization can be re-conceptualized in discursive terms. In particular, descriptions of 'out-groups' can be constituted by moral boundaries that such groups are seen to transgress, positioning them outside of what is considered acceptable, civilized, and even 'normal' social behaviour, thereby legitimating exclusionary practices against such groups (Tileagă, 2007). We aim to demonstrate below how such practices of dehumanization can be evidenced in the language used in newsprint media when reporting on events and matters pertaining to asylum seekers, in particular, on unauthorized boat arrivals to Australia.

The Language of Asylum

Discursive psychologists have been at the forefront of systematically analysing how issues pertaining to asylum seekers and refugees are articulated in everyday talk and public discourse. As Kirkwood, Goodman, McVittie, and McKinlay

(2016) argue, the use of specific categories and terms to reference asylum seekers and their right to seek asylum is central to understanding how their relationship with members of the host country are developed and understood. Media reporting of what has become an increasingly contentious and polarized issue worldwide is central to how public debates about asylum seekers are framed and understood. There is now a significant body of discursive research demonstrating how the very terms commonly used by the media for the depiction of asylum seekers and refugees works to represent this group as deviant and criminal, specifically by reference to their supposed unlawfulness. For example, categories such as 'illegal immigrants', 'illegals', or 'queue jumpers' have been found to be ubiquitous, not only in media reporting, but also in political discourse in Australia (Every, 2006; O'Doherty & LeCouteur, 2007; Pickering, 2001; Saxton, 2003). Moreover, asylum seekers have been frequently constructed as 'bogus' and therefore not genuine refugees but rather economic migrants who are circumventing legitimate channels of entry (see Kirkwood & Goodman, this volume). As many have argued, these negative terms function to undermine the legitimacy of the status of asylum seekers as people who are genuinely escaping from threat and persecution. In this way, asylum seekers are frequently recast as threats to a nation's sovereignty over its borders. Such representations arguably function to strip asylum seekers of their humanity in order to legitimize increasingly restrictive border protection policies.

These findings have been mirrored in media research conducted in several English-speaking countries, including Australia (Every, 2006; O'Doherty & LeCouteur, 2007; Pickering, 2001; Saxton, 2003), the UK (KhosraviNik, Krzyzanowski, & Wodak, 2012; Kirkwood et al., 2016; Krzyzanowski & Wodak, 2009; Lynn & Lea, 2003; Messer, Schroeder, & Wodak, 2012), and Ireland (Coole, 2002; Haynes, Devereux, & Breen, 2006). Indeed, as Pickering (2001) argues, public discourse on refugees and asylum seekers predominantly revolves around maintaining the 'integrity' of the nation-state and its border security. In Australia, media coverage of asylum seekers and border security is often presented within metaphors of war, which explicitly position asylum seekers as on a different 'side' to the nation (Pickering, 2001). In this way, asylum seekers are implicitly represented as 'an enemy' of the nation, thereby justifying harsh border security measures such as mandatory detention in both on-shore and off-shore camps (including children) as a necessary response to this threat. Furthermore, border security is frequently represented as in a state of 'crisis', and in need of 'protection'; thus legitimating what could otherwise be considered the dehumanizing treatment of asylum seekers (Klocker & Dunn, 2003; Macken-Horarik, 2003; Pickering, 2001).

Discursive research has also highlighted that the media rarely gives a voice to asylum seekers or provides any context to the conditions that led to their displacement in their countries of origin. Asylum seekers are thus dehumanized by the language used to describe them as well as by their lack of voice in traditional media (Haynes et al., 2006; Klocker & Dunn, 2003; Pickering, 2001).

The Present Research

In previous research, we have demonstrated how nationalist rhetoric (O'Doherty & Augoustinos, 2008) and a neoliberal bureaucratic discourse (Lueck, Due, & Augoustinos, 2015) works together to position asylum seekers as undesirable to the host nation. In this chapter, we specifically focus on how practices of dehumanization are accomplished through the reporting practices of the newsprint media and the implications these constructions have for how asylum seekers are perceived by the wider polity. We argue that these dehumanizing practices not only contribute to the social exclusion or 'othering' of asylum seekers; they also facilitate and legitimate acts of direct and structural violence to control and restrict their mobility.

We specifically focus on a period of time in Australia's recent history (2009), where a combination of 'push' and 'pull' factors generated an increase in the number of boats arriving in Australian territorial waters carrying asylum seekers. The focus on this period of time allows us to examine the ways in which Australia's domestic political interests dominated media discourse about the large number of boat arrivals during this time, thereby allowing the government to cast those on board the boats as unlawful and therefore justify exclusionary policies and, more specifically, mandatory offshore detention on the Pacific islands of Manus and Nauru.

While previous research from Australia has mainly focused on media and political discourse related to asylum seekers under the Howard Government (primarily during 2001–2007), we will focus on representations of asylum seekers in the news media in relation to two incidents that occurred during the Rudd Labor Government. By the time Kevin Rudd became Prime Minister in 2007, unauthorized boats arriving in Australian waters had decreased from previous levels seen between 2001 and 2003, with just over 200 people arriving between mid-2004 and mid-2008 (Parliament of Australia, 2010). However, the end of the civil war in Sri Lanka led to a resurgence in boat arrivals in Australia in 2008–2009. By March 2010 the 100th boat arrived since the Rudd Labor government came to power in November 2007, carrying an overall total of around 4500 asylum seekers (van Onselen, 2010). This created a significant political problem for the Rudd government who came to power with a mandate to enact 'more compassionate' policies for unauthorized arrivals, such as the dismantling of the off shore system of processing asylum seekers (referred to as the 'Pacific Solution'), and ending the mandatory detention of children. The media and the government's political opponents on the right attributed the resurgence of boat arrivals in 2008 to the dismantling of these harsh policies, positioning Rudd and his government as directly responsible for producing a new 'crisis' which had to be managed (Fox, 2010).

The analysis will focus on two events that occurred in October 2009. The first of these occurred on 9 October 2009 when an Indonesian navy patrol vessel intercepted 255 asylum seekers travelling on the cargo vessel, the *Jaya Lestari 5,* after Australian Prime Minister Kevin Rudd reportedly phoned Indonesian President Susilo Bambang Yudhoyono requesting that he intercept the boat. Asylum seekers on the vessel were then escorted back to the Indonesian port of Merak where they refused to disembark. Once there, two spokespeople aboard the vessel, Sanjeev Kuhendrarajah, (commonly referred to as 'Alex') and a 9-year-old girl, Brindha, made public pleas for help.

The second incident occurred shortly after the *Jaya Lestari 5* was intercepted. On 18 October 2009, the Australian customs vessel the *Oceanic Viking* came to the aid of a boat carrying 78 asylum seekers that was in distress. The asylum seekers and crew were transferred to the *Oceanic Viking*, which then travelled to Indonesia where the asylum seekers on board also refused to disembark. Eventually, all asylum seekers had left the vessel by 17 November 2009, after reports of them receiving a 'special deal' to fast-track their claims instead of spending months, or even years, in Indonesian detention centres.

These two events were chosen for analysis specifically because they occurred during the period of the Rudd Labor government, which came into office advocating for more humanitarian policies in the treatment of asylum seekers. These incidents reignited heated debates within Australia concerning whether asylum seekers should be 'allowed' to come to Australia—thus demonstrating explicitly the enacting of national sovereignty in relation to attempts to maintain control over who crosses Australian borders. Given the hiatus of boat arrivals during the latter part of the previous Howard government—which was largely attributed to its harsh border protection policies—these incidents became highly politicized and made asylum seeker policies once again a highly salient issue of national and public concern.

Data and Analytic Approach

Data on Asylum Seekers Arriving by Boat

Data were collected from the twelve Australian daily newspapers with the highest circulation (Australian Press Council, 2007). These newspapers included: *The Herald Sun*, *The Daily Telegraph*, *The Courier Mail*, the *Sydney Morning Herald*, *The Age*, *The West Australian*, *The Advertiser*, *The Australian*, *The Australian Financial Review*, *The Mercury*, *The Canberra Times,* and *The Northern Territory News*.

A search was conducted on the Factiva data base, using the search keywords 'Oceanic Viking', 'Jaya Lestari', and '(Brind* OR Alex) AND ('asylum seeker*' OR refugee*)' for all articles published during the period 1/10/2009–30/4/2010.[1] A total of 699 articles were returned. Initial analysis identified 59 articles that were not relevant to the analysis (e.g. the customs vessel Oceanic Viking was also used to monitor Japanese whaling vessels in the southern oceans, which a number of these

---

[1] Although the asylum seekers had all disembarked by November 2009, we included the wider date range to April because the incident (along with a continued increase in boat arrivals during this time) was still being widely reported in the Australian media in the early part of 2010.

articles reported on). Across all three searches 146 articles were identified as 'soft' news articles and excluded from further analysis, leaving a total of 494 relevant 'hard news' articles for analysis.

'Hard' news is generally defined as news within which evaluative meanings or attributions by the author are constrained (White, 2006). Thus, 'hard' news is differentiated from other journalism that appears in newspapers such as editorials and opinion pieces, which are marked by commentary and individual viewpoints. Traditionally, this type of news reporting has claimed to be objective, and to only report the 'facts' (Fowler, 1991). While news reporting claims to be 'factual', the recent uptake of discursive methods of analysis, particularly in relation to the language of asylum, has increasingly challenged such claims to impartiality and neutrality (e.g. Kirkwood et al., 2016).

Discursive Psychological Approach

The discursive psychological approach we adopt in this chapter to analyse our data corpus draws upon the principles of both discursive psychology (Edwards & Potter, 1992; Potter, 1996; Wetherell & Potter, 1992) and rhetorical psychology (Billig, 1987, 1991). Both of these have as their focus the ways in which discourse and rhetoric actively construct particular versions of social reality, which in turn, accomplish particular social objectives such as explaining, justifying, blaming, and defending. This approach not only emphasizes the action-orientation of discourse, but also its rhetorical organization to undermine competing or alternative accounts. Specifically, the current analysis is concerned with identifying the discursive practices and rhetorical resources evident in the purported 'factual' reporting of the *Oceanic Viking* and *Jay Lestari* incidents. Our analysis examines how the asylum seekers on board these two vessels were represented and depicted by the newsprint media: what kinds of identities were made available to readers, how were they categorized and described, and how were their claims to asylum constructed? This involved examining the fine detail of descriptions and accounts of the two incidents, focusing on the use of recurring linguistic categories, terms, and metaphors, and how these functioned to dehumanize this group, thereby facilitating the justification of *homo sacer* and justifying the re-introduction of punitive government policies towards asylum seekers—namely, their forced removal from Australian territorial waters and their detention in the Pacific Islands of Manus and Nauru.

Analysis and Discussion

The newsprint media typically represented asylum seekers arriving by boat as 'illegal', as 'threatening', and as 'non-genuine'; all of which functioned to dehumanize them and to render them as undesirable to Australia. The analysis below will focus specifically on three recurring and pervasive patterns in the media reporting of the *Oceanic Viking* and the *Jaya Lestari* incidents: (1) the construction of asylum seekers from Sri Lanka as 'illegal' or 'unlawful', (2) how their voices were predominantly erased or rendered illegitimate, and (3) how the use of both direct and structural violence against those aboard these vessels were legitimated through these discursive constructions.

Unlawfulness

Constructions of 'unlawfulness' appeared regularly in our data corpus and represent the ways in which in-group/out-group categories are constructed in discourse to position certain groups as outside the law, demonstrating Agamben's (1998, 2005) concept of bare life (*homo sacer*). In doing so, the asylum seekers in question are seen as undeserving of state protection. These extracts frequently used categories of 'unlawfulness' to justify their exclusion from the Australian nation-state, thereby evoking the state of exception:

> Extract 1: 'Rudd Needs to Prepare for Next Boat', *The Courier Mail*; 31 October 2009, p. 21.
>
> 1   The combination of a bloody aftermath to a civil war in Sri Lanka - which has left
> 2   more than a quarter of a million displaced people in camps trying to flee the
> 3   country - and Australia's relatively humane and civilised treatment of asylum-
> 4   seekers who do reach this country have combined to set off a new wave of boats
> 5   carrying people trying their luck across the Indian Ocean or through Indonesia.
> 6   Australians want the Government to implement and observe a strong border-
> 7   protection regime, which deters people from going around the UN mechanisms for
> 8   seeking asylum. To allow the Sri Lankans automatic entry to an Australian facility
> 9   on Christmas Island or the mainland would be a signal of weakness – something
> 10 the Government understands. This is why Mr Rudd has no choice but to sit out the
> 11 stubborn refusal of those on the Oceanic Viking.

Although this article begins by describing the conditions from which the asylum seekers have fled, (line 1: the 'bloody aftermath' of the civil war in Sri Lanka), this is subsequently undercut by reference to Australians' desire to 'implement and observe a strong border protection regime' (6–7). The call for enhanced border protection is made through the voice of 'Australians' (6) to warrant this view as consensual. This positioning works in several ways. First, it utilizes a consensus warrant (Potter, 1996), locating those calls as something that 'Australians' want, and therefore as necessary within a democracy. Thus, border protection is positioned as the prerogative of majority opinion within a democratic nation state. Second, reference to 'Australians' in this way works to explicitly position asylum seekers as outside of, and as not belonging to, Australia.

This is contrasted with the asylum seekers who are described here as 'going around the UN mechanisms for seeking asylum' (7–8). This positions those seeking asylum as failing to observe UN protocols and as such, as acting unlawfully. The very phrase 'trying their luck' (5) implicitly suggests that asylum seekers arriving by boat are opportunistic and/or strategic, and are behaving outside of international standards, thus calling into question their morals and values. This suggests that there are 'proper' and 'improper' channels, but without reference to the many difficulties and barriers to accessing UN sanctioned channels for seeking asylum (Mares, 2001). By calling into question their genuineness and indeed their moral integrity, these asylum seekers are delegitimized (Haslam, 2006).

Correspondingly, the need for stronger border protection is worked up in the extract in the context of Australia becoming a 'soft touch' for asylum seekers. Specifically, the juxtaposition of the need to not be seen as 'weak' and the argument that Australia's treatment of asylum seekers is 'relatively humane and civilized' (3) works to support the claim that Australia can afford to be 'tougher' thereby justifying calls for the need for stronger border protection. Being seen to be 'weak' is constructed here as inherently undesirable, the implication being that such weakness will only attract more (unwanted) asylum seekers.

In the final line, asylum seekers are described as stubborn and recalcitrant ('stubborn refusal', 11): arguably qualities that do not represent 'refined' emotions (see Haslam & Loughnan, 2014) and which justify the punitive handling of asylum seekers by the Australian Government.

In Extract 2, asylum seekers are repeatedly referred to as 'unlawful entrants', again positioning asylum seekers as outside the law and as such undeserving of state protection.

Extract 2: 'Sri Lankans Face Detention Centre Lock-up', *The Courier-Mail*; 27 October 2009, p. 7.

1 A group of unlawful entrants at the centre of the nation's most heated
2 immigration debate since the 'children overboard affair' in 2001 will today face
3 the harsh realities of an Indonesian detention centre. The 78 Sri Lankans, who
4 have been on board the Australian Customs vessel Oceanic Viking for more than
5 a week, were last night near the port of Tanjung Pinang and were due to be taken
6 by Indonesian authorities when tides changed. With the men ending their hunger
7 strike - sparked after being told they would not be taken to Australia – reports
8 emerged that some detainees had been beaten by Indonesian guards. Foreign
9 Affairs Minister Stephen Smith said any allegations would be investigated.
10 However, the circumstances behind private negotiations with Prime Minister
11 Kevin Rudd and Indonesia to intercept the unlawful entrants earlier this month
12 has been attacked by the Opposition, which has argued 'Australia is the new
13 destination' for people smugglers because of relaxed immigration laws. Almost
14 40 unlawful boats have arrived in Australian waters since Labor won office.

The term 'unlawful' is used three times in this extract: 'unlawful entrants' (twice: 1, 11) and 'unlawful boats' (14). This discourse of 'unlawfulness' functions primarily to represent asylum seekers' claims to refuge in Australia as a criminal matter rather than a humanitarian issue that is mandated under the Refugee Convention, which states that refugees must be afforded protection in countries that they enter.

This construction explicitly positions the asylum seekers on board the Australian customs vessel and within Australian territorial waters as outside the law and therefore as *homo sacer*. As *homo sacer*, then, the people on board the *Oceanic Viking* can be represented as undesirable to Australia and as deserving of any harsh treatment that they receive (e.g. the 'harsh realities of an Indonesian detention centre' (3)).

Furthermore, the construction of these asylum seekers as outside the law further legitimizes calls for stricter border protection measures since, as unlawful, Australia has no obligation towards them. Thus, the extract effectively justifies the existence of a state of exception in relation to asylum seekers arriving by boat.

Extract 3 reports on the latest boat arrival in Australian waters carrying asylum seekers on New Year's Eve 2009/2010:

Extract 3: Tillett, A. 2010. 'Boat arrivals hit 8-year high', *The West Australian*; 2 January 2010, p. 12

1 The arrival of the 60th boat carrying asylum seekers on New Year's Eve has
2 marked the end of the biggest yearly influx of boat people since 2001.
3 [13 lines omitted]
4 Prime Minister Kevin Rudd has faced pressure to stop the surge in boats, with
5 the coalition accusing him of going soft on border protection and encouraging
6 people smugglers.
7 [1 line omitted]
8 The mass arrival of boat people has put a strain on Christmas Island's detention
9 camp and forced the Government to ship demountable huts and pitch tents to
10 ease overcrowding. More than 1400 people are now detained on the island, with
11 passengers from some of the latest boats still en route where they will undergo
12 identity, security and health checks. The Government's sensitivity to the boat
13 people issue has seen it cut a special deal to resettle 78 Tamils who refused for a
14 month to get off the Australian Customs vessel Oceanic Viking, and led to Mr
15 Rudd personally asking Indonesian President Susilo Bambang Yudhoyono to
16 stop another boat carrying almost 250 Tamils from reaching Australian waters.

The need to protect Australia's borders is made rhetorically self-sufficient in this extract by reference to the number of boats arriving in Australia in 2009 (1), and the number of individuals detained on Christmas Island (10). The use of terms such as 'biggest yearly influx' (2), 'mass arrival' (8), and 'the surge in boats' (4) all function to imply that these numbers are large, despite the fact that they are relatively small in relation to other forms of unauthorized arrivals.

The 'pull factor' (i.e. Rudd's 'soft' policy which has made Australia an attractive destination) is emphasized (4–5) at the expense of any mention of the 'push' factors that have led the asylum seekers to flee Sri Lanka. The privileging of pull factors in this way functions to deny the subjectivity of asylum seekers from Sri Lanka (Nussbaum, 1999) and their 'secondary emotions' (Haslam & Loughnan, 2014). The erasure of any political or social context of the plight of those seeking asylum at the end of the civil war does not allow for any emotional understanding (empathy) that could generate a connection to their essential humanity. The repeated use of the term 'boat people' in reference to the asylum seekers is notable in this respect. Instead, what this extract emphasizes are domestic political concerns, in particular the political pressures faced by Prime Minister Rudd from opposition claims that his 'soft' border protection policies are to blame for the increase in boat arrivals by encouraging 'people smugglers'. As such, the global responsibility of accepting asylum seekers is here hijacked by domestic Australian anxieties over border control and national security (discussed further below).

The article continues to construct the number of boat arrivals as excessive through the use of the term 'mass arrival' (8) and further emphasizes its excessive nature by describing Australia's lack of preparation and facilities to accommodate them. This construction of excessive numbers here achieves two things: the first is the creation of a sense of 'crisis' (Kirkwood et al., 2016). Secondly, this move allows Australia to be relinquished of its obligation to accept people who are seeking asylum by constructing the number of arrivals as extreme, again invoking Agamben's state of exception and implicitly justifying the detention of people who arrive by boat in detention centres. This continues with the use of the number '1400' (10) and the suggestion that there are more people still to arrive. Again, this construction invokes a sense of 'crisis', thereby legitimizing the representation of these asylum seekers as outsiders and therefore existing in a state of exception. Moreover, the three-part list, 'identity, security and health risks' (12) constructs people who arrive by boat as potential 'risks' to the nation and as such, undesirable.

The Voice of Asylum Seekers

The use of reported speech in newspaper reporting is a common and pervasive practice that is used to give a story credibility and legitimacy, providing human actors central to the story an opportunity to validate the reporter's claims and to serve as evidence of how events unfold (Krestel, Bergler, & Witte, 2008). During the Howard government era (2001–2007), significant restrictions were put in place to deny the Australian media access to asylum seekers who were mandatorily detained in onshore and off shore detention centres—restrictions that are still in place (Mares, 2001). Arguably this has restricted the media from presenting more humanizing representations of the plight of those seeking asylum. For example, the graphic portrayal of the lifeless body of 3-year-old Syrian refugee Alan Kurdi attempting to cross the Mediterranean made headlines in September 2015 and led to an unprecedented international response (see Byford, this volume). The *Oceanic Viking* and *Jaya Lestari* incidents represented rare occasions when the media had direct access to people seeking asylum in Australia, primarily because their boats were forcibly docked in Indonesia. Despite this access, the voices of asylum seekers remained largely disregarded in the newsprint coverage of these events. Even though refugees aboard the boats spoke directly to the media, particularly on the *Jaya Lestari 5* where spokesman Alex and 9-year-old Brindha were confined, the pleas made by them to Australia were rarely reported on within a human-interest frame, and their 'voice', when present, was insufficiently reported to create a context for their plight.

The use of reported speech in newspaper stories is also used by authors to align the reader with his or her views (Smirnova, 2009). In this sense, the author chooses speech that they consider necessary and important, thereby serving as a rhetorical technique to construct a particular version of events. In Extract 4, we demonstrate how the voice of Alex, the spokesperson for the people aboard the *Jaya Lestari*, is used in such a way that their defiance and the extreme nature of their plight are used to make salient the potential risk they pose to Australia's security.

Extract 4: Lewis, S. 2009, 'Refugee Tide is at Crisis Point', *Daily Telegraph*; 16 October 2009, p. 2

1 Australia will send police and hi-tech gear into several Asian hot-spots in a
2 frantic bid to stem the flow of asylum seekers. With secret intelligence warning
3 of a continuing surge in illegal arrivals, Australian Federal Police commissioner
4 Tony Negus held emergency talks with his Sri Lankan and Indonesian
5 counterparts this week
6 [2 lines omitted]
7 Sources said Cabinet was also expected to consider extra funding for border
8 protection, on top of the $650 million announced in the May Budget in a bid to
9 stem the tide.
10 [6 lines omitted]
11 More than 250 Tamil asylum seekers caught by Indonesia authorities en route to
12 Australia yesterday spent another day aboard their rickety cargo boat, refusing to
13 set foot on land in the west Java port of Merak until they receive asylum from a
14 Western country. "If you come see the situation in Sri Lanka where most Tamils
15 live ... you can see it's a lot worse than living on this ship", said the group
16 spokesman, known only as Alex.

Discourses of 'illegality' and asylum seekers as a 'threat' are explicitly drawn upon, with direct reference to a 'continuing surge in illegal arrivals' (3), and references throughout to 'secret intelligence' (2), 'border protection' (7–8), and the need for a police presence in areas from which asylum seekers may come (1). We again see here references to the scale of the economic cost to the government which is reported to be considering 'extra funding' on top of an already significant budget for border protection and security (7). Thus, unauthorized arrivals are not only represented as a threat to national security and sovereignty, but also an economic threat.

The reference to the 'rickety cargo boat' (12) implies the risk-taking behaviour of the asylum seekers with little consideration of the 'push' factors that led them to take such drastic measures, again providing no account that could help generate empathy from the Australian public. This group is constructed as both risky and defiant (11–14), with the voice of Alex used in this context to support this construction. Alex (16), who emphasizes the harsh living conditions in Sri Lanka in comparison to the conditions on the boat, could be viewed unsympathetically as displaying a flagrant disregard of Australian authorities: after all, he is the spokesperson for a group of people who have wilfully engaged in a 'standoff' with the Australian government, refusing to disembark the boat until they are assured asylum. In this way, the 'voice' of asylum seekers is not used to provide a human-interest frame that could serve to position them as deserving of an empathic response. Instead, this 'voice' is used to support constructions of this group as defiant and as a potential security threat.

In Extract 5, we can see how the pleas made by Brindha (a 9-year-old girl) are explicitly reported as 'staged', and thus their genuineness undermined:

In Extract 5, we can see how the pleas made by Brindha (a 9-year-old girl) are explicitly reported as 'staged', and thus their genuineness undermined:

Extract 5: Fitzpatrick, S. 2009, 'Hunger-Strikers Flag in Heat', *The Australian*; 17 October 2009, p. 7
    1   Alex has become the voice of the group largely because of his facility in the
    2   language, though others including a nine-year-old girl named Brindha have also
    3   played a role in the group's media strategy. Brindha was coached by adults on the
    4   boat to make an emotional plea as journalists were invited aboard for a staged
    5   visit on Wednesday night. "Please help us and save our lives; we are your
    6   children. Please think of us", she said.

Brindha's emotional plea to Australian journalists is described as 'coached' and as part of the asylum seekers' 'media strategy' (3). Such claims function to reinforce the view that asylum seekers attempting to arrive by boat are non-genuine refugees. Thus, despite the opportunity here to present asylum seekers on their own terms, the news media instead attributed Brindha's emotional pleas for help as a manipulative performance. The authenticity and legitimacy of Brindha's pleas are thus called into question. In this way, moral boundaries are drawn around the adults' behaviour— 'coaching' Brindha as part of a media strategy is arguably morally questionable behaviour. As Tileagă (2007) argues, such moral boundary work serves to justify exclusionary practices because such acts are treated as transgressions of 'normal' and acceptable moral standards.

Legitimating Force and Violence Against Asylum Seekers

Previous Australian research has demonstrated how nationalist rhetoric can be used to justify and legitimate the use of military action against asylum seekers (O'Doherty & Augoustinos, 2008). The next two extracts demonstrate how the dehumanization of asylum seekers legitimated the use of violence to forcibly remove them from the boat in the stand-off between them, the Australian government and Indonesian authorities:

Extract 6: Viellaris, R. 2009. Hopefuls in limbo refuse to co-operate—Facing a forceful exit, *The Courier-Mail*; 29 October, 2009, p. 4
    1   Unlawful entrants stranded off Indonesia could remain at sea until next month,
    2   leaving the Rudd Government with weeks of more political pain. As Australian
    3   officials were last night deciding whether to forcibly remove the 78 Sri Lankan
    4   unlawful entrants from the Australian Customs vessel Oceanic Viking, an
    5   Indonesian official warned they might not be allowed on the mainland until talks
    6   between Jakarta and Canberra at an APEC meeting on November 14.
    7   The unlawful entrants, who have spent nearly two weeks in limbo on the Customs
    8   ship, are refusing to co-operate with Indonesian officials.

Political interests rather than people's lives are made salient in Extract 6, with the emphasis being on the 'weeks of more political pain' for the Australian government and their Indonesian counterparts. The asylum seekers, once again referred to as 'unlawful entrants' (1, 4, 7), and their purported 'refusal to co-operate' (8) combine to construct them as difficult and uncooperative, thereby legitimizing the potential use of force to remove them from the boat. This construction of their motivations, rather than the desperate nature of their plight, arguably renders them inert and not in control of their own stories (Nussbaum, 1999). It is against the backdrop of the denial of the asylum seekers' subjectivity that the use of force and violence can be considered reasonable options.

A similar account is again invoked in Extract 7, where the possibility that a small number of the asylum seekers may have ties to the Tamil Tiger militant group is used as justification for the use of potential violence by Indonesian officials:

> Extract 7: Fitzpatrick, S. & Maley, P. 2010, Jakarta set to force refugees off boat, *The Australian*; 14 January, 2010, p. 2
> 1 Indonesia will force 240 Sri Lankan asylum-seekers into immigration detention by
> 2 the end of next week, at gunpoint if necessary, after admitting it has concerns there
> 3 are former Tamil Tigers militants among the group. As the opposition stepped up
> 4 its attack on the government over its decision to bring to Australia four Tamils
> 5 deemed a security risk by ASIO, Indonesian immigration officials said they
> 6 suspected the three-month standoff at the port of Merak was being directed by
> 7 Tamil militants on the boat. Tony Abbott yesterday called on the government to
> 8 explain what it would do with five Tamils whom ASIO deemed a threat to national
> 9 security.

Extract 7 draws on explicit constructions of violence to justify the forced removal of the asylum seekers ('by gunpoint if necessary'; 2). As with previous extracts, Extract 7 draws upon a discourse of unlawfulness (through reference to possible 'militant Tamil Tigers among the group'; 3, 7) to legitimate violence against this group. Of note is the justification of the forced removal of all 240 asylum seekers, despite only four from previous arrivals having been deemed a security risk. Thus, the dehumanized status of asylum seekers in general without any civil or human rights can be justified on claims that a small minority posed a security (read 'terrorist') threat. Once asylum seekers are constructed in this way (as a potential terrorist threat), Australia's refusal to accept them or to use violence against them becomes rhetorically self-sufficient, requiring no further warrant or justification.

Conclusion

In this chapter, we have argued that asylum seekers arriving by boat are routinely dehumanized in the mainstream news media, and that these discursive practices allow the government to justify policies such as the mandatory detention of asylum seekers in off-shore detention centers. This dehumanization was accomplished in several ways; specifically, by constructing asylum seekers as unlawful and therefore operating outside the normal processes for seeking asylum, and erasing or restricting their voices in ways that present them as manipulative, stubborn, and uncooperative. Moreover, we see a number of practices documented by Haslam (Haslam, 2006; Haslam & Loughnan, 2014) and Nussbaum (1999) that were mobilized by the Australian newsprint media to deny asylum seekers' human attributes; specifically, their delegitimization, and their denial of subjectivity and voice, which all combine to justify their social exclusion and denial of legal protection (Livingstone-Smith, 2014).

Moreover, asylum seekers were not only constructed as unlawful and as a threat to the nation, but both physical and symbolic violence against asylum seekers was justified on the basis of their status as outside the law. As *homo sacer* or 'bare life', asylum seekers are essentially stripped of fundamental human rights and as such can be subjected to state-sanctioned violations from which citizens are routinely protected. In this way, the potential use of force and physical violence against asylum seekers can be justified and legitimated. Indeed, their mandatory detention (including women and children) in both onshore and offshore centers has become a routine and widely accepted practice in Australia since the 1990s. Rather than personalizing or humanizing the plight of asylum seekers then, the Australian newsprint media instead largely politicizes their claims to seek refuge in Australia, turning the debate into one of border security and dangerous mobilities rather than one of humanitarian responsibilities in a globalized world.

Finally, it is of concern and worth noting that the highly restrictive policies towards asylum seekers that have evolved in Australia since 2001 and that have received bipartisan support are increasingly being advocated by European nations as a political solution to the refugee crisis. The so-called 'Australian Model' has not only been strongly endorsed by the political right (e.g., UKIP former leader Nigel Farage) but also by parties of the centre, despite having been heavily criticized by the United Nations Human Rights Council (UNHRC) for violating the 1951 Refugee Convention. Indeed, the dehumanizing practices we have described in this chapter are being increasingly witnessed all over the world as those fleeing war, persecution, and intergroup conflict are being demonized in public discourse as dangerous threats to sovereign borders and nation states. The increasing dehumanization of people seeking asylum by depicting them as potential or actual 'enemies' to be feared and rejected not only serves to maintain intergroup conflict but also denies displaced persons the social justice they are entitled to.

References

Agamben, G. (1998). *Homo sacer: Sovereign power and bare life* (D. Heller-Roazen, Trans.). Stanford, CA: Stanford University Press.

Agamben, G. (2005). *State of exception* (K. Attell, Trans.). Chicago, IL: The University of Chicago Press.

Alverez, A. (1997). Adjusting the genocide: The techniques of neutralization and the Holocaust. *Social Science History, 21*, 139–178.

Andreas, P. (2003). Redrawing the line: Borders and security in the twenty-first century. *International Security, 28*, 78–111.

Australian Press Council. (2007). *State of the news print media in Australia: A supplement to the 2006 report*. Retrieved from http://www.presscouncil.org.au/snpma/index_snpma2007.html

Billig, M. (1987). *Arguing and Thinking: A rhetorical approach to social psychology*. Cambridge: Cambridge University Press.

Billig, M. (1991). *Ideology and opinions: Studies in rhetorical psychology*. London: Sage.

Bourdieu, P. (1991). *Language and symbolic power*. Cambridge: Polity Press.

Browning, C. (1992). *The path to genocide*. Cambridge: Cambridge University Press.

Carrington, K. (2006). Law and order on the borders in the neo-colonial Antipodes. In S. Pickering & L. Weber (Eds.), *Borders, mobility and technologies of control*. Berlin: Springer Verlag.

Coole, C. (2002). A warm welcome? Scottish and UK media reporting of an asylum seeker murder. *Media, Culture and Society, 24*, 839–852.

Edwards, D. & Potter, J. (1992). *Discursive psychology*. London: Sage.

Every, D. (2006). *The politics of representation: A discursive analysis of refugee advocacy in the Australian parliament*. Doctoral thesis, University of Adelaide.

Fernandez, C., Gill, M., Szeman, I., & Whyte, J. (2006). Erasing the line, or, the politics of the border. *Ephemera: Theory and Politics in Organization, 6*, 466–483.

Fowler, R. (1991). *Language in the news: Discourse and ideology in the press*. London: Routledge.

Fox, P. D. (2010). International asylum and boat people: The Tampa affair and Australia's Pacific solution. *Maryland Journal of International Law, 25*, 356–373.

Galtung, J. (1969). Violence, peace, and peace research. *Journal of Peace Research, 6*, 167–191.

Galtung, J. (1990). Cultural violence. *Journal of Peace Research, 27*, 291–305.

Hagan, J., & Rymond-Richmond, W. (2008). The collective dynamics of racial dehumanization and genocidal victimization in Dafur. *American Sociological Review, 73*, 875–902.

Haslam, N. (2006). Dehumanization: An integrative review. *Personality and Social Psychology Review, 10*, 252–264.

Haslam, N., Bain, P., Douge, L., Lee, M., & Bastian, B. (2005). More human than you: Attributing humanness to self and others. *Journal of Personality and Social Psychology, 89*, 937–950.

Haslam, N., & Loughnan, S. (2014). Dehumanization and infrahumanization. *Annual Review of Psychology, 65*, 399–423.

Haslam, N., Rothschild, L., & Ernst, D. (2000). Essentialist beliefs about social categories. *British Journal of Social Psychology, 39*, 113–127.

Haslam, N., Rothschild, L., & Ernst, D. (2002). Are essentialist beliefs associated with prejudice? *British Journal of Social Psychology, 41*, 87–100.

Haynes, A., Devereux, E., & Breen, M. (2006). Fear, framing and foreigners: The othering of immigrants in the Irish print media. *International Journal of Critical Psychology, 16*, 100–121.

Kelman, H. G. (1973). Violence without moral restraint: Reflections on the dehumanization of victims and victimizers. *Journal of Social Issues, 29*, 25–61.

Kelman, H., & Hamilton, V. L. (1989). *Crimes of obedience: Toward a social psychology of authority and responsibility*. New Haven, CT: Yale University Press.

KhosraviNik, M., Krzyzanowski, M., & Wodak, R. (2012). Dynamics of representation in discourse: Immigrants in the British press. In M. Messer, R. Schroeder, & R. Wodak (Eds.), *Migrations: Interdisciplinary perspectives* (pp. 283–296). New York: Springer.

Kirkwood, S., Goodman, S., McVittie, C., & McKinlay, A. (2016). *The language of asylum: Refugees and discourse*. London: Palgrave McMillan.

Klocker, N., & Dunn, K. (2003). Who's driving the debate?: Newspaper and government representations of asylum seekers. *Media International Australia, Incorporating Culture and Policy, 109*, 71–92.

Krestel, R., Bergler, S., & Witte, R. (2008). Minding the source: Automatic tagging of reported speech in newspaper articles. *Reporter, 1*, 4.

Krzyzanowski, M., & Wodak, R. (2009). *The politics of exclusion: Debating migration in Austria*. New Brunswick, NJ: Transaction Publishers.

Livingstone-Smith, D. (2014). *Dehumanization, essentialism, and moral psychology*. Cambridge: Cambridge Working Paper.

Lueck, K., Due, C., & Augoustinos, M. (2015). Neoliberalism and nationalism: Representations of asylum seekers in the Australian mainstream news media. *Discourse and Society, 26*, 608–629.

Lynn, N., & Lea, S. (2003). 'A phantom menace and the new apartheid': The social construction of asylum seekers in the United Kingdom. *Discourse and Society, 14*, 425–452.

Macken-Horarik, M. (2003). Working the borders in racist discourse: The challenge of the 'children overboard affair' in news media texts. *Social Semiotics, 13*, 283–303.

Mares, P. (2001). *Borderline*. Sydney: University of New South Wales Press.

McMaster, D. (2002). Asylum seekers and the insecurity of a nation. *Australian Journal of International Affairs, 56*, 279–290.

Messer, M., Schroeder, R., & Wodak, R. (2012). *Migrations: Interdisciplinary perspectives*. New York, NY: Springer.

Nussbaum, M. C. (1999). *Sex and social justice*. Oxford: Oxford University Press.

O'Doherty, K., & Augoustinos, M. (2008). Protecting the nation: Nationalist rhetoric on asylum seekers and the Tampa. *Journal of Community and Applied Social Psychology, 18*, 576–592.

O'Doherty, K., & LeCouteur, A. (2007). 'Asylum seekers', 'boat people' and 'illegal immigrants': Social categorization in the media. *Australian Journal of Psychology, 59*, 1–12.

Parliament of Australia. (2010). *Boat arrivals in Australia since 1976*. Retrieved 17 September, 2010, from http://www.aph.gov.au/library/pubs/bn/sp/BoatArrivals.htm#_Toc233686296

Perera, S. (2002). What is a camp...? *Borderlands e-journal, 1*(1).

Pickering, S. (2001). Commonsense and original deviancy: News discourses and asylum seekers in Australia. *Journal of Refugee Studies, 14*, 170–186.

Pickering, S. (2004). Border terror: Policing, forced migration and terrorism. *Global Change, Peace and Security, 16*, 211–226.

Potter, J. (1996). *Representing reality: Discourse, rhetoric and social construction*. London: Sage.

Pugh, M. (2004). Drowning not waving: Boat people and humanitarianism at sea. *Journal of Refugee Studies, 17*, 50–69.

Rothbart, M., & Taylor, M. (1992). Category and social reality: Do we view social categories as natural kinds? In G. R. Semin & K. Fieder (Eds.), *Language and social cognition* (pp. 11–36). London: Sage.

Saxton, A. (2003). 'I certainly don't want people like that here': The discursive construction of 'asylum seekers. *Media International Australia, Incorporating Culture and Policy, 109*, 109–120.

Smirnova, A. V. (2009). Reported speech as an element of argumentative newspaper discourse. *Discourse & Communication, 3*, 79–103.

Tileagă, C. (2007). Ideologies of moral exclusion: A critical discursive reframing of depersonalization, delegitimization and dehumanization. *British Journal of Social Psychology, 46*, 717–737.

van Onselen, P. (2010, 3 April). Who's afraid of 4500 boat people? *The Australian*.

Walters, W. (2006). Border/control. *European Journal of Social Theory, 9*, 187–203.

Wetherell, M. & Potter, J. (1992). *Mapping the language of racism: Discourse and the legitimation of exploitation*. London: Harvester Wheatsheaf.

White, P. R. R. (2006). Evaluative standpoints and ideological positioning in journalistic discourse: A new framework for analysis. In I. Lassen, J. Strunck, & T. Vestergaard (Eds.), *Mediating ideology in text and image* (pp. 37–69). Amsterdam: John Benjamins Publishing.

Chapter 12
Constructing the "Refugee Crisis" in Greece: A Critical Discursive Social Psychological Analysis

Lia Figgou, Martina Sourvinou, and Dimitra Anagnostopoulou

Introduction

As other commentators have argued "it has become utterly banal to speak of 'the crisis' in Europe" (De Genova et al., 2016, p. 2). This is particularly true for Greece. In various discursive contexts—in public rhetoric, as well as in everyday interactions—"crisis" is a category commonly mobilized and used with multifaceted connotations and consequences. It was used in the context of discussing Greece's bail out by its international creditors (in 2010 and in 2012) and the subsequent austerity policies imposed. More recently, it is also mobilized in the context of discussing the movement of hundreds of thousands of refugees who, after having risked their lives in the attempt to cross the Aegean Sea, have been trapped in Greece as a result of border closings along the Balkan route to Northern Europe.

Our focus in this chapter is on the way in which leading politicians in Greece mobilize the category of "crisis" in parliamentary discourse on the refugee issue. Adopting a critical discursive social psychological perspective (Wetherell, 1998), the chapter considers the consequences of the construction of the current population movement as "a crisis" in political discourse. The analytic focus is on the ways in which its constitution as *a crisis* affects the construction of relevant social actors and the attribution of responsibility.

It would also be a truism to maintain that immigration and human mobility are issues that concern Peace Psychology. Given the more recent interest of peace psychology in studying both direct episodic violence (which harms people directly) but also (and even more emphatically) structural violence (referring to the effects of social inequalities and deprivation) (Christie, 1997, 2006a, 2006b; Pilisuk, 1998), it can be said that the population movement to Europe that is usually described as the "refugee crisis" or "migrant crisis" involves both forms of violence, or rather it is an

L. Figgou (✉) · M. Sourvinou · D. Anagnostopoulou
Aristotle University of Thessaloniki, Thessaloniki, Greece
e-mail: figgou@psy.auth.gr

© Springer Nature Switzerland AG 2018
S. Gibson (ed.), *Discourse, Peace, and Conflict*, Peace Psychology Book Series,
https://doi.org/10.1007/978-3-319-99094-1_12

indication of their interrelation. The movement of people who risk their own and their children's lives in the Aegean Sea and face some of the most detrimental forms of episodic violence is the result of inequality and violence built into the fabric of international socio-political and economic systems. Amongst the priorities of Peace Psychology is also to highlight how immigration and human mobility are embedded in and shaped by wider social, cultural, and political contexts. This interest constitutes common ground with a critical discursive social psychological analysis of the refugee issue. Critical discursive social psychology is also interested in the historical and contextual specificity of discourses/social representations. Apart from looking to the historical and structural constitution of phenomena, though, it also aims to shed light on the way in which historically sedimented representations are actively mobilized to constitute the phenomena in microcontextual interactional contexts, and the implications of that mobilization. In other words, a critical discursive analytic framework is sensitive to the echoes of historical discourses deployed to legitimate social inequality but also to the complex ways in which fragments of discursive resources are invoked in the ever-changing flux of everyday interactional life (Gibson, 2015).

Crisis as a Meaning Making and Consequential Category

Tracing the genealogy of "crisis" as a historical-philosophical concept, authors seem to agree that the term—which originally comes from the Greek verb κρίνω which means decide or judge—was coined in the context of Hippocratic medicine, to signify a turning point, a decisive moment in the course of a disease (Koselleck, 1988; Shank, 2008; Starn, 1971). According to Koselleck and Richter (2006), until the seventeenth century there were three main uses/significations of the term: the medical (crisis is used to signify recurrence and transition), the judicial-political (the term takes the meaning of judgment), and the theological (the term acquires an eschatological meaning, signifying the Last Judgment). Koselleck and Richter (*ibid.*, p. 358) also maintained that it was not until the period of the great revolutions of the eighteenth century that "crisis" entered the vocabulary of everyday life and became a central "catch-word." In their own words "by its application to the events of the French and American revolutions, the apocalyptic vision of the last judgment now acquired a secular meaning" (*ibid.*, p. 358).

Since the middle of the nineteenth century, "crisis" has been used to signify the greatest economic, political, as well as cultural, events. The representation of history as progress determined by turning points and transitions, tensions and revolutions, was developed hand in hand with a representation of historical consciousness as a "consciousness of crisis" (*ibid.*, p. 398). According to this approach, while crises are unique, they should be considered as structurally recurrent (Koselleck & Richter, 2006). These assumptions, according to Koselleck and Richter (2006), are to some extent reflected in Marxist writings, which constituted two interpretations of crisis, between economic analysis (the recurrent imbalance of production and consumption in capitalism) and revolutionary hope (as a prerequisite for revolution).

By the 1990s, according to Hay (1995), "crisis" had become a ubiquitous concept in social and political analyses: "all understandings of (state) failure are necessarily accessed through perceptions, narratives, and hence constructions of crisis" (p. 64). Reflecting on the consequences of this use of the concept, Hay articulates his thesis on the "symbolic violence of abstraction" (p. 72). According to this thesis, to apply the (meta)narrative of crisis—through a series of distorting generalizations—to social events means to construct a certain line of causality and responsibility. Specifically, crisis narratives often become rhetorically effective not because they manage to reflect the complex webs of causation (of factors that interact in order to co-produce certain effects), but because of their ability to provide an account flexible enough to identify a great variety of symptoms, while also being simple in their attribution of responsibility.

In the same vein, Janet Roitman (2014) cautions that crises are events in need of explanation. By the adoption of a "crisis" narrative, Roitman argues that the uniqueness of events "is abstracted by a generic logic"; crisis is a term that seems "self-explanatory" (p. 3). Crisis construction seems to have a normative dimension "because it requires a comparative state for judgment: crisis compared to what?" (p. 4). That question goes beyond the questions of "what went wrong?" and "who is to blame" in a manner that allows the focus to be put on "the significance of crisis as an axiological problem," or "the questioning of the epistemological or ethical grounds of certain domains of life and thought" (*ibid.*, p. 4). This point of view indicates, indeed, that the implications of the political uses of "crisis" may need to be unpacked.

In such an attempt to unfold the implications of recent "economic crisis" narratives in public political dialogue, Agamben (2013a, p. 3) notes that "the judgment is split from its temporal index and coincides now with the chronological course of time, so that, not only in economics and politics, but in every aspect of social life, the crisis coincides with normality and becomes, in this way, just a tool of government." Agamben's attention is paid to the banality of the concept's use which seems to result in a banalization of emergency and in turn to the legitimation of certain governmental interventions (Agamben, 2013b). The latter are usually predicated upon the pressure of time, meaning that only the most urgent needs are addressed, with the real decisions being postponed.

Agamben (2013a) uses two central concepts in order to explain the way in which this governmentality is performed: The first one is *the state of exception* paradigm according to which a government operates by overlooking the limitations of the law, in the name of an emergency situation (see also Agamben, 2003; Augoustinos, Due, & Callaghan, this volume). The second is the "paradigm of security and the security apparatuses" (Agamben, 2013a, p. 6), the technological and economic mechanisms used to manage the effects of troubles, caused by non-preventive political choices. This point of view has been drawn upon in the exploration of the implications of current discourses on the "refugee crisis" (De Genova et al., 2016). According to De Genova et al. (2016), the narrative of a "refugee crisis" in 2015 evoked decisions and actions at the EU level that were oriented to the development of technologies of border control and state security. This fed into the politics of externalization of crisis and the management of numbers—both in relation to people and to financial-humanitarian interventions—in the name of security. Crisis in this case was used as a ready-made, self-explanatory concept that blurred agency (or in Roitman's term the question "Whose is this crisis?"). At the same time though, political decisions and actions taken seem to recognize it as basically "Europe's security crisis."

Discursive Social Psychological Work on Refugee Crises

There is already a large body of discursive social psychological research on population movements as "crises." Existing literature has applied discourse analytic tools and concepts in the study of migratory movements that have been constructed as crises in different national contexts. Studies conducted in Australia (Every & Augoustinos, 2008; Gale, 2004; O'Doherty & Lecouteur, 2007) have focused on the interweaving and multifaceted factors (notions of nationalism, illegality, cultural difference) that are mobilized in public discourse in order to construct the (ab) normality of refugees. In the Canadian context, Hier and Greenberg (2002) showed how the arrival of a few refugees by boat was represented as a threat with emphasis placed on the risk to the moral order by the "invasion." Hier and Greenberg argued that this constituted a *moral panic*. In the United Kingdom, discursive representations of refugees in public discourse have been mainly pejorative, including accusations of being "bogus" (Lynn & Lea, 2003); or nonsensical, such as the construction "illegal refugees" (Gabrielatos & Baker, 2008).

Recently, there has been a proliferation of discursive studies on the construction of the movement of refugees to Europe. Goodman and colleagues, for example, have considered the rhetorical implications of shifting the construction of the particular population movement from *refugee crisis* to *migrant crisis* and vice versa (Goodman, Sirriyeh, & McMahon, 2017). In a similar vein, Gilbert (2013) has argued that the construction of a Mexican "refugee crisis" in Canada is based on arguments concerning the illegality of refugees, which is considered to undermine their right to humanitarian protection (Rowe & O'Brien, 2014). Hence, it becomes evident that "crisis," or rather the construction of mass movement as a "crisis," is based upon the concept of the "illegality" of people, even though the notion of "illegality" has no clear boundaries (and see Kirkwood & Goodman, this volume).

Nevertheless, representations of refugees have not always been pejorative, and public as well as everyday discourse has been reported to include sympathetic arguments. For example, sympathetic arguments concerning the human qualities of both refugees and "us" can serve to make social or institutional actors morally accountable for protecting refugees (Kirkwood, 2017). However, as other commentators maintain, arguments which deploy "humanitarian" themes are not necessarily oriented to challenge social exclusion (Nightingale, Quayle, & Muldoon, 2017). Furthermore, they potentially draw on the same stock of common places as nationalistic discourse, constructing national sovereignty as part of a natural order (Hanson-Easey & Augoustinos, 2011).

To sum up, the above studies on the discursive construction of refugee movements have largely considered the way in which the construction of these movements is bound up with certain representations of the moving populations (e.g., as illegal), and the ways in which these constructions function to maintain social exclusion. Our study aims to extend this by focusing on political discourse and by exploring the way in which the category "crisis" becomes a resource mobilized in an attempt to manage responsibility and to construct agency for the recent refugee movement in a specific national context. This context is contemporary Greece in which, as already mentioned, a narrative of crisis seems to dominate social and political life due to the country's recent "bailout" and the severe austerity measures imposed.

Background and Methods

Since early 2015 about one million people (coming mainly from Syria, Afghanistan, and Iraq) have entered the Greek territories with the intention of traveling through the adjacent Balkan countries towards Northern and Western Europe (UNHCR, Global Report 2015).

In early 2016, a series of regional political developments in Europe, including the sealing of borders with Greece by key Balkan countries, severely impaired the movement of refugees[1] (Amnesty International Report, 2015/2016). In general, the EU appeared reluctant to guarantee legal and safe pathways for the movement of refugees and to agree to an effective redistribution and relocation mechanism.

As a result of the above, Greece has turned from a short-term transit country to a long-term host country. Without having the necessary reception framework or infrastructure, this poses severe threats to the well-being of the refugee population. According to UNHCR (2016), more than 55,000 people have been registered as permanent residents in settlements throughout Greece.

On 18 March 2016, in an effort to control the flow of migrants to the shores of Greece, the EU entered into an agreement with Turkey. In a joint statement, the EU and Turkey stated that all irregular migrants arriving in Greece after March 20, 2016 would be returned to Turkey. For every Syrian being returned to Turkey from the Greek islands, another Syrian would be resettled to the EU. Moreover, Turkey would take any necessary measures to prevent new sea or land routes for irregular migration opening from Turkey to the EU[2] (http://europa.eu/rapid/press-release_MEMO-16-963_el.htm).

---

[1] A regional agreement between some EU Member States (Austria, Croatia and Slovenia) and non-EU countries (the Former Yugoslav Republic of Macedonia and Serbia) led to the closure of the Greek-FYRoM border, which in turn blocked the migration route out of Greece.

[2] It is beyond the scope and the space limits of this chapter to consider this agreement in all its details.

The effectiveness of this agreement has been seriously questioned as refugees and migrants continue to arrive on the Greek shores. Furthermore, the agreement–or rather the deportation of all the people who do not have a right to international protection–raised serious human rights concerns amongst policymakers and NGOs. The necessity for, and the implications of, the EU agreement have constituted matters of heated political debate in the Greek parliament. A few days after the agreement (on 23rd March 2016), the leader of the opposition party (New Democracy), Kyriakos Mitsotakis, requested a pre-agenda debate on security. His request was largely predicated upon what he called the "*dramatic situation concerning the refugee-migrant issue.*"

Analytic Corpus

The parliamentary debates that followed from the agreement constituted the analytic material of the present study. In particular, our analytic corpus consisted of the proceedings of the following:

(a) The 94th plenary session of the Greek parliament (which included a discussion on the interpellation of twelve New Democracy MPs regarding the implementation of the European Program "Actions for Immigration") (21 March 2016)
(b) The pre-agenda debate on the subject "Citizens' Security" (20 April 2016)

The proceedings are posted on the official website of the Greek Parliament (http://www.hellenicparliament.gr). The proceedings of the plenary session consist of 35 pages—numbered from 6940 to 6974. The proceedings of the pre-agenda debate on "Citizens' Security" consist of 45 pages—numbered from 8763 to 8808.

The material is transcribed mainly for content–although it may also include information on interruptions and applause–and it is edited to avoid repetitions and apparent mistakes. After considering (reading and re-reading) the original corpus, it was decided to focus exclusively on the discourse of the Government (Syriza, a self-identified leftist party, which won the elections mainly by adopting an anti-austerity rhetoric) and the Opposition (the right-wing New Democracy party, which consistently retained an anti-immigration agenda) and not to include the discourse of other political parties. This is because–as the two key parliamentary parties–representatives of Syriza and New Democracy frequently directly addressed each other in the debate, lending their interactions an explicitly dialogical quality.

Analytic Concepts and Procedure

The analysis draws on the rhetorical approach to categorization (Billig, 1987) and considers categorical constructions of "crisis" as argumentative resources in the context of political debate. Categories, according to rhetorical psychology, are always open to contestation on a number of levels, as social actors argue about how categories are defined, how particular instances relate to categories or even what the argument itself is all about (see also Reicher & Hopkins, 2001). By treating social categorization as a rhetorical phenomenon, we are able to appreciate how category meanings are established in lines of argument in which speakers–in our case politicians–construct versions of group interests and argue for the legitimacy of particular policies (Condor, Tileagă, & Billig, 2013). Furthermore, by approaching categories as aspects of rhetoric, we are able to appreciate their dialogic qualities considering each version in juxtaposition to the one it aims to undermine. Such a perspective is particularly relevant in an analysis of political discourse (Finlayson, 2007).

Analysis also used tools and concepts from critical discursive social psychology (Wetherell, 1998). This approach considers categories as rhetorical devices which are used to manage local interactional business (Edwards, 1991; Tileagă, 2010), but also as fragments of broader historically specific and culturally available discursive resources.

A first stage of the analytic procedure involved coding of the material and extracting from the corpus of data all the relevant extracts in which explicit references to "crisis" were made. At this stage, the analysis erred on the side of over-inclusion in order to avoid decontextualizing and fragmenting the data. The second stage involved identification of the argumentative lines (coherent sets of statements justifying a certain premise) within which constructions of crisis were nested. Finally, analysis proceeded to point to the potential local functions of categorizations and to the corollaries of the use of categories in talk. For the purposes of the present analysis, extracts have been translated from Greek to English. Needless to say, such translation unavoidably involves the danger of losing subtleties of meaning.

Analysis

Whose Crisis? Whose Problem? Constructing Agency for the "Refugee Crisis"

As other commentators (Hay, 1995; Roitman, 2014) have argued, to apply the (meta)narrative of crisis means to construct a certain line of causality and agency. In the parliamentary discourse analyzed, "refugee crisis" constituted a common-place resource in a "blame game" between the Government and the Opposition party.

According to a line of argument identified in the discourse of the Opposition, crisis has been facilitated by acts and omissions on the part of government. The government is accused of exacerbating the crisis by being incompetent in its attempts to manage its more dramatic consequences. For example, the first extract features Olga Kefalogianni, who was one of the twelve New Democracy MPs who in the context of the 94th plenary session questioned the Government's implementation of the European "Actions for Immigration" program. Immediately prior to her talk quoted in Extract 1, Kefalogianni had argued that the European

Continent is faced with the biggest "refugee crisis" since the Second World War and emphasized that Greece has the most significant involvement in this crisis, being faced with its most dramatic consequences. Her use of extreme case formulations (Pomerantz, 1986) (*the biggest crisis, the most dramatic consequences*) and the use of the category of *crisis* itself preface her move to consider matters of responsibility:

Extract 1: The government did anything possible to "facilitate" the crisis.

1. All of the above obviously do not lessen the responsibility of the government in
2. the management of the refugee and immigration crisis. On the contrary. The
3. government did anything possible to 'facilitate' the crisis. And it was not just
4. its ideological rigidity. It was above all its inability to work in a coordinated
5. way, to get the state to work, to absorb the European financial aid, to
6. negotiate with our European partners [...] Due to the fact that you
7. underestimated the refugee and immigration problem at the beginning, you
8. ended up with closed borders, a humanitarian crisis and, of course, zero
9. credibility.

Olga Kefalogianni (New Democracy), 21st March 2016

Kefalogianni emphasizes the responsibility of the Greek government; she does not blame, however, the government for generating the crisis. Crisis is constructed as a category that pre-exists the actions of all potential actors (the government, Europe, Greece's European partners). The government is blamed for *facilitating* the crisis and exacerbating its symptoms, amongst which are Greece's closed borders, a humanitarian crisis and the lack of credibility with European partners. In common with other analyses of immigration discourse (Every & Augoustinos, 2008; Gale, 2004; O'Doherty & Lecouteur, 2007), immigration is constructed as a problem to be managed and the restriction of immigration is treated as self-evidently desirable. It is also worth pointing to the *banal nationalistic* assumptions (Billig, 1995) that underlie this construction. Population movements constitute a problem for specific nation-states in a world of nation-states. Refugees end up constituting a problem for Greece, to the extent to which other countries have closed their borders and they remained trapped in Greece. Hence, arguing for border security in one's country goes hand in hand with appeals to other countries to open their borders and to accept immigrants.

The constitution of refugee movement as a crisis in Extract 1—and in others similar to this one—is not only used to challenge particular policy choices on the part of the Greek government. It also mobilizes arguments about the involvement and agency of the EU (Sambaraju, McVittie, & Nolan, 2017). According to this line of argument, the refugee crisis is mainly a Greek problem, albeit one which Greece's European partners can help to solve by providing support and resources. In doing so, however, there is a recognition that those EU partners will be evaluating the way in which these resources are used, and the credibility of the Greek government. Thus, the way in which Europe and Greece are positioned in relation to one another, and the concern to obtain European "credentials" by being institutionally efficient (*getting the state to work*) reflects hegemonic constructions/explanations of *another crisis* that troubles the country, namely the economic crisis. This reproduces the powerful ideological distinction between a superior (in terms of efficiency) West and an inferior East (Bozatzis, 2014). In these accounts, Greece is positioned as "lacking Europeanness" (see also Andreouli, Figgou, Kadianaki, Sapountzis, & Xenitidou, 2017).

One further point of note in the account quoted in Extract 1 is the way in which the failure of governmental immigration policy is grounded on a juxtaposition between ideology and inability/efficiency. According to the speaker, although it could be argued that a specific ideologically loaded immigration policy (driven by ideological rigidity) has resulted in the worsening of the crisis, *it was above all the inability to get the state to work that should be blamed.* Such a construction seems to be oriented to very important functions in the local interactional context, since it serves to manage the speaker's accountability as an Opposition MP by ensuring that she is not seen to be basing her argument on purely ideological grounds. It also seems to reproduce an assumption–commonly found in neoliberal politics–that all social issues (including immigration) can be dealt with through effective management (through getting the state to work) and indisputable technocratic practices which are constructed as consensual and above politics (Andreouli & Figgou, in press; Figgou, 2016).

Extract 2 is from the same plenary session as the previous extract and the speaker, Vassilis Kikilias, is also an opposition MP. In common with the speaker in the previous extract, Kikilias constructs crisis as—at least partly—a consequence of a policy of *open borders* that the government adopted, despite the warnings of the Opposition:

Extract 2: "Differentiating between immigration flows": Refugees and economic immigrants.

1. We warned you to adopt a strategy of preventing and differentiating between
2. the immigration flows […] We warned you to stop the policy of the open
3. borders. You maintained that the war in Syria was the main cause. Only, Mr
4. Minister, the war in Syria cannot really explain why the Greek islands were
5. chosen for the entry of refugees into Europe, nor does it explain why in
6. January 2015 only sixteen Pakistanis entered, while in December of the
7. current year three thousand seven hundred and thirty-three people from
8. Pakistan entered Greece. The current crisis, the crisis we experience is to an
9. extent the result of this policy […] You put in the same boat refugees, who
10. have fled from their home-country forced by war and economic migrants.
11. And sending them all to the northern borders you give Europe the right to
12. react Europe as it reacted.

Vassilis Kikilias (New Democracy), 21st March 2016

It is again noteworthy and seemingly paradoxical that Kikilias criticizes the open borders policy of the Greek government (lines 2–3) and at the same time constructs the closed borders policy of Europe as something that we should have avoided (lines 11–12). Although the way in which Europe reacted is depicted as undesirable, it is not however represented as illegitimate by the speaker. On the contrary, Europe is depicted as having the right to react as it actually reacted because it could not possibly accept all people that were sent to its borders. As other commentators have argued, space metaphors and references to spatial limitations impose particular understandings of immigrants (as invaders); at the same time, by grounding immigration control on practical criteria (Charteris-Black, 2006; Chilton, 2004) they also serve to manage moral accountability concerns. Europe, as a limited space, can accept only a certain number of immigrants. Detailed numbers are used by the speaker in an attempt to further warrant exclusion.

In common with the previous extract, the superior and most efficient European (occidental) institutions are depicted as being endangered by Greece's (oriental) inefficiency and the inability to control immigration. It is not however the only way in which Greece is positioned vis a vis Europe in this extract. Despite the lack of (occidental) efficiency credentials, Greece is constructed as–at least spatially–a *sine qua non* part of Europe, as *the entry* to Europe. Hence, concerns over immigration policy are not only national concerns, they are also European concerns that reflect other juxtapositions and ingroup-outgroup constructions.

In Extract 2, the rationale for exclusion and border control also features a distinction between refugees (people who are forced to leave their home country) and economic immigrants that has been commonly identified in anti-immigration discourse (Figgou, 2015; Kirkwood, Goodman, McVittie, & McKinlay, 2016; Rojo & van Dijk, 1997). Discursive research has highlighted the contingency of these categories, showing that they constitute epiphenomena of immigration policy since the boundaries between them are largely determined by certain policy decisions. Research has also highlighted the connotations of the prefix "economic" in this particular context. As other authors have maintained, it is seemingly paradoxical that in the neoliberal era of globalized and open economic activity it is possible to apply the term "economic" with pejorative connotations in immigration discourse. In this context, the term is used to refer to people who allegedly have nothing to offer "us," but who opt to take advantage of "our" employment or welfare opportunities (Lueck, Due, & Augoustinos, 2015).

Extract 3 is an exchange between Ioannis Mouzalas, the Deputy Minister for Home Affairs, and the Opposition MP Georgios Koumoutsakos. Mouzalas has taken the floor as the Deputy Minister who is responsible for immigration issues, and his speech follows from the contributions of the Opposition MPs considered above:

Extract 3: Crisis as a natural disaster.

1. **Ioannis Mouzalas**: Please do not talk about 'unattended borders'. It harms
2. our country. The whole of NATO is struggling to reduce the refugee flows. The
3. whole of Europe is pushing for a reduction in flows. It is not our diplomatic
4. failure. It is not our own military failure. There is no reason to blame the
5. Government. Blaming the Government for what; because NATO has been
6. unable to succeed? [...] The same phenomenon that we had in Idomeni and
7. Mitilini in September, has been witnessed in America when 'Katrina[3]'
8. occurred. For months the situation was very bad. NGOs were uncontrolled.
9. **Georgios Koumoutsakos**: 'Katrina' was unpredictable, Mr Minister. Do not
10. make comparisons between different situations.
11. **Ioannis Mouzalas**: We have a different view, Mr Koumoutsakos. You think

---

[3] Hurricane Katrina, which struck the Gulf coast of the United States in August 2005, was one of the most intense hurricanes in US history.

12. the refugee crisis could have been predicted. It was not foreseen by anyone.
13. The first European Union report on the refugee issue is in May 2015. Excuse
14. me but there is no previous study.
   Georgios Koumoutsakos (New Democracy) & Ioannis Mouzalas (Syriza), 21st March 2016

Since Mr. Mouzalas is the appropriate person to account for governmental immigration policy, it is notable that throughout most of his speech he avoids adopting the footing of the government official. Rather, by using inclusive "we"/"our" constructions, he works up his identity as a representative of the country instead of a representative of a political party or government, and at the same time constitutes the issue under consideration as an issue that necessitates unanimity. The minister also makes explicit appeals to political consensus in the name of "our country" by asking the opposition MPs to abandon its rhetoric on unattended borders. Seeking consensus serves again to construct immigration policy as an issue that is above ideological/political controversy (Weltman & Billig, 2001). It is also noteworthy that Mouzalas does not downgrade closed borders as a potential objective of immigration policy. Rather, he considers public rhetoric on unattended borders as potentially harmful and problematic for the image of the country.

After appealing to consensus and constructing immigration reduction as an indisputable policy objective, Mouzalas proceeds to warrant government policy and to counter the accusations of the opposition by constituting two main representations of the refugee issue. First is the construction of refugee movement as a problem that concerns not only Greece, but also other supranational agents. It is common place in the discourse of Government officials that Greece has been loaded with a disproportionately big burden and has taken on a responsibility that concerns the whole of Europe, or which even transcends the boundaries of Europe. This functions to position Greek action as insufficient by itself, and thereby to manage issues of blame (Sambaraju et al., 2017). As Mouzalas puts it, if NATO cannot manage to reduce "flows" then Greece cannot be blamed for being ineffective.

There seems to be another way, however, in which Mouzalas's discourse is oriented to agency/responsibility concerns in attempting to downgrade the challenges of the Opposition: the constitution of the refugee issue as a natural disaster. Such metaphors constitute a common place in political discourse advocating immigration restriction (e.g., Charteris-Black, 2006). Drawing comparisons with natural phenomena and their operation (flows, storms) not only dehumanizes immigrants and refugees, and constructs population movement as necessarily and inevitably bad, but it also sets limits on possible actions. There is not much that someone could do in order to manage the consequences of a hurricane. The situation on the island of Lesvos (the main entry point of refugees) and Idomeni (a makeshift camp created in the north of Greece as a result of the closure of the Balkan route to western Europe) are compared with the situation in the United States after hurricane Katrina in that both were impossible to plan for. The Opposition MP challenges the metaphor and predicates his objection on the premise that a hurricane is something unpredictable and by the same token attributes responsibility to the Greek government for not having predicted the phenomenon. To this challenge, the deputy minister responds by making the logic underpinning the analogy explicit and constructing the refugee crisis as something that was not foreseen by anyone, and to buttress his argument he refers to the exact month in which the first EU report was circulated.

Crisis, Security, and Border Control

The following extract is from the pre-agenda debate on security and in particular from the speech of Kiriakos Mitsotakis, the leader of the Opposition party (ND) who requested the debate. The piece of talk quoted below follows from the initial speech of the Greek Prime Minister whose main argument was that Greece is a safe and secure country:

Extract 4: Europe at 'real war'.

1. Security requires constant concern and care, especially in our times, times of
2. economic, social and institutional crisis, times of dramatic geopolitical changes,
3. tensions and conflicts in the wider region and, of course, times of continuous
4. widening and growing asymmetric threats of any form, from Islamic terrorism to
5. natural disasters and from organized crime violence to cyber attacks [...] And would
6. you like to know something more, mister Tsipras, because this is also a common
7. argument between the members of SYRIZA? It is at least naive to believe that our
8. country is by definition safe, a priori safe, thanks to our traditionally good
9. relationships with the Arabic world. You know very well that Europe is at war-real
10. war!- and the western way of life and social organization are challenged. Our very
11. freedom is, finally, challenged.

Kiriakos Mitsotakis (New Democracy), 20th April 2016

Accounting for the necessity of the debate on security in the Greek Parliament, Kiriakos Mitsotakis predicates his request on two temporal constructions: First, that security presupposes constant concern and continuous care and that there is no such thing as normality in security issues; second, that security is a topical issue, a concern related to historically specific changes. By this twofold construction, in combination with the speaker's list (Edwards & Potter, 1992) of other types of "crises" (economic, social, institutional, environmental) which are located in a rather non-specific space (the region), a ubiquitous (Hay, 1995) and, at the same time, urgent (Koselleck & Richter, 2006) threat is rhetorically constituted.

However, apart from co-constructing an omnipresent danger, the vague formulation of "changes in the region" and the reference to multiple crises could be considered to be oriented to the speaker's social accountability concerns. To explicitly relate the refugee issue to security concerns is rhetorically consequential, and although the leader of New Democracy put forward such an argument in his letter to the president of the Greek Parliament, as mentioned earlier, he avoids such an explicit connection in the initial part of his speech. However, amongst these vaguely formulated multiple crises and "natural disasters," there is one threat that is more precise: "Islamic terrorism." This threat has a specific origin and is frequently included in narratives of security and immigration in western political discourse. As other authors have shown, after the events of 11th September 2001, Islamic terrorism has become one of the narratives most frequently used by European politicians in order to "institutionalize a diverse range of security governance technologies" (Hassan, 2010, p. 445), especially in relation to border control.

Having constructed a crucial threat that necessitates attentiveness, the speaker prepares the ground for responsibility attribution and the construction of agency. He then proceeds to blame the government not only for failing to pay the necessary attention to national safety issues, but for adopting a naïve stance by considering Greece by definition safe, due to its traditionally good relationships with the Arabic world. In what follows a war metaphor is introduced and the alleged security threat to Greece is constituted as part of a general war against Europe: the war between the European (Western) way of life and social organization and the Arabic world. Greece's position in this war is undeniably, according to Mitsotakis, on the side of Europe, while the superiority of the West is grounded on the criterion used to differentiate between these ways of life, between the West and the Rest (Said, 1995): Freedom. While the former values freedom, the latter does not.

In Mitsotakis's narrative, we can identify an interesting intertextuality as he seems to echo media and political discussions after the terrorist attacks in Paris of November 2015. In these formulations, terrorists' access and movement around Europe has been depicted as having been facilitated by the "migrant crisis." Moreover, differences in culture were used to foreground issues of incompatibility and to warrant exclusion (Goodman et al., 2017). Finally, the construction of the situation as an emergency, or even a war (worked up by extreme case formulations and repetitions on lines 9–11) is used to emphasize security issues and to put asylum processes and migration regulations aside.

A Crisis of European Values

The last extract we will consider is from the Greek Prime Minister's speech (which follows from the speech of the Opposition leader quoted in Extract 4 above). As we will show, Alexis Tsipras does not oppose Mitsotakis's premise that European values are at stake, but constructs the conflict of values as taking place *within* Europe. In so doing, Tsipras invokes a meeting between the Christian religious leaders Pope Francis, Archbishop Ieronymos II and Ecumenical Patriarch Bartholomew, which took place in Lesvos on the 16th of April 2016:

Extract 5: A value conflict within Europe.

1. And it is not just a matter of international concern that the leaders of Christianity are
2. meeting in Greece; it is also the venue of this meeting which constitutes a boundary
3. within Europe between humanism on the one hand and - in a wider sense - what could
4. be termed progressive and liberal thinking and on the other hand the black
5. obscurantism, the reactionary world view, which is expressed in the name of

6. Christian Europe. Religious leaders met there in order to put forward that this Europe
7. which raises walls and fences cannot be considered Christian, this xenophobic
8. Europe; humanism and solidarity constitute our values, our principals. What happened
9. last week constituted a major historical event.
10. And I wonder: Could this happen in Lesvos and could our country become a synonym
11. for solidarity and humanism, had we followed all this time another policy on the
12. refugee issue? If we followed what, in any case, is in your announcements, the strict
13. and crude repulse? Is it, so, or isn't it an honor for our country this recognition of its
14. leading role in handling the refugee issue, always with respect to international
15. legitimacy and human rights? It seems that some of us are not ready to give the
16. obvious answer.

Alexis Tsipras (Syriza), 20th April 2016

In contrast with the quotation from the deputy minister of his government considered in Extract 3, who emphasized the need for consensus on immigration policy, the Prime Minister highlights the differences between the immigration policy of his government and that of the Opposition. To this end, Tsipras refers to the fact that the three religious leaders, despite their differences, met on a Greek island in order to appeal for international attention and solidarity on the refugee issue. This is not only constructed as a major historical event, but is also represented as validating his own policy and as something that would not have been possible had he adopted the political agenda of the Opposition. Hence, the Government's position on the refugee issue is depicted as coinciding with the values of Christianity and humanism, while the opposition is constructed as standing apart from them.

The values of Christianity, which in Tsipras's account go hand in hand with the values of liberalism, are depicted not only to differentiate the government from the opposition. They are also used to draw a hard-and-fast line between the two different faces of Europe. The Europe of humanism, liberal values, tolerance, and solidarity with the refugees is juxtaposed with the xenophobic Europe that constructs fences and walls. The leaders of Christianity are depicted as having met in Lesvos in order to underscore this crisis of values in Europe, and to castigate reactionary policies towards the refugees. This value crisis constitutes a "conflict within" since the threat is *the European other.* Within this internal conflict Greece has a prominent position. The island of Lesvos is constituted as the symbolic boundary between the progressive and the repressive face of Europe, while Greece has become synonymous with solidarity and humanism. In other words, it has become synonymous with the real values and principles of Europe. Therefore, if in the quotations considered previously the positioning of Greece in Europe was undermined due to its inefficient institutions and policies, in this account Greece is depicted as quintessentially European and as the cradle of European (liberal) values and principles. It has become the "guardian" of European values in the era of (their) crisis.

Concluding Remarks

Our aim in this chapter was to consider the ways in which the category of "crisis" is mobilized in parliamentary discourse on the refugee issue in Greece. Analysis indicated that the constitution of the refugee movement as a crisis is a resource that parliamentarians use to warrant or to challenge particular policy choices and to construct responsibility and agency. Specifically, whereas government officials could construct it as a natural disaster that could not be predicted and which necessitated urgent solutions, the Opposition sought to frame some of the most dramatic consequences of the crisis as being at least partly the result of the Government's inadequacies. Moreover, while in some contexts crisis was mobilized to highlight the "in principle" ideological differences between the two political parties, in others it was used to appeal for consensus and unanimity and to construct *a state of exception* (Agamben, 2003) within which there are no alternatives and the management of immigration (and more often than not the restriction of it) operates by overlooking legal limitations and ideological principles.

Apart from constituting a central resource in the blame game between government and opposition, narratives of crisis also involve arguments about the positioning and agency of other supranational agents and, in particular, of Europe (De Genova et al., 2016; Sambaraju et al., 2017). Nevertheless, as Billig's (1995) account of banal nationalism has indicated, the invocation of international entities is not necessarily in ideological contradiction with nationalism. On the contrary, nationalism and internationalism seem to constitute different sides of the same coin reproducing–in banal ways–nations in a world of nations. Hence, in many cases, Parliamentarians of both parties negotiate the positioning of Greece within Europe by constructing frontiers and alliances and by asking other European nation-states to open their borders when border control is constructed as the only desirable end of immigration policy for Greece. These contradictory goals (for Greece and its European partners) are usually accounted for through recourse to the same stock of values grounded in the common places of liberalism. Security and border control are warranted through invocations of Islamic terrorism which threatens "our" freedom and creates a value crisis. Closed borders, on the other hand, are depicted as a policy that reveals an internal conflict in which the European, progressive humanistic values are violated. Hence, the whole debate is conducted not only within the context and limitations of nationalism (Hanson-Easey & Augoustinos, 2011) but also with the resources and dilemmas of liberalism (Billig et al., 1988) and neoliberalism (Lueck et al., 2015).

To sum up, the constitution of refugee movement as a crisis goes hand in hand with certain perspectives on the temporality/historicity of the phenomenon and has implications for the ways in which responsibility might be attributed. More often than not, crisis narratives direct attention to the symptoms of a phenomenon and, by the rhetoric of emergency, allow for the warranting of a policy that allows for few alternatives. The key questions thus go beyond "what went wrong?" and "who is to blame" (Roitman, 2014, p. 3). They are the questions that constitute a priority for Peace Psychology and aim to shed light on the structural causes of immigration and refugee movements, as well as highlighting the ways in which social inequality and violence are built into the fabric of international socio-political and economic systems (Christie, 1997, 2006a, 2006b).

References

Agamben, G. (2003). *State of exception* (K. Attell, Trans.). Chicago, IL: University of Chicago Press.

Agamben, G. (2013a). For a theory of destitute power. *Critical Legal Thinking*. Retrieved from http://criticallegalthinking.com/2014/02/05/theory-destituent-power/

Agamben, G. (2013b). The endless crisis as an instrument of power: In conversation with Giorgio Agamben. Verso Blog (04 June 2013). Retrieved from http://www.versobooks.com/blogs/1318-the-endless-crisis-as-an-instrument-of-power-in-conversation-with-giorgio-agamben

Amnesty International (2015/2016). *Amnesty International report 2015/2016*. Retrieved from https://www.amnesty.org/en/latest/research/2016/02/annual-report-201516/

Andreouli, E., & Figgou, L. (in press). Critical social psychology of politics. In K. O'Doherty & D. Hodgetts (Eds.), *Sage handbook of applied social psychology*. London: Sage.

Andreouli, E., Figgou, L., Kadianaki, I., Sapountzis, A., & Xenitidou, M. (2017). "Europe" in Greece: Lay constructions of Europe in the context of Greek immigration debates. *Journal of Community and Applied Social Psychology, 27*, 158–168.

Billig, M. (1987). *Arguing and thinking: A rhetorical approach to social psychology*. Cambridge: Cambridge University Press.

Billig, M. (1995). *Banal nationalism*. London: Sage.

Billig, M., Condor, S., Edwards, D., Gane, M., Middleton, D., & Radley, A. R. (1988). *Ideological dilemmas: A social psychology of everyday thinking*. London: Sage.

Bozatzis, N. (2014). Banal occidentalism. In C. Antaki & S. Condor (Eds.), *Rhetoric, ideology and social psychology: Essays in honor of Michael Billig*. London: Routledge.

Charteris-Black, J. (2006). Britain as a container: Immigration metaphors in the 2005 election campaign. *Discourse & Society, 17*, 563–581.

Chilton, P. (2004). *Analysing political discourse: Theory and practice*. London: Routledge.

Christie, D. J. (1997). Reducing direct and structural violence: The human needs theory. *Peace and Conflict: Journal of Peace Psychology, 3*, 315–332.

Christie, D. J. (2006a). What is peace psychology the psychology of? *Journal of Social Issues, 62*, 1–17.

Christie, D. J. (2006b). Post–Cold War peace psychology: More differentiated, contextualized, and systemic. [Special issue]. *Journal of Social Issues, 62*(1), 1–17.

Condor, S., Tileagă, C., & Billig, M. (2013). Political rhetoric. In L. Huddy, D. O. Sears, & J. S. Levy (Eds.), *The Oxford handbook of political psychology* (pp. 262–300). Oxford: Oxford University Press.

De Genova, N., Tazzioli, M., Álvarez-Velasco, S., Fontanari, E., Heller, C., Jansen, Y., et al. (2016). Europe/crisis: New keywords of 'the crisis' in and of 'Europe'. *Near Futures Online, 1*, 1–45.

Edwards, D. (1991). Categories are for talking: On the cognitive and discursive bases of categorization. *Theory & Psychology, 1*, 515–542.

Edwards, D., & Potter, J. (1992). *Discursive psychology*. London: Sage.

Every, D., & Augoustinos, M. (2008). Constructions of Australia in pro-and anti-asylum seeker political discourse. *Nations and Nationalism, 14*, 562–580.

Figgou, L. (2015). Constructions of 'illegal' immigration and entitlement to citizenship: Debating an immigration law in Greece. *Journal of Community and Applied Social Psychology, 26*, 150–163.

Figgou, L. (2016). Everyday politics and the extreme right: Lay representations of the electoral performance of the neo-Nazi political party "Golden Dawn" in Greece. In C. Howarth & E. Andreouli (Eds.), *The social psychology of everyday politics* (pp. 206–221). London: Routledge.

Finlayson, A. (2007). From beliefs to arguments: Interpretive methodology and rhetorical political analysis. *The British Journal of Politics and International Relations, 9*, 545–563.

Gabrielatos, C., & Baker, P. (2008). Fleeing, sneaking, flooding: A corpus analysis of discursive constructions of refugees and asylum seekers in the UK press, 1996-2005. *Journal of English Linguistics, 36*, 5–38.

Gale, P. (2004). The refugee crisis and fear: Populist politics and media discourse. *Journal of Sociology, 40*, 321–340.

Gibson, S. (2015). From representations to representing: On social representations and discursive-rhetorical psychology. In G. Sammut, E. Andreouli, G. Gaskell, & J. Valsiner (Eds.), *The Cambridge handbook of social representations*. Cambridge: Cambridge University Press.

Gilbert, L. (2013). The discursive production of a Mexican refugee crisis in Canadian media and policy. *Journal of Ethnic and Migration Studies, 39*, 827–843.

Goodman, S., Sirriyeh, A., & McMahon, S. (2017). The evolving (re) categorisations of refugees throughout the 'refugee/migrant crisis'. *Journal of Community and Applied Social Psychology, 27*, 105–114.

Hanson-Easey, S., & Augoustinos, M. (2011). Complaining about humanitarian refugees: The role of sympathy talk in the design of complaints on talkback radio. *Discourse & Communication, 5*, 247–271.

Hassan, O. (2010). Constructing crises, (in)securitising terror: The punctuated evolution of EU counter-terror strategy. *European Security, 19*, 445–466.

Hay, C. (1995). Rethinking crisis: Narratives of the New Right and constructions of crisis. *Rethinking Marxism, 8*, 60–76.

Hier, S. P., & Greenberg, J. L. (2002). Constructing a discursive crisis: Risk, problematization and illegal Chinese in Canada. *Ethnic and Racial Studies, 25*, 490–513.

Kirkwood, S. (2017). The humanisation of refugees: A discourse analysis of UK parliamentary debates on the European refugee 'crisis'. *Journal of Community and Applied Social Psychology, 27*, 115–125.

Kirkwood, S., Goodman, S., McVittie, C., & McKinlay, A. (2016). *The language of asylum: Refugees and discourse*. Basingstoke: Palgrave Macmillan.

Koselleck, R. (1988). *Critique and crisis. Enlightenment and the pathogenesis of modern society*. Cambridge, MA: The MIT Press.

Koselleck, R., & Richter, M. (2006). Crisis. *Journal of the History of Ideas, 67*, 357–400.

Lueck, K., Due, C., & Augoustinos, M. (2015). Neoliberalism and nationalism: Representations of asylum seekers in the Australian mainstream news media. *Discourse & Society, 26*, 608–629.

Lynn, N., & Lea, S. (2003). 'A phantom menace and the new Apartheid': The social construction of asylum-seekers in the United Kingdom. *Discourse & Society, 14*, 425–452.

Nightingale, A., Quayle, M., & Muldoon, O. (2017). 'It's just heart breaking': Doing inclusive political solidarity or ambivalent paternalism through sympathetic discourse within the 'refugee crisis' debate. *Journal of Community and Applied Social Psychology, 27*, 137–146.

O'Doherty, K., & Lecouteur, A. (2007). "Asylum seekers", "boat people" and "illegal immigrants": Social categorization in the media. *Australian Journal of Psychology, 59*, 1–12.

Pilisuk, M. (1998). The hidden structure of contemporary violence. *Peace and Conflict: Journal of Peace Psychology, 4*, 197–216.

Pomerantz, A. (1986). Extreme case formulations: A way of legitimizing claims. *Human Studies, 9*, 219–229.

Reicher, S., & Hopkins, N. (2001). Psychology and the end of history: A critique and a proposal for the psychology of social categorization. *Political Psychology, 22*, 383–407.

Roitman, J. (2014). *Anti-crisis*. Durham, NC: Duke University Press.

Rojo, L. M., & Van Dijk, T. A. (1997). "There was a problem, and it was solved!": Legitimating the expulsion of illegal migrants in Spanish parliamentary discourse. *Discourse & Society, 8*, 523–566.

Rowe, E., & O'Brien, E. (2014). 'Genuine' refugees or illegitimate 'boat people': Political constructions of asylum seekers and refugees in the Malaysia Deal debate. *Australian Journal of Social Issues, 49*, 171–193.

Said, E. W. (1995). *Orientalism: Western conceptions of the Orient.* Harmondsworth: Penguin Books.

Sambaraju, R., McVittie, C., & Nolan, P. (2017). 'This is an EU crisis requiring an EU solution': Nation and transnational talk in negotiating warrants for further inclusion of refugees. *Journal of Community and Applied Social Psychology, 27*, 169–178.

Shank, J. B. (2008). Crisis: A useful category of post–social scientific historical analysis? *The American Historical Review, 113*, 1090–1099.

Starn, R. (1971). Historians and 'crisis'. *Past & Present, 52*, 3–22.

Tileagă, C. (2010). Cautious morality: Public accountability, moral order and accounting for a conflict of interest. *Discourse Studies, 12*, 223–239.

United Nations High Commissioner for Refugees (2015). *Global report 2015.* Retrieved from http://www.unhcr.org/gr15/index.xml

United Nations High Commissioner for Refugees (2016). *Syria regional refugee response – regional overview.* Retrieved from http://data.unhcr.org/syrianrefugees/regional.php

Weltman, D., & Billig, M. (2001). The political psychology of contemporary anti-politics: A discursive approach to the end-of-ideology era. *Political Psychology, 22*, 367–382.

Wetherell, M. (1998). Positioning and interpretative repertoires: Conversation analysis and post-structuralism in dialogue. *Discourse & Society, 9*, 387–412.

Chapter 13
Citizenship, Social Injustice and the Quest for a Critical Social Psychology of Peace: Majority Greek and Immigrant Discourses on a New Migration Law in Greece

Antonis Sapountzis and Maria Xenitidou

Introduction

Peace psychology claims its historical roots in World War II and the Cold War (Christie, 2006; Christie, Tint, Wagner, & Winter, 2008; Deutsch & Coleman, 2012; Wessells, 1996) during which time the prevention of war, conflict resolution and nuclear deterrence were the main topics that seemed to draw its attention (Christie et al., 2008). Nonetheless, researchers started to recognize that in order to avoid war and conflict certain prerequisites should be put in place such as respect for human rights and social justice (Deutsch & Coleman, 2012). As early as 1969, Galtung introduced the term 'structural violence' to denote institutional arrangements that promote the interests and power of certain groups of people while at the same time depriving other groups, thereby leading to suffering by indirect means. Leaving certain groups of people for example outside the umbrella of welfare or access to a health system may lead these groups to unfair treatment or even death (Galtung, 1969). Therefore, nowadays, peace psychology emphasizes equality, respect for human rights and social justice. This emphasis is often described in terms of 'positive peace' (Christie et al., 2008) or a 'culture of peace' (Adams, 2000; Fry & Miklikowska, 2012; Mayor, 1995). Within this framework, equality in terms of rights and political participation is seen as a necessary component for peace (Fry & Miklikowska, 2012). In this chapter, we examine the possible intersections between peace psychology and another topic that has gained prominence within social

A. Sapountzis (✉)
Democritus University of Thrace, Komotini, Greece
e-mail: ansapoun@psed.duth.gr

M. Xenitidou
Democritus University of Thrace, Xanthi, Greece

University of Surrey, Surrey, UK
e-mail: m.xenitidou@surrey.ac.uk

© Springer Nature Switzerland AG 2018
S. Gibson (ed.), *Discourse, Peace, and Conflict*, Peace Psychology Book Series,
https://doi.org/10.1007/978-3-319-99094-1_13

psychology recently, namely, the psychology of citizenship (Condor, 2011a; Stevenson, Dixon, Hopkins, & Luyt, 2015; Xenitidou & Sapountzis, 2018). Since citizenship is seen as a necessary condition for full civic and political rights, it can be argued that depriving individuals of citizenship is an instance of structural violence. Elsewhere we have maintained that discursive approaches are particularly fruitful in examining the way notions of citizenship are negotiated by social actors (Xenitidou & Sapountzis, 2018). Our focus here is on how both immigrants and Greek majority members construct citizenship in the aftermath of a new citizenship bill which contained favourable conditions for the acquisition of citizenship by immigrants. It is argued that a discursive approach to citizenship can help us examine the way people (immigrants and majority members) manage dilemmas of citizenship. This line of research can offer new insights into how we can promote and assist people to build a culture of peace.

Peace Psychology, Social Justice and Human Rights

The pursuit of peace is considered as the main focus of peace psychology. Yet peace is often not defined in abstract terms, but as the lack of its opposite; Galtung (1969), for example, notes how peace has conventionally been understood as the 'absence of violence'. By contrast, recent decades have seen a shift of emphasis whereby peace psychologists are more concerned with identifying and implementing (if possible) the necessary conditions for peace. Galtung (1969) has made an important contribution towards this shift: he introduced the term 'structural violence' to denote instances where violence is not actively practised by social actors, but is embedded within the social and institutional fabric of society. When populations do not enjoy full human rights and are deprived of access to welfare, medical care or valuable resources, their well-being may be heavily impeded and even lead to their extermination. Within this framework, approaches that aim at developing societal and institutional arrangements that promote social justice and equality seem to play a pivotal role. These types of approaches are often described in terms of 'positive peace' (Christie et al., 2008), 'sustainable peace' (Deutsch & Coleman, 2012), or as cultivating a 'culture of peace' (Anderson & Christie, 2001; Fry & Miklikowska, 2012; Mayor, 1995).

Respect for human rights is often seen as an important component of peace, while their abuse has been seen as an instance of structural violence (Lykes, 2001). Drawing on this, a strand of peace research has attempted to examine how people understand human rights and human rights abuse. Researchers have tried to examine the different personality factors, values and political orientations that seem to play a role in the support for human rights (e.g. Cohrs, Maes, Moschner, & Kielmann, 2007; McFarland, 2010, 2015). Different and often contradictory results have been yielded in different countries, suggesting that human rights are understood in different ways in different contexts (Ife, 2007). It can be argued that the political and citizenship rights of immigrants constitute human rights (Proto &

Opotow, 2012; Reardon, 2012). Therefore, withholding citizenship rights from immigrants can be considered an instance of structural violence: while they may be permanent inhabitants/residents, if the nation-state in which they reside does not grant them citizenship, they do not have the right to participate in democratic procedures, cannot hold office and in most cases, they cannot work in the public sector. Although the right to democratic participation in political procedures is clearly recognized in the International Covenant on Civil and Political Rights (1966), this right is conceded only to the citizens of a country, deferring, in this way, the decision of granting the right of participation in politics/citizenship to nation-states. To an extent this is understandable, since the UN—recognizing that the nation-state is the basic unit of sovereignty—cannot enforce certain migration policies upon its members. Not all countries of course hold the same laws and constitutions regarding citizenship. Even within the EU, where there are mandates demanding uniformity in some laws, there are great variations in citizenship rights (Koning, 2011). While in some countries naturalization procedures are straightforward, in others immigrants have to wait for a long time and meet difficult requirements before they are eligible to apply for citizenship. In that respect, researchers argue that universal human rights have failed to provide equal opportunities to citizens and non-citizens (Nash, 2009).

Citizenship, Migration and Social Psychology

Citizenship has recently attracted the interest of social psychologists (Condor, 2011a; Stevenson et al., 2015; Xenitidou & Sapountzis, 2018). To a large extent, the study of citizenship intersects with the phenomenon of migration and participation in a new national polity. In this respect, it relates closely to issues of social justice, democratic participation and access to welfare which, as we have argued, are essential features of human rights. It is generally acknowledged in the social sciences that the phenomenon of migration poses challenges to nation-states (Bloemraad, Korteweg, & Yurdakul, 2008). Citizenship, among other things, is a sense of belonging to, and participation in, a national community. Hence, in many countries citizenship is granted upon demonstration of adapting to the mores, values and culture of the host nation. Nevertheless, at the same time citizenship is closely linked to rights and a status that are conceded to those that earn and/or deserve it (Bloemraad et al., 2008). Of course, things are not straightforward: deciding who 'deserves' citizenship depends on how each nation-state defines itself at certain points in time and also on what counts as 'successful integration'. In the social sciences, it is generally acknowledged that two different conceptions of national belonging play a role in how a national identity is understood and therefore on who can become a member of the national polity. Ethnic nationalism considers the national community to be an aggregate of people who share the same culture, language and more or less share the same ethnic descent. Civic nationalism, on the other hand, considers the national community to be a collective of people who share the same political vision and concede voluntarily their individual freedoms to be handled democratically by the nation-state (Brubaker, 1992; Connor, 1993; Kohn, 1945, 1955; Pearton, 1996). Although this distinction has been used to classify countries, critics argue that it is overstated, and a mix of definitions is usually found in most countries (Medrano & Koenig, 2005). Koning (2011), for example, suggested that the ethnic-civic distinction should be considered as a continuum rather than as a dichotomy of national identification.

This distinction has ramifications for the guiding principles for awarding citizenship in different countries. In countries that are closer to the ethnic end of the continuum, the *jus sanguinis* principle applies (which is the official legal terminology), according to which citizenship is granted upon proof of sharing origin, culture or bloodline with the nation-state. In countries that are close to the civic end, the *jus soli* principle applies, which postulates that potentially all people within the nation-state can become its citizens (Brubaker, 1992). In countries where the official policy is closer to an ethnic understanding of national identity, it is more difficult for immigrants to acquire citizenship (Koning, 2011). Within social psychology, research has attempted to examine how different understandings of national identities may relate to attitudes towards immigrants. In general, this research demonstrates that the closer a definition is to an ethnic understanding of a national identity, the more negative the attitudes towards immigrants are (Meeus, Duriez, Vanbeselaere, & Boen, 2010; Pehrson & Green, 2010; Pehrson, Vignoles, & Brown, 2009).

Discourse analytic research on citizenship has emphasized the dilemmatic and highly contextual nature of constructions of citizenship (Barnes, Auburn, & Lea, 2004; Haste, 2004). In addition, discursive researchers have paid close attention to the ideological premises upon which arguments concerning citizenship are constructed and how these are flexibly mobilized in talk. For example, in the UK, while on the one hand multiculturalism is celebrated and racism is castigated, at the same time British citizens are considered to have more rights in legal terms, but also more rights to cultural expression (Condor, 2011b; Gibson & Hamilton, 2011). Research on naturalization procedures in the UK has also demonstrated the interplay between official understandings of citizenship and the ones mobilized by immigrants (Andreouli & Howarth, 2013). Although naturalization procedures (e.g. formal citizenship testing) seem to set the wider framework for how people understand themselves as citizens, they do not inhibit argumentation and deliberation upon these issues. Rather citizenship testing itself seems to carry its own contradictions and ideological dilemmas. It assumes a common set of values, which unavoidably bears the question of whose values should be endorsed, it examines technical skills (such as language and knowledge of the constitution) without assessing whether they are endorsed and yet it assumes that identity and the endorsement of these values and skills are the key criteria for integration (Gray & Griffin, 2014).

In Greece, the issue of citizenship has been quite contested since the end of the 1980s, when immigration began to rise. Discursive research reveals the dilemmas people face when they talk about citizenship and migration within the Greek context. In parliamentary debates on a new citizenship law, political leaders drew on discourses of illegal entrance to a nation-state to deem immigrants as a priori unlawful. At the same time though, in other accounts the process of granting citizenship to immigrants was called into question and they were constructed as 'legalized immigrants' undermining the institutional process that regulated their presence in Greece (Figgou, 2016). In the accounts of educators talking about their pupils' cultural background, on the one hand there is a plea for respecting their cultural difference, while, on the other, they argued that they should be awarded citizenship on the basis that they do not differ from pupils of the host society. In addition, while they were in favour of granting citizenship to immigrants' children, this was not seen as paving the way to further civic rights (Figgou, 2017).

In this chapter, we examine the ways in which Greek majority members and immigrants construct citizenship within the Greek context. This is crucial in so far as relations between naturalization, civic participation and civic rights are embedded and afforded in these constructions of citizenship. In relation to migration, these are entangled with social justice, a necessary prerequisite for a 'culture of peace'.

Background to the Study

The collapse of the communist regimes in eastern Europe led to increased immigration flows towards Greece at the end of the 1980s and the beginning of the 1990s. It was estimated that more than one million immigrants were living in Greece at the beginning of 2010 (Triandafyllidou, 2010; see also Baldwin-Edwards 2004). Most of the immigrants (more than 60%) came from neighbouring Albania, while the second biggest group (around 300,000) is people from the ex-Soviet Republics. More recently, immigrants and also refugees from Africa and Asia started to arrive in Greece. Greece seemed to lack both the infrastructure and the legal framework to help with the reception and adaptation of immigrants (Anagnostou, 2011). Although several presidential decrees were signed to settle the residency conditions and procedures of immigrants in Greece, the criteria that were applied were strict, making it difficult for immigrants to meet them, usually meaning that a large proportion of immigrants remained undocumented (Maroukis, 2012).

In addition, Greek national identity has been conceptualized in the Greek constitution and legal frameworks mainly in ethnic terms. This official emphasis on the *jus sanguinis* principle (Christopoulos, 2012) has made immigrant naturalization extremely difficult (Koning, 2011). Moreover, it has also meant that immigrants who are thought to be of Greek ethnic descent have had more access to welfare and benefits as well as a better chance of acquiring Greek citizenship (Kokkinos 1991). This has led to an alarming problem since large numbers of people in Greece have not enjoyed full citizenship rights. The institutional denial of rights for long-term residents within a country can be considered as an incident of structural violence: in not acknowledging the new demographic reality, and in applying an outdated naturalization law for a long period of time, the Greek state withheld political and civic rights from many first- and second-generation immigrants.

Things seemed to change in 2010 when the newly elected government of PASOK passed a new naturalization law which introduced principles of *jus soli* to Greek legislation. The law made it easier for first- and second-generation immigrants to acquire Greek citizenship, since some of the criteria were easy to meet (i.e. by birth, or education if the immigrants' children successfully attended 6 years of Greek schooling). Nonetheless, in February 2011, the Supreme Constitutional Court in Greece decided that the new law violated the Greek constitution, because it allowed the naturalization of second-generation immigrants without examining whether they share bonds with the Greek nation. This decision was heavily influenced by the *jus sanguinis* principle which is prominent in the Greek constitution. In May 2015, the new SYRIZA government passed a revised code of citizenship in the parliament which linked naturalization of immigrants' children to education in the form of schooling (e.g. enrollment in primary school from the first grade onwards for children born in Greece and successful completion of nine grades or six grades in secondary education for children not born in Greece). The research on which this chapter draws was conducted in the liminal period during which the bill introduced by PASOK was frozen and eventually deemed unconstitutional. The research examined how both immigrants and Greek majority members construct citizenship and citizenship criteria.

Method

The research was conducted in Thessaloniki, Greece. Thessaloniki is the second biggest city in Greece with a population of more than one million people. The percentage of immigrants in Thessaloniki is estimated at around 7% (Katsavounidou & Kourti, 2008). Participants were immigrants ($N = 25$) and Greek majority people ($N = 25$). The country of origin of the immigrants varied: the majority were from Albania ($N = 16$), followed by participants from Georgia ($N = 5$), Ukraine ($N = 1$) and Romania ($N = 1$). Most of them worked as unskilled workers while there was one doctor, one nurse and a self-employed/freelance translator. A few of them ($N = 6$) had a university degree, or were in the process of studying for one; others had completed vocational training ($N = 4$). All of the immigrants were documented (or in the process of acquiring documentation), but lacked Greek citizenship. Participants were approached in certain workplaces where it was expected that Greek majority people interact with immigrants: construction, tourism and hospitality, food, service and recreational industries, domestic work, public and health services, schools, parents' groups, etc. The interviews were mainly conducted at coffee shops or in the houses of the participants after working hours.

We conducted both individual interviews ($N = 24$) and group interviews ($N = 10$) in the present research. Group interviews were used because they are closer to naturally occurring talk and allow more in-depth discussion. It has to be stressed though that we did not find any differences between group and individual interviews in terms of the themes and interpretative repertoires participants mobilized. All interviews were conducted by the second author. The interviews covered a very wide array of topics: the current crisis in Greece, participants' daily activities, whether and how the crisis has affected their lives, migration, how they define citizenship, what they think of the measures on migration the Greek state has enacted, and so forth. Data were translated from the original Greek and transcribed using a simplified version of Jefferson's transcription system (Jefferson, 1984; see Appendix). Where there are no exact equivalents in English for a term used by participants, the closest alternative possibilities are indicated using a forward slash. For example, because English, unlike Greek, does not have a straightforward non-gendered singular pronoun, 'he/she' is used in the translated transcripts.

Initial analysis focused mainly on content: at that stage, we identified the main interpretative repertoires (Potter & Wetherell, 1987) or rhetorical themes (Billig, 1987) participants mobilized in the course of the interviews. For the analysis of the data we employed Critical Discursive Social Psychology (CDSP) (Bozatzis, 2009; Edley, 2001; Wetherell, 1998). Similarly to discursive psychology, this approach is concerned with how accountability is managed in verbal interaction turn-by-turn. As a result, it pays close attention to the micro-social context examining how people employ rhetorical strategies and what they achieve in discourse. At the same time though, it acknowledges that interpretative repertoires or themes are embedded within a wider social context. Within these contexts certain repertoires may be more prominent, common-sensical, or simply more relevant than others. CDSP thus allows for the drawing of links between the micro-management of accountability and more macro-social concerns. This is important in the case of citizenship since how our participants manage their accountability and the resources they draw upon can be traced in the socio-historical processes leading to the emergence of the notion of citizenship with Greece.

In the next section, we examine how participants—both Greeks and immigrants—construct citizenship in Greece in talking about the new citizenship law in group and individual interviews. Both Greeks and immigrants seem to draw on an essentialized notion of Greekness in talking about Greek citizenship. Citizenship is constructed as a sense of belonging, on the basis of which arguments in support of or against citizenship acquisition are formulated. Therefore, we noted a symmetry in drawing on an essentialized notion of Greekness and citizenship-as-belonging and in managing the dilemma of integration which manifested a persistent relationship between citizenship and nationalist ideology. We also noted that some participants (majority group members mainly but also immigrants) prioritized the notion of 'earned citizenship', while some others (immigrants mainly but also majority group members) emphasized 'the largely unconsummated citizenship obligations' of the Greek state towards immigrants. The ways in which belonging is constructed and accountability is managed, as well as the symmetries and asymmetries between accounts, are discussed in terms of the ideological implications they hold for the notion of citizenship and its role in encouraging peaceful co-existence.

Analysis and Discussion

In this section, we discuss the ways in which citizenship in Greece is constructed by Greeks and immigrants in talking about the new citizenship law in group and individual interviews. As indicated in the previous section, a commonplace identified in these constructions is that participants draw on an essentialized notion of Greekness while negotiating their different stakes. In addition, we note that this essentialized notion of Greekness commonly constructs Greekness as belonging. However, this construction may be used to achieve different rhetorical ends; for example, it may be used in arguments in support of or against the acquisition of citizenship by immigrants. In what follows, therefore, we discuss the ways in which citizenship is constructed by participants by focusing on extracts that exemplify these constructions. The first four extracts are from discussions with members of the Greek majority population while extracts 5–8 come from discussions with immigrants. The aim of this structure is to highlight symmetries and asymmetries between and across participants rather than reifying immigrants or Greeks as essentialized categories.

The first extract follows from a question posed by the interviewer with regard to the new citizenship law:

Extract 1
```
  Gavriela: FFFFF I am against the ((right)) to vote and the
((right)) to be elected. (…) with the Greek citizenship that
they got because of bi:rth now in the six yea:rs I am also
against to become (.) for a child to be born here and become
eighteen years o:ld (.) and ask for Greek citizenship I saw
this as more right but because he/she went six years to school
(.) and acquired the Greek citizenshi:p (.) I don't think so.
I have a child ((who lives)) opposite to me that was born here
in Greece >just opposite my house< they haven't spoke:n to him
in Greek. He doesn't go to school yet (.) they speak to him
in Albanian so that he does not forget his language. Is it
possible that this child will ever feel Greek? (.)
  (Individual    interview:    Gavriela,    Greek,    50,    public
services)
```

Gavriela develops an argument against the acquisition of citizenship by the children of immigrants through birth or schooling. In this argument, she draws on an essentialized notion of Greekness, constructing it in terms of 'feeling Greek'. While in principle Greek citizenship is presented as a legitimate claim if the conditions of birth (*jus soli*) and adulthood (maturity) are met, in practice this right is not divorced from national belonging. Gavriela builds the facticity of her account by claiming witness status mobilizing the vivid image of a child who lives opposite her home. She presents as a fact the observation that the child is only spoken to in his first language — constructing language as a precondition of 'feeling Greek'—and with the use of a rhetorical question the result of this fact is established: the child will not feel Greek. In this way, the participation in the national polity is constructed as contingent upon the development of a personal bond with Greece. In the extract Gavriela engages in stake management on two levels, as her argument may be accused of being against the both rights of immigrants and also against the rights of a child. She manages this by introducing values of liberal democracy: people have the right to determine their own fate freely—rather than have a fate imposed upon them—and this should be a mature decision (of adulthood). Previous research has discussed the ways in which citizenship acquisition or categorization on the same terms as the national majority may be problematic in so far as it may be seen as an imposition of identity upon immigrants and minorities on the part of Greeks (see Figgou, 2017). In this case, however, it is the parents who are positioned as potentially imposing a categorical membership on the child, and thereby denying the child the possibility of feeling Greek. In this way, Gavriela argues against the acquisition of citizenship by the children of immigrants drawing on a commonplace notion of citizenship as 'feeling Greek' while managing her accountability by appealing to principles of liberal democracy.

The next extract follows a discussion of the new citizenship law, with the interviewer subsequently asking if people living in Greece should apply for Greek citizenship:

Extract 2
```
    Zisis: >That is if I went to Holland I wouldn't be inter-
ested< to be: called Dutch or to feel Dutch. This I wouldn't
I wouldn't (.) want to feel Dutch (.) necessarily. I would
want my everydayne:ss to be functional where I live >but I
think I would understand< also a: priority of the Dutch on
some issues that concern them that is (.) I wouldn't vote for
their problems with the: I don't know if they have problems
with Belgium for example °now I say something°. I wouldn't
consider it fair to have a say on this.
    (Individual interview: Zisis, 36, Greek, teacher)
```

In the above extract, Zisis discusses the need to differentiate between citizenship as a purely formal status and citizenship as requiring a sense of identity (*feeling*). This distinction is embedded in two terms that translate to the word 'citizenship' in Greek (see Christopoulos, 2012), and has been shown to commonly function as an argumentative resource to argue for differentiated levels of membership in Greek society (Figgou, 2017). 'Ithageneia' ('directly descended') refers to citizenship in ethnic terms, and is portrayed as a higher form of citizenship reserved for native Greeks. By contrast, 'ypikooita' ('subject of') refers to citizenship as civic status, and is presented as a more limited type of membership that is appropriate for migrants. In the extract above, Zisis orients to this distinction in formulating an argument against granting full citizenship rights to migrants. Zisis uses an argument by analogy hypothesizing that he migrates to Holland—thus putting himself in the position of a migrant abroad. Through this hypothetical condition Zisis claims entitlement to speak as a migrant, and thereby manages his potential stake as a member of the majority group arguing against granting full citizenship rights to migrants. The hypothesis functions rhetorically to construct, inter alia, what he would do as a moral directive: both what migrants (should) want *and* the logical and responsible thing for them to do. This is manifested through a distinction between national belonging—being and feeling Dutch—and functional 'everydayness', with the latter reserved for migrants. Functional everydayness is constructed as both more relevant *and* more important for migrants than being categorized with the national majority and acquiring a national feeling about the host country. Migrants and locals are constructed as two naturally distinct groups with naturally different issues, concerns and interests. On these grounds, Zisis' account makes a claim for restricted political participation for migrants while catering for the accountability that such a line may bear by being hypothetically positioned as a migrant abroad himself and by making a distinction between access to citizenship and functional everydayness. Therefore, similarly to Gavriela's account above, Zisis' account also indicates that a discussion on citizenship acquisition by migrants is not divorced from national belonging. In comparison to Gavriela though, the stakes this dilemma of inclusion/ exclusion bears are managed by arguing for a 'higher form' of citizenship for ethnic Greeks and a 'lower form' of functional recognition for migrants as normal, natural and as desired by migrants themselves.

The next extract follows from a discussion on the new citizenship law and in response to a direct invite by the interviewer to the participants to voice their opinion on whether people who come to Greece should be assessed for their Greekness. This question was based on a question used in a study by Gibson and Hamilton (2011) which invited young people in the UK to discuss a statement which read: 'Some people have suggested that people who move to this country should take a test to see how British they are. Do you think this is a good idea?' (p. 234):

Extract 3

```
    Georgia: no but for me that is for me the basic and nodal
is that he/she has that many rights in order that he does not
see the acquisition of citizenship ((ithageneia)) as a way to
be able to live
    Evi: in total
    Georgia: in a country well (.) because I believe that most
people that want to obtain the Greek citizenship it i:s not
for reasons that >they feel so much citizens of this country<
a:nd have a desire let's say to vote to play an active role.
They have so condensed rights as immigrants (.) that is why
they    turn   to   the   acquisition   o:f   Greek   citizenship
((ypikootita)) (.) and I believe that there should be strict
criteria in e:h someone acquiring the citizenship ((ypikootita))
e:h o:f in Greece (.) as far as though he/she has very specific
rights a:s a subject of a third country
    (Group interview: Georgia, 42, Evi, 43, civil servants)
```

The rationale developed in Georgia's account is that the granting of 'specific' rights to migrants will make up for the rights they acquire through citizenship so that they don't 'need' to acquire Greek citizenship. This is reminiscent of Zisis' argument above that the important thing for migrants themselves is that their 'everydayness' is functional. In this way, Georgia dissociates migrants' rights from citizenship. Her position is potentially accountable as it is against granting citizenship to migrants *and* also constructs citizenship as something potentially beyond civic rights, as 'feeling'. This is managed in two ways—by speaking on behalf of migrants as, on the one hand, not feeling themselves to be citizens of Greece and/or caring about being active citizens, while, on the other hand, being in need of specific rights (that enable them to live well). A sense of citizenship-as-feeling is thus safeguarded as something only granted when strict criteria have been met, while at the same time not depriving migrants of basic rights and decent living conditions in Greece. In this way, similarly to Zisis above, a dilemma of liberalism which associates civic rights with 'feeling' Greek is managed through a seemingly liberal account which argues for basic rights to be granted to non-citizens. As in Gavriela's account above, this is again positioned as respecting migrants' own wishes in not having this specific notion of citizenship imposed upon them in order to live well in Greece.

Therefore, in the previous three extracts participants argued against the granting of citizenship to immigrants by drawing on a notion of citizenship as national feeling and constructing citizenship in terms of national belonging. At the same time, they managed their accountability by appealing to (other) values of liberal democracy—the right to self-determination and maturity—and/or by allowing for migrants to enjoy *some* rights. In this way, participants negotiate the boundaries of citizenship by arguing for a 'higher form' of citizenship for ethnic Greeks and a 'lower form' of functional recognition for migrants, which leaves the status quo intact (see Andreouli, Kadianaki, & Xenitidou, 2017). This is in line with Ariely's (2011) discussion of 'civic' tokenism: granting some civic rights to minority groups but not all citizenship rights to avoid shifting power relations.

The next extract follows from a discussion about a specific article of the new citizenship law related to immigrants' rights of political participation. The interviewer notes that this article was deemed unconstitutional by the Supreme Court on the grounds that it alters the electoral base. She then invites the participant to comment on that:

Extract 4
```
    Katia: Eh it is unfair okay when someone lives here perma-
nently and has years and especially for the children that are
born here (.) and grow up here (.) it is unfair. I see it a
little racist that is (.) you discriminate and that is why:
there is such a/that reaction from the: (.) the way they see
thi:ngs (.) the: the migrants in Greece (.) that is they don't
feel the country as their country (.) eh this keeps them at a
distance any way you see it when you live in a country and
it does not accept you your country (.) but they accept to pay
them taxes and to work as normal in this country and pay (.)
it goes without saying tha:t (.) it isn't right (.) it seems
irrational to me basically
    (Individual interview: Katia, 36, Greek, civil servant)
```

As noted in relation to previous extracts, Katia constructs a commonplace association between rights and feeling. However, in contrast to the previous extracts where participants argued for restrictions on migrants' rights on the grounds that they lacked national feeling, here political rights are treated as a precondition for the development of feeling. Nevertheless, the absence of feeling is presented using a categorical modality, which builds on the facticity of the statement, 'they don't feel the country as their country'. Migrants are constructed not only as not sharing in the national feeling, but also as having a potentially negative reaction to Greece. This could be treated as problematic for different reasons and audiences: for migrants, it functions to factualize an image of them as distant and reactionary; for majority members, Katia's account may come across as an accusation of unfairness. She manages these implications through an argument by analogy which builds on the liberal notion of rights and obligations: since migrants have obligations they should have rights. In this way, her claim that they don't feel Greece is their country is minimized while also appealing to a rational argument of fairness. While Katia's account is in support of granting political rights to immigrants (as part of citizenship), similarly to the previous extracts this negotiation is not divorced from the dilemmas of liberal ideology: political rights are not divorced from feeling. Therefore, citizenship values and nationalist ideology go hand-in-hand in accounts for or against citizenship acquisition by migrants.

Interestingly, immigrants in our sample also drew on essentialist notions of citizenship and constructed it in terms of belonging. As we noted above, belonging in the accounts of majority members was constructed as feeling Greek. Immigrants constructed belonging in terms of *bonding*, feeling that one is a member of Greek society, participating in Greek life, cultural belonging, and having a Greek mentality. As in the extracts above, in this orientation to citizenship, the construction of belonging was used in arguments for and against granting full citizenship rights to immigrants (but commonly against the preconditions set out in the law, on the grounds of proof, relevance and fairness as above) and functioned to construct different groups of others with variable access to rights and citizenship.

For example, in extract 5, we see a distinction drawn between the length of time one has been in Greece and the level of 'bonding' one feels with Greece. In the talk immediately preceding the extract, the interviewer mentioned in passing that the law was deemed unconstitutional by the Supreme Court and that it is up for revision, and then invited participants to discuss what they consider the preconditions for acquiring Greek citizenship should be:

Extract 5
```
    Soula: eh these what you have mentioned before I thi:nk if
you have been born here yes. He/she should shouldn't he/she
take? I believe he/she should and also a:nd with the years of
study.
    Thekla: I don't know if it is this exactly because there
are children that are six years in school (.) bu:t they are
just here in Greece and then they leave and study in their
countries. I don't think that identity ((card)) >citizenship
anyway< should be give:n to them. I don't know how it should
be assessed but it is an internal matter that is (.) I don't
know how you will understand if the other truly deserves to:
(.) e:h to get citizenship. >that is the matter is not practi-
cal< (.) how many yea:rs e:h let's say you are in school or
how many years you are here. There are people that are here
but they have nothing to do with e:h Greece (.) they are just
```

```
here and they work (.) inevitably (.) it is not a matter of
time (.) it is how much you bond.
   (Group interview: Thekla and Debora, 18, South Albania,
students; Soula, 18, Georgia, working in tourism/catering/
cleaning)
```

While Soula tentatively argues in support of granting citizenship to immigrants on the basis of birth and years of study in Greece, Thekla treats the conditions of the law as technicalities which cannot prove if bonding with Greece is established. In this way, she draws on an essentialized notion of citizenship as an 'internal matter', which consists of 'bonding' and is thus difficult to assess. In her account, she positions those to be assessed as 'others' ('people that are here but they have nothing to do with … Greece'), constructing a distinction between them and locals and shifting footing between addressing them directly and talking about them. The way in which her account is framed, constructing bonding as a precondition for Greek citizenship, does not seem to allow for Greek citizenship to be accessed by immigrants simply by virtue of time spent working in Greece.

Notably, Thekla argues against granting citizenship to immigrants, despite being an immigrant herself. She manages this on the one hand by differentiating herself from the immigrants she speaks of *and* by making a distinction between simply living in a country and bonding with it, implying that immigrants only do the former and in any case the latter cannot be assessed. In orienting to citizenship in this way, immigrants are not excluded from living and working in Greece, but are excluded from access to citizenship. However, by distancing herself from the immigrants she speaks of, she implicitly positions herself as being on the 'bonded' side of this distinction.

In the next extract, Costas also dismisses the preconditions of the law as technicalities by explicitly juxtaposing his personal experience and constructing belonging as a more important criterion:

Extract 6
```
   Costas: I think that thi:s (.) I mentioned this also ear-
lier that is someone (.) I that in this country live as Greek
(.) I don't think tha:t I should feel the preconditions (.) I
don't think that I should go six yea:rs ((to school)) I
shouldn't have to go (.) to read history and write exams for
the other to see if I am Greek. That is I felt from the begin-
ning I felt a member of thi:s e:h society don't know since I
took part in whatever was happening.
   (Individual interview: Costas, 24, Albania, civil engineer/
construction and food services)
```

As with Thekla in extract 5, Costas treats the preconditions as poor indicators of citizenship. However, rather than treating them as *insufficient* criteria on which to grant Greek citizenship to migrants, Costas mobilizes his own felt sense of being 'a member of this society' to argue that they are *unnecessary*. Through his example, belonging is treated as the main criterion of citizenship. Belonging here is constructed as feeling that one is a *member of* Greek society, and that one is *participating* in it ('I took part in whatever was happening'). It still holds, however, that while private feelings cannot be easily disputed, they are also difficult to assess. By linking them to active participation in Greek society, Costas points to the ways through which he came to feel 'a member of this society'. In contrast to Thekla's account above, therefore, where bonding seems to be taken implicitly for granted for some while not being assessable for immigrants in general, for Costas, feeling oneself to be a member of Greek society *could* be proven through being an active member in Greek society. In the way in which Costas' account is framed, therefore, while Greek citizenship is constructed as belonging, immigrants are not excluded from it; rather, by constructing belonging and feeling like a Greek citizen in terms of cultural assimilation an appeal to inclusion is made. Note, however, that Costas does not claim to feel *Greek* specifically, but rather to feel *membership* of Greek society. This enables him to claim inclusion while not challenging the status quo by laying claim to Greek identity.

Overall, it seems that making a distinction between technicalities and 'what really matters' provides the grounds for an association between formal recognition and feelings of belonging. On this basis claims to Greek citizenship can be made by migrants (cf. Andreouli et al., 2017), or in the name of migrants, or else such claims can be denied by migrants and majority members. Importantly, as indicated in the next extract as well, a sense of citizenship-as-belonging is negotiated so as not to exclude or be excluded.

Extract 7 comes at the beginning of the interview, in response to a question on what it means to be a Greek citizen and before any mention of the new law or citizenship acquisition by immigrants in Greece:

Extract 7
```
    Toula: E:h (.) ok I will resp- (.) let's say I that I am a
foreigner (.) to me what does it mean to be a Greek citizen
(.) I will tell you this very procedurally (.) e:h that at
least ten years have to pass to be able to get the citizenshi:p
what does that mean? >We have to pass an interview in which
we have to know the language (.) and the history< (.) despite
all these I don't think that these are enough to be citizen
of a country (.) e::h (.) in order for you in order for some-
one to be Greek citizen (.) look (.) he has to fee:l (.) the
values o:f Greekness ((Hellenism)) (.) that is I don't know
if someone who (.) is from abroad (.) and does not understand
what is happening around if he can indeed be a Greek citizen
(.) like I don't think that you should definitely be born here
(.) to be a Greek citizen (.) you could be: more Greek than
the Greeks (.) without being a Greek citizen (…) e:h for some-
one to be a Greek citizen (.) nice question (…) look (.) again
I say that obviously to belong in a culture (.) to have grown
up with some mores and traditions (.) e:h to: have Greek (.)
how should I tell you (.) to say it Greek mentality is too
much* to say it this way (.)
    (Individual interview: Toula, 37, Romania, translator)
```

Initially, Toula positions herself as a foreigner and orients to Greek citizenship procedurally listing the formal stages and preconditions. As in extracts 1 and 5 above, these are explicitly treated as insufficient criteria for Greek citizenship, which is subsequently constructed as feeling the values of Greekness, being immersed in and accustomed to Greek everydayness, belonging in a culture, having grown up with certain mores and traditions. While Toula states that adding Greek mentality may be 'too much', *jus soli*—birth—and *jus sanguinis*—Greek origin—are not constructed as proof of being a Greek citizen. In this way, citizenship is constructed as Greekness, which is nevertheless not a consequence of formal citizenship, nor of origin. In Toula's account, therefore, non-indigenous residents could be included despite their origin and civic status, but also excluded if they do not fulfil this notion of Greekness as cultural belonging. In this way, Toula manages the dilemma of citizenship by not excluding immigrants *tout court*, but also not including all immigrants as of right. By distinguishing the technicalities of citizenship acquisition from what citizenship *really* is, Toula claims category entitlement, aligning herself with those who know what Greek citizenship really is about.

Therefore, as in the two previous extracts Toula draws on an essentialized notion of citizenship, constructing it as cultural belonging, which seems nevertheless difficult to pinpoint (and assess). Similarly, the procedural aspect of citizenship is treated as a technicality, which while not dismissed or criticized per se (see extracts 5 and 6 respectively) is nevertheless treated as insufficient. Constructing citizenship as more than that—as requiring cultural belonging—allows for the inclusion and exclusion of others while leaving an essentialized sense of citizenship as Greekness intact.

All in all, similarly to the Greek majority members considered in extracts 1–3, the immigrants in extracts 5–7 negotiated citizenship in Greece by drawing on essentialized notions of identity. These are used in accounts which treat citizenship as a sense of belonging. Belonging is constructed as something that the law misrepresents or disrupts and is used to help formulate arguments for or against the acquisition of citizenship by migrants. In either case, participants are faced with a dilemma of integration and prejudice: namely, how not to exclude (and face the stigma of prejudice) or be excluded, while retaining the status quo of keeping Greekness intact. This suggests that the negotiation of citizenship is not divorced from the ideology of nationalism. While this is to some extent expected as interrupting Greekness could threaten the inclusion of majority members, the terms on which it is negotiated—belonging as feeling, bonding, cultural assimilation—suggest that ethnic nationalism is prevalent in these negotiations in Greece, with (some form of) civic status treated as important yet distinct from this notion of citizenship (extracts 2, 3, 7; cf. 4). Importantly, this relationship between nationalism and citizenship is also manifested in immigrants' accounts. Finally, this relationship is not only manifested in accounts that make an argument *against* the acquisition of citizenship by migrants, but also in accounts that argue explicitly *for* it. In such arguments, rather than constructing civic status as 'distinct' from this notion of citizenship, it is treated as a prerequisite for it (see extract 4 above and 8 below). This is manifested in the final extract, which is taken from a discussion of rights to political participation:

Extract 8

```
Roula: Very important to me ((the right to elect and be
elected)). It makes me (.) if I had this right they would make
me love more this country. Why? Because it would give me an
additional right to engage myself even more actively wi:th
political action (.) and with what goes on politically. Now I
hate her ((the country?)) politically I do not even want to
follow what is going on because it is all ridiculous all i:s
(.) lies a:nd (.) orchestrated that i:s completely (.) mechan-
ically all the words that come out everything set up nicely
(.) set up in a way to pass it on to a people with the/this
education that it has (.) either second rate it is or third
rate because first rate it is not for sure, okay? And with the:
(.) with ou:r culture (.) with our mentality (.) either to
digest it either to believe it either to pass us something
else. But it would have given me (.) a lot (.) of enthusiasm
(.) to engage with it. Do you understand? That is I have been
to Albania when I became eighteen they happened to have elec-
tions (.) and I have been over there a:nd I have: (.) taken
part >don't know< in the elections and I have felt very nice.
Without bei:ng (.) without living over there. Without in
essence to: (.) change my life much this the flow of the polit-
ical situation there to expect something to change very dras-
tically. Though just that I took part made me engage more.
That is I read about what is going on: what the parties
believe: about the law:s for this for that. Now I don't care
(.) and this is wrong (.) to discredit something (.) that is
so important.
        (Individual   interview:   Roula,   22   Albania,   tourism
industry)
```

Similarly to Katia in extract 4 above, Roula associates giving rights with the process of building bonds with a country, with the former being presented as a precondition for the latter (rather than the latter being a precondition for the former, which is the case in all other extracts). Roula talks about the Greek political system as corrupt, positioning herself with 'the people'. She then shifts footing to present the people as inadequately educated—and thus seemingly deserving this political system—and then aligns herself explicitly with the majority of the Greek people in talking about culture, mentality and being manipulated by politicians. Against that background—the blunt Greek political reality—she indicates that her personal feelings would be different if she had been able to participate in the elections. She supports this by drawing on her personal experience in Albania as proof of her intentions, and of the effect of actively engaging with politics, in a place which would not even affect her everyday life. Thus she claims that granting the right to vote can help to create responsible citizens who will engage in politics, and who will make rational, informed, choices. The fact that she does not participate in politics is accountable both as regards her extent of love for Greece *and* her civic responsibilities. However, ultimate responsibility for this falls on the shoulders of the Greek state, which does not grant citizenship rights and, thus, inhibits the full bonding which would make migrants into responsible citizens. As in previous extracts, here again talking about rights to political participation is not divorced from talking about national feeling.

This appears to be a commonplace in talking about citizenship in Greece in the discourse of both Greeks and immigrants. Citizenship is essentialized as belonging, and—as noted above—this may be drawn upon in formulating arguments in support of, or against, the acquisition of citizenship by migrants. Roula's account, for example, enables her to argue *against* the state and *for* full citizenship rights drawing on a notion of citizenship which associates civic status with feeling, with the former being a prerequisite for the latter (see also extract 4). In other extracts, participants oriented to this notion of citizenship in accounts that functioned to exclude all migrants (extract 1), or some migrants (extracts 5 and 7), from full citizenship (extracts 2 and 3), or in accounts which argued for inclusion (extracts 6 and 7).

Conclusions

The present analysis set out to explore the ways in which majority members and immigrants in Greece construct citizenship in the aftermath of a new citizenship law which contained comparatively more favourable conditions for the acquisition of citizenship by immigrants than had been the case in the past. By employing a discursive approach to citizenship, we discussed the ways in which people (immigrants and majority members) managed the dilemmas that were made relevant in this context. The findings indicated that, in talking about citizenship and political participation in Greece, both Greeks and immigrants seem to draw on *essentialized* notions in negotiating citizenship, constructing it in terms of *belonging*. While the ways in which belonging is constructed each time may vary (feeling Greek, feeling oneself to be a Greek citizen, a member of Greek society, participating in everyday 'Greekness', bonding, cultural belonging, love) this commonplace engaged participants in managing the *dilemmas of integration*: how not to exclude (and bear the stigma of prejudice) or be excluded, while maintaining this notion of citizenship. There are three further points to be made about this commonplace: first, this version of citizenship underpins arguments both *for* and *against* citizenship acquisition by migrants; second, it is drawn upon in both immigrants' *and* Greeks' accounts; and third, participants manage their own position within this dilemma, with the basic assumption of citizenship-as-feeling underpinning a range of specific arguments concerning the relationship between formal citizenship and a more elusive psychological sense of belonging/feeling. Thus formal citizenship could be treated both as a condition for a felt sense of belonging, and a sense of belonging could be treated as a condition for formal citizenship.

   Other commonalities in the way in which Greeks and immigrants talk about citizenship have been noted elsewhere (Andreouli et al., 2017). In the present analysis, we see a dilemma of liberal ideology between civic values and a feeling of belonging to a country. The boundaries and meaning of citizenship can be negotiated within the terms of this dilemma, which nevertheless provides the grounds for resistance to change and for safeguarding the status quo. For Greeks, the dilemma is used to 'construct a hierarchy of belonging that constrains migrants' abilities to make claims that they are 'truly' Greek' (Andreouli et al., 2017, p. 99), and, on those grounds, argue against granting full citizenship rights to immigrants. For migrants, the dilemma seems to 'allow them to make claims for citizenship either because they can argue that they fulfill the conditions of 'true' Greekness' (ibid.), *or* by constructing a hierarchy of 'others'. The crucial issue for the purposes of this chapter is the way in which these prevalent ways of talking about citizenship in Greece play out with regard to claims-making and the perpetuation of structural violence insofar as all these constructions share a common assumption of an essentialized notion of citizenship. If citizenship-as-belonging underpins accounts for *and* against citizenship acquisition, and sustains hierarchies of belonging constructed by both immigrants *and* majority members, then it may be that, rather than (or in addition to) a citizenship law, another avenue is required to enable immigrants to enjoy full rights in Greece.

Appendix

Transcription Notation
= no discernible gap between utterances
((text)) researcher's comments
CAPITALS louder speech
°text° quieter speech[overlapping speech
Text emphasised speech
"text" quoted speech
Te::xt extension of preceding vowel
(.) short pause
>text< speeded-up speech
Text* original (i.e. English) term used

All other punctuation marks (commas, full stops) are based on their regular usage (in both English and Greek).

References

Adams, D. (2000). Toward a global movement for a culture of peace. *Peace and Conflict: Journal of Peace Psychology, 6*, 259–266.
Anagnostou, D. (2011). *Citizenship policy making in Mediterranean EU states: Greece. Comparative report, RSCAS/EUDO-CIT-Comp. 2011/12*. Retrieved from http://cadmus.eui.eu/bitstream/handle/1814/19599/EUDO-CIT_2011_02_Comp_Greece.pdf?sequence=1
Anderson, A., & Christie, D. J. (2001). Some contributions of psychology to policies promoting cultures of peace. *Peace and Conflict: Journal of Peace Psychology, 7*, 173–185.
Andreouli, E., & Howarth, C. (2013). National identity, citizenship and immigration: Putting identity into context. *Journal for the Theory of Social Behavior, 43*, 361–382.
Andreouli, E., Kadianaki, I., & Xenitidou, M. (2017). Citizenship and social psychology: An analysis of construction of Greek citizenship. In C. Howarth & E. Andreouli (Eds.), *The social psychology of everyday politics* (pp. 87–101). London: Routledge.
Ariely, G. (2011). Exploring citizenship spheres of inclusion/exclusion: rights as "potential for power". *Patterns of Prejudice, 45*(3), 241–258.

Baldwin- Edwards, M. (2004). Στατιστικά δεδομένα για τους μετανάστες στην Ελλάδα: Αναλυτική μελέτη για τα διαθέσιμα στοιχεία και προτάσεις για τη συμμόρφωση με τα standards της Ευρωπαϊκής Ένωσης [Statistics on immigrant numbers in Greece: An analytic study of existing figures and suggestions for the compliance to the European standards]. Athens: I.ME.ΠO.

Barnes, R., Auburn, T., & Lea, S. (2004). Citizenship in practice. *British Journal of Social Psychology, 43*, 187–206.

Billig, M. (1987). *Arguing and thinking: A rhetorical approach to social psychology*. Cambridge: Cambridge University Press.

Bloemraad, I., Korteweg, A., & Yurdakul, G. (2008). Citizenship and immigration: Multiculturalism, assimilation, and challenges to the nation-atate. *Annual Review of Sociology, 34*, 153–179.

Bozatzis, N. (2009). Occidentalism and accountability: Constructing culture and cultural difference in majority Greek talk about the minority in western Thrace. *Discourse & Society, 20*, 431–453.

Brubaker, R. (1992). *Citizenship and nationhood in France and Germany*. Cambridge, MA: Harvard University Press.

Christie, D. J. (2006). What is peace psychology the psychology of? *Journal of Social Issues, 62*, 1–17.

Christie, D. J., Tint, B. S., Wagner, R. V., & Winter, D. D. (2008). Peace psychology for a peaceful world. *American Psychologist, 63*, 540–552.

Christopoulos, D. (2012). *Who is Greek citizen? The status of citizenship from the foundation of the Greek state until the early 21st century*. Athens: Vivliorama.

Cohrs, J. C., Maes, J., Moschner, B., & Kielmann, S. (2007). Determinants of human rights attitudes and behavior: A comparison and integration of psychological perspectives. *Political Psychology, 28*, 441–469.

Condor, S. (2011a). Towards a social psychology of citizenship? Introduction to the special issue. *Journal of Community & Applied Social Psychology, 21*, 193–201.

Condor, S. (2011b). Rebranding Britain? Ideological dilemmas in political appeals to "British multiculturalism". In M. Barrett, C. Flood, & J. Eade (Eds.), *Nationalism, ethnicity, citizenship: Multidisciplinary perspectives* (pp. 101–134). Newcastle upon Tyne: Cambridge Scholars.

Connor, W. (1993). Beyond reason: The nature of the ethnonational bond. *Ethnic and Racial Studies, 16*, 373–400.

Deutsch, M., & Coleman, P. T. (2012). Psychological components of sustainable peace: An introduction. In P. T. Coleman & M. Deutsch (Eds.), *The psychological components of sustainable peace* (pp. 1–14). New York: Springer.

Edley, N. (2001). Analysing masculinity: Interpretative repertoires, ideological dilemmas and subject positions. In M. Wetherell, S. Taylor, & S. J. Yates (Eds.), *Discourse as data: A guide for analysis* (pp. 189–228). London: Sage.

Figgou, L. (2016). Constructions of "illegal" immigration and entitlement to citizenship: Debating an immigration law in Greece. *Journal of Community & Applied Social Psychology, 26*, 150–163.

Figgou, L. (2017). Multiculturalism, immigrants' integration, and citizenship: Their ambiguous relations in educators' discourse in Greece. *Qualitative Psychology, 5*, 117–134.

Fry, D. P., & Miklikowska, M. (2012). Culture of peace. In P. T. Coleman & M. Deutsch (Eds.), *The psychological components of sustainable peace* (pp. 227–243). New York: Springer.

Galtung, J. (1969). Violence, peace, and peace research. *Journal of Peace Research, 6*, 167–191.

Gibson, S., & Hamilton, L. (2011). The rhetorical construction of polity membership: Identity, culture and citizenship in young people's discussions of immigration in northern England. *Journal of Community and Applied Social Psychology, 21*, 228–242.

Gray, D., & Griffin, C. (2014). A journey to citizenship: Constructions of citizenship and identity in the British citizenship test. *British Journal of Social Psychology, 53*, 299–314.

Haste, H. (2004). Constructing the citizen. *Political Psychology, 25*, 413–439.

Ife, J. (2007). Human rights and peace. In C. Webel & J. Galtung (Eds.), *Handbook of peace and conflict studies* (pp. 160–172). New York: Springer.

Jefferson, G. (1984). Transcription notation. In J. M. Atkinson & J. Heritage (Eds.), *Structures of social action: Studies in conversation analysis* (pp. ix–xi). Cambridge: Cambridge University Press.

Katsavounidou, G., & Kourti, P. (2008). La présence à Thessalonique de migrants omogeneis venus de l'ex-Union soviétique et la transformation des quartiers ouest de la ville. *Migrance, 31*, 61–70.

Kohn, H. (1945). *The idea of nationalism.* New York: Macmillan.

Kohn, H. (1955). *Nationalism: Its meaning and history.* Princeton, NJ: D. Van Nostrand.

Kokkinos, D. (1991). The Greek's state overview of the Pontian issue. *Journal of Refugee Studies, 4*, 312–314.

Koning, E. A. (2011). Ethnic and civic dealings with newcomers: Naturalization policies and practices in twenty-six immigration countries. *Ethnic and Racial Studies, 34*, 1974–1994.

Lykes, M. B. (2001). Human rights violations as structural violence. In D. Christie, R. V. Wagner, & D. Winter (Eds.), *Peace, conflict, and violence* (pp. 158–167). Upper Saddle River, NJ: Prentice-Hall.

Maroukis, T. (2012). *The number of irregular immigrants in Greece at the end of 2010 and 2011.* ELIAMEP Briefing Notes.

Mayor, F. (1995). How psychology can contribute to a culture of peace. *Peace and Conflict: Journal of Peace Psychology, 1*, 3–9.

McFarland, S. (2010). Authoritarianism, social dominance, and other roots of generalized prejudice. *Political Psychology, 31*, 453–477.

McFarland, S. (2015). Culture, individual differences, and support for human rights: A general review. *Peace and Conflict: Journal of Peace Psychology, 21*, 10–27.

Medrano, J., & Koenig, M. (2005). Nationalism, citizenship and immigration in social science research: Editorial introduction. *International Journal on Multicultural Societies, 7*, 82–89.

Meeus, J., Duriez, B., Vanbeselaere, N., & Boen, F. (2010). The role of national identity representation in the relation between in-group identification and out-group derogation: Ethnic versus civic representation. *British Journal of Social Psychology, 49*, 305–320.

Nash, K. (2009). Between citizenship and human rights. *Sociology, 43*, 1067–1083.

Pearton, M. (1996). Notions in nationalism. *Nations and Nationalism, 2*, 1–15.

Pehrson, S., & Green, E. G. (2010). Who we are and who can join us: National identity content and entry criteria for new immigrants. *Journal of Social Issues, 66*, 695–716.

Pehrson, S., Vignoles, V. L., & Brown, R. (2009). National identification and anti-immigrant prejudice: Individual and contextual effects of national definitions. *Social Psychology Quarterly, 72*, 24–38.

Potter, J., & Wetherell, M. (1987). *Discourse and social psychology: Beyond attitudes and behaviour.* London: Sage.

Proto, C. M., & Opotow, S. (2012). Justice, activity, and narrative: Studying of the World March for peace and nonviolence. In P. T. Coleman & M. Deutsch (Eds.), *The psychological components of sustainable peace* (pp. 177–196). New York: Springer.

Reardon, B. A. (2012). Education for sustainable peace: Practices, problems and possibilities. In P. T. Coleman & M. Deutsch (Eds.), *The psychological components of sustainable peace* (pp. 325–352). New York: Springer.

Stevenson, C., Dixon, J., Hopkins, N., & Luyt, R. (2015). The social psychology of citizenship, participation and social exclusion: Introduction to the special thematic section. *Journal of Social & Political Psychology, 3*, 1–19.

Triandafyllidou, A. (2010). Aspects and characteristics of migration to Greece. In A. Triandafyllidou & T. Maroukis (Eds.), *Migration to Greece in the 21st century* (pp. 57–96). Athens: Kritiki.

Wessells, M. G. (1996). A history of division 48 (peace psychology). In D. A. Dewsbury (Ed.), *Unification through division: Histories of the divisions of the American Psychological Association* (Vol. 1, pp. 265–298). Washington, DC: American Psychological Association.

Wetherell, M. (1998). Positioning and interpretative repertoires: Conversation analysis and post-structuralism in dialogue. *Discourse & Society, 9*, 387–412.

Xenitidou, M., & Sapountzis, A. (2018). Qualitative methodologies in the study of citizenship and migration. *Qualitative Psychology, 5*, 77–84.

Part IV
Conceptual and Methodological Reflections

Chapter 14
Discursive Psychology and Social Practices of Avoidance

Cristian Tileagă

Discursive Psychology

Over the last 30 years discursive psychology (henceforth DP) has developed into a massively influential field which has impacted on a range of academic disciplines in addition to psychology itself (Tileagă & Stokoe, 2015).

DP's roots lie in a variety of theoretical-philosophical and empirical traditions. In addition to ethnomethodology and conversation analysis, these include the language philosophy of Wittgenstein (1958) and Austin (1962), constructivist approaches to human development (e.g., Vygotsky, 1978), and social studies of science (e.g., Gilbert & Mulkay, 1984). DP's early eclecticism has sprung into a systematic approach to all things social—from everyday interactional encounters to institutional settings and the analysis of wider social issues and social problems. DP's key contribution to psychology and the social sciences lies in its revolutionary approach to how we understand and study psychology and particularly how we conceptualize language and social action.

Since its inception in the late 1980s and early 1990s, DP has developed along two main trajectories. DP's original engagement with ethnomethodology and conversation analysis substantially influenced the evolution of its methods and analytic focus and, in recent years, has, in turn, influenced many in conversation analysis, particularly with regard to debates about action description (e.g., Edwards, 2005) and cognition (e.g., van Dijk, 2006). A second, "critical" DP strand is more closely aligned to post-structuralism, with approaches to analysis combining attention to conversational detail with wider macro structures and cultural-historical contexts (Wetherell, 1998).

C. Tileagă (✉)
Loughborough University, Loughborough, UK
e-mail: C.Tileaga@lboro.ac.uk

© Springer Nature Switzerland AG 2018   245
S. Gibson (ed.), *Discourse, Peace, and Conflict*, Peace Psychology Book Series,
https://doi.org/10.1007/978-3-319-99094-1_14

These two traditions have resulted in quite distinct bodies of empirical work. On one hand, CA-aligned DP has focused on understanding the way psychological matters, understood as oriented-to issues in interaction, impact on the design and organization of everyday and institutional encounters, from child protection helplines (e.g., Hepburn & Potter, 2012) to police interviews with suspects (e.g., Stokoe & Edwards, 2007), and from interaction in care homes for disabled persons (e.g., Antaki, 2013) to investigating psychiatric assessments of different patient groups (e.g., Speer & McPhillips, 2013). On the other hand, the "critical" DP strand has generated studies of how interaction, conversation, and texts operate within wider social, cultural, and political contexts (Augoustinos, Hastie, & Wright, 2011; Tileagă, 2011).

It is perhaps appropriate to restate here (see Tileagă & Stokoe, 2015 for the original account) the three most important characteristics that should find their way into any description of DP. These deal with what DP is not.

First, as Potter argues, "DA/DP is neither a self-contained paradigm nor a stand-alone method that can be easily mix-and-matched with others" (Potter, 2003, p. 787). Historically, DP has not been overly concerned with offering strict methodological guidelines, but rather with providing a grounding for a certain philosophy, or orientation, to researching everyday and institutional practices.

Second, DP is not a universal approach to discourse, talk-in-interaction, or ideology, but is concerned with particular claims in particular settings that have particular consequences. DP offers particularistic answers to general questions and reframes debates around psychology's central quandaries (experience, mind-body, the nature of self and identity, categorization, prejudice, and so on). Those who equate DP's particularism with reductionism routinely miss DP's central epistemological thrust as well as its theoretical, and empirical, diversity.

Third, there is a tendency to cluster DP with qualitative approaches. Although it can be broadly situated within "qualitative psychology," it does not share its overall ontological and epistemological orientation. Neither does it share its methods; the main proponents of DP study the world using what Stokoe (2012) describes as "designedly large-scale" qualitative data (see also Stokoe, this volume)—that is, databases of hundreds of instances of recorded encounters, rather than small-scale interview studies of talk generated through a researcher. This does not mean, however, that DP cannot and does not enter into a constructive dialogue with the different/various branches of qualitative inquiry such as action research, narrative research, ethnography, and other styles of doing discourse analysis.

Although some caricature DP as ignoring issues of power, conflict, social justice, and social problems, DP engages directly with such issues as both resource and topic. The example of numerous applied interventions designed around researching and unpacking interactional practices (Stokoe, Hepburn, & Antaki, 2012), as well as the example of research studies using interviews or public texts to explore the reproduction of inequality and unequal power relations (Augoustinos, Due, & Callaghan, this volume; Stokoe, this volume; Tileagă, 2005), are all examples of DP in the service of some particular critical agenda.

To do DP "is to do something that psychology has not already done in any systematic, empirical, and principled way, which is to examine how psychological concepts (memory, thought, emotion, etc.) are shaped for the functions they serve, in and for the nexus of social practices in which we use language" (Edwards, 2012, p. 427). In the context of peace psychology, I suggest, to do DP is to examine psychological or sociological variables (things like interpersonal or group conflict, reconciliation for social justice, etc.) not as conventional "input" and "output" variables but as live and situated discursive actions (cf. also Gibson, 2011).

In this chapter I use the example of a key theme in peace psychology—that of promoting social justice or "positive peace" (Christie & Montiel, 2013) through reconciliation/coming to terms with the past—to show how discursive psychology might inform the study of how communities engage with the historical and social legacy of communism.

The Official Condemnation of Communism and Archival Memory

In the majority of former communist states, reckoning with a troubled and painful communist past has presupposed a strong dimension of recuperation and reassessment of communist memory and history through empowering the victims, identifying the victimizers, and revealing the nature and the extent of crimes and abuses perpetrated by the defunct communist regime (see Stan, 2007; Tismăneanu, 2008). The official condemnation of the communist regime in Romania in the so-called "Tismăneanu Report," that is, the final report of the Presidential Commission for the Analysis of the Communist Dictatorship in Romania, chaired by Professor Vladimir Tismăneanu, was a case in point. As an initiative unmatched by any other Central and Eastern European country except Germany, which constituted two history commissions in 1992 and 1994, the Presidential Commission set out to give a definitive account of the crimes and abuses of communism in that country (1945–1989).[1] The avowed ambition of the Tismăneanu Report was to provide a synthetic and rational account of the history of communism and, in doing so, to facilitate the creation of a unified collective memory of communism capable of overriding lay, individual experiences or perspectives (Tismăneanu, 2007a).

The leading author of the Report was Vladimir Tismăneanu, an internationally renowned expert (political scientist and historian) on communism. The Report consisted largely of an account of communism's political methods and institutions. It aimed at documenting the repressive and criminal nature of the totalitarian society and giving an exhaustive account of communism as a self-perpetuating political system. In December 2006, in front of the Romanian Parliament, President Traian Băsescu officially condemned the crimes and abuses of the communist regime, declaring communism as "illegitimate" and criminal. This is demonstrated by the following three excerpts from the Report:

---

[1] For more details on the structure, scope, and reactions to the Tismaneanu Report, see Ciobanu (2009), Cesereanu (2008), Tănăsoiu (2007), and Tismăneanu (2007a).

Excerpt 1

Condemning communism is today, more than ever, a moral, intellectual, political, and social duty/obligation. The democratic and pluralist Romanian state can and ought to do it. Also, knowing these dark and saddening pages of 20th century Romanian history is indispensable for the younger generations who have the right to know the world their parents lived in.

(Tismăneanu, Dobrincu, & Vasile, 2007 pp. 35–36)

Excerpt 2

Against the facts presented in this report, it is certain that genocide acts have been committed during 1945–1989, and thus the communist regime can be qualified as criminal against its own people.

(*ibid.*, p. 211)

Excerpt 3

Taking act of this Report, the President can say with his hand on the heart: the Communist regime in Romania was illegitimate and criminal.

(*ibid.*, p. 776)

As I showed elsewhere (Tileagă, 2009), by emphasizing the criminality and illegitimacy of the communist regime, the Report creates, affirms, and legitimates a narrative for a normative ethics of memory whose main purpose is to transmit responsibilities to a new generation. The key implication that can be derived from the Report is that the political category of "communism" belongs to an exceptional class of political categories. The Report is nonetheless careful to openly announce the conception of memory that it uses in framing the criminality and illegitimacy of communism. Gleaning the "incontestable facts that demonstrate the systematic, methodical, antihuman, and utterly repressive nature of the communist regime," as the Report puts it, presupposes working with raw historical materials and repositories—"testimonies, recollections, reports, information notes, meetings of the Political Bureau." (Tismăneanu et al., 2007, p. 35). These statements reflect an archival conception of memory based on the notion that the collective memory of communism is purportedly inscribed in documents, and documentary traces, and mediated by personal and institutional archives. This way, the historian of communism is akin to the ethnographer of institutions, as DeVault and McCoy (2006) suggest: "to find out how things work and how they happen the way they do, a researcher needs to find the texts and text-based knowledge forms in operation" (p. 33).

The emerging collective memory of communism is therefore inextricably tied to "text-based knowledge forms" (ibid.) provided by personal and institutional archives. In this context, what matters primarily for the historian of communism is the *correspondence* between experience and its representation in documents. Moreover, this process is perceived as "a necessary step in the development of the group's ability to speak in one voice or be a political actor in the process of its mobilization" (Misztal, 2005, p. 1329).

The archival conception of memory reflected in the Report is based on one of the most entrenched and enduring ways of thinking about memory: the idea of memory as storage of information, encoding and retrieval—the idea of memory as archive.

The "archive" metaphor is constitutive of everyday and scientific meanings of memory around the permanence and solidity of memory. According to Brockmeier (2010), "Western common sense, both in everyday life and in science, assumes that there *is* a specific material, biological, neurological, and spatial reality to memory—something manifest—in the world." (p. 6).

Institutional and personal archives are the place for historical encoding and storage of information, and they are followed by contemporary retrieval based on the principles of accessibility and activation. In the process of reckoning with a troubled past, texts, documents, etc. are activated by the gaze of the historian, and made to speak of, and stand for, the vital memories of millions of people who lived under communism. Their accessibility is also crucial to this entire process. Although accessibility does not guarantee truthfulness, accessibility is a key criterion for judging their inclusion in the encoding-storage-retrieval sequence.

The model of encoding-storage-retrieval of information proposes a nomothetic, normative, version for writing about a specific collective memory of communism. The hallmark of creating and reproducing social memory in the public sphere is represented by a "dogmatic commitment to one – and only one account of the past." (Wertsch, 2002, p. 125).

The communal memory of communism that is centered on the notions of criminality and illegitimacy, and is reflected in the Tismăneanu Report, is produced by probing the social organization of textual archives that reproduce a closed, self-perpetuating, system of inquiry. The archive model is firmly grounded in an individualistic and positivist view of human nature.[2] The archive model of memory limits our vision of how individual and collective memories are formed, how they are affirmed, how they are resisted, and how they are transformed (Tileagă, 2013).

In the case of the official condemnation of communism that took place in Romania at the end of 2006, the archives of the communist secret political police, the notorious and much-feared Securitate, become a "privileged space" (Lynch, 1999), a space of discovery, from where carefully selected details are used to support the perspective offered. The key (self-assigned) task of the historian or political scientist is to construct a representation of the recent past by uncovering "the facts about the past" and recounting them "as objectively as possible" (Skinner, 2002, p. 8). Archives, and texts/documents contained therein, "universalize or objectify, create forms of consciousness that override the 'naturally' occurring diversity of perspectives and experiences" (Smith, 2004, pp. 195–196). Yet, the communist regime was not only what Smith (1974, p. 261) would call "an administratively constituted knowledge," but also knowledge incorporated into various types and kinds of witnessing and testimonies, and various other public sources of memory. In order to appreciate the multitude of public sources of memory one needs to be able to reject a naïve notion of the past as a repository of social meaning, and of memory as solidly preserved permanently in a material (or mental) archive.

---

[2] As Brockmeier (2010) argues, what is lacking from the archive model of memory is a perspective on "human beings as persons who remember and forget, embedded in material, cultural, and historical contexts of action and interaction." (p. 9).

Social Memory and Social Practices of Avoidance

We take it now for granted that collective remembering is not simply a process of social representation. Memory manifests itself and takes various forms at different levels of social and political organization, in public and in private, in elite discourse and in lay meanings, in the guise of personal as well as societal remembering. Researchers working within and across disciplines research memory for the social functions it fulfills, and for how it assumes collective relevance in the cultural, social, as well as political web in which it is entangled (Keightley & Pickering, 2012, 2013; Wagoner, 2015).

The struggle to find socially and individually acceptable stories, the mediation of vital memories by personal and social relationships, and by material environments, is typically portrayed as a contingent, active and conscious social activity. Yet, I want to argue that the unconscious also plays a part in the mediation of these vital memories. A closer inspection of narratives and accounts reveals gaps, silences, avoidances, ambivalence and, more generally, a tension between wanting to express the uniqueness of painful, shameful experiences and wanting to repress these same experiences. This tension arguably points to deeper difficulties that people (and collectives) experience when encountering, and facing, a painful, troubled past. "One wants to get free of the past," Adorno (1986) admitted, "one cannot live in its shadow," but the "past one wishes to evade is still so intensely alive." (p. 115).

In this section, I focus on one set of social practices that are relevant to understanding the official appraisal of communism in public consciousness. I call these practices "social practices of avoidance."

One of my main concerns here is with understanding the role of what Billig (1999) calls "social repression" and what Frosh (2010) describes as "resistance." Billig's account of repression stresses the importance of social practices of "avoidance" that are part and parcel of conversational practices around topics or feelings that are too "difficult" to discuss.[3] Resistance refers to "something to be overcome"; analysis is a process of understanding the mind that is "at war with itself, blocking the path to its own freedom." (Rose, 2007, cited in Frosh, 2010, p. 166). Also, I am guided here by LaCapra's insights on the foundational problem that is facing historians and concerns "how to articulate the relation between the requirements of scientific expertise and the less easily definable demands placed on the use of language by the difficult attempt to work through transferential relations in a dialogue with the past having implications for the present and future." (LaCapra, 1994, p. 66).

In his work on the Holocaust, LaCapra distinguishes between "constative" historical reconstruction and "performative" dialogic exchange with the past. As he argues, this latter "performative" dialogic exchange relies on certain unconscious memory activities. The process of canonization of a single collective narrative around the nature of communism in Romania has been, predominantly, a constative historical reconstruction based on the factual reconstruction of experiences and an

---

[3] In a different, yet related, context see Tileagă (2015) for the relevance of "social repression" in the analysis of extreme prejudice against ethnic minorities.

archival conception of memory. In contrast, according to a psychosocial conception, whatever comes out of the past, whatever is "discovered" in dusty, previously unexplored corners of mental and physical archives, can trigger resistance, repression, and avoidance and can activate unconscious fears, phantasies, unexpected identifications, as well as unresolved conflicts.

In the remainder of this chapter, I focus on describing the performative dialogic exchange with the past in the Tismăneanu Report. I follow LaCapra in the assumption that the basis of a performative dialogic exchange with the past is rooted in the notion of "working-through" taken-for-granted ethical and political considerations. As LaCapra argues, "working-through implies the possibility of judgment that is not apodictic or ad hominem but argumentative, self-questioning, and related in mediated ways to action." (LaCapra, 1994, p. 210).

Perhaps the most striking aspect of the representation of communism in the Tismăneanu Report is the image of communism as the Other (Tileagă, 2012). Throughout the Report, communism is described in general terms as a "regime" and an "ideology," a "utopian conception," an "enemy of the human race" that instituted "the physical and moral assassination" and survived "through repression." However, communism is also described in national terms: a "(foreign) occupation regime," "criminal towards its own people," and "antinational," among others (Tileagă, 2009). To write of communism in the Report means to narrate the (Romanian) nation and its past, present and future. In doing so, the Report is proposing a specific method of reasoning about Romanian history and memory that constitutes communism as the Other, not quite "us." Interestingly, the narrative of communism is not self-condemnatory or self-blaming, but rather communism is distanced from (the national) self. This is demonstrated by the following excerpts:

Excerpt 4

> The total Sovietisation, through force, of Romania, especially during the period 1948-1956, and the imposition under the name 'dictatorship of the proletariat' of a despotic political system ruled by a profiteering caste (nomenklatura), tightly united around its supreme leader.

> (Tismăneanu et al., 2007, p. 774)

Excerpt 5

> Pretending to fulfill the goals of Marxism, the regime has treated an entire population as a masse of lab mice part of a nightmarish social engineering experiment.

> (*ibid.*, p. 775)

Excerpt 6

> ...the imposition of a dictatorial regime totally surrendered to Moscow and hostile to national political and cultural values.

> (*ibid.*, p. 774)

Excerpt 7

> The Romanian Popular Republic, who has come into being through diktat, or more exactly, through a coup d'état, symbolizes a triple imposture: it wasn't even a Republic (in the full sense of the phrase), it wasn't popular, and, most certainly, it wasn't Romanian.

> (*ibid.*, p. 765)

In the Tismăneanu Report, the communist regime is also found "responsible" for crimes "against the biological makeup of the nation." Through references to physical and psychological effects (for example, "psychological weakening and disheartenment of the population," and "decreased capacity for physical and intellectual effort") (Tismăneanu et al., 2007, pp. 461-462) communism is externalized and objectivized (van Leeuwen, 1995) as a sui generis political ideology designed to undermine the Romanian ethos. The Report describes communism as "antipatriotic" (Tismăneanu et al., 2007, p. 765), whereas the Romanian communist leaders are portrayed as lacking "patriotic sentiments" (ibid., p. 773), and Romanian communist politics are described as not representing the affirmation of a "patriotic spirit/will" (ibid., p. 30).

Paradoxically, the basic premise for the condemnation of Romanian communism is to construe communism as the Other, in other words as not reflecting Romanian values and national interests. This is not only in stark contrast with how ordinary people have experienced communism in both its positive and negative consequences (see Bucur, 2009, for an example), but this also encapsulates an active avoidance of the implication that communism may have been in any way a "criminal" ideology that reflected, and furthered, national interests. This position can be seen as an example of how a progressive, social justice repertoire masks and represses an insufficiently worked-through transferential relation with a controversial past. The textual construction of the negative qualities of communism in the Tismăneanu Report ("enemy of human rights"; "illegitimate"; "criminal") opens the way for the operation of social repression, the suppression of the socially inappropriate thought that communism may have been historically part and parcel of national identity. In this context, what is not said is even more significant than what is said. The negative attributes of communism are distanced from the (national) self. One can see how the writings of the professional historians of communism, who are adhering strictly to the conventions of their field, actively resist alternative ideological implications, especially those that closely reflect nationalist representations of communism in popular culture. As Frosh notes, resistance is a useful notion for understanding the subtleties of ambivalence. "Resistance," Frosh (2010, p. 167) points out, "has general significance as a way of indicating how a person might want something but not want it at the same time."

The topics of repression and resistance in the Romanian context will vary from those of other Central and Eastern European countries. Any thorough analysis of social repression and resistance will need to identify and explore general, but also specific, topics subject to repression and resistance. Post-communist transition has developed its own complex social conventions and discursive codes that resist and repress the topic of collective involvement in the perpetuation of the communist system. By constructing communism as the Other, paradoxically, even progressive texts such as the Tismăneanu Report are engaging in collective avoidance of this very sensitive topic. As new generations of young people participate in the public debate on the nature of communism, they acquire specific routines of thought, and in addition they learn the accepted and acceptable social conventions and discursive codes that present communism, and its legacy, as the Other (not "us"!). Building a mnemonic community implies a process of formal mnemonic socialization (through museums and history textbooks, for example), as well as less formal mnemonic socialization (families) into what must be remembered or forgotten, what must be expressed or repressed. According to the Report, the idea the "we" (Romanians) may have had anything to do with the perpetuation of the communist regime must be suppressed from national consciousness.

There is an inherent conflict present in any attempt to constitute a unitary and coherent version of the communist past. For the general public, communism is constructed as oppressive, persecutory, destructive, and aggressive. There are various powerful reminders of individual and collective powerlessness and suffering mentioned in the Tismăneanu Report. Yet, from the individual, professional perspective of the historian of the communist regime, communism does not seem so; it is rather something tamed, something already understood, as Tismăneanu himself acknowledges:

Excerpt 8

> For me, as historian and political scientist, the verdict of such a commission was not needed in order to argue that 'communism has been an aberrant system, criminal, inhuman'.

(Tismăneanu, 2007b, p. 42).

The double self-categorization as "historian" and "political scientist" indexes and legitimizes Tismăneanu's scientific, academic credentials and prepares the ground for the public expression of a moral judgment. It is interesting to note how any affective and relational aspects are subordinated to knowing rationally, intentionally, as well as scientifically (cognitively) the *true* characteristics of communism. For the professional historian, communism is both an object of loathing and desire. A process of "canonization" of a unique representation of recent history requires that alternative experiences, perspectives, and interpretations are actively suppressed. "Self-sufficient" professional research endeavors, to use LaCapra's (2001) term, are most effective in shielding official ideologies and images from the impact, contradictions, and paradoxes of memory.

Discussion

The vagaries and difficulties of a clean and ultimate break with the recent communist past in Central and Eastern Europe have been extensively documented (Galasińska & Galasiński, 2010; Petrescu & Petrescu, 2007; Stan, 2006; Waśkiewicz, 2010). One key insight coming out of the majority of studies is that the question of how to take communism into public consciousness arguably remains the greatest political, epistemological, and ethical challenge facing the post-communist states.

The conventional historical attitude is that "telling the truth" about the past and making it public will enlighten people and change perceptions. If one can only find the "right" words to describe the past, its nature (essence) will "reveal" itself to everyone. "Telling the truth" about the past is also seen as a progressive attempt to stifle and "control" the return of "negative currents" (for example, revisionist accounts and nostalgia), to bring the "repressed" oppressive ideology and effects of communism into public consciousness, and thus to banish the risk (and fear) of repetition. Yet, at the same time, the same progressive conventional historical attitude can obscure, mask, and suppress, as much as it reveals, key ideological aspects of the appraisal of communism in public consciousness.

This position should not be seen as denying the significance and overall social value of the conventional ways in which historians, political scientists, and sociologists approach the issue of coming to terms with the recent communist past. Historical knowledge of the objective (ideological) makeup of political regimes and other social formations should be continually sought as a remedy for half-truths, political manipulation, or simply ignorance. Yet, such knowledge, when used and reproduced as a "matter of fact," is arguably inadequate for handling the dilemmas and ambiguities of collective memory or for the development of broader social scientific frameworks of analysis. One needs to strive to find the meaning of the collective memory of communism in the sometimes contradictory, paradoxical attitudes and meanings that members of society uphold and negotiate, and not only in and through official representations of recent history "compressed into generalities" (Veyne, 1984, p. 63).

A parallel can perhaps be drawn between psychological therapy and historical enquiry. In *Analysis Terminable and Interminable*, Freud contemplated an answer to the question: "is there such a thing as a natural end to an analysis?" (Freud, 1937, p. 219). The conditions that must be fulfilled for a "terminated" analysis are extremely complex, but they involve three key aspects: "that so much of repressed material has been made conscious, so much that was unintelligible has been explained, and so much of internal resistance conquered, that there is no need to fear a repetition of the pathological processes concerned." (ibid., p. 219). Freud was skeptical of the idea that "it were possible by means of analysis to attain to a level of absolute psychical normality – a level, moreover, which we could feel confident would be able to remain stable, as though, perhaps, we had succeeded in resolving every one of the patient's repressions and in filling in all the gaps in his memory" (pp. 219–220).

It is resistance that "reveals the existence of an unconscious wish that gives glimpses of a subject's desire" (Frosh, 2010, p. 167). It is the *wish* for an all-encompassing narrative of communism that has led some historians and political scientists to believe that one could attain a level of absolute certainty that would resolve, once for all, the concurrent societal dilemmas, and societal struggles with consensus. It is not surprising that the Report was perceived as more a "spin-off of spin" (Wertsch & Karumidze, 2009, p. 388) than a genuine attempt at reconciliation with the past.

There is no "natural end" to understanding the recent past; there is no ultimate story. The imperative of a "shared memory" entails the "integration" and "calibration" of different perspectives and stances (Margalit, 2002). This means, primarily, the integration and calibration of what is not yet worked-through, of ambivalent and suppressed meanings. Moreover, social/collective memory is also multidirectional memory: it points in different directions, and operates on many fronts, at both conscious and unconscious levels (Rothberg, 2009). The implication of this is that "the haunting of the past cannot be harnessed in the present without unforeseen consequences" (Rothberg, 2009, p. 223).

Furthermore, this *wish* for an all-encompassing narrative of communism can be seen as a claim of (explanatory) ownership of its (negative) aftereffects. Yet, as LaCapra rightly argues, "the after effects ... of traumatic events are not fully owned by anyone and, in various ways, affect everyone." (LaCapra, 2001, xi). That is indeed the case of the Romanian official appraisal of communism. Any attempt at a definitive description of its aftereffects has been met with fierce, direct, and/or passive/aggressive resistance. The fixation on a single, unique, all-or-nothing description of the nature of (Romanian) communism has led to resistance. Resistance is puzzling to historians and political scientists; it is misunderstood by being attributed to and explained with reference to the internal psychology of the person and the democratic "competence" of individuals:

> the population lacks a sophisticated understanding of 'suffering' during the communist regime. One needs to explain, in order to make one's own, the criminal nature of dictatorship ... Perceiving yourself as a victim of a totalitarian regime entails a full understanding of the inner workings of the regime ... there is a danger of creating a selective memory of communism, based primarily on personal experience and which disregards the repressive nature of the regime (Iacob, 2010)

The core assumption here is that the ordinary person is "ideologically innocent" (Kinder & Kam, 2009, p. 232) and lacks political sophistication (cf. Converse, 1964). The commentator's views express an entrenched attitude that actively downplays the value of the everyday morality of (social and political) experiences (see Tileagă, 2013, for an extended critique of this position). Yet, as Todorov has argued, "if historians are going to further their understanding, to collect as many facts as possible and formulate the most accurate interpretations, then they must not decide ahead of time what morality they want to see in the end. History comprises very few pages written in black and white only" (Todorov, 2009, pp. 89–90). It also downplays the multiplicity of social sources of memory, and it treats people as "memory consumers" (Kansteiner, 2002, p. 180). Individual and collective memories are neither fixed nor given once and for all, but can be shaped and transformed into specific forms by cultural, societal, and political/ideological constraints.

Can issues of retrospective justice really be "fixed for all time," to use Teitel's (2000) words? The analysis of social practices of avoidance is largely absent from the agenda of historians and political scientists working on transitional justice. The analysis of social practices of avoidance is also largely absent from the work of peace psychologists. By taking social practices of avoidance seriously historians and political scientists of transitional justice, as well as peace psychologists, may be in a better position to appreciate the fluidity of collective (psychic) life that turns the "real" into "fantasy," the "unsettledness of psychic life, in which the tendency to rest at ease with oneself is undermined by the appalling capacity of unconscious elements to introduce something fantastic and full of desire" (Frosh, 2010, p. 6). By analyzing the sociocultural workings of social repression and resistance, the analyst engages in ideological analysis and social critique of what it means to *come to terms with* the past. As Billig (1997) argues, when one engages in ideological analysis one shifts the focus from the individual unconscious to the social and collective constitution of the unconscious. Frosh also reminds us that "psychoanalysis has an intrinsic link to radical social critique, because its concern is with unconscious impulses understood as destabilizing and subversive of social as well as personal norms" (Frosh, 2010, p. 12).

An analysis of practices of avoidance is not sufficient, on its own, in addressing the challenges of conceptualizing historical redress in historical/political science analysis. As LaCapra has shown in his wide-ranging studies of the Holocaust, adapting psychoanalytic concepts to historical analysis can present advantages as well as disadvantages. On one hand, they can help support "sociocultural and political critique in elucidating trauma and its aftereffects in culture and in people" (LaCapra, 2001, p. ix).[4] On the other hand, concepts derived from psychoanalysis should not "become a pretext for avoiding economic, social and political issues" (ibid., p. ix).

Researchers of transitional justice ought to consider archival, relational, and psychosocial understandings of memory as complementary, mutually informing positions. A deeper appreciation of the role of different conceptions of memory for memorialization and historical redress will hopefully lead to dispelling the illusion of a linear relationship between the accumulation of "positive" knowledge and the creation of "shared" collective narratives. In doing so, researchers of communism and transitional justice should be able to more clearly theorize and take into account the cross-cutting possibilities and challenges of researching vital memories. Any hope of full mastery of historical events—of the "last word"—is a regressive step. Historians of communism should perhaps appreciate more the subtle consequences of the psychic operations of "definitive closure … and radically positive transcendence." (LaCapra, 2001, p. 71). The task of the historian of communism is to produce an integrated view of coming to terms with the recent past, to introject or incorporate into the (master) narrative both aspects of an idealized, virtuous (national) self and aspects perceived as uncharacteristic of the (national) self. As a nation, a liberal polity that 'aspires to justice' (Nussbaum, 2013, p. 3), Romania has sustained a strong, unfailing commitment to meaningful, official and unofficial memory and identity projects of coming to terms with the communist past. It has overcome numerous barriers and, over the years, it has created a "vigilant critical culture" (ibid., p. 124) that has supported transitional justice, and the continuation of liberal and democratic values. This vigilant critical culture, however, is not devoid of ambivalence; it is not immune to the operations of repression and resistance. There is a need to excavate the nature of this ambivalence, to unearth more of the nature of repression and resistance that may stand in the way of a full understanding, and ownership, of a myriad of vital memories of communism.

---

[4] See also Frosh (2010) on the implications of drawing upon psychoanalysis "outside the clinic" and the contributions in Stevens, Duncan & Hook (2013) on the role of psychoanalytic vocabulary for working through the socio-historical trauma of apartheid racism.

Conclusion

As this chapter, and others in this collection, hopefully show, DP can be a useful tool for analyzing practices of human accountability - and human affairs in general - in and as part of everyday and institutional practices.

DP has developed, and transformed, into an original and innovative program of research with far-reaching impact for psychology and its sub-disciplines. Peace psychology can benefit from incorporating discursive psychology among its existing approaches. But this would constitute more than a methodological addition—it would imply developing novel and sophisticated ways to understand human sociality and practices based on the study of talk and text as an action-oriented, world-building resource, rather than a tool of transmission and communication from one mind or setting to another. A discursive peace psychology—that is, a renewed peace psychology based on the study of language practices—can establish itself to be, in the long term, a viable intellectual home for any researcher that takes seriously the study of situated social practices.

As Derek Edwards notes, DP "rests upon a very different, and non-causal conception of what makes social actions orderly and intelligible" (Edwards, 2012, p. 432). The upshot of developing the meaning of this description rests with promoting new ways of thinking about the epistemological and methodological *grounds* of what peace psychologists do, the ideas they explore, the critiques they develop, the research avenues they take, and the impact that some of their ideas have (or might have in the future).

Acknowledgments I am grateful to John Wiley & Sons, Routledge, and Cambridge Scholars Publishing for permitting me to reproduce and adapt material published elsewhere.

References

Adorno, T. (1986). What does coming to terms with the past mean? (trans. T. Bahti & G. Hartman). In G. Hartman (Ed.), *Bitburg in moral and political perspective* (pp. 114–129). Bloomington: Indiana University Press.

Antaki, C. (2013). Two conversational practices for encouraging adults with intellectual disabilities to reflect on their activities. *Journal of Intellectual Disability Research, 57*, 580–588.

Augoustinos, M., Hastie, B., & Wright, M. (2011). Apologizing for historical injustice: Emotion, truth and identity in political discourse. *Discourse & Society, 22*, 507–531.

Austin, J. L. (1962). *How to do things with words*. Oxford: Clarendon Press.

Billig, M. (1997). Discursive, rhetorical and ideological messages. In C. McGarty & S. A. Haslam (Eds.), *The message of social psychology*. Oxford: Blackwell.

Billig, M. (1999). *Freudian repression*. Cambridge: Cambridge University Press.

Brockmeier, J. (2010). After the archive: Remapping memory. *Culture & Psychology, 16*, 5–35.

Bucur, M. (2009). *Heroes and victims: Remembering war in twentieth-century Romania*. Bloomington: Indiana University Press.

Cesereanu, R. (2008). The final report on the Holocaust and the final report on the Communist dictatorship in Romania. *East European Politics and Societies, 22*, 270–281.

Christie, D., & Montiel, C. (2013). Contributions of psychology to war and peace. *American Psychologist, 68*, 502–513.

Ciobanu, M. (2009). Criminalising the past and reconstructing collective memory: The Romanian Truth Commission. *Europe-Asia Studies, 61*, 313–336.

Converse, P. E. (1964). The nature of belief systems in mass publics. In D. Apter (Ed.), *Ideology and discontent* (pp. 206–261). New York: Free Press.

DeVault, M., & McCoy, L. (2006). Institutional ethnography: Using interviews to investigate ruling relations. In D. Smith (Ed.), *Institutional ethnography as practice* (pp. 15–44). Lanharn: Rowman & Littlefield.

Edwards, D. (2005). Moaning, whinging and laughing: The subjective side of complaints. *Discourse Studies, 7*, 5–29.

Edwards, D. (2012). Discursive and scientific psychology. *British Journal of Social Psychology, 51*, 425–435.

Freud, S. (1937). Analysis terminable and interminable. *SE, 23*, 209–253.

Frosh, S. (2010). *Psychoanalysis outside the clinic: Interventions in psychosocial studies.* Basingstoke: Palgrave Macmillan.

Galasińska, A., & Galasiński, D. (Eds.). (2010). *The post-communist condition: Public and private discourses of transformation.* Amsterdam: John Benjamins.

Gibson, S. (2011). Social psychology, war and peace: Towards a critical discursive peace psychology. *Social and Personality Psychology Compass, 5*, 239–250.

Gilbert, G. N., & Mulkay, M. (1984). *Opening Pandora's Box: A sociological analysis of scientists' discourse.* Cambridge: Cambridge University Press.

Hepburn, A., & Potter, J. (2012). Crying and crying responses. In A. Peräkylä & M.-L. Sorjonen (Eds.), *Emotion in interaction* (pp. 194–210). Oxford: Oxford University Press.

Iacob, B. C. (2010). *Avem nevoie de o pedagogie a memoriei colective a trecutului comunist.* Retrieved from http://www.evz.ro/detalii/stiri/bogdan-cristian-iacob-avem-nevoie-de-o-pedagogie-a-memoriei-colective-a-trecutului-comunist-90689.html

Kansteiner, W. (2002). Finding meaning in memory: A methodological critique of collective memory studies. *History & Theory, 41*, 179–197.

Keightley, E., & Pickering, M. (2012). *The mnemonic imagination: Remembering as creative practice.* London: Palgrave Macmillan.

Keightley, E., & Pickering, M. (2013). Painful pasts. In E. Keightley & M. Pickering (Eds.), *Research methods for memory studies* (pp. 151–166). Edinburgh: Edinburgh University Press.

Kinder, D. R., & Kam, C. D. (2009). *Us against them: Ethnocentric foundations of American opinion.* Chicago: Chicago University Press.

LaCapra, D. (1994). *Representing the Holocaust: History, theory, trauma.* Ithaca, NY: Cornell University Press.

LaCapra, D. (2001). *Writing history, writing trauma.* Baltimore, MD: Johns Hopkins University Press.

Lynch, M. (1999). Archives in formation: Privileged spaces, popular archives and paper trails. *History of the Human Sciences, 12*, 65–87.

Margalit, A. (2002). *The ethics of memory.* Cambridge, MA: Harvard University Press.

Misztal, B. (2005). Memory and democracy. *American Behavioral Scientist, 48*, 1320–1338.

Nussbaum, M. (2013). *Political emotions: Why love matters for justice.* Cambridge, MA: Harvard University Press.

Petrescu, C., & Petrescu, D. (2007). Mastering vs. coming to terms with the past: A critical analysis of post-communist Romanian historiography. In A. Antohi, B. Trencsenyi, & P. Apor (Eds.), *Narratives unbound: Historical studies in post-communist Europe* (pp. 311–408). Budapest: CEU Press.

Potter, J. (2003). Discursive psychology: Between method and paradigm. *Discourse & Society, 14*, 783–794.

Rose, J. (2007). *The last resistance.* London: Verso.

Rothberg, M. (2009). *Multidirectional memory: Remembering the Holocaust in the age of decolonization*. Stanford, CA: Stanford University Press.

Skinner, Q. (2002). *Visions of politics: Regarding method* (Vol. I). Cambridge: Cambridge University Press.

Smith, D. (1974). The social construction of documentary reality. *Sociological Inquiry, 44*, 257–268.

Smith, D. (2004). *Writing the social: Critique, theory and investigations*. Toronto: University of Toronto Press.

Speer, S., & McPhillips, R. (2013). Patients' perspectives on psychiatric consultations in the gender identity clinic: Implications for patient-centered communication. *Patient Education and Counseling, 91*, 385–391.

Stan, L. (2006). The vanishing truth: Politics and memory in post-communist Europe. *East European Quarterly, 40*, 383–408.

Stan, L. (2007). Comisia Tismăneanu: Repere internaţionale. *Sfera Politicii, 126-127*, 7–13.

Stevens, G., Duncan, N., & Hook, D. (Eds.). (2013). *Race, memory and the Apartheid archive: Towards a transformative psychosocial praxis*. Basingstoke: Palgrave Macmillan.

Stokoe, E. (2012). Moving forward with membership categorization analysis: Methods for systematic analysis. *Discourse Studies, 14*, 277–303.

Stokoe, E., & Edwards, D. (2007). 'Black this, black that': Racial insults and reported speech in neighbour complaints and police interrogations. *Discourse & Society, 18*, 337–372.

Stokoe, E., Hepburn, A., & Antaki, C. (2012). Beware the "Loughborough School" of social psychology: Interaction and the politics of intervention. *British Journal of Social Psychology, 51*, 486–496.

Tănăsoiu, C. (2007). The Tismăneanu report: Romania revisits its past. *Problems of Post-Communism, 54*, July/August.

Tileaga, C. (2005) Accounting for extreme prejudice and legitimating blame in talk about the Romanies. *Discourse & Society, 16*(5), 603–624.

Tileagă, C. (2009). The social organization of representations of history: The textual accomplishment of coming to terms with the past. *British Journal of Social Psychology, 48*, 337–355.

Tileagă, C. (2011). (Re)writing biography: Memory, identity, and textually mediated reality in coming to terms with the past. *Culture & Psychology, 17*, 197–215.

Tileagă, C. (2012). Communism in retrospect: The rhetoric of historical representation and writing the collective memory of recent past. *Memory Studies, 5*, 462–478.

Tileagă, C. (2013). *Political psychology: Critical perspectives*. Cambridge: Cambridge University Press.

Tileagă, C. (2015). *The nature of prejudice: Society, discrimination and moral exclusion*. London: Routledge.

Tileagă, C., & Stokoe, E. (Eds.). (2015). *Discursive psychology: Classic and contemporary issues*. London: Routledge.

Tismăneanu, V. (2007a). Confronting Romania's past: A response to Charles King. *Slavic Review, 66*, Winter.

Tismăneanu, V. (2007b). *Refuzul de a uita: Articole şi comentarii politice (2006–2007)*. Iasi: Curtea Veche.

Tismăneanu, V. (2008). Democracy and memory: Romania confronts its communist past. *The Annals of the American Academy of Political and Social Science, 617*, 166–180.

Tismăneanu, V., Dobrincu, D., & Vasile, C. (2007). *Raport final: Comisia prezidentiala pentru analiza dictaturii comuniste din Romania*. Bucuresti: Humanitas.

Todorov, T. (2009). *In defence of the enlightenment*. London: Atlantic Books.

van Dijk, T. A. (Ed.). (2006). Discourse, interaction, and cognition [special issue]. *Discourse Studies, 8*(1).

van Leeuwen, T. (1995). Representing social action. *Discourse & Society, 6*, 81–106.

Veyne, P. (1984). *Writing history: Essay on epistemology*. (M, Moore-Rinvolucri, Trans. Middletown, CT: Wesleyan University Press.

Vygotsky, L. S. (1978). *Mind in society: The development of higher psychological processes.* Cambridge, MA: Harvard University Press.

Wagoner, B. (2015). Collective remembering as a process of social representation. In G. Sammut, E. Andreouli, G. Gaskell, & J. Valsiner (Eds.), *The Cambridge handbook of social representations* (pp. 143–162). Cambridge: Cambridge University Press.

Waśkiewicz, A. (2010). The Polish home army and the politics of memory. *East European Politics and Society, 24*, 44–58.

Wertsch, J. (2002). *Voices of collective remembering.* Cambridge: Cambridge University Press.

Wertsch, J., & Karumidze, Z. (2009). Spinning the past: Russian and Georgian accounts of the War of August 2008. *Memory Studies, 2*, 377–391.

Wetherell, M. (1998). Positioning and interpretative repertoires: Conversation analysis and post-structuralism in dialogue. *Discourse & Society, 9*, 387–412.

Wittgenstein, L. (1958). *Philosophical investigations.* Oxford: Blackwell.

Chapter 15
Structure and Agency in Peace Psychology: Temporality as Mediating Gesture Between Abstract and Concrete Intervention

Kevin McKenzie

My interest in this chapter will be to explore how an orientation to different aspects of temporality affords a way of managing contrastive demands for moral account-ability in descriptions of conflict intervention by peace psychologists and other third-party actors. More specifically, I will be concerned to explore how the professional activities of those outside parties involved in managing the various effects of armed conflict are afforded moral legitimacy through the selective appeal to both structural and agentive accounts of related violence, and will consider the way that these different forms of explanation are variably invoked to underwrite the legitimacy of activities on the part of these professional practitioners. We will begin by examining the text of a programmatic description taken from the literature of peace psychology (Christie, Tint, Wagner, & Winter, 2008; see also Christie, 2006 and Christie & Montiel, 2013), and then move on to consider a number of examples of talk recorded in face-to-face interviews with representatives of various humanitarian aid organizations that operate in Israel and the Occupied Palestinian Territories.[1] An especially significant feature of the different modes of accountability we will consider is that of the descriptive placement of the particulars of armed conflict along a temporally unfolding trajectory, such that concrete events of violent

---

[1] These conversational materials were recorded over a six-week period in early 2004 while I was a Visiting Research Scholar at the University of Cyprus, and are comprised of open-ended discussions with some 43 different speakers representing various high-profile and lesser-known humanitarian aid organizations. These include various UN agencies, the International Committee for the Red Cross, Care International, Médecins Sans Frontières, Save the Children, and others. Participant identities in the transcripts presented here have been systematically obscured through the use of pseudonyms and the alteration of otherwise revealing details (see below for Appendix detailing transcript conventions). I am grateful to Dr. Eleni Theocharous MEP of the Cyprus chapter of Médecins du Monde, as well as staff of the Palestinian Red Crescent Society for their generous assistance in the collection of these materials.

K. McKenzie (✉)
Independent Researcher (formerly at University of Cyprus and Qatar University),
Brooklyn, New York, USA

© Springer Nature Switzerland AG 2018 261
S. Gibson (ed.), *Discourse, Peace, and Conflict*, Peace Psychology Book Series,
https://doi.org/10.1007/978-3-319-99094-1_15

confrontation are related to a noumenal order of explanatory reasoning wherein those particulars are taken as documentary evidence of the transcendent, structural origins out of which they (those particulars) are said to emerge. Both structural and agentive modes of explanation are made relevant to justify the relationship that third-party actors have with the antagonists of conflict, both for the positive effects those relations are presumed to have on the relationship between said antagonists, and for the entitlement of those outside parties to act upon the related affairs in question.

As discussed in the introduction to this volume, discursive psychology (hereafter DP) is an endeavor under whose rubric a variety of different (and arguably incompatible) analytic practices are carried out. These range anywhere from that involving a strict focus on the action-orientation of scholarly and lay representations of cognition (and their putatively underlying operations), to critical analyses that reify the social as an autonomous domain through their treatment of participant formulations as documentary evidence. Despite the not insignificant differences between such discrete lines of analysis, a common feature they share is that of an approach to discursive representation as a *constructive* (or *formal*) *analytic* undertaking.[2] This draws on Harold Garfinkel's radical program of analytic re-specification wherein the situated, practical uses that get made of everyday description are examined as investigative phenomena in their own right (rather than as epiphenomenal indices of underlying causes for the remote activities and events to which they ostensibly refer).[3] Operational questions related to such a program are thus not to do with the plausibility of the specific claims that are entailed in mundane assertions—arrived at on independent grounds, as it were—but with how social order is immanently accomplished in and as the conduct of the methodical procedures by which the relevance of such claims is furnished.[4] Put differently, ethnomethodologists regard social order to be immanently realized in the emergent details of its situated conduct. Moreover, the evidentiary status of emergent detail is reflexively made available both by and for members themselves as a necessary condition of social order production. Providing for a common perspective on the evidentiary (or documentary) status of some particular detail (vis-à-vis the category of which that detail is

---

[2] The principal distinction between these related forms of DP can be attributed to how assiduously that approach is adopted (see McKenzie, Forthcoming).

[3] Along these lines, Lynch (1993) notes that (p. 190): "ethnomethodologists try to characterize the organized uses of indexical expressions, including the various lay and professional uses of formulations. Inevitably, ethnomethodologists engage in formulating, if only to formulate the work of doing formulating, but unlike constructive analysts, they "topicalize" the relationship between formulations and activities in other than truth-conditional terms. That is, they do not treat formulations exclusively as true or false statements; instead, they investigate how they act as pragmatic moves in temporal orders of action."

[4] The related literature here is voluminous and a bibliographic catalogue of its contributions would run into many pages. A reasonable starting point into that literature, however, would include (Garfinkel, 2002, especially see Ann Warfield Rawls' editorial introduction, pp. 1–76), Heritage (1984), Hilbert (1992, 2009), Korbut (2014), Sharrock and Anderson (1986), as well as contributions to Button (1991) and Coulter (1990).

taken to be a manifestation) is thus a joint undertaking whose collaborative conduct is constitutive of social order itself. Social actors work to make evident to one another what it is they are doing, in and as the course of that activity's conduct. The phenomena for investigation that ethnomethodology takes up is the detailed exploration of exactly how that work gets done, and of how members' practical agreement concerning the methodical nature of that work's uniquely detailed operation is definitive of social order.[5]

Against this background, questions of social accountability are taken up for how they feature as participant concerns. This means that the various accounts which social actors formulate in order to make sense of their own and others' actions (including those said to have taken place in remote circumstances) are examined not for their accuracy as determined by some set of criteria independent to the occasions where their relevance is furnished, but as a phenomenon in which the explanations that underwrite shared reasoning are collaboratively assembled. Accounts are not examined primarily for the sense they furnish of the remote events and activities to which they refer, but for how that sense is made operational to the situated purposes of their production. What are the presumptive suppositions that such accounts furnish, and how are they made to operate in the circumstances where they are made available? These are questions that DP also pursues in its own examination of how the considerations whose investigation has traditionally been taken to define the discipline of social psychology are themselves made to feature as participant concerns (see related discussion in Coulter 1999, 2004; Potter & Edwards, 2003). In what follows, I will examine the specific considerations attending peace psychology's own distinctive undertakings (especially as these are said to warrant its practical interventions), and will further go on to explore how these are similarly made to feature in mundane accounts of humanitarian aid. In both of these cases, my concern will be with how the use of related accounts is oriented to providing the justification for external involvement on the part of professional practitioners who work in settings of armed conflict.

Mapping Peace Psychology

Our point of departure is the review article by Daniel Christie, Barbara Tint, Richard Wagner, and Deborah DuNann Winter entitled "Peace Psychology for a Peaceful World" (Christie et al., 2008). This comprehensive overview of both theoretical and

---

[5] In her introduction to Garfinkel's (2002) monographic description of ethnomethodology's program, Rawls addresses this specific point, elaborating upon the critical significance it might otherwise be taken to have (p. 56): "Social structure is produced locally. Institutional orders are maintained through accounting practices and they also, in spite of the tension involved, require the cooperation of populational cohorts. The fact that persons may be required to reproduce the very social forms that oppress them is a much more powerful and frightening vision of tension and inequality than the idea that independent individuals exist in some sort of primeval struggle against society."

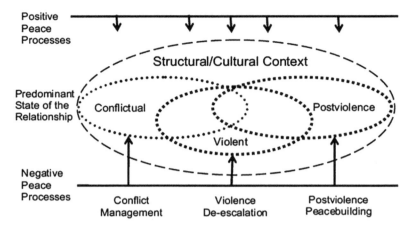

Fig. 15.1 Christie et al.'s (2008, p. 547) multilevel model of negative and positive peace process

applied work in peace psychology catalogues related developments that make up that endeavor under a synoptic framework relating otherwise disparate examples of work within a conceptually integrated whole. Beginning with the distinction between positive peace and negative peace initially developed in the seminal work of Johan Galtung (1969, see also Galtung, 1975, 1990; Galtung & Tschudi, 2001), Christie and his colleagues elaborate upon how the different undertakings of peace psychology can be distinguished either on the basis of their significance for effecting the structural (and, by extension, cultural[6]) conditions that are said to be necessary for peace, or for how they contribute to managing the effects of "direct" violence that are emergent within an unfolding trajectory of real-time development. The interventions attending this latter category are further distinguished for their placement along a trajectory of events described in three different phases, as: (1) leading up to, (2) emergent as, or (3) following on from the episodes of concrete violence that negative peace initiatives describe (with corresponding interventions glossed as *peacekeeping*, *peacemaking*, and *peacebuilding*, respectively). Represented schematically, these different forms of peace psychology are summarized in Fig. 15.1.

While Christie et al.'s review elaborates some rather subtle differences between the distinct categories of peace psychology that it describes,[7] the overall classification

---

[6]The cultural aspect here is differentiated in terms of some shared set of (prejudicial) beliefs (p. 543): "Closely related to structural violence is cultural violence (Galtung, 1996), which refers to the symbolic sphere of our existence that reinforces episodes or structures of violence." Note the designative transformation here between the referential terms that culture is meant both to index and to describe: *cultural violence* is variably taken to refer both to concrete manifestations of, as well as abstract conditions for, violence.

[7]Describing the figures they employ to depict these categories, Christie et al. (2008) note (pp. 544, 547): "The ovals … represent three different and potentially overlapping kinds of relationships. Moving from left to right, the first oval depicts a conflictual relationship in which the perception of incompatible goals dominates the relationship. The overlap of the "Conflictual" oval with the

of related initiatives is nevertheless relatively straightforward. Broadly speaking, work in peace psychology is classified into two main categories reflecting a basic axiomatic distinction that informs the social sciences across a range of otherwise disparate analytic endeavors.[8] Referred to variously with different terms, the distinction Christie et al. elaborate here delineates an explanatory commonplace characteristic of mundane accountability, one in which detailed particulars are rendered intelligible with reference to abstract categories of classification by which they are described, while such classificatory formulations, in their turn, are rendered intelligible in view of the detailed specifics that are organized under their respective rubrics.[9] Together, this makes for a methodical interpretation of documentary forms in which the particulars that negative peace interventions are meant to remedy are related to the structural generalities whose causal manifestations those particulars are said to exhibit. Moreover, in this case, the temporal trajectory traced by the various forms of negative peace is related to the generalities of a structural account at the end points of buildup-to and aftermath-of the emergent episodes of direct violence which that account describes. Glossed by Christie et al. with the terms *conflictual* and *postviolence* (respectively), the mode of description that these endpoints articulate operates conceptually so as to depict the noumenal domain of positive peace in relation to the phenomenal particulars of direct confrontation (i.e., negative

---

"Violent" oval suggests that conflictual relationships may become destructive, that is, marked by periodic episodes of violence. The "Violent" oval depicts a relationship that is dominated by violent behavioral episodes; here there is the potential to move the relationship away from violence and toward an examination of the conflicted features of the relationship (i.e., the overlap between Violent and Conflictual) or beyond violence toward a postviolence arrangement. The "Postviolence" oval indicates the relationship is dominated by nonviolence but has the potential to return to conflictual perceptions or violent actions. [...] [These] relationships (whether primarily in a conflictual, violent, or postviolent state) occur within a structural and cultural context. Whereas negative peace processes have three conceptually distinct entry points, contingent on the predominant state of the relationship, opportunities for positive peace processes are ubiquitous and can take place at any point in the relationship whenever social injustices are present, that is, regardless of whether the predominant state of the relationship is conflictual, violent, or postviolent."

[8] Watson and Coulter (2008) describe this axiomatic distinction as grounding theoretical debates that are foundational to the modern European understanding of human conduct (p. 1): "There have been some broadly accepted terms to this debate, which has been cast in terms of a set of binary conceptual opposites such as 'individual'-'society', 'subjectivity'-'objectivity', 'agency'-'structure', 'psychological'-'social' and so on. These oppositions are still preserved, largely uncritically, and this has tended to ossify the debate (Sharrock & Watson, 1988). Over the years, this ossification has taken on a bureaucratic incarnation, given that the conceptual oppositions in which it is rooted have come to gain expression in departmental divisions between disciplines—notably those of sociology and psychology." In the discussion to follow, I shall simply refer to this distinction with the glosses *structure* and *agency* in order to maintain consistency with the terminology Christie et al. employ.

[9] Drawing on Mannheim (1952), Garfinkel (1967) refers to this aspect of mundane sense-making with the term *documentary method of interpretation* (p. 78): "The method consists of treating an actual appearance as 'the document of,' as 'pointing to,' as 'standing on behalf of,' a presupposed underlying pattern derived from its individual documentary evidences, but the individual documentary evidences, in their turn, are interpreted on the basis of 'what is known' about the underlying pattern. Each is used to elaborate the other."

Fig. 15.2 Revised model

peace). That is, in describing violence as an event whose emergence from and eventual re-submergence into the notional domain of positive peace, the various negative peace interventions portray time as a manifestation of the structural domain (from which it is distinguished as that domain's concrete realization). It does this by relating the details of violence to a structural depiction at the discarnate endpoints of a temporally linear (or narrative) trajectory.

This latter interpretative reading can be represented similarly to the way that Christie et al. present their summary in Fig. 15.1 if we first move the rings out and apart slightly in order to accentuate the temporal aspect of conflict's unfolding trajectory, and then turn the diagram on its side, thus making visible the co-implicative relationship between structural violence and direct violence via the links that delineate the endpoints of the narrative formulation (the before and after phases of the emergence of a violent episode in and across real time, see Fig. 15.2).

The noumenal realm of purely structural (i.e., positive) peace is related to the details of conflict's phenomenal operations (i.e., negative peace) by means of the projective and retrospective glosses that describe peacekeeping and peacebuilding as the endpoints of a temporally unfolding trajectory whose site of emergence into the phenomenal realm delineates the outbreak of violent activity which peacemaking interventions are meant to rectify. Put differently, the preventive and reparative formulations justify negative interventions in view of the concrete specifics relative to which those formulations are rendered significant *as constituents of the time line to which they belong*. That is, the apprehension these endpoints furnish is not, strictly speaking, phenomenal, but derives its transformation *into* the phenomenal by virtue of the particulars whose noumenal significance it renders visible (by pointing inward toward the trajectory's midpoint or outbreak of direct violent activity). Put differently still, the endpoints of the time line have a dual function in not only describing the outbreak of violence to which they serve as preceding and following moments (rendering that outbreak with the significance it has), but also in transforming those direct outbreaks into conditions amendable to a structural depiction. Thus, on the assumption that conflict has its basis in disruptions to the structural conditions which positive peace processes describe, the relating of those conditions to the particulars of violence within the linear account traces a hermeneutic circuit wherein those particulars are rendered meaningful relative to the structural-universal they document (and vice versa). In this way, the intelligibility of either analytic gesture is made available relative to its contrasting alternative. The formulation of temporality here is the capacitating device that realizes the operation of the documentary method in virtue of the transformative status furnished by the liminal endpoints of its episodic trajectory.[10]

This hermeneutic circuit exhibits an elegance uncomplicated by the details of violent conflict it invokes. At the same time, it provides for the accountability of intervention in and at all points of conceptual justification. Pointing this out here is not meant as a critique of that operation, but instead is intended to highlight how it brings together the significance of the different and variable analytic accounts it assembles under an overarching synoptic description. One risk involved in pointing all of this out as I have here, however, lies in the potential to overlook the selective ways that the otherwise disparate accounts are drawn upon to provide for the moral intelligibility of action by professional practitioners. More specifically, it potentially overlooks how disparate accounts render related interventions answerable to the demands for moral accountability that one or the other depiction makes available relative to its counterpart. For instance, where sympathetic affiliation with the parties victimized by events of conflict is invoked to justify intervention, this has the potential to be seen as neglecting the moral implications attending a structural account of conflict's root causes.[11] Conversely, an account which attends exclusively to the moral imperatives furnished in a structural depiction could be seen to neglect the practicalities that a phenomenal-agentive account entails, thereby potentially exacerbating the circumstances whose deleterious effects it would otherwise be directed toward mitigating (see McKenzie, 2009, 2012). Pie-in-the-sky theoretical formulations (of structure) are called to account by the practical imperative to alleviate the suffering that a temporal account of direct violence highlights, while the alleviation of suffering is made to answer to an account of underlying structural causes.

It is beyond the modest scope of a single chapter to examine the details of the voluminous literature that Christie et al. outline in their summary review, but in order better to clarify how the operative distinction is selectively deployed, we shall examine details of related account formulations in mundane talk from interviews

---

[10] In his introduction to the 1831 edition of Schelling's *Die Weltalter* [*Ages of the World*], Žižek addresses this relationship in remarks concerning Hegel's treatment of the ontological significance afforded with a distinction between temporality and the eternal (Žižek & von Schelling, 1997: 15): "We must be careful not to miss this crucial point: as with Hegel, the problem is not how to attain the noumenal In-itself beyond phenomena: the true problem is how and why at all does this In-itself split itself from itself, how does it acquire a distance toward itself and thus clear the space in which it can appear (to itself)." That appearance, according to (Žižek's reading of) Hegel, is what time effectuates, not as the condition of its fulfillment, but as its immanent realization.

[11] This is also the position developed in certain critically oriented approaches to the study of discursive interaction, including that of some contributors to DP (see Hepburn & Jackson, 2009; Hopkins & Reicher, 2011; Hopkins, Reicher, & Levine, 1997; Parker, 2012; Wetherell, 1998, 2001, 2007). To the extent that such work deploys its analysis of participants' endogenously furnished sensemaking as a way to interject itself into what is, after all, the business of others (and not the analytic business of examining how that participant work is carried out), it departs from the ethnomethodological heritage, abandoning the latter's distinctive and unique character (Bogen & Lynch, 1990; Garfinkel & Sacks, 1970). Related appeals to eclecticism sacrifice conceptual clarity to the fetish of collegiality, usually without achieving either.

collected as part of a research project to explore the everyday understanding of humanitarian aid in settings of armed conflict. As we shall see, the different modes of sense-making attending the structural and the agentive (or positive and negative peace) formulations are variably furnished in speakers' strategic efforts to manage the different demands for accountability they each entail. In other words, we will examine how speakers attend to both of the moral demands in the respective accounts that Christie et al. delineate, as well as how the pertinence of either is not only occasioned by its counterpart, but rendered intelligible in relation to it.

Structure and Agency as the Formulation of Moral Accountability

The distinction Christie et al. elaborate invokes various suppositions relative to which different kinds of intervention on the part of peace psychology are made accountable. This interpretative practice relating noumenal and phenomenal accounts is one that proceeds from first principles involving the supposition of intervention's legitimacy. What are made to look like the reasons for various kinds of intervention on the part of peace psychology are accounts wherein the supposition of legitimacy is a condition of their intelligibility.[12]

One way of approaching these different explanations of professional activity is to consider the distinct demands for moral accountability they are oriented to furnishing (either by way of substantiation or as a way to foreclose the potential accusation of negligence), and to examine the different assumptions they invoke to furnish the intelligibility of the activities they reference. Here the explanatory domain does not resolve the tension between the diverse suppositions. Not only are otherwise antithetical assumptions about the nature of violence drawn upon to make sense of intervention, but the relevance of any given assumption is rendered available by the demands for accountability that its alternative assumption furnishes (Billig, 1991, 1996). The universe of intelligibility is sustained in suppositional antinomy (Billig et al., 1988).[13] In the terms that Christie et al. employ in their review, this involves a translation of abstract formulation into the particulars of concrete detail (see Latour, 1993). The (measurable) scarcity of resources, the

---

[12] Elaborating on this same point in her discussion of the way time features in ethnomethodology, Rawls (2005) notes (pp. 177–178): "Instructed action is not a process of bringing an anticipation to reality. In fact, it is the reverse; a process of bringing reality to an anticipation. That is, anticipation is vague, or abstract, until one begins to work out how things might go together. Like a conversation — one starts with something that is constantly changing and becoming something else."

[13] The dialectic relationship involved here is described by Žižek (1993) in his exploration of the German Idealist tradition in philosophy (p. 122): "What Hegel calls "the unity of the opposites" subverts precisely the false appearance of … a complementary relationship: the position of an extreme is not simply the negation of its other. Hegel's point is rather that the first extreme, in its very abstraction from the other, is this other itself. An extreme "passes over" into its other at the very moment when it radically opposes itself to this other …."

(ratifiable) effects of political oppression (described in terms of voting rights and other activities regarded as instrumental expressions of the structural abstraction they are taken to manifest), etc. are only rendered intelligible in virtue of their specificity. This reciprocal transformation of structural abstraction and detailed specifics is what makes the accountability of professional intervention available, and the moral demand that one kind of explanation answers to is occasioned by the alternative kind with which it is contrasted.

As will become evident, such a transformation also occurs in the spoken accounts of humanitarian aid workers. The mutually co-occasioning, yet (seemingly) contradictory suppositions that comprise the universe of intelligibility can be referred to in the following two general ways: as answering to the assumption (1) that the legitimacy of social-cultural-political change necessary to resolve the tension manifested in violent conflict is solely the entitlement of antagonists to determine, and (2) that the debilitating consequences of violent conflict preclude the carrying out of such structural changes, and thus intervention by external parties is required. In the talk we will consider below, external interventions are seen to provide for conditions that would enable adversaries to bring about structural change, but in such a way as not to encroach upon the exclusive entitlement of those parties in bringing such change to fruition. Managing the availability of these different suppositions so as to provide for the relevance of one without undermining its alternative is the practical undertaking by which the moral accountability of humanitarianism is formulated. The professional detachment of the external parties derives its warrant precisely from the prospect of effecting change, while still remaining within the legitimacy afforded by their status as independent brokers.

Let us begin here by examining talk from an interview with the president and CEO of a non-governmental organization (NGO) that provides medical relief aid to the community of Palestinian refugees in the West Bank and Gaza Strip, primarily through that organization's logistic and fundraising efforts in arranging for medical experts from outside the region to volunteer their services on short-term medical missions. As a part of this job, the CEO and his staff spend a significant amount of their time meeting with potential donors from the United States and elsewhere. The transcript below begins at a point in the conversation where the interviewee (Clark) discusses the relationship that his organization has with other NGOs that carry out similar work among the same target community of aid recipients.

Extract 1.1 [palis19a, 18:33-20:48]

1	**Int**	Tell me a bit about maybe how w- you relate with: uh other NGOs that
2		work here. Y'know meh- ih you've mentioned that there's some kind of
3		competition (here), [xx-]
4	**Clark**	[I don't think the] competition it ↑here- well, actually
5		there is some competition here, u:m: I mean the competition that I was
6		addressing was more to do with the: organizations in the ↑States,=
7	**Int**	=Uh huh,=
8	**Clark**	=who a:re >y'know< chasing after the money from the Palestinian
9		com↓munity, which is limited and which is overly burdened by trying to
10		raise money,
11		((*some lines omitted*))

12	**Clark**	here in Palestine the NGO situation is much <u>different</u>, >y'know< the
13		fundraising aspect comes from um governments, the European Community
14		and the inter↑na↓tional community [is]
15	**Int**	[but] you don't have any of that, your
16		organ[ization- uh-]
17	**Clark**	[I <u>don't</u> get any of] that no, u:m which kind of keeps me out of the
18		NGO um ↑cul↓ture here, and I've made a conscious effort on the
19		ad<u>mini</u>strative level to stay out of the NGO culture.=
20	**Int**	=Uh huh=
21	**Clark**	=Meaning- >I mean and there< i:s this kind of NGO <u>net</u>work which e↑xists
22		↓here which is more po<u>liti</u>cal than it is um dealing with specific u:h
23		humanitarian issues.
24		(.)
25	**Int**	Like how. What is:- [what's that mean I (mean)-]
26	**Clark**	[Well, I mean y'know] there are- dealing with issues
27		relating to occu↑pa↓tion. Which >y'know< I- I have no ↑personal problem
28		with whatso↑e↓ver I also support their ↑mea↓sures but as a- as an NG↑O↓:
29		we have limited resources and limited u:m >y'know< ability to focus on
30		specific ↑issues and we have enough work cut out for us trying to run our
31		projects on a shoestring budget a:nd not to: be distracted about what the
32		wa- where the wall's being built and-=
33	**Int**	=Mm hm=
34	**Clark**	=I mean these are all relevant <u>issues</u> and I'm concerned as a human <u>being</u>
35		about them as ↑we↓:ll but I can't go to meetings and sit and discuss how
36		we're going to confront the wa:ll I uh- that's not the role of (*name of*
37		*organization*).=
38	**Int**	=Mm [hm mm hm]
39	**Clark**	[I mean we're trying] to deal with children who have specific
40		medical surgical needs and find so↑lutions for ↓them and where the wall's
41		being built is a- >y'know< it's a- in- it's a war crime it's a inter↑national
42		crime but it's not something I can get (*name of organization*) involved in.
43		(.)
44	**Int**	Mm hm mm hm
45		(.)
46	**Clark**	We're dealing with specific medical issues.

Here, Clark first responds to the interviewer's initial prompting to discuss competition between NGOs with a somewhat cursory account of the different resourcing demands at both local and international levels of operation (lines 4–14). Following this, he goes on to develop a motive account distinguishing between his own professional activity and that of other NGO operatives working in the same region; differentiating between strictly humanitarian efforts, on the one hand, and actions that are directed toward political protest, on the other ("this kind of NGO network which e↑xists ↓here which is more po<u>liti</u>cal than it is um dealing with specific u:h humanitarian issues," lines 21–23). That is, Clark distinguishes between the practical considerations attending relief aid, and the theoretical concerns that inform a structural understanding of the conflict resulting in such needs. Note that the relevance of this difference is not based on the legitimacy attributed to the respective activities (the practical and the theoretical), but rather on the demands for accountability that their respective orientations address. Though Clark initially describes this in terms of comparative efficiency (lines 29–32), elsewhere in the same interview he recounts a range of considerations that answer to the legitimacy of his organization in confining itself to the provision for medical relief (a point he reiterates here in remarking upon the "specific[ally] medical" nature of his organization's activities, lines 39–40, 46). He thereby concedes the legitimacy of respective undertakings while nonetheless distinguishing between efforts that are confined to alleviating the adverse effects of conflict from those that attend the political considerations otherwise understood as related to them. The comparative activity of those with whom he contrasts his own efforts is directed toward impacting specific, concrete events—in this case, the construction of the security barrier separating Israel from the Palestinian Territories[14]—belying Clark's gloss on their status as *political.*

Such a formulation answers to the demand for a sympathetic appreciation of the direct repercussions of the region's conflict upon the population of those adversely effected by its conduct. Yet, the contrastive case Clark describes, in which he argues for the distinction between his own efforts and those of the more politically motivated NGOs, is potentially hearable in analogous terms. In other words, there is nothing to prevent arguing that opposition to building the separation barrier is motivated by a concern to manage the concrete effects of the regional conflict; nor, on the other hand, is there anything to prevent arguing that the attention to "specific medical" concerns is itself politically motivated. The contrasting arguments are translatable into one another's terms. Indeed, as we shall see, this latter possibility is one that Clark goes on to develop in the course of warranting his activities against the demands for accountability to the "political" concerns with which he here compares his own efforts. What is said to distinguish his own professional activities from those of the "NGO culture" or "network[s]" (lines 19, 21) which are "dealing with issues relating to occupation" (lines 26–27) is only intelligible in virtue of an interpretative reading wherein documentary evidence is selectively underwritten in such a way as to warrant that distinction. Note, the issue here is not the exclusion of one concern as against its alternative, but the relevance that the two are taken to have relative to one another, along with the demands for moral accountability implicated within the configuration of intelligibility their respective descriptions furnish. Thus, Clark's "administrative" position neither excludes from consideration, nor is a principled critique, of the efforts of those with whom he contrasts his own professional activities (lines 27–28, 40–41). Rather it implicates certain assumptions about the way that concrete interventions are related to the abstract formulation of their causes.

While this political versus humanitarian distinction employs glosses that differ from those in Christie et al.'s synoptic description, it nevertheless portrays that difference in much the same way as that of structural causes and their concrete effects. What makes this complicated is that the structural (or "political")

---

[14] This interview was carried out as the separation barrier was initially being constructed, during which time the highly controversial project was the object of widespread condemnation from various quarters both locally in Palestine and internationally (see Barak-Erez, 2006; Kelly, 2005).

gloss is invoked by references to specific activities (viz., the strategic planning of protest and the like in response to the building of the barrier). This kind of referential transformation, however, is neither distinctive of Clark's description, nor is it problematic for the conceptual integrity of the contrast. Instead, it articulates a method of interpretation whereby the differentiation is rendered available as a condition of each gesture's intelligibility. Put differently, it is the transposition of the structural and agentive (or, as Galtung puts it, the "structural" and the "direct") modes of explanation into one another's terms that makes them individually visible. It is that conceptual distinction that the interviewer then goes on to interrogate in the exchanges that immediately follow on from the talk represented in Extract 1.1, above.

Extract 1.2 [palis19a, 20:49-22:52]

47	**Int**	.hh uh- then- that's ↑interesting cuz that touches on >obviously a kind of
48		debate in the ↑field< which is >y'know< to what extent u::m u:h
49		humanitarian assistance: should or should not be:: politically committed=
50	**Clark**	=Hm=
51	**Int**	=um and >yeah, I- I mean< the counter argument would be something like
52		"Well" >y'know< "look, these ↑circumstances that you: work to al↑leviate
53		in some sense they: very much are- they have their ↑source uh in:
54		[the-] the political [↑conflict and therefore] not to deal [with that] is to
55	**Clark**	[Right.] [I understand that] [mm hm]
56	**Int**	kind of m- >y'know< close your eyes or-=
57	**Clark**	=No:: I mean the- that's certainly- that's a perspective that could be ↑argued
58		but I could counter by saying >y'know< Look I̲ think by saving the lives
59		of Palestinian children by using our limited resources and our limited
60		↑ti↓:me to address the life and death existential issues that are facing some
61		of the children that we ↑ha↓:ve is far more of a political contribution than
62		standing in- at a demonstration and shouting s̲l̲o̲g̲a̲n̲s̲. We're saving the
63		lives of children who in the ↑future might grow up and be able to ex↑ist on
64		t̲h̲i̲s̲ land and provide some form of solution for their people whereas
65		>y'know< my role in standing and- and demonstrating or- or dealing with
66		po↑l̲i̲tical issues takes away from my ability to provide a real u::m u:h
67		solution for specific individual c̲a̲s̲e̲s̲.=
68	**Int**	=Mm hm,=
69	**Clark**	=I define this conflict- my personal definition is one of existence for the
70		Palestinian people at this point now we're beyond the stage of struggling
71		for specific causes now its ju- simply whether the nation will e̲x̲i̲s̲t̲ or not
72		and our ro:le by saving the lives of the ↑children in this country and
73		providing them medical services that they otherwise can't ↑ge↓:t is in m̲y̲
74		abil- in my ↑p̲e̲r̲sonal definition a political a↓:ct
75		(.)
76	**Int**	°Mm hm [mm hm°]
77	**Clark**	[and I] don't think it's- I uh- >y'know< it's fine for some of
78		these guys who want to demonstrate and want to um y'know uh put ads in
79		the newspaper: denoucing this or denouncing that that's their right and
80		their cho↓ice (0.8) and they're more than welcome to ↑make those choices
81		that's something t̲h̲e̲y̲ have to do but for me I consider it equally or even a
82		stronger political act to: provide the type of services we are to Palestinian
83		children under occu↑pation

Here, the dichotomy between the concrete or direct (medical) needs of those effected by violent conflict and the pursuit of abstract "political contribution[s]" (line 61) is mediated in Clark's efforts to translate the one into its contrasting, alternative terms. That is, the concrete activities of providing medical attention are elaborated in terms of the abstract, "existential" (lines 60, 69) implications they are said to bear ("at this point now we're beyond the stage of struggling for specific causes now its ju- simply whether the nation will exist or not," lines 70–71). The moral intelligibility of the practical interventions is rendered available in and through their translation into the abstract terms of reference by which their political significance is described. At the same time, political abstraction is translated back into its opposite moment, as where the protests against Israel's security barrier is regarded to be the concrete manifestation of just such abstraction (Extract 1.1, lines 35–36; Extract 1.2, lines 77–81). Note that while Clark's description of those NGO activities that he distinguishes from his own professional activities could be heard as a complaint (Schegloff, 2005), neither Clark nor the interviewer treat them as such. Instead, their relevance is here limited to the extent that their translation into the realm of the concrete-particular circumscribes the limitations of their effectiveness in that domain. The moral intelligibility of the respective activities is thus furnished in a documentary interpretation where the one set of suppositions regarding the accountability of activities is rendered intelligible in view of the contrasting alternative. Clark's professional activities are rendered morally accountable precisely insofar as they can be related to the abstract-political considerations whose pursuit they are said to make possible, while the moral accountability of others' political protests is made visible in what might otherwise be seen as a criticism of its efficacy.

Sustaining the intelligibility of such moral reasoning here is such that not only are the dichotomous terms of reference translated into one another's idiom, but their autonomy is also (and simultaneously) rhetorically safeguarded. This is what takes place in the following set of exchanges from an interview with the CEO (*Brad*, together with his partner *JoAnn*) of an organization that offers material and logistic support services to NGOs operating within the same community of aid recipients in the Palestinian Territories where Clark works.

Extract 2 [palis25; 46:12-48:07, 49:33–51:08]

```
1   Brad   Well if I- >y'know< if I was involved in some (1.6) level of: u:h
2   Int    (clears throat)
3          (.)
4   Brad   political persuasion or political discourse here u:h=or >y'know< supporting
5          one party versus a↑nother party, but [>y'know<] I'm supporting grassroots
6   Int    [Mm hm?]
7   Brad   NGOs. [I'm] supporting community groups. [U:h that are] trying to uh put
8   Int    [Mm hm?] [Mm hm, mm hm?]
9   Brad   together a u:h after school program so the kids aren't out on the streets where
10         it's very dangerous right now, uh but th- [>y'know<] they have a place to go
11  Int    [°Mm hm°]
12  Brad   to u:m- >y'know< ↑feeding programs >y'know< emergency water supplies
13         u::m (2.1) uh=I can't help but to think that uh- I hope that uh (2.3) I can feel
14         completely comfortable and confident that I'm not involved in that political
15         [dialogue right now]
```

```
16   Int      [Mm hm, mm hm, mm hm,] mm hm,=
17   Brad     =u:h what I'm trying to do is I'm trying to work with the people who are the
18            victims
19            (0.6)
20   JoAnn    of [that political di]alogue. Yeah=
21   Brad     [of that violence.]
22   Brad     =Yeah=
23   Int      =[Mm] hm, mm hm,
24   JoAnn    =[yeah]
25            (.)
26   Brad     A:nd u:m:=
27   JoAnn    =Let the poli↑ticians deal with political dialogue=
28   Int      =[°↑We↓:ll-°]
29   Brad     =[and-] and the- an:d y'know this has been going on for- >y'know< the
30            intifada's for three and a half yea::rs and the conflict has been going on for
31            .hh >°y'know°< sixty seventy years and if you look at histori- historically it's
32            been going on for ↑thousands of years so [y'know]
33   Int      [Mm hm]
34   Brad     u[:m]
35   JoAnn    [It's not gon]na end in our lifetime I don't think,
36            (.)
37   Brad     Well I don't know. Y'know I'm an ↑optimist uh
38            (…) ((some lines omitted, relating details of experience in another country))
39   Brad     I'm the eternal ↑op↓timist and I guess I wouldn't be in this lifestyle if I didn't
40            have that. Because if I ↑didn't have that I think >you're right< there'd days is
41            that the bruises would be on my ↑fore↓head .hhh instead of inside my ↑the↓art
42            u::m so no. U:h I'm always a believer that change can hap↓pen u:h and
43            positive change can happen and there can even be a positive change here. We
44            had Oslo: y'know we had a- a start u::m obviously it was a long time ago and
45            I think we all forget Oslo u:m but y'know all it takes is dynamic leadership.
46            What ↑happened in South Af↓rica >y'know< we had dynamic- dynamic
47            >↑leadership.< We had a Nelson Mandela, and we had a de Kle↓rk. U:m we
48            had people that had a vision that they ri:- they ↑rose above petty (0.7)
49            personal (1.0) egos (0.3) politics (0.3) economic wealth (0.2) economic gain
50            (0.2) and they came to the table and they made ↑mo:numental deci↓sions and
51            then they brou↑:ght the forces with ↓them- >their respective political forces
52            with them< to an ama::zing a↑chieve↓ment. Y'know it probably one of the
53            most beautiful things that've happened in the twenty first ↑century was what
54            happened in South ↑Africa. Can we have a repeat of something like that here?
55            And people say "Oh=hh °no way°" but if you don't be↑lie↓:ve (1.1) then you
56            shouldn't be ↓here. (0.8) Y'know >especially outsiders< if they don't believe
57            (0.7) that there can be: (0.5) positive (0.5) peaceful (0.5) mira:culous r- um
58            tsk (0.3) ↑change ↓here the:n anyone who's from the outside shouldn't be
59            here.
```

There are, of course, a great many things that take place in this exchange. Perhaps the most poignant feature here, however, is the contrast that Brad draws between the concrete, practical considerations attending the work of "grassroots NGOs" (lines 5–12), and the celebration of political activism (or "dialogue") as a means to bring about positive change. On initial examination, this appears as a rather straightforward distinction between the abstract considerations that stand outside of his own professional sphere of activity and the concerns that animate his own endeavors (lines 17–24). Both Brad and JoAnn work collaboratively to delimit the parameters of the political realm with the professional management of its practical effects, distinguishing their own (and others') efforts as non-members or outsiders (lines 13–22). They take as problematic the possibility of conflating the two kinds of activity. More than just this is happening here, however. The very distinction is the condition for understanding the moral account-ability of the respective domains of activity. This is not so much the case where Brad distinguishes, say, the "leadership" of the principals in negotiating the Oslo Accords or the dismantling of the apartheid system in South Africa. Rather, this occurs precisely where the supposition of the related endeavor's legitimacy is taken to warrant the distinct undertakings which Brad pursues ("but if you don't be↑lie↓:ve (1.1) then you shouldn't be ↓here. (0.8) Y'know > especially out<u>sid</u>-ers< if they don't be<u>lie</u>ve (0.7) that there can <u>be</u>: (0.5) positive (0.5) peaceful (0.5) mi<u>ra:</u>culous r- um tsk (0.3) ↑change ↓here the:n anyone who's from the outside shouldn't be here.", lines 55–59). Just as we saw in Extract 1.2 how Clark relates the carrying out of his professional activities as the necessary, "existential" condition for the resolution of abstract political conflict, similarly here Brad relates the abstract realm of eventual political resolution to the accountability of his professional activities. The difference is one of directionality (or conceptual starting point): where in Clark's account, intervention is a condition of political resolution, in Brad's account, the supposition of political resolution warrants the pursuit of humanitarian intervention. In both cases, the warrant of the one is derived from its relation with the other. Just as relief aid is justified to the extent that it contributes to the resolution of political conflict, so too it is the eventuality of political resolution that justifies the carrying out of relief aid.

In analyzing how scientists provide for the legitimacy of experimental conclusions in light of the ephemerality of theory, Gilbert and Mulkay (1984) point out how a common feature of related accounts involves portraying meaning as temporally manifest in the developmental trajectory which the experimental process realizes (something Gilbert and Mulkay refer to with the term "truth will out device [TWOD]"; for related discussion see Potter & Wetherell, 1987, pp. 153–155). Similarly, here the teleological unfolding that Brad and JoAnn invoke constitutes the suppositional background that warrants the pursuit of temporally situated activities (with what might be referred to, using a more generic term, as a Temporally Mediated Resolution Device [TMRD]). The point here is that the reference to time functions as a device by which the hermeneutic circle of abstract and concrete is made visible as a problematic whose resolution is achieved by the unfolding of events. The transcendent significance of concrete particulars (as manifestations of the abstract realm they are taken to exhibit) is made visible through the dichotomous (but ultimately connected) resolution between abstract-universal and concrete-particular that time both creates and resolves. In the formulation Christie et al. develop, that teleological potential is translated from the abstract of political resolution into the cyclical dimensions of concrete interventions associated with negative peace initiatives. Similarly, in the talk among aid workers examined above, the co-implicative mode of accountability is made available in the conceptual distinction between aid and activism. The accountability of either is furnished by the conceptual distinction in and through which they are mediated. That any sort of political resolution can be said to take place is an eventuality that justifies aid intervention both as its condition and as its motivation. A requisite for the intelligible operation of such mundane reason is the transmutation of the abstract (of political resolution) into the realm of temporal development, the conditions for which are said to be furnished by the specific, concrete activities of intervention.

Conversely, such a documentary interpretation is also furnished in efforts to shore up the distinction where it might otherwise be called into question, as seen in the following exchange taken from a later point in the same interview represented in Extract 2. Here, Brad and JoAnn address the legitimacy of that distinction in view of the potential confusion that arises when the political entitlement and concrete support are conflated.

Extract 3 [palis25, 53:10-55:21]

1	Brad	We:ll °I think there's° a little bit of the:: u:h I'm gonna go out and save the
2		world mentality (0.4) I think I started off with that ↑too↓: I think that a lot of
3		people get- get involved in this uh- >y'know< you come into that-
4		[come into this]
5	JoAnn	[You learn very] quickly.=
6	Brad	=work [but you know le↓arn. You learn.]
7	JoAnn	[heh heh heh heh You lea(h)rn ve↑ry(h)] qui(h)ck↓ly(h)=
8	Brad	=U:m=
9	JoAnn	=that you're not gonna save the world. >You might save< one person.=
10	Brad	=My favorite [saying]=
11	JoAnn	[°heh° heh]=
12	Int	=°hehh heh heh°=
13	Brad	=that I used to s-=uh tell all my (*name of organization*) volunteers was uh-
14		°when I was the° director >y'know I (had)< literally hundreds and hundreds
15		of (1.2) young idealistic u::m (1.3) Americans coming out from middle
16		America or from (1.0) very privileged backgrounds in most cases uh "out to
17		do goo:d" and they were gonna "s:ave the wo:rld" y'know,
18	(.)	
19	Int	°heh° [heh heh]
20	Brad	[and my] uh- >and uh< y'know that's fi↓:ne and I never
21		dis[[cou↓rage- and I never discou:rage them]] cuz I said "Yes!=
22	Int	[[£How swee:t£ heh heh .hhh]]
23	JoAnn	=Well they've got to have that [ener]gy.
24	Brad	[↑Do it!"]
25		(.)
26	Int	[Mm]
27	Brad	[Cuz I] said on the one hand y'know, I said one person ca:n change the world
28		y'know if you look at a Václav- Václav Havel or if you look at a Lech Wałęsa
29		at the time, if you look at a Nelson Mandela, if you look at people that really
30		through their perso↑nalities (1.0) >y'know< throu:gh- >y'know,< individuals
31		that just cha:nged so↑cie↓ty uh it ca:n happen. Uh at the same time >y'know<
32		that u:h- you have to be so: realistic and you have to be so careful that you
33		don't go out there- cuz you can raise expectations to the point that you
34		actually are ↑hurting ver[sus] hel↓ping. So my (1.0) motto was "You're
35	JoAnn	[Mmm]

36	**Brad**	coming fr- from a society that taught you don't just stand there ↑<u>do</u>
37		something." And I told them "For the next six months don't just do something
38		↑STAND THERE.=
39	**Int**	=Right right
40		(.)
42	**Brad**	U::h take a look around you. Understand the people. Understand the culture.
43		Don't feel you have to go out there and (1.0) "↑GIVE them something.
44		BUILD them a school." You don't know if that's really what they nee:d.
45		[U:h just] be invo:<u>l</u>ved. <u>Lis</u>ten to them. Just be <u>part</u> of it. Just ex<u>pe</u>rience it.
46	**Int**	[Mm hm,]
47	**Brad**	And then slow:ly ↑with ↓them listen to what they're saying (.) what <u>the:y</u>
48		want to do: (.) and see if you can contribute in some meaningful way
49		>y'know< in the course of your two years.

What perhaps begins here as a description of naïve idealism is treated as a vital, essential factor in moral accountability. That is, even though the initial mention of what Brad refers to as a "go out and save the world mentality" (lines 1–2) is tentatively treated by the interviewer as a critical gloss on the credulousness of rookie volunteers (lines 19–22), JoAnn immediately mitigates that depiction in her remarks identifying such enthusiasm as a necessary source of vital energy (line 23), with Brad going on to elaborate and document the political changes he invokes through mention of certain episodes of celebrated, high-profile political change (lines 27–31). The nuts-and-bolts activities of aid workers are portrayed as motivated by the desire for world-changing transformation otherwise achieved by the sort of charismatic personalities to whom Brad refers (lines 28–29).[15] Thus, Brad in particular distinguishes such political activities from the work of aid providers, not on the basis of a motive account, but by translating the terms of political abstraction into the concrete particulars that are treated as documentary evidence of how "one person <u>ca:n</u> change the world" (line 27). Conversely, he also works up humanitarian activities in theoretical terms that necessitate abstract contemplation and a restraint from concrete actions until ratified in terms attributed to and warranted by the entitlement appertaining to the target population of aid recipients ("And then slow:ly ↑with ↓them listen to what they're saying (.) what <u>the:y</u> want to do: (.) and see if you can contribute in some meaningful way," lines 47–48).

The noumenal is transformed into the concrete terms of phenomenal instantiation, and conversely, the phenomenal is rendered with the legitimacy appertaining to its documentary counterpart in virtue of the gesture of transcendent restraint (or withholding of action) ("So my (1.0) motto was "You're coming fr- from a society that taught you don't just stand there ↑<u>do</u> something." And I told

---

[15] This appeal to the individual dynamism of such politically charismatic personalities is redolent of Max Weber's interpretative sociology (see Giddens, 1971, "Part 3: Max Weber," esp. pp. 119–181). Note too how, through the use of the indefinite article, references to such persons get formulated in terms that transform the recognition which their detailed specificity otherwise furnishes into a manifestation of abstraction ("a Nelson Mandela," "a de Kle↓rk," Extract 2, lines 46–47; "a Václav- Václav Havel," "a Lech Wałęsa," "a Nelson Mandela," Extract 3, lines 28–29).

them "For the next six months don't just do something ↑STAND THERE.","
lines 34–38). The latter gesture is additionally ratified with an appeal to the category entitlement of aid recipients in a rhetorical move that conflates that recipient status with cultural identity (lines 42–49).[16] Both the abstract-political and
the concrete-particular are transformed into one another's terms, but in just such
a way that retains their respective entitlements. Put differently, the documentary
accounts of political change are evidenced by historical examples only to the
extent that those examples warrant claims about the plausibility of the distinct
category entitlements which they reference. The concrete-practical category is
rendered visible precisely by efforts to delineate its parameters in the notional
terms of reference with which it is contrasted, while the remote category of political (or "change-the-world") entitlement is made visible in reference to the historical examples that are said to be its manifestations. The difference in
entitlements (between those-who-can-change-the-world and those-who-make-it-
possible-for-such-world-changers-to-act) is one of linear progression. These distinct entitlements are not merely oriented to delimiting the parameters of moral
accountability, but such entitlements also delineate a set of relational possibilities which their conceptual parameters define. Work of just the sort which charismatic politicians are able to conduct is made possible by the efforts of those
who attend to the otherwise debilitating effects of conflict that would prevent
them from successfully carrying out such work. The intelligibility of those
respective entitlements are organized within a temporally mediated relationship:
the work of humanitarian intervention enables efforts to change (or to bring
peace to) the world, and the emergence of violence from out of that world of
peaceful relations is remedied on the other end of a cyclical process.

Conclusion

I started off this chapter by considering the distinction made in the peace psychology literature between the abstract formulations of structure-culture that
delineate positive peace processes and the negative peace initiatives which have
as their concern the alleviation of conditions attending concrete episodes of

---

[16] This way of invoking the entitlement of aid recipients as a warrant for humanitarian intervention
is recurrent in the corpus of talk from which these extracts are taken, and is also pervasive in the
way that cultural identity is made to feature as a participant concern (both in efforts to corroborate
speaker claims and to foreclose the potentially damaging implications that would otherwise be
relevant for an account of refugee recalcitrance, see McKenzie, 2009, 2012). This deployment of
category entitlement is similarly carried out by Clark in remarks taken from a later point in the
same interview represented above, where he explains (palis19a, 28:27–28:44): "I've never had e:h
a Palestinian accuse me of do̲ing that. And saying go away you're helping the occupation by doing
what you're doing and I think that's one of the barometers I also ↑use to determine whether
>y'know < we're focusing in the right way or ↑no↓:t is the response of the: Palestinian commu̲nity
here."

violent conflict. We noted that the distinction between these categories is belied by efforts to translate the terms of the one mode of formulation into those of its counterpart. In the synoptic terms of description employed by Christie et al., that relationship is formulated in efforts to translate the abstract-structural into the concrete-particular of temporal placement within an unfolding trajectory organized around emergent episodes of violence, with the concrete-particular translated into the abstract-structural by means of the beginning and end points of a teleological progression in linear time. I hope to have made clear that the conceptual translation of the different formulations (whether glossed in terms of positive and negative peace, or in the descriptive terms relating the structural-political to the specificity of concrete programs of aid) is oriented to providing for the moral accountability of activities on the part of different actors. There is no one-to-one, homologous relationship between the structure-agency (or abstract-temporal) dichotomy and the recipient–provider distinction such that they map onto one another in a consistently analogous fashion. Rather, the distinction is deployed as an explanatory resource to delineate the parameters of entitlement for action on the part of the respective parties (of aid providers and aid recipients). It is not simply a matter of who can act, but of who can act in respect to the external relationship invoked in accounts of the conflict. The work that the abstract-structural versus concrete-temporal distinction accomplishes is that of managing the accountability of both aid provider and aid recipient actions vis-à-vis the remote, third-party relationship. In both the synoptic account that Christie et al. formulate, and in the mundane accounts of the speakers whose talk we have examined, what actions are considered to be concrete manifestations of abstract-structural conditions are a factor of category entitlements that furnish them with their warrant. The translation of the one set of terms into its alternative (as in the case we saw where Clark describes the activities of his NGO as contributing to the politics of the conflict) is a way in which the category entitlement of both aid recipient and aid provider is related to the conflict that is said to occasion the provider's intervention in the first place.

Another way of saying all of this is that it is not category membership which determines who-can-do-what, but rather it is the formulation of distinctions in what-kind-of-thing-it-is-that-can-accountably-get-done which establishes membership. To conceive of actions in either abstract-structural or concrete-particular terms is to express an assumption about the accountable nature of entitled activity. Such formulations answer to the suppositions about category entitlement which they make relevant for an understanding of the activities they describe. My saying this is not meant to undermine the efficacy of such formulations by disclosing their trick, as it were, but to explore how the intelligibility of action is rendered available in accounts of its category relevance. Everyday spoken accounts and the scholarly formulation of different activity types are both oriented to making that category entitlement relevant. Furthermore, these observations are not meant to undermine peace psychologists' descriptive assertions about the individual psychological nature of their interventions. Rather, the related claims are approached for the action orientations they realize in accounting for the events and activities they describe on the part of antagonists in the related conflict. Constructive analysis of the sort examined here is thus not regarded as a shortcoming or mistake, rather, it is seen as an analytic phenomenon—one which ethnomethodology and DP (to the extent that it partakes in the ethnomethodological heritage) takes as its task to investigate.

Appendix: Transcription Conventions

The transcription of talk that appears above is based on the well-known set of conventions initially developed by Gail Jefferson (1985, see also Sacks, Schegloff, & Jefferson, 1974), and extended by John Du Bois and his colleagues (Du Bois, 1991; Du Bois, Schuetze-Coburn, Susanna, & Paolino, 1993). Included among these conventions in the extracts above are the following:

Explanation	Example
full stop indicates completion intonation	NGOs that work here.
Comma indicates continuing intonation	some competition here,
Underlining indicates additional stress	on the administrative level
Prolongation of sound indicated with colon	u:m: I mean the competition
	young idealistic u::m
False starts indicated with a dash followed by a single space	there are- dealing with issues
Voiceless articulation indicated with ° symbol	°Mm hm mm hm°
Talk delivered with an increase in speed indicated with inward pointing arrows	that I think >you're right<
All caps indicate increase in volume	BUILD them a school
Indistinguishable speech indicated with x for each syllable of such talk	xxx-
Quotation as a presentational feature indicated with double quote	in most cases uh "out to do goo:d"
Up/down arrows precede marked rise or fall in intonation	NGO um ↑cul↓ture here
Equal sign indicates no space between two speaker turns at talk or in single speaker articulation	**Int** politically committed= **Clark** =Hm uh=I can't help
Untimed pause indicated by a full stop enclosed in parentheses	(.)
Timed pause in talk indicated to	(0.7)
tenth of a second	(1.2)
Speaker overlap indicated with	**Clark** community [is]
square brackets	**Int** [but] you
Audible inbreath of varying length	.hh .hhh
Audible outbreath of varying length	hh hhhh

Explanation	Example
Description of articulatory detail in single parentheses, italicized	(*clears throat*)
Obscured word or phrase in single parentheses, italicized	all my (*name of organization*)
Editorial comment indicated with remark in double parentheses, italicized	((*some lines omitted, relating details of experience in another country*))
Syllables of laughter	heh heh
Interpolated particles of aspiration inserted into words, indicated with (h)	You lea(h)rn ve↑ry(h) qui(h)ck↓ly(h)

References

Barak-Erez, D. (2006). Israel: The security barrier—between international law, constitutional law, and domestic judicial review. *International Journal of Constitutional Law, 4*, 540–552.

Billig, M. (1991). *Ideology and opinions: Studies in rhetorical psychology*. London: Sage.

Billig, M. (1996). *Arguing and thinking: A rhetorical approach to social psychology* (2nd ed.). Cambridge: Cambridge University Press.

Billig, M., Condor, S., Edwards, D., Gane, M., Middleton, D., & Radley, A. (1988). *Ideological dilemmas: A social psychology of everyday thinking*. London: Sage.

Bogen, D., & Lynch, M. (1990). Social critique and the logic of description: A response to McHoul (1988). *Journal of Pragmatics, 14*, 505–521.

Button, G. (1991). *Ethnomethodology and the human sciences*. Cambridge: Cambridge University Press.

Christie, D. J. (2006). What is peace psychology the psychology of? *Journal of Social Issues, 62*, 1–17.

Christie, D. J., & Montiel, C. J. (2013). Contributions of psychology to war and peace. *American Psychologist, 68*, 502–513.

Christie, D. J., Tint, B. S., Wagner, R. V., & Winter, D. D. (2008). Peace psychology for a peaceful world. *American Psychologist, 63*, 540–552.

Coulter, J. (Ed.). (1990). *Ethnomethodological sociology*. Northampton, MA: Edward Elgar.

Coulter, J. (1999). Discourse and mind. *Human Studies, 22*, 163–181.

Coulter, J. (2004). What is "discursive psychology"? *Human Studies, 27*, 335–340.

Du Bois, J. W. (1991). Transcription design principles for spoken discourse research. *Pragmatics, 1*, 71–106.

Du Bois, J. W., Schuetze-Coburn, S., Susanna, C., & Paolino, D. (1993). Outline of discourse transcription. In J. A. Edwards & M. D. Lampert (Eds.), *Talking data: Transcription and coding in discourse research* (pp. 45–89). Hillsdale, NJ: Lawrence Erlbaum.

Galtung, J. (1969). Violence, peace, and peace research. *Journal of Peace Research, 6*, 167–191.

Galtung, J. (1975). Three approaches to peace: Peacekeeping, peacemaking and peacebuilding. In *Peace, war and defence—essays in peace research* (Vol. 2, pp. 282–304). Copenhagen: Christian Ejlers.

Galtung, J. (1990). Cultural violence. *Journal of Peace Research, 27*, 291–305.

Galtung, J. (1996). *Peace by peaceful means: Peace and conflict, development and civilization*. London: Sage.

Galtung, J., & Tschudi, F. (2001). Crafting peace: On the psychology of the TRANSCEND approach. In D. J. Christie, R. V. Wagner, & D. D. Winter (Eds.), *Peace, conflict, and violence: Peace psychology for the 21st century*. Englewood Cliffs, NJ: Prentice-Hall.

Garfinkel, H. (1967). *Studies in ethnomethodology*. Englewood Cliffs, NJ: Prentice-Hall.

Garfinkel, H. (2002). In A. W. Rawls (Ed.), *Ethnomethodology's program: Working out Durkheim's aphorism*. Lanham, MD: Rowman & Littlefield.

Garfinkel, H., & Sacks, H. (1970). On the formal structures of practical action. In J. C. McKinney & E. A. Tiryakian (Eds.), *Theoretical sociology* (pp. 338–366). New York: Appleton-Century-Crofts.

Giddens, A. (1971). *Capitalism and modern social theory: An analysis of the writings of Marx, Durkheim and Max Weber*. Cambridge: Cambridge University Press.

Gilbert, G. N., & Mulkay, M. (1984). *Opening Pandora's box: A sociological analysis of scientists' discourse*. Cambridge: Cambridge University Press.

Hepburn, A., & Jackson, C. (2009). Rethinking subjectivity: A discursive psychological approach to cognition and emotion. In D. Fox, I. Prilleltensky, & S. Austin (Eds.), *Critical psychology: An introduction* (2nd ed., pp. 176–194). Los Angeles, CA: Sage.

Heritage, J. (1984). *Garfinkel and ethnomethodology*. Cambridge, MA: Polity Press.

Hilbert, R. A. (1992). *The classical roots of ethnomethodology: Durkheim, Weber, and Garfinkel*. London: University of North Carolina Press.

Hilbert, R. A. (2009). Ethnomethodology and social theory. In B. S. Turner (Ed.), *The new Blackwell companion to social theory* (pp. 159–178). Chichester: Wiley-Blackwell.

Hopkins, N., & Reicher, S. (2011). Identity, culture and contestation: Social identity as cross-cultural theory. *Psychological Studies, 56*, 36–43.

Hopkins, N., Reicher, S., & Levine, M. (1997). On the parallels between social cognition and the "new racism.". *British Journal of Social Psychology, 36*, 305–329.

Jefferson, G. (1985). An exercise in the transcription and analysis of laughter. In T. A. van Dijk (Ed.), *Handbook of discourse analysis 3: Discourse and dialogue* (Vol. 3, pp. 25–34). London: Academic Press.

Kelly, M. J. (2005). Critical analysis of the International Court of Justice ruling on Israel's security barrier. *Fordham International Law Journal, 29*, 181–228.

Korbut, A. (2014). The idea of constitutive order in ethnomethodology. *European Journal of Social Theory, 17*, 479–496.

Latour, B. (1993). *We have never been modern* (C. Porter, Trans.). London: Prentice-Hall.

Lynch, M. (1993). *Scientific practice and ordinary action: Ethnomethodology and social studies of science*. Cambridge: Cambridge University Press.

Mannheim, K. (1952). On the interpretation of Weltanschauung. In P. Kecskemeti (Ed.), *Essays in the sociology of knowledge* (pp. 53–63). London: Routledge & Kegan Paul.

McHoul, A. W. (1988). Review article: Language and the sociology of mind: A critical introduction to the work of Jeff Coulter. *Journal of Pragmatics, 12*, 339–386.

McKenzie, K. (2009). The humanitarian imperative under fire. *Journal of Language and Politics, 8*, 333–358.

McKenzie, K. (2012). Formulating professional identity: The case of humanitarian aid. *Pragmatics and Society, 3*, 31–60.

McKenzie, K. (Forthcoming). Discursive psychology's ethnomethodological heritage.

Parker, I. (2012). Discursive social psychology now. *British Journal of Social Psychology, 51*(3), 471–477.

Potter, J., & Edwards, D. (2003). Rethinking cognition: On Coulter on discourse and mind. *Human Studies, 26*, 165–181.

Potter, J., & Wetherell, M. (1987). *Discourse and social psychology: Beyond attitudes and behaviour*. London: Sage.

Rawls, A. W. (2005). Garfinkel's conception of time. *Time & Society, 14*, 163–190.

Sacks, H., Schegloff, E. A., & Jefferson, G. (1974). A simplest systematics for the organization of turn-taking for conversation. *Language, 50*, 696–735.

Schegloff, E. A. (2005). On complainability. *Social Problems, 52*, 449–467.

Sharrock, W., & Anderson, B. (1986). In P. Hamilton (Ed.), *The ethnomethodologists*. London: Tavistock.

Sharrock, W., & Watson, R. (1988). Autonomy among social theories: The incarnation of social structures. In N. G. Fielding (Ed.), *Actions and structure: Research methods and social theory* (pp. 56–77). Newbury Park, CA: Sage.

Watson, R., & Coulter, J. (2008). The debate over cognitivism. *Theory, Culture & Society, 25*, 1–17.

Wetherell, M. (1998). Positioning and interpretative repertoires: Conversation analysis and post-structuralism in dialogue. *Discourse & Society, 9*, 387–412.

Wetherell, M. (2001). Debates in discourse research. In M. Wetherell, S. Taylor, & S. J. Yates (Eds.), *Discourse theory and practice: A reader* (pp. 380–399). London: Sage.

Wetherell, M. (2007). A step too far: Discursive psychology, linguistic ethnography and questions of identity. *Journal of Sociolinguistics, 11*, 661–681.

Žižek, S. (1993). *Tarrying with the negative: Kant, Hegel, and the critique of ideology*. Durham, NC: Duke University Press.

Žižek, S., & von Schelling, F. W. J. (1997). *The abyss of freedom/Ages of the world: An essay by Slavoj Žižek and the complete text of Schelling's Die Weltalter (second draft, 1813) in English translation by Judith Norman* (J. Norman, Trans.). Ann Arbor, MI: University of Michigan Press.

Chapter 16
The Emotional and Political Power of Images of Suffering: Discursive Psychology and the Study of Visual Rhetoric

Jovan Byford

On September 2, 2015, the body of the 3-year-old Syrian boy Alan Kurdi washed up on a beach near the resort town of Bodrum in western Turkey. The boy had drowned earlier that morning, alongside his 5-year-old brother Galib and mother Rehan, when the small inflatable boat in which they tried to reach the Greek island of Kos capsized shortly after setting off on the precarious night-time voyage.[1]

Alan Kurdi's name and tragic fate would probably have remained unknown to the wider world were it not for the series of photographs of the boy's dead body taken by the Turkish journalist Nilüfer Demir. Although Demir took several dozen photographs of the aftermath of the boating tragedy, two images (of which there are several versions) captured the imagination of the public: one was of the boy's body lying face down in the surf, and the other of a Turkish policeman cradling the lifeless toddler in his arms.

Mainly through the power of Twitter and other social media platforms, these photographs became an instant internet sensation, reaching over 20 million users in less than 24 hours (D'Orazio, 2015). Instrumental in their global diffusion was widespread coverage in the mainstream media, which devoted attention not just to the boy's fate and the broader refugee crisis, but also the seemingly unprecedented impact of the photographs on public imagination and political discourse, and the ethical issues surrounding their publication. Within days, the death of Alan Kurdi became a potent symbol of the plight of refugee children, and a reminder of the, at least temporary, political power of visual images.

The role of photographs as vehicles for imagining and remembering war and notable peace-time disasters is well documented. Since the early twentieth century,

---

[1] The deceased boy's name was initially reported as Aylan Kurdi, before it was changed to Alan, the correct transliteration of the Kurdish name. This chapter will refer to the boy as Alan throughout, except when quoting from sources where the different spelling appears in the original.

J. Byford (✉)
The Open University, Milton Keynes, UK
e-mail: jovan.byford@open.ac.uk

© Springer Nature Switzerland AG 2018
S. Gibson (ed.), *Discourse, Peace, and Conflict*, Peace Psychology Book Series,
https://doi.org/10.1007/978-3-319-99094-1_16

dramatic events have been frequently represented through symbolic and poignant images that captured (but also produced and perpetuated) what was deemed to be the essence of human suffering (Sontag, 2003; Zelizer, 2004). However, the impact of the Kurdi images was seen by many as novel and unique. In the modern, digital age, defined by the ubiquity of the camera, the hyperproduction of visual images and their instant dissemination via the internet, it seemed remarkable that a single photographed event was still able to provoke such outpouring of sympathy and generate a sense of common purpose. Thus, many saw the responses to the death of Alan Kurdi as a radically new phenomenon, the marker of a new 'regime of visuality' for the social media age, and a new form of global citizenship exercised through an internet 'meme', through an image gone 'viral' (Goriunova & Vis, 2015).

Responses to the publication of the photographs of Alan Kurdi's body touch upon issues that are of intrinsic interest to peace psychologists. First is the apparent *emotional* power attributed to the photographs. Responses from journalists, politicians, representatives of advocacy groups, ordinary members of public and so on, especially in the west, were replete with references to emotional states provoked by the images—shock, outrage, compassion—but also bodily reactions—the sense of being 'punched in the stomach', 'gut-wrenched', 'heart-wrenched', 'sickened', 'moved to tears', etc. These strong, affective reactions were, for the most part, treated as natural, involuntary responses to the sight of the dead boy, reinforcing the widely held belief that visual images more so than other modes of representation (news reports, documentary evidence, or testimonies) have the power to elicit emotions, and move the audience on an instinctive, 'visceral' level (e.g. Butler, 2007; Goldberg, 1991; Sontag, 2003; Zelizer, 2004).

The second and related issue is that the emotional experiences, or, more specifically, the publicly avowed claims to those experiences, were as much about social relationships, identity and norms that govern pro-social behaviour and civic responsibility, as about internal mental states. An imagined, transnational 'community of mourning' (Kear & Steinberg, 1999) formed around a shared cluster of emotions, and did so in a way that was directly political. The boy's death was a summons to *do* something, or at least to take a stance.

This chapter looks more closely at the link between visual images of human suffering, emotions and political mobilisation. How do we account for this, seemingly inevitable, link? Also, how are images constituted as emotionally and politically moving, and how does an instance of suffering become a symbol for public consumption? Finally, what is it specifically about the images of Alan Kurdi's dead body that made them uniquely newsworthy, affecting, and recognisable as a source of emotional investment?

The starting point of the present analysis is the discursive psychological approach to the study of emotion. Ever since the late 1980s, discursive psychologists have argued that verbal or embodied expressions of feelings should be regarded not as more or less accurate descriptions of a corresponding internal, mental state, but as discursive phenomena and social acts. When people use emotion words, when they avow, describe, ascribe, deny, or account for emotions, their own and those of other people, they are doing socially and rhetorically meaningful things (Edwards, 1997, 1999; Harré, 1987; Harré & Gillett, 1994, see also Childs & Hepburn, 2015; Hepburn, 2004; Wetherell, 2012). For instance, the claim to have been 'upset' or 'made angry' by something, or that someone has acted 'emotionally' carries specific moral weight in the context of an argument and can be mobilised to justify or contest a position or interpretation, manage accountability, persuade others and so on (Potter, 2012). The focus of much discursive psychological work on emotion has been on how the rich thesaurus of emotion terms is deployed in everyday, often mundane, situations to manage some relevant social, or interactional, 'business'.

This chapter, however, seeks to move beyond this kind of 'micro' analysis of discourse, centred on the occasioned use of emotion terms. Common-sense understanding of emotions, and the normative order that governs their public display and rhetorical use—what Wetherell (2012, p. 93) calls the 'lay ethnopsychologies of emotion'—are embedded in structured, but also inherently argumentative, interpretative frameworks and social practices which configure human experience (also Wetherell, 1998). Examining these frameworks and practices requires a shift away from looking at specific instances of *how* people use the vocabulary of feelings to manage accountability and negotiate their way through the prevailing moral order, to exploring *why*, in a specific social, cultural and historical context, certain kinds of emotions or emotional responses are constituted as relevant, and recognised as an appropriate (albeit contestable) resource for 'doing' things. Or indeed why some objects, such as photographs, or events, such as a death, are constructed as 'shocking', 'heart-breaking', or 'harrowing'. Crucially, this broader, 'macro' analysis does not preclude analysing the situated use of emotion terms and details of rhetoric. On the contrary it involves doing so, but while also broadening the examination to 'how discursive threads with longer histories and conventional and communal powers weave in and out of the local order' and permeate the texture of everyday talk, and experience (Wetherell, 2012, p. 100; also Wetherell, 1998).

This chapter will, therefore, use the Kurdi photographs to explore the culturally specific conventions and codes through which the assumption about the emotional and political power of images, and specifically *these* images, is constituted and maintained as part of the ideological common sense. The specific focus of the chapter is *spectatorial sympathy*, as a distinct social practice which mediates the relevance of particular emotions and emotional reactions to images of suffering, and through which certain images are constituted as topics of humanitarian concern.

In examining the impact of the Kurdi photographs, we will also take a road less travelled in discursive psychology and consider the possibilities of extending this approach more directly towards the study of visual material. Historically, analyses of discourse have privileged talk and text as the 'primary arena for human action, understanding and intersubjectivity' (Potter, 2012, p. 114), acknowledging visual material solely as a topic of conversation. Edwards and Middleton's (1988) analysis of conversational remembering around family snapshots is a relevant example. In the study, the authors showed that looking through, and talking about, family photographs provides a rich social and communicative setting within which children develop the skills of joint, conversational remembering and learn how to 'take meaning' from a photograph. However, while Edwards & Middleton (1988, p. 7) acknowledge that photographs are 'semiotically and culturally meaningful things' whose form, content, creation, and usage are regulated by a set of culturally specific conventions, their analysis focused entirely on conversations *about* photographs. The family snapshots were neither shown, nor examined. They were occasionally described, with the descriptions restricted to those features that were attended to by the participants. The emphasis was, therefore, on photographs as a 'rich stimulant of joint remembering' (Edwards & Middleton, 1988, p. 7), without acknowledging that the photographs themselves (i.e. their content, form and composition, and their existence as material objects), as well as the complex social practices involved in their creation and preservation, are also constitutive of, and intrinsic to, the activity of joint, family remembering.

The reluctance within discursive psychology to engage more directly with visual material can be attributed to the fact that its theoretical, philosophical and empirical roots lie in traditions and approaches that focus on written and spoken language and offer tools for their analysis. Also, as Frith, Riley, Archer, and Gleeson (2005) point out, there is a deeply entrenched belief within psychology more generally that the polysemic nature of images and the subjective nature of what Stuart Hall (1973) calls their 'connotative code', makes them less amenable to systematic, empirical examination of the kind that might be possible with verbal data. The assumed 'subjective' nature of images is, arguably, why talk *about* images is deemed such a useful tool in the study of subjectivity (Reavey & Johnson, 2008).

Yet when examining discourses surrounding iconic images of human suffering, the neglect of visual analysis becomes hard to justify. How can we study the emotional and political power of images without analysing photographs themselves, without examining their aesthetic features, their symbolism and connotative force, or without scrutinising what they show and what they conceal? After all, visual methodologies developed over the past half century which ushered in a 'pictorial turn' in arts and humanities (Mitchell, 1994) have supplied ample evidence of the benefits of engaging in interpretation of symbols, cultural signs and meanings in visual texts, particularly when unpicking the ideological power of images (e.g. Barthes, 2000, 2009; Berger, 2013; Hall, 1973; Helmers & Hill, 2004; Sontag, 1977, 2003). More recently, several authors have emphasised the inherently performative nature of photography, arguing that visual images are themselves rhetorical and action-oriented; they are stances in an argument, deployed, often alongside words, to get things done (Asch, 2005; Azoulay, 2008; Levin, 2009). So, this chapter can be seen as a preliminary inquiry into how one might bring the analysis of visual rhetoric into discursive analysis, and enrich the examination of talk *about* images, with a closer look at their aesthetic and symbolic properties, and institutional and social practices that inform their production and dissemination.

Looking as a Morally Accountable Activity

In accounts of the public impact of the death of Alan Kurdi, there has been a tendency to assume that, because Twitter and Facebook played an important role in the dissemination of the photographs, this was a spontaneous, global, 'bottom up' phenomenon, which largely bypassed traditional, more institutionalised channels through which news about humanitarian crises are usually disseminated. The public's emotional reaction was seen as the *source* of the media story, in that the traditional media found themselves merely reporting on, or responding to, an unprecedented and unforeseen outburst of sympathy.

However, the analysis of the evolution of the story on Twitter in the hours immediately after the images first appeared on the website of the Turkish news agency DHA, suggests otherwise (D'Orazio, 2015). Among the first disseminators of the images were journalists and activists campaigning on behalf of Syrian refugees, who by the very nature of their social, and professional, networks had a comparatively large number of followers. Their activity enabled the images to cascade down not just to more users, but also to other influential individuals, among them fellow journalists and charity workers, politicians, public figures and so on, many of whom were similarly eager to turn Alan Kurdi's death into a humanitarian cause (see Fehrenbach & Rodogno, 2015). This eventually ensured the uptake of the images by the mainstream media, including all the major outlets in the UK. It was, in fact, only after the images went 'mainstream' that they also went 'viral' on social networks (D'Orazio, 2015).

The role of the mass media in the global diffusion of the Kurdi images is important because it suggests that between the photographs and the public's emotional response, was a complex process of mediation, what Zelizer (2004, p. 115) defined as the 'maze of practices and standards, both explicit and implicit, by which photographers, photographic editors, news editors, and journalists decide how war can be reduced to a photograph'. In this case, mediation involved working up the images as an emotionally relevant, viewable object of humanitarian interest.

Whenever there is a conflict or natural disaster, newspaper picture desks face an influx of troubling imagery, often involving children, which come in via news agencies, or increasingly, social networks (Tooth, 2014). Such images present a quandary for mainstream news outlets. Western media generally refrain from publishing graphic images of death and suffering, particularly those showing children, mainly because of concerns about the dignity of the victims, and to avoid offending the sensibilities of the audience. Moreover, dissemination of distressing images leaves the media open to accusations that they are engaging in sensationalism, or that they are seeking to profit from the disaster by satisfying the public's morbid curiosity and unsavoury need for 'atrocity porn'. At the same time, not publishing distressing images leaves them exposed to charges that they are concealing the 'truth' or sanitising the brutal realities of war. News editors as 'visual gatekeepers' must therefore make, and justify, decisions that will often test the boundaries of responsible, ethical journalism, and balance the competing demands of, on the one hand, newsworthiness, and on the other hand, public sensibility, and the dignity and privacy of victims.

Shahira Fahmy (2005) has shown that despite the existence of various codes of practice and ethics guidelines, editorial decisions about the use of controversial imagery are inherently subjective, and based mainly on journalistic 'instinct', political leanings and actual, or anticipated, actions of competitors. The images of Alan Kurdi's body offer a good example of how the media manage competing obligations, and how the framing of images, and the emphasis on their emotional resonance, becomes inherently tied up with the media's handling of their own accountability for publishing photographs of a dead child.

As soon as the images of Alan Kurdi's body appeared on the front covers of newspapers, the decision to publish them became part of the news story. Many daily newspapers explicitly acknowledged the controversial nature of their decision and sought to justify it. Consider the following examples:

> We didn't rush to publish [...] We verified the photographs and waited for a full story before publication. The enormous poignancy and potential power of the photographs was evident from the start. Could they be the images that provided a tipping point? Would public sympathy, and perhaps anger at Britain's role as an apparent bystander in this saga, be moved by them? We decided that both of these were highly likely. Those factors had to be balanced again [sic] the real shock that some readers would feel. (Paul Johnson, *Guardian* web editor, in Fahey, 2015)

> Ultimately, we felt – and still do – that the power to shock is a vital instrument of journalism, and therefore democracy. Our motivation wasn't avaricious; it was to shock the world into action, to improve refugee policy – which is why the accompanying editorial and petition had clear policy recommendations – and to put pressure on a Prime Minister whose behaviour in this crisis has been embarrassing. We hoped some good may yet be salvaged from the appalling fate of poor Aylan, and thousands like him. (*The Independent*; Rajan, 2015)

> "the world must see the truth in order to change". Strong photos "arouse emotions. They show beautiful, but also cruel moments. They let us sympathise with other people." (editorial in the German daily *Bild*, cited in Henley, 2015)

> The image is not offensive, it is not gory, it is not tasteless — it is merely heartbreaking, and stark testimony of an unfolding human tragedy that is playing out in Syria, Turkey and Europe, often unwitnessed [...] We have written stories about hundreds of migrants dead in capsized boats, sweltering trucks, lonely rail lines, but it took a tiny boy on a beach to really bring it home to those readers who may not yet have grasped the magnitude of the migrant crisis. (Kim Murphy, the assistant managing editor of *The Los Angeles Times*, cited in Mackey, 2015)

Evident in these examples is a surprisingly uniform, threefold argument for why the images were printed. First, claims such as that the world 'must see the truth in order to change' or that it is the task of newspapers to 'bring it home' imply that publication was necessary, because of the need to draw attention to an important, tragic event, which would otherwise have been overlooked. Second, it is assumed that this had to be done through images because of their 'enormous poignancy and potential power'. Crucially, this power lay not in their evidentiary or documentary value, but in their ability to 'arouse emotion' and 'shock the world into action'. Third, it was implied that the Kurdi images were exceptional, in their horror and emotional impact: they had a unique ability to capture the 'magnitude of the migrant crisis', succeed where 'stories' failed and offer a potential 'tipping point'. The emphasis on the singularity of the Kurdi images is unsurprising, because editorial decisions to print graphic images of violence are related to (and can be accounted for by) the perceived scale of the event. The more significant or extraordinary a news story, the less important it becomes to 'hold anything back' (Fahmy, 2005, p. 159).

Identical arguments were to be found even in publications such as *The Sun*, or the *Daily Mail*, which have traditionally taken a less sympathetic and occasionally hostile stance towards refugees. The *Daily Mail* stated on its front page that the images 'could not be more harrowing—but must be seen to comprehend the gravity of the migrant crisis engulfing Europe', while *The Sun* described the images as a 'heartbreaking symbol of the migrant crisis' and demanded of the government to 'solve this tragedy'. Therefore, across the political and media spectrum, the initial decision to publish the images was presented as controversial, but well thought through, in the public interest, and well intentioned. What is more, it was argued that what made these images publishable was not that they were not excessively distressing, but on the contrary, that the images *must* be seen, and disseminated, *because* they are 'shocking' and 'heart-breaking', and because they can make a difference. As Burns (2015, p. 38) put it, the message being conveyed was that it was 'acceptable to look at and share a photograph of a dead child if that is perceived to do something, or somehow improve the situation that otherwise seems overwhelmingly complex'.

This framing of the images as belonging to the genre of 'photography of conscience' (Sontag, 2003) was not limited to opinion pieces which reflected on the journalistic decision; it featured in the descriptions of the very event being reported. The headline on the front page of *The Independent* on the day after the body of Alan Kurdi was discovered, is probably the most illustrative example, because it captured, within a single sentence (one character short of the length of a Twitter post), all the elements of the aforementioned threefold argument: '*I*F THESE EXTRAORDINARILY POWERFUL IMAGES OF A DEAD *S*YRIAN CHILD WASHED UP ON A BEACH DON'T CHANGE *E*UROPE'S ATTITUDE TO REFUGEES, WHAT WILL?' (*The Independent*, September 3, Rajan, 2015). Kurdi photographs were introduced as an *extraordinary* instance of a category of images that are inherently *powerful* and have the capacity to *change attitudes*. The account *of* the images was, therefore, at the same time an account *for* looking at, or publishing them.

Importantly, it was not just the media that had to manage their moral accountability for viewing and disseminating the images, and in doing so negotiate a normatively positive place for themselves within the prevailing moral order. Looking at the images of a dead child is, in most contexts, an accountable activity. Politicians, journalists, activists, commentators, but also ordinary members of the public communicating via social media, all engaged in similar rhetorical work. When describing and discussing the images, they too appealed to the link between images, emotion and action, they worked up their feelings about the boy's death as natural, appropriate and genuine, and accounted for the sincerity of their motives and actions. They endeavoured to show that they gazed at or even shared photographs of a dead child, but that their motives for doing so were benevolent rather than self-serving, or perverse.

And yet, all this accounting contained an important omission. The assumption that visual evidence in general, and the Kurdi images in particular, possess superior ability to provoke sympathetic concern, was taken for granted. Nowhere were we told *why* the world needs to 'see the truth in order to change it', or why images succeed where 'stories' fail. Or what made the 'enormous poignancy and potential power' of these images immediately obvious, and what differentiated them, in terms of their emotional power, from other images of dead children. These assumptions, and the corresponding sentiments, were all meant to be understood and accepted instinctively, and unquestioningly, by the good-hearted audience who, operating within the same framework of meaning and moral order, would recognise, and share them. In other words, speakers were relying on, and reproducing an ideological common sense about the intrinsic link between images, emotions and action.

'Moving Images' and the Practice of Spectatorial Sympathy

In recent years there have been some, largely speculative, attempts to provide a scientific explanation for the association between images, emotion and social action, drawing on neuroscience and evolutionary biology. Joshua Sarinana, a neuroscientist at the Harvard Medical School, writes, for instance, that the link between photography, empathy and altruism is 'deeply ingrained into the architecture of our brain' and that 'photography plays a unique role in triggering the network of brain regions that underlie empathy'. Therefore, he suggests, photographs '*undoubtedly* appeal to our emotions and our yearning to help those in need' (Sarinana, 2014, emphasis added).

Such essentialist explanations do not stand up to scrutiny, however. There is nothing inevitable, or natural, about human empathy. Children are frequent casualties of war, and images depicting their dead bodies are not uncommon. Yet few make it to the front pages of newspapers or become part of a humanitarian cause. So, as Gregory (2015) points out, the peculiar thing about images depicting the dead, the injured or the needy is not that they provoke a wave of compassion, but that they do so rarely. Also, the power of images of suffering is short lived: according to the European Journalism Observatory, which examined the coverage of the Kurdi death in eight countries across Europe, any notable effect on public debate all but disappeared within just 10 days (European Journalism Observatory, 2015).

The common-sense assumptions about the power of images can be much more productively explored as products of culture rather than nature, as ideological constructs with a distinct social and cultural history. In fact, until the eighteenth century, the contention that one might feel emotionally moved by the suffering of strangers would have seemed distinctly alien: the 'affective barrier' between any individual and the outside world seldom extended further than the immediate family, friends or community (Friedland, 2012). People were seen as predisposed mainly towards self-interest and self-love (Fiering, 1976), and while Christian iconography was replete with imagery of suffering, the emphasis there was on the inevitability of pain and its redemptive potential, not empathy (Eisenman, 2007).

It was only in the 1700s that the broader project of Enlightenment ushered in a 'sentimental revolution' which instituted the idea of visually mediated humanitarian concern as an intrinsic, and divinely ordained part of human 'nature' (Fiering, 1976, p. 212, also Arendt, 1963). At that time, a new generation of moral philosophers including the Third Earl of Shaftsbury, William Wollaston, Francis Hutcheson and Adam Smith offered a view of 'human nature' as defined by a fundamental moral sense and benevolence towards others (Halttunen, 1995). The emerging doctrine of 'irresistible compassion' manifested itself as a basic psychological principle, namely that 'men [*sic*] irresistibly have compassion for the suffering of others and are equally irresistibly moved to alleviate that suffering' (Fiering, 1976, p. 195). This 'secular sanctification of compassion' (ibid, p. 198) and its key corollary, the view of pain as unacceptable and repulsive, gained wider social and political currency in part because it offered an intellectual and moral standpoint from which to advocate humanitarian reform, namely, the abolition of slavery, torture, corporal punishment and other violent practices which were now deemed cruel, offensive, uncivilised and 'unnatural' (Halttunen, 1995).

In articulating the idea of a natural humanitarian impulse, writers were heavily influenced by John Locke's emphasis on vision as the primary sense. *Viewing* the anguish of others was believed to enhance psychological proximity to the suffering of strangers and was thus instrumental in triggering empathy. The assumed association between compassion and spectatorship, which Dwyer (1987) labelled *spectatorial sympathy*, leads to a proliferation of visual representations of suffering, initially in the form of sentimental art. Humanitarian reformers also embraced the assumed power of the visual, and supplemented the often sensationalist descriptions of violence with artistic representations of the most brutal practices which they sought to outlaw, all with the aim of awakening, and cultivating, humanitarian sensibility in the audience.

The link between humanitarian advocacy and spectatorial sympathy became even more prominent in the late nineteenth and early twentieth century, when the rapid development of photographic technology, with its rhetoric of realism and truth, revolutionised how evidence of suffering could be presented visually (Fehrenbach & Rodogno, 2015). Photographic images have been at the core of humanitarian campaigns ever since, underpinning the 'manipulative emotional appeals' which remain an inherent feature of organised humanitarianism (Rozario, 2003, p. 419).

In constructing human compassion as instinctive and 'natural', eighteenth-century moral philosophy was effectively establishing a new moral order and initiating a new 'historical stage in the education of the emotions' (Fiering, 1976, p. 212). It did so by turning empathy towards strangers into a marker of virtue. Compassion became something to be *displayed* and *performed* through emotionally charged words and actions (gasping or recoiling when faced with evidence of suffering), through charity work and philanthropy, or simply by calling for something to be done. Therefore, spectatorial sympathy refers not just to an abstract link between emotion, spectatorship and action, but to a set of discursive and embodied *practices* through which a visually facilitated humanitarian sentiment is articulated, and enacted.

Importantly for the present discussion, the practice of spectatorial sympathy had, from the outset, an argumentative texture, driven by a fundamental contradiction: it mandated engagement with visual material that was often constructed as too repulsive to watch. The same sentimental ethics that made the pain of others intolerable, made it also a source of public fascination. This revealed the possibility that the pain of others was a potential source of *pleasure*: the pleasure of one's own virtue manifested in the experience of empathy, or relief provoked by the realisation that one has been spared from the observed suffering. Susan Sontag (2003) alluded to a further dimension of the pleasures of spectatorship when she wrote that moral satisfaction can be derived both from the act of flinching before images of unbearable suffering, and from the knowledge that one can look at the image *without* flinching.

The prospect of pleasure being derived from watching images of death and suffering, but also the emerging concern that indulgence in such material might stifle one's instinctive humanitarian response, or even worse, arouse a perverse affinity for cruelty, shaped the argumentative context within which images of suffering have been circulating ever since (Halttunen, 1995). In fact, when one reads the late eighteenth and early nineteenth-century writing about the natural humanitarian impulse, it is striking how closely the arguments align with those in evidence today, in both academic and popular discourse. Then, just like today, those participating in the spectacle of suffering 'filled their writing with close descriptions of their own immediate emotional response' to demonstrate the purity of their sensibilities (Halttunen, 1995, p. 326), they linked the act of viewing to meaningful action lest they should be seen as merely 'feasting upon the consciousness of our own virtue' (Barbauld, 1773, p. 174), or 'gratifying a morbid appetite' (Wright, 1846, p. iii). They debated the relationship between 'feeling' and 'doing': talking about what one has seen and how they were personally affected was, just like today, intrinsically tied up with the act of *adopting a stance*, or committing to a cause (Boltanski, 1999).

Tracing the history of spectatorial sympathy is important because it suggests that emotional displays, verbal or otherwise, that permeated the responses to the images of Alan Kurdi, are embedded in culturally specific discourses and practices, which shape both the sources of moral accountability associated with the act of looking at an image of a dead child, and the ways of managing them. And yet, as we shall see, spectatorial sympathy does not influence just the reading of, and responses to, images. It influences also the images themselves; it informs the various representational practices and aesthetic conventions that makes some images recognisable icons of suffering, and renders some deaths more visible, politically consequential and 'grievable' than others (Butler, 2007).

Images of Suffering Children and the Aesthetics of Humanitarianism

The central feature of the Kurdi images, from which they draw their symbolic power, is undoubtedly that they represent a dead *child*. Ever since the movement to end the atrocities in the Belgian Congo in the 1890s, photographs of suffering or dead children have been a staple ingredient of visually mediated compassion (Fehrenbach & Rodogno, 2015). The coming together of spectatorial sympathy, and the nineteenth-century invention, and idealisation, of childhood (and especially the motifs of innocence and vulnerability) have encouraged campaigners to develop a distinct 'iconography of childhood' which includes the trope of the lone suffering child, or the child being cradled by an adult in the manner of the Pietà (Fehrenbach, 2015, p. 166). There is no doubt that, out of several dozen images taken that day on the beach near Bodrum, the two 'iconic' images of Alan Kurdi's body were selected for dissemination because they fitted the established conventions of humanitarian photography, and in the knowledge that they would be read as such.

In fact, the familiar 'iconography of childhood' can be said to have influenced the *creation* of the images in the first place. As Zelizer (2004) points out, in today's highly competitive media market, what makes a news image stand out, and more importantly, what makes it memorable and durable, 'defining' and 'iconic' is that it meets certain aesthetic expectations and is recognisably symbolic, connotative, dramatic and vivid. This leads to a reliance on a set of interpretative strategies, and familiar visual tropes, including that of the dead child. The point being made here is not that Nilüfer Demir, the photographer behind the Kurdi images, was intentionally reproducing a photo-journalistic cliché, but rather that what made that scene worth photographing is that it conformed to a set of established conventions, well represented in the history of award-winning news photography, or compilations of 'iconic', 'heart-breaking' images.

And yet, the image of a dead child does not in itself make a global phenomenon. So, what is it about the Kurdi images that made them such a prominent icon of the refugee experience?

The rhetorical use of visual images of suffering involves a specific moral framing, based on what Azoulay (2008, p. 25) calls the 'pragmatics of obligation'. Recipients of the humanitarian message are not just expected to care; they are expected to accept responsibility for the problem and take appropriate action. The audience must be *shamed* into doing something to alleviate the observed suffering (Asch, 2005). For this moral rhetoric to work in the contemporary political context, both the 'problem' and the 'solution' need to be distinctly *humanitarian* in nature, and 'we' (often 'the west', to whose gaze the victims are exposed) need to be identifiably accountable.

In the case of the Kurdi images, this rhetoric of shaming is revealed in the location of the boy's body (the beach) and the cause of death (drowning). Had the image been of a child killed by the so-called Islamic State, the Syrian Army or Russian air strikes, it would have been much more difficult to frame the death in strictly humanitarian terms and invoke the rhetoric of shame. Blame would have been attributable to a specific side in the military conflict, rather than the 'inaction' of those for whom the image was intended. It also would have introduced the option of western military action, a controversial proposition in the post-Iraq world characterised by intervention fatigue. The fact that Alan Kurdi drowned on Europe's border, rather than being killed, for instance, on the streets of Aleppo, allowed for the geographical, and political, distance to be maintained between the plight of the refugees, and its underlying (military) cause. It allowed for the problem to be constituted as *humanitarian* as opposed to *military*, and it foregrounded the accountability of western governments on whose 'doorstep' the boy died. Therefore, the image itself reflected, while at the same time reinforcing, a particular framing of the refugee crisis, its causes and possible solutions.

Also, the photographs of Alan Kurdi's body are inherently ambiguous. On the one hand, they are highly graphic in their portrayal of violent death: they show the body of a child that the viewer knows is dead. Yet at the same time, the body does not 'look' dead. There are no signs of putrefaction or bloating, common in cases of drowning, there is no blood or other signs of physical trauma. In fact, in responses to the photograph of the body lying face down in the sand, one frequently encounters comparisons to a 'sleeping child': the posture of the body is said to be reminiscent of the 'awkward sleeping position' of toddlers (Drainville, 2015, p. 47). The sanitised and aestheticised representation of death makes the image seem 'taboo breaking'—in the context of journalistic conventions that generally proscribe the publication of images of dead children—but also inoffensive, because it aligns with the sensibilities of an audience accustomed to funereal practices that make the dead look as if they are asleep. This ambiguity made the photograph of Alan Kurdi's body both controversial and publishable and, therefore, inherently newsworthy. What is more, the condition of the body itself appeals to the sense of shame in the audience: it suggests that the boy had only just died, and therefore, that assistance, symbolised by the figure of the Turkish policeman, arrived just a little too late. In the best known of the Kurdi images, in which the boy's body is lying alone, face down in the sand, the viewer is effectively invited to look at the boy through the gaze of the first responders, and reflect on their culpability for not 'getting there' (in terms of responding to the refugee crisis) sooner.

The ambiguity of the images is important also because it captured the two lenses through which the refugee crisis in the Mediterranean is often perceived: the forensic lens, which views dead or suffering migrant bodies as evidence of a crime (war crimes, trafficking, but also the western governments' inaction), and the lens of memory whereby the body becomes the 'reference point for mourning and the addressing of trauma' (Kovras & Robins, 2016). The photograph of the body in the sand resembles, at the same time, an artistically unpretentious forensic photograph, which gives it an aura of authenticity and referentiality (McCabe, 2015), and a work of art that uses the moral figure of the child and the motif of childhood innocence, to capture the tragedy of the refugee experience. The latter dimension is especially apparent in the large number of 'surrogate' images, artistic manipulations of the original photographs created by illustrators and graphic designers, which sought to moderate the explicitness of the original photographs, while foregrounding their wider symbolism (Drainville, 2015).

Perhaps most importantly, the images of Alan Kurdi's body owe their public prominence to the fact that they struck a balance between the rhetoric of similarity and difference that underpins humanitarian photography. Since its inception, humanitarian imagery has been instrumental in representing *distant suffering*, the anguish of people who are both culturally and geographically removed from those to whose gaze they are being subjected. Distance, after all, is what made Alan Kurdi's dead body visible in the first place: no British media outlet would ever have published an explicit image of a dead British child washed up on a beach.

There are two principle reasons for this emphasis on *distant* suffering. The first and obvious reason is that only distant suffering needs to be 'brought home' through affecting images. Suffering close by is already visible, or perceptible in other ways. The second reason is that historically, humanitarian imagery has been instrumental in fostering the ideology of racial and class difference, presenting populations in need as 'passive but pathetic objects capable only of offering themselves up to a benevolent, transient gaze' of those on whose compassion they supposedly depend (Tagg, 1988, p. 12). The sense of entitlement to watch the suffering of distant others, supposedly for their benefit, is inherent in the practice of spectatorial sympathy and the moral order underpinning international humanitarianism.

The distance between the spectator and the suffering victim is never absolute, however. Humanitarian mobilisation depends on the process of identification: the distant victim must be made to resemble 'us' (Douglas, 1994). Thus, in accounting for why they were moved by the death of Alan Kurdi, journalists, public figures and users of social media often focused not just on the boy's pose, but also his attire, especially his shoes (Procter & Yamada-Rice, 2015; Tharoor, 2015). This focus on shoes was facilitated by the fact that in one of the widely circulated versions of the image, the angle of the shot and the composition of the image made the boy's feet a salient feature. On a symbolic level, the shoes are evocative of childhood innocence, and the fragility and dependency of children. Yet, the point here was not that Alan Kurdi was wearing shoes (why wouldn't a Syrian child wear them?) but, rather, that he was wearing shoes (and clothes) like those worn by children in the west. It provided a point of visual similarity between a Syrian child and 'our' children, and a source of identification.

This kind of identification seems unproblematic at first. Recent work on altruism and social identity has shown that people are more likely to help those who resemble them in terms of some socially relevant, or salient criterion (e.g. Levine, Prosser, Evans, & Reicher, 2005). This might include a mundane point of similarity, such as someone's clothing, which acts as an external marker of cultural affiliation. However, in the context of the history of humanitarianism, the importance attributed to identification has a troubling legacy. For over a century, campaigners seeking to 'bring home' the suffering of distant peoples have known that, to inspire sympathy, they must make non-Europeans look more 'European'. In the 1920s, humanitarian campaigners went as far as to lighten the skin of Armenian children to inspire compassion among western audiences (see Fehrenbach & Rodogno, 2015). Such extreme practices are uncommon today, but the fact remains that issues of racial and cultural similarity and difference still inform the choice of subject of humanitarian photography and the reading of images (ibid.). Humanitarian campaigners will choose humanitarian causes, and images to represent them, according to these parameters, and draw attention to issues and features that they believe will promote identification, and, by extension, enhance empathy.

This of course does not mean that people reacted emotionally to images of Alan Kurdi's body simply *because* he resembled a child of European descent, or that they would not have done so if he was black or had been wearing attire that explicitly marked him as culturally different. Nor does the analysis of the images, their symbolism and ideological message, imply that their capacity to elicit an emotional or political response lies exclusively, and inexorably, in their visual, or aesthetic qualities. Rather, the point being made is that the practice of spectatorial sympathy has a political and ideological dimension which is reflected not just in how we make sense of images of suffering or how we feel about them, but also in which dead bodies we get to gaze at, get 'shocked' by, and care about in the first place.

Conclusion

This chapter examined the responses to the images of Alan Kurdi as a manifestation of *spectatorial sympathy*, a practice that shapes the prevailing cultural assumptions about the link between images, emotion and political mobilisation, and determines the parameters within which the appropriateness of emotional and political responses to images of suffering is negotiated. Being shocked, disturbed or saddened by the photograph of a suffering body is not a visceral *reaction* to a tragic event or its technologically mediated representation, but a form of social *action*. It is a way of suffusing the photograph with moral and political significance, redefining the death represented in it as an emergency that demands urgent collective response, and accounting for the act of looking.

Spectatorial sympathy, which informed the social life of the Kurdi images from the moment they were taken on the beach in Bodrum, to when they were displayed on millions of computer screens and on front covers of newspapers around the world, is inherently multimodal. It is constituted not just through avowals of emotions (both verbal and embodied), and the debates about their meaning and appositeness, but also through images themselves. The inherent link between what is *seen* and what is *felt* suggests that in studies of discourse, visual images and their symbolism deserve to be recognised as an object of analysis, and not, as is often the case, a prop used to stimulate talk. Focusing simply on what participants *say* about an image leads us to miss the complex dynamic by which that image became visible to them, and instituted as something worth talking about.

Acknowledging the fact that the visual is an intrinsic part of everyday social and emotional life does not require a break with discursive psychology's broader intellectual project. Especially in the early stages, discursive approaches were defined by intellectual open-mindedness and eclecticism that was (and still is) missing from mainstream psychology. The argument was frequently made that scholarship (Billig, 1988; Gill, 1996) is as important as a specific method of analysis, especially when it comes to the study of ideology. As Billig (1988, p. 199–200) put it, in the study of ideological phenomena, using 'intellectual experience', 'scholarly judgment', 'hunches' and 'specialist knowledge' to place specific patterns of thought within longer traditions of explanation, and one might add, ways of seeing, is often more illuminating than following 'formally defined procedures'. There is no reason these skills cannot be productively mobilised to explore more fully the interplay between verbal and visual rhetoric, especially in terms of how images come to serve 'as the index of an ideological theme' (Hall, 1973, p. 184). Given that contemporary political and media cultures are becoming increasingly reliant on both visual communication and emotion, perhaps it is time to challenge the 'hegemony of verbal texts' (Helmers & Hill, 2004, p. 19–20) and consider how words and images work together in shaping human experience, and how they inform what we see and feel, and perhaps more importantly, what we don't see and don't feel.

References

Arendt, H. (1963). *On revolution*. New York: Viking Press.

Asch, S. (2005). The Barnardo's babies: Performativity, shame and the photograph. *Continuum: Journal of Media & Cultural Studies, 19*, 507–521.

Azoulay, A. (2008). *The civil contract of photography*. New York: Zone Books.

Barbauld, A. L. (1773/1825). On romances: An imitation (1773). In L. Aikin (Ed.), *Works of Barbauld* (pp. 171–175). London: Longman Hurst.

Barthes, R. (2000). *Camera lucida*. London: Vintage.

Barthes, R. (2009). *Mythologies*. London: Vintage.

Berger, J. (2013). *Understanding a photograph*. London: Penguin.

Billig, M. (1988). Methodology and scholarship in understanding ideological explanation. In C. Antaki (Ed.), *Analysing everyday explanation: A casebook of methods* (pp. 199–215). London: Sage.

Boltanski, L. (1999). *Distant suffering: Morality, media and politics*. Cambridge: Cambridge University Press.

Burns, A. (2015). Discussion and action: political and personal responses to the Aylan Kurdi images. In O. Goriunova & F. Vis (Eds), *The iconic image on social media: A rapid research response to the death of Aylan Kurdi* (pp. 38–39). Visual Social Media Lab. Retrieved from http://visualsocialmedialab.org/projects/the-iconic-image-on-social-media

Butler, J. (2007). Torture and the ethics of photography. *Environment and Planning D: Society and Space, 25*, 951–966.

Childs, C., & Hepburn, A. (2015). Discursive psychology and emotion. In C. Tileagă & E. Stokoe (Eds.), *Discursive psychology: Classic and contemporary issues* (pp. 114–128). London: Routledge.

D'Orazio, F. (2015). Journey of an image: From a beach in Bodrum to twenty million screens across the world. In O. Goriunova & F. Vis (Eds.), *The Iconic image on social media: A rapid research response to the death of Aylan Kurdi* (pp. 11–18). Visual Social Media Lab. Retrieved from http://visualsocialmedialab.org/projects/the-iconic-image-on-social-media

Douglas, S. (1994). A three-way failure. Progressive, July 1994, p. 15.

Drainville, R. (2015). On the iconology of Aylan Kurdi, alone. In O. Goriunova & F. Vis (Eds), *The iconic image on social media: A rapid research response to the death of Aylan Kurdi* (pp. 47-49). Visual Social Media Lab. Retrieved from http://visualsocialmedialab.org/projects/the-iconic-image-on-social-media

Dwyer, J. (1987). *Virtuous discourse: Sensibility and community in late eighteenth-century Scotland*. Edinburgh: John Donald.

Edwards, D. (1997). *Discourse and cognition*. London: Sage.

Edwards, D. (1999). Emotion discourse. *Psychology and Culture, 5*, 271–291.

Edwards, D., & Middleton, D. (1988). Conversational remembering and family relationships: How children learn to remember. *Journal of Social and Personal Relationships, 5*, 3–25.

Eisenman, S. F. (2007). *The Abu Ghraib effect*. London: Reaktion Books.

European Journalism Observatory. (2015). *Research: How Europe's newspapers reported the migration crisis*. Retrieved from http://en.ejo.ch/research/research-how-europes-newspapers-reported-the-migration-crisis

Fahey, J. (2015, September 7). The Guardian's decision to publish shocking photos of Aylan Kurdi. *The Guardian*. Retrieved from https://www.theguardian.com/commentisfree/2015/sep/07/guardian-decision-to-publish-shocking-photos-of-aylan-kurdi.

Fahmy, S. (2005). US photojournalists' and photo editors' attitudes and perceptions: Visual coverage of the 9/11 and the Afgan war. *Visual Communication Quarterly, 12*, 146–163.

Fehrenbach, H. (2015). Children and other civilians: Photography and the politics of humanitarian image-making. In H. Fehrenbach & D. Rodogno (Eds), *Humanitarian photography: A history* (pp. 165–199). Cambridge: Cambridge University Press.

Fehrenbach, H., & Rodogno, D. (2015). "A horrific photo of a drowned Syrian child": Humanitarian photography and NGO media strategies in historical perspective. *International Review of the Red Cross, 97*, 1121–1155.

Fiering, N. S. (1976). Irresistible compassion: An aspect of eighteenth-century sympathy and humanitarianism. *Journal of the History of Ideas, 37*, 195–218.

Friedland, P. (2012). *Seeing justice done: The age of spectacular capital punishment in France*. Oxford: Oxford University Press.

Frith, H., Riley, S., Archer, L., & Gleeson, K. (2005). Imag(in)ing visual methodologies. *Qualitative Research in Psychology, 2*, 187–198.

Gill, R. (1996). Discourse analysis: Practical implementation. In J. T. E. Richardson (Ed.), *Handbook of qualitative research methods for psychology and the social sciences* (pp. 141–158). Leicester: British Psychological Society Books.

Goldberg, V. (1991). *The power of photography: How photographs changed our lives*. New York: Abbeville Press.

Goriunova, O., & Vis, F. (Eds.). (2015). *The iconic image on social media: A rapid research response to the death of Aylan Kurdi*. Visual Social Media Lab. Retrieved from http://visualsocialmedialab.org/projects/the-iconic-image-on-social-media

Gregory, S. (2015). When should we share distressing images? Seeing Aylan Kurdi. In O. Goriunova & F. Vis (Eds), *The iconic image on social media: A rapid research response to the death of Aylan Kurdi* (pp. 61–63). Visual Social Media Lab. Retrieved from http://visualsocialmedialab.org/projects/the-iconic-image-on-social-media

Hall, S. (1973). The determination of news photographs. In S. Cohen & J. Young (Eds.), *The manufacture of news: Social problems, deviance and the mass media* (pp. 226–247). London: Sage.

Halttunen, K. (1995). Humanitarianism and the pornography of pain in Anglo-American culture. *The American Historical Review, 100*, 303–334.

Harré, R. (1987). *The social construction of emotions*. Oxford: Blackwell.

Harré, R., & Gillett, G. (1994). *The discursive mind*. London: Sage.

Helmers, M., & Hill, C. A. (2004). Introduction. In C. A. Hill & M. Helmers (Eds.), *Defining visual rhetorics* (pp. 10–23). Mahwah, NJ: Lawrence Erlbaum.

Henley, J. (2015, September 9). Bild's stance over Alan Kurdi image a typically bold move. *The Guardian*. Retrieved from https://www.theguardian.com/media/2015/sep/09/bilds-stance-over-alan-kurdi-images-a-typically-bold-move

Hepburn, A. (2004). Crying: Notes on description, transcription and interaction. *Research on Language and Social Interaction, 37*, 251–290.

Kear, A., & Steinberg, D. L. (1999). *Mourning Diana: Nation, culture and the performance of grief*. Abingdon: Routledge.

Kovras, I. & Robins, S. (2016). Death as the border: Managing missing migrants and unidentified bodies at the EU's Mediterranean frontier. *Political Geography, 55*, 40–49.

Levin, L. (2009). The performative force of photography. *Photography and Culture, 2*, 327–336.

Levine, M., Prosser, A., Evans, D., & Reicher, S. (2005). Identity and emergency intervention: How social group membership and inclusiveness of group boundaries shapes helping behaviour. *Personality and Social Psychology Bulletin, 31*, 443–453.

Mackey, R. (2015, September 2). Brutal images of Syrian boy drowned off Turkey must be seen, activists say. *The New York Times*. Retrieved from https://www.nytimes.com/2015/09/03/world/middleeast/brutal-images-of-syrian-boy-drowned-off-turkey-must-be-seen-activists-say.html

McCabe, E. (2015). Why we press the shutter. *British Journalism Review, 26*, 17–21.

Mitchell, W. J. T. (1994). *Picture theory: Essays on verbal and visual representation*. Chicago: University of Chicago Press.

Potter, J. (2012). Discourse analysis and discursive psychology. In H. Cooper (Editor-in-Chief), *APA handbook of research methods in psychology: Vol. 2. Quantitative, qualitative, neuropsychological, and biological* (pp. 111–130). Washington, DC: American Psychological Association Press.

Procter, L. & Yamada-Rice, D. (2015). Shoes of childhood: Exploring the emotional politics through which images become narrated on social media. In O. Goriunova & F. Vis (Eds), *The iconic image on social media: A rapid research response to the death of Aylan Kurdi* (pp. 57–60). Visual Social Media Lab. Retrieved from http://visualsocialmedialab.org/projects/the-iconic-image-on-social-media

Rajan, A. (2015, September 5). Letter from the editor: If you were shocked by Aylan Kurdi's picture, we did our job. *The Independent*. Retrieved from http://www.independent.co.uk/voices/editorials/letter-from-the-editor-if-you-were-shocked-by-aylan-kurdis-picture-we-did-our-job-10488122.html

Reavey, P., & Johnson, K. (2008). *Visual methods in psychology: Using and interpreting images in qualitative research*. London: Routledge.

Rozario, K. (2003). "Delicious horrors": Mass culture, the Red Cross, and the appeal of modern American humanitarianism. *American Quarterly, 55*, 417–455.

Sarinana, J. (2014, October 25). Photography and the feelings of others: From mirroring emotions to the theory of mind. *Petapixel*. Retrieved from http://petapixel.com/2014/10/25/photography-feelings-others-mirroring-emotions-theory-mind/

Sontag, S. (1977). *On photography*. London: Penguin.

Sontag, S. (2003). *Regarding the pain of others*. London: Penguin.

Tagg, J. (1988). *The burden of representation*. Minneapolis: University of Minnesota Press.

Tharoor, I. (2015, September 2). A dead baby becomes the most tragic symbol yet of the Mediterranean refugee crisis. *Washington Post*. Retrieved from https://www.washingtonpost.com/news/worldviews/wp/2015/09/02/a-dead-baby-becomes-the-most-tragic-symbol-yet-of-the-mediterranean-refugee-crisis/?noredirect=on&utm_term=.47601eac93f4

Tooth, R. (2014, July 23). Graphic content: When photographs of carnage are too upsetting to publish. *The Guardian*. Retrieved from https://www.theguardian.com/world/2014/jul/23/graphic-content-photographs-too-upsetting-to-publish-gaza-mh17-ukraine

Wetherell, M. (1998). Positioning and interpretative repertoires: Conversation analysis and post-structuralism in dialogue. *Discourse and Society, 9*, 431–456.

Wetherell, M. (2012). *Affect and emotion: A new social science understanding*. London: Sage.

Wright, H. C. (1846). *Defensive war proved to be a denial of Christianity and of the government of God: With illustrative facts and anecdotes*. London: Charles Gilpin.

Zelizer, B. (2004). When war is reduced to a photograph. In S. Allan & B. Zelizer (Eds.), *Reporting war: Journalism in wartime* (pp. 115–135). London: Routledge.

Chapter 17
Charlie Hebdo and the Prophet Muhammad: A Multimodal Critical Discourse Analysis of Peace and Violence in a Satirical Cartoon

Laura Kilby and Henry Lennon

Introduction

In this chapter, we examine how ideologies of peace and violence can be (re) produced and communicated via multiple semiotic forms that include, but are not restricted to, language. We grapple with the complexity and importance of the situated-ness of peace and violence, and consider what does peace, indeed what *can* peace, look like in a social context where meaning and expression are both multiple and contested. To this end, we undertake a case study analysis, exploring how a multimodal text might be variously interpreted as an explicit display of peace and forgiveness, and yet simultaneously as an oppressive act which knowingly causes offence. In addressing these issues, we relate to Galtung's (1996, p. 196) typology of violence, and we consider the issue of cultural violence, which he defines as 'those aspects of culture, the symbolic sphere of our existence […] that can be used to legitimize direct or structural violence'.

Discursive Psychology, Critical Discourse Studies and Multimodal Discourse Analysis

Since the 1980s, three broadly separable strands of discourse analysis (DA) have evolved from origins which can be traced back to critical linguistics, the work of Foucault, and the sociology of scientific knowledge (Wooffitt, 2005), although there are many cross-fertilisations between these origins which can be found amongst the body of discursive psychology (DP) research. The range and flexibility of DP

L. Kilby (✉) · H. Lennon
Sheffield Hallam University, Sheffield, UK
e-mail: L.Kilby@shu.ac.uk

© Springer Nature Switzerland AG 2018
S. Gibson (ed.), *Discourse, Peace, and Conflict*, Peace Psychology Book Series,
https://doi.org/10.1007/978-3-319-99094-1_17

approaches bring to the fore an assortment of issues for researchers related to research questions, data, analysis and interpretation in the research process. This leads us to the relationship between more traditional DP (e.g. Edwards, 1997; Edwards & Potter, 1992; te Molder & Potter, 2005) and critical discourse studies (CDS), an umbrella term for discursive work which sets out with an explicit agenda to examine and challenge social problems and inequalities, and study relations of power and institutional systems and practices (e.g. Fairclough, 1989, 2001; Fairclough & Wodak, 1997; van Dijk, 2001, 2015; Wodak & Meyer, 2015). CDS bears an important, yet sometimes contentious, relation to DP, where some consider *all* DP to be critical, whilst others within CDS argue that much of DP is not critical enough (for discussion of this, see Wooffitt, 2005). Moreover, not all advocates of more traditional discursive analytic methods are at ease with the critical ambitions of CDS (see Schegloff, 1997). When orienting to these issues, it can be helpful to consider how one's use of theory, choice of analytical objects, cultural and historical contextualisation, and political advocacy is arranged to determine where one's own work fits (Meyer, 2001).

In this chapter we are concerned with examining how power, psychology and language are interwoven and how they shape and constrain social action institutionally and interactively, thus we align our work with critical discourse studies. However, we have a further ambition to examine how multiple semiotic components are arranged, articulated and interpreted in the construction of a given discourse. We therefore position our approach as a 'multimodal critical discourse analysis' (MCDA). Multimodal practitioners view discourse as incorporating diverse semiotic forms such as language, imagery, sound and gesture to construct meaning. Rather than focussing solely on language, within the analytic process they seek to incorporate as much 'semiotic complexity and richness' as possible (Iedema, 2003, p. 39). The field of multimodal studies (Kress & van Leeuwen, 2001, 2006; van Leeuwen, 1999, 2005) is increasingly driven by recognition that contemporary technologies are re-shaping communicative practices, and the reach of multimodality extends to newly innovated technologies as well as those that were previously the preserve of more mono-modal communications (Levine & Scollon, 2004). Iedema (2003) argues that 'the increased ubiquity of sound, image, film, through TV, the computer and the internet is undoubtedly behind this new emphasis on and interest in multi-semiotic complexity' (p. 33). However, this multimodal turn has not only been prompted by attempts to comprehend postmodernity. As van Leeuwen (2004) notes when considering the famous British military recruitment poster of 1914 featuring Lord Kitchener ('Your country needs YOU') it would be naive to evaluate all forms of discourse *solely* in terms of their language when imagery and graphics can also contribute to the construction of communicative acts. Machin and Mayr (2012, p. 76) argue that a range of features, including verbal description, gaze and pose 'can be used to implicitly communicate kinds of identities and in turn evaluate the actions of participants'. Thus, to solely focus on language in a discourse which incorporates a range of semiotic forms can lead to under-analysis or, potentially, misleading interpretations.

Given our undertaking to adopt a *critical* multimodal approach, it is helpful to note that CDS scholars do typically conceptualise discourse in its broadest semiotic sense, with discourse understood to incorporate all manner of meaningful signs (Fairclough, 2001), albeit the majority of CDS research to date has focussed solely upon the study of talk and text (Machin, 2016). There is, however, a growing interest in studying multimodality within a critical framework (e.g. Carter, 2011; Catalano & Waugh, 2013; Djonov & Zhao, 2014; Machin, 2013; Richardson, 2016; Richardson & Wodak, 2009). Following a review of studies which employed MCDA to examine a range of media, including photographs, toys and music, Carter (2011, p. 61) argues that in each case, MCDA serves to 'better understand how language and other types of semiotic signs are used together to construct, express, and challenge social power'. The focus of our analysis is a political cartoon; hence, we are engaging with a discourse where the visual and textual are heavily interwoven. Any attempt to discursively examine this medium, we suggest, must therefore consider both the textual and the visual components, addressing how they interrelate in the construction and communication of a discourse.

MCDA as Applied to Political Cartoons

According to El Refaie (2009, p. 175), the function of political cartoons is 'to represent an aspect of social, cultural or political life in a way that condenses reality and transforms it in a striking, original and/or humorous way'. They are a fruitful site of investigation because they display culturally embedded values and perpetuate widely shared beliefs. They identify with ideas, address issues, and highlight contrasts between differing groups (Mazid, 2008). Their achievement of meaning is typically managed through satirical humour and use of metaphor. James Gillray's 'Little Boney in a Strong Fit' (published in 1803), depicting Napoleon I's obsession with the British, is a good example. The physical illustrations of his imperial ambitions such as the Roman consular chair, globe, and his triumphal hat all corroborate criticism of his military and political goals.[1] A more contemporary example is Jonathon Shapiro's cartoon, published in September 2008, with the then-President of South Africa Jacob Zuma grinning as he unzips his trousers in front of a group of men (with political abbreviations on their hats), holding down a blindfolded woman in distress wearing a ribbon titled 'Justice System', an allegorical criticism reminiscent of criminal charges that were being made against Zuma.[2] From these two examples we can see that the communicative functions of cartoons are achieved through both visual metaphors and their situated textual claims. Further, we see how 'parody, borrowing, plagiarism, generic and/or thematic similarity' are achieved through both literal interpretation and through a layer of 'cultural, emotional, or ideological overtones and undertones' (Mazid, 2008, p. 440).

In his extensive discussion of cultural violence, Galtung (1996) highlights that in secularised Western nations where concerns with categories of 'Self' and 'Other'

---

[1] For the cartoon, see the British Museum website (http://tinyurl.com/James-Gillray-Maniac-Raving-s).

[2] For the cartoon, see Zapiro's website (https://www.zapiro.com/cartoons/080907st).

have come to reign, ideology is a key driver of cultural violence. Galtung (1996, p. 204) states 'Combine nationalism with steep Self Other gradients, and statism with the right, even the duty to exercise ultimate power and we get the ugly ideology of the nation-state'. Applying MCDA to the genre of political cartoons offers an excellent opportunity to explore the semiotic construction of ideological messages of Western nation-states. Indeed, the study of ideology is not uncommon within MCDA research (e.g. Gamson & Stuart's [1992] study on the 'symbolic contest' between universal and national frames of reference in nuclear weapon cartoons). More recently, Mazid (2008) considers how verbal and visual signs were used to construct meaning in the context of (de)legitimation of ideological claims. Analysing two particular cartoons in a corpus of President Bush and Osama Bin Laden cartoons, Mazid shows how differing stylistic and generic features were engaged to commonly invoke God and the belief in righteous action to justify their opposition to one another. It is notable that in both cases, despite being presented as oppositional characters, they are commonly ridiculed as being similarly hateful, bloodthirsty, and as the antonym to the 'holy fighters' (p. 452), personas which they both seek to uphold (cf. Leudar, Marsland, & Nekvapil, 2004). Elsewhere, Müller, Özcan, and Seizov (2009) investigate three related cases of cartoon controversies, including one case of direct relevance to us, concerning the Muslim prophet Muhammad published in the Danish newspaper Jyllands-Posten. Noting the general pattern to denote Muhammad in unpleasant and threatening ways, Müller et al. (2009) argue that the tendency to present Muhammad in the cartoons with an aggressive demeanour produces stark conflations between Islam and violence/terrorism (e.g. by having a bomb as a turban). Despite a potential for reading cartoons such as 'Bomb in the Head' as bringing a satirical challenge to extremist fundamentalism which claims to act in the name of Muhammad, the satirising components of the cartoon also present an inflammatory conflation of violent fundamentalism with the peaceful practice of Islam. The same can be said of 'Muhammad in the Desert', in this case the decision to feature a donkey in the cartoon alongside Muhammad allows for ambivalent interpretations, ranging from pilgrimage and humility (judged by the audience in Denmark), to stupidity (amongst some of the wider international audience). In both cases, Müller et al. (2009) note that the cartoons employ 'stereotypical and offensive depictions of another culture to make a statement' (p. 33), and present Islam as a 'cradle for mass-murderers and lunatics' (p. 35).

The Case Study: Charlie Hebdo and the 'Survivors' Issue' Cover

Charlie Hebdo is a satirical weekly magazine that publishes in France, self-defining as a 'secular, political and jubilant' periodical that 'draws, writes, interviews, ponders and laughs at everything on this earth which is ridiculous, giggles at all that is absurd or preposterous in life'.[3] Of interest to us is the controversy surrounding

---

[3] See https://charliehebdo.fr/en/

the successive publication of cartoons featuring the prophet Muhammad. Widely reported across global media, their cartoons have been variously interpreted as contentious provocations toward Islam which disregard iconographic norms and thereby ride roughshod over Muslim cultural sensitivities, and/or as depicting Islam in crude, stereotypical and offensive fashion. In contrast, other commentators have applauded the magazine, viewing these cartoons as the expression of universal civic rights of free speech, secularism and equality.

We can trace this controversy to the period following Charlie Hebdo's 2006 reprinting of the Jyllands-Posten series of Muhammad cartoons (see Müller et al., 2009). The reprinting in Charlie Hebdo stimulated debates over whether depictions of Muhammad saying 'it's hard being loved by jerks' promoted Islam as a mainstream religion with small minorities of fundamentalist followers, or if it was a blatant display of editorial conflation between Muslims in general and Muslim extremists. Later, a renaming of the editor-in-chief as Muhammad with the caption '100 lashes of the whip if you don't die laughing' (following pronouncements of Sharia law in Libya and Islamist party electoral success in Tunisia) was met with a similar reception. It was also followed by a firebombing of their offices and a subsequent hacking of their website. Across these instances, government ministers and journalists alike expressed a range of contradictory messages, ranging from condemnations of violence, disappointment over their alleged provocation, to universal support for free speech and the right to present any subject matter. Such contrasting responses highlight the situated and contextual qualities of interpretation, and in this context, the ethnic, cultural, political and religious identities of the audience are key, with the potential for political satire to perform cultural violence (Galtung, 1996).

On January 7th 2015 two armed men attacked the Charlie Hebdo offices in Paris. In total 12 people were killed, including Charlie Hebdo staff, one visitor and two police officers. Responsibility was subsequently claimed by Al Qaeda, allegedly operating within Yemen (Aboudi, 2015). The attacks were internationally condemned amongst the Western media and public, and the phrase 'Je suis Charlie' circulated in a flurry of support for Charlie Hebdo's stance on maintaining their satirical defiance. In response to the attack, Charlie Hebdo announced an increase in publication for the next edition, labelling it the 'Survivors' Issue'. It is the front page of this 'Survivors Issue' which provides the focus for our analysis. Adopting an MCDA approach, we endeavour to demonstrate how the combined affordances of varied semiotic forms enable the development of a discourse which engenders multiple and conflicting interpretations related to ideas and possibilities, both for peace and for violence.

Methodology

Aligning with Mazid (2008, p. 435), we view cartoons as a 'hybridization of a variety of codes – language, picture, colour and sometimes movement' which require analysis of the verbal and non-verbal content, and the interactions between the two, in order to develop an appreciation of the complex multimodal action of the discourse. According to Kress and van Leeuwen (2006), visuals involve both represented participants (those people, places and things depicted in the visual) and interactive participants (the producers, and the receivers of the visual). The visual provides a medium through which interactive participants communicate with one another as they undertake to 'produce and make sense of images in the context of social institutions which, to different degrees and in different ways, regulate what may be 'said' with images, how it should be said, and how it should be interpreted' (p. 114). Within the genre of political cartoons, the regulatory norms which govern how represented participants are depicted are expected to differ from those which routinely apply to other, more traditional forms of visual discourse. Indeed, the capacity to subvert and satirise is the basis of the genre, thus political cartoons are able to resist the constraints of traditional visual discourse, and thereby provoke different possibilities regarding 'what can be said'. However, as Mazid (2008, p. 435) notes, the interactive potential of the political cartoon remains embedded within a given context, such that 'wherever they might be on the true-untrue continuum, political cartoons can only be produced and perceived in a socio-historical background'. Our case study analysis of the Charlie Hebdo 'Survivors'Issue' front page draws upon the methods of visual analysis developed by Kress and van Leeuwen (2006) (see also Kress & van Leeuwen, 2001; van Leeuwen, 2005; van Leeuwen & Jewitt, 2001) to undertake a close examination of both the textual and visual components, and to further consider how the textual and the visual intersect, and how they interact with pre-existing, situated, contingent layers of social and cultural meaning and group-based identities.

Analysis

We proceed by analysing the visual components and the textual components in turn, we then draw this together and consider how the visual and the textual are interwoven in the construction of a situated discourse.

Composition Overview

The overall page comprises a limited number of visual elements arranged in a simple composition. The central represented participant is a head and shoulders cartoon caricature of a single male figure. This is widely accepted to be a portrayal of the prophet Muhammad, and the artist confirmed this to be the case ('How I created Charlie Hebdo', 2015). Throughout our analysis, we therefore refer to this represented participant as Muhammad. Muhammad is drawn centrally on the page, occupying a sizeable section of the overall visual. Alongside him, two additional elements appear. One is a three-word headline (TOUT EST PARDONNÉ [ALL IS

FORGIVEN]), which is located above the head of Muhammad, the other is a placard which is held in front of his upper torso. A further three words (JE SUIS CHARLIE [I AM CHARLIE]) are written on the placard. The only other components on the page are the standard magazine mast head, the artist signature and the optical bar-code. The overall organisation of the page, and the represented participants, provide the reader with a 'visual syntax' (Jewitt & Oyama, 2001), which, in this cartoon, is highly simplistic. We note that such simplicity is not typical for the genre of political cartoons, and this syntax distinguishes our data from many prior Muhammad cartoons published on the front page, and within the pages of Charlie Hebdo.[4]

Jewitt and Oyama (2001) describe visual syntax as a 'matter of spatial relationships, of 'where things are' in the semiotic space and of whether or not they are connected through lines, or through visual 'rhymes' of colour, shape and so on' (p. 141). Aligning with Kress and van Leeuwen (1996) they distinguish between narrative and conceptual syntactic patterns. Narrative patterns are those which present sequences of actions, turns of events or processes of change, whilst conceptual patterns represent more generalised, often more stable qualities, or essences. Conceptual patterns do not represent something as 'doing', but rather 'as being something, or meaning something, or belonging to some category, or having certain characteristics or components' (Jewitt & Oyama, 2001, p. 141). According to Kress and van Leeuwen (2006), the distinction between narrative and conceptual representations can be made dependent on the presence of vectors, which are only found in narrative structures. Vectors are visual elements that often form a clear diagonal line, the function of which is to express a 'dynamic 'doing' or 'happening' kind of relation' (Jewitt & Oyama, 2001, p. 141) (e.g. connective arrows in a diagram or an outstretched, pointing finger). In contrast, conceptual patterns often engage classification processes which provide some means for relating people, places and things to each other within the process of representation. The dearth of vectors in our data (note: we do identify one vector which we address later), coupled with the spatial composition of the page, indicates a conceptual visual syntax, and as our analysis progresses we will examine each element outlined above in detail and consider how the conceptual syntax serves the production of semantic meaning. However, our first point of analysis begins with a consideration of colour.

Colour

There are only four colours used in the cartoon. Black is used for outlining Muhammad, outlining the placard, writing the text on the placard, and scribing the headline. The facial features of Muhammad are also drawn in black. White is used for his eyes, and for all his clothing. A beige tone is used for the face and hands, and also the placard. The final colour, and the only primary or secondary colour to feature, is a vivid pea green. This colour provides a solid background colour to the

---

[4] For some examples of prior Charlie Hebdo front page portrayals of Muhammad, see Taibi (2015).

whole page. The scale of its use and the absence of other colours make green a significant component of the cartoon. Kress and van Leeuwen (2006) refer to colours as signifiers which 'carry a set of affordances from which sign-makers and interpreters can select according to their communicative needs and interests in a given context' (p. 232). They point to the 'provenance' of colour, it's common associations with existing forms of meaning, and the potential for colour to carry 'significant symbolic value in the given sociocultural context' (p. 233). They further point to the potential diversity and multiplicity of the communicative affordances of colour, highlighting that the analyst should take close account of how colours might be understood to variously contribute to the construction of the discourse for a given audience. For example, in the contemporary UK context, the use of red, white and blue in a political cartoon whose subject matter is 'Brexit' might be understood to introduce discourses of national identity into the fray, at least for a UK audience. Thus, colour can perform interdiscursive work, in this example, weaving concerns with national identity into debates about political exit from Europe.

Taking account of the points above, and recognising that colour has a 'cultural history' (Kress & van Leeuwen, 2001) with implications for how it is received by a given audience, we suggest that the use of green in this cartoon does rhetorical work. In Islamic culture, the colour green is widely viewed as the 'colour of Islam' (see Abu Bakar, n.d.). Thus, it has important communicative functions for a Muslim audience. Use of a green background in other 'Muhammad' cartoons, and the Islamic cultural significance of this is elsewhere discussed in the analysis by Müller et al. (2009), and we also note that two previous Charlie Hebdo 'Muhammad' front covers published in 2012 and 2013 similarly use a solid green background (see Taibi, 2015). Drawing on the work of Michael Halliday, Kress and van Leeuwen (2006) distinguish between three communicative semiotic metafunctions: ideational, interpersonal and textual. The ideational function of colour relates to the ways in which colour 'can be used to denote people, places and things as well as classes of people, places and things, and more general ideas' (Kress & van Leeuwen, 2006, p. 229). We argue that the extensive use of green in this cartoon fulfils an ideational purpose, saturating the discourse with potentially variable communicative affordances.

Given the significance of green in Islamic culture, its use in this cartoon makes available a discourse in which Islam is central. The extensive use of green coupled with the absence of any other primary or secondary colours ensures that this reference is not a subtle backgrounding. What is especially key however is the potential that colour avails for differing interpretations depending on how green features in the 'cultural history' of the audience. We suggest that for a Muslim audience, the extensive use of green flags Islam as a critical element of the discourse, asserting Muslim category membership as salient, and Islam as integral to the Charlie Hebdo attacks. In many respects, the cartoon can be understood to promote and cohere with the prevailing Western discourses surrounding the Charlie Hebdo attacks, and the subsequent response to those events. However, as we have indicated, such a reading may differ depending on the symbolic relevance that the audience attaches to the colour. Non-Muslim audiences may fail to attach any meaning to the use of green. Alternatively they may be aware of the Islamic cultural significance of the colour, thus they may similarly locate Islam as central to the discourse. However, the non-

Muslim audience would do so in the context of being *not* Muslim, hence a concern with the Muslim 'other' is foregrounded. These differing interpretative possibilities linked to colour reveal an initial indication of varying communicative potentials of the cartoon. Against this culturally loaded background, we now examine all the represented participants (people, objects, things) that feature on the page.

Represented Participants

When it comes to visual representations of people, portrayals of closeness and distance communicate something about the social relations between the represented participant and the viewer. Kress and van Leeuwen (2006) propose that the represented participant is evaluated by the viewer in accordance with the normative degrees of physical closeness and distance that are maintained between people in everyday social interactions. In the 'Survivors' Issue' front page, the head, shoulders and upper torso of Muhammad are presented in a style typically referred to as a close-up, thereby communicating the potential for closeness between the represented participant and the audience.

Muhammad is depicted with a closed and distinctly downturned mouth conveying an unambiguous display of sadness. His eyes are wide and looking outward from the page in a direct gaze. From the left eye, a single tear is falling. The use of direct gaze in our data contrasts notably with the cartoons analysed by Müller et al. (2009). They state that in the cartoon labelled 'Muhammad in the Desert', 'his gaze is defiant and unfriendly' (p. 31), whilst in the other two cartoons analysed, the authors report a complete lack of eye contact with the viewer. According to Kress and van Leeuwen (2006), there is a crucial difference between images in which represented participants look directly at the viewers' eyes, and images where this does not occur. In direct gaze images 'vectors, formed by the participants' eyelines, connect the participants with the viewer. Contact is established, even if it is only on an imaginary level … [thereby creating] a visual form of direct address' (p. 117). Kress and van Leeuwen (2006) theorise that such images constitute an 'image act', whereby the image makes a form of demand on the viewer. They highlight that the significance of direct gaze, or 'demand' images, has been studied by art historians who point to the development of this type of gaze as an innovation in portraiture, whereby the gaze of the subject instils a sense of scrutiny in the viewer, or requires some form of reciprocity. The 'demand' which the image makes upon the viewer is often signified by other elements of the visual, for example, an accompanying hand gesture, or facial expression, might invite the viewer closer or insist they stay back. Relating this to our analysis, the direct gaze of Muhammad, coupled with the close-up portrayal which implies closeness with the audience, can be understood to construct a direct communication between Muhammad and the viewer, through which the sorrowful facial expression both conveys and seeks a unifying emotional experience. Thus, where colour can be understood to elevate cultural and religious boundaries between Muslim and non-Muslim, gaze and positioning potentially downplay these boundaries.

Like many prior Charlie Hebdo portrayals of Muhammad, in the 'Survivors' Issue' Muhammad is portrayed with a bulbous, drooping nose. The shape and size of the nose conveys a highly stereotypical physiognomic depiction of the Muslim 'other', which is similarly reported by Müller et al. (2009). The portrayal of a 'Central Asian nose' to convey stereotypical notions of a homogenised Muslim 'other' is also noted by Moloney, Holtz and Wagner (2013, p. 291) in their analysis of Australian political cartoons. These authors suggest that such stereotypical tendencies are common across the Western world. Interestingly however, whilst we see this stereotypical facial feature of the Muslim 'other' in our data, we also identify clear differences with respect to the portrayal of other facial features. Specifically, in our data, Muhammad's beard is conservatively drawn, leaving much of the face on display, above and below the mouth. This contrasts with the findings of Moloney et al. (2013) where beards of Muslim men were found to be heavily exaggerated. Our findings similarly contrast with Müller et al.'s (2009) analysis of other Muhammad cartoons. Analysing the cartoon which they label as 'Muhammad with Scimitar and Two Veiled Women', Müller et al. (2009, p. 32) report that Muhammad is portrayed with a 'long wild beard, a moustache, and thick eyebrows'. Similar findings are also reported for the cartoon 'Bomb in the Head'. It appears that the 'Survivors' Issue' portrayal of Muhammad walks a line between maintaining the salience of Muslim identity and minimising religious or cultural boundaries between Muhammad as representative of Islam, and the Muslim/non-Muslim audience.

Turning to consider clothing, Muhammad is depicted wearing a simple white robe and turban. There is no shading to suggest movement or volume in the clothing, and no indication of anything concealed within the clothing. Again, we witness interesting contrasts between our data, and the depiction of clothing in each of the three cartoons analysed by Müller et al. (2009), the most provocative of which portrays Muhammad wearing a large black turban drawn to appear as 'a large bomb with a fuse on top that has already been lit' (p. 31). Moloney et al. (2013) similarly report the subversion of traditional female Muslim dress in the cartoon referred to as 'Does my bomb look big in this' which portrays two women each wearing a full veil whilst concealing explosives beneath their black robes. This kind of visual subversion is typical of political cartoons and, as Moloney et al. (2013, p. 289) maintain, emphasising the traditions of Muslim dress promotes an 'essentialist perception that "Muslims are all the same"', and elevates the construction of a violent and dangerous Muslim 'other'. It is striking that such subversion is absent in the 'Survivors' Issue' cartoon.

Perspective, Angles and Power

Drawing upon studies in the history of Art, Kress and van Leeuwen (2006) propose that since the Renaissance, images in Western culture can be categorised as being either with or without a central perspective. Subjective images (with central perspective) are understood to present the viewer with a particular viewpoint, whilst objective images (without central perspective) seek to convey to the viewer all that can be known. Jewitt and Oyama (2001) further outline how the development of visual perspective during the renaissance facilitated the development of visual 'points of view'. Referring to previous visual analysis undertaken by Jewitt (1997, 1999), these authors suggest that 'frontal angle' can be used to 'increase audience identification and involvement with represented participants' (p. 138). Relating this to the frontal angle used to depict Muhammad in the 'Survivors Issue' front page, we can theorise that the use of frontal angle here provides a further means by which a connection between Muhammad and the audience is offered.

It is also notable in the 'Survivors' Issue' front page that the frontal angle and the perspective used constructs an openness to the image of Muhammad which lacks the usual satirical subversion, or any suggestion that there is something 'more' than meets the eye going on. The sole object in the cartoon is a placard which Muhammad holds in front of his chest with both of his hands visible either side of the placard. There is nothing to suggest that anything is hidden about his person, or that anything more can be known about the image. This certainty about what is contained in the image contrasts with other cartoons already discussed. As we noted earlier, in the cartoon labelled 'Bomb in the Head' it is the subversion of the turban as a bomb which acts as a focal object through which a demonisation and othering of Muslim culture is achieved. In 'Muhammad with Scimitar and Two Veiled Women' the prophet holds a sabre, which the authors suggest constructs an 'aggressive dagger-wielding impression' (Müller et al., 2009, p. 32). Elsewhere, in an analysis of cartoon portrayals of Osama bin Laden and George Bush, Mazid (2008, p. 447) notes that Bin Laden is portrayed in traditional Muslim dress 'sitting on a prayer-carpet, keeping his exceptionally long, flowing beard, yet still carrying his berretta on his left shoulder'. The similarity of the portrayals of the prophet Muhammad and of Osama bin Laden in previous cartoons not only serve to construct the two protagonists as members of a shared Muslim category, but the portrayal of these men in traditional Muslim dress, whilst also wielding deadly weaponry again conflates everyday Muslim norms (i.e. the mundane practice of wearing traditional dress), with practices of extreme violence. Again, the contrast between previously analysed cartoons, and the way in which the 'Survivors Issue' presents Muhammad, is clear. Overall then we see how the use of perspective has implications for the rhetorical work of multimodal discourse.

Linked to the communicative functions of perspective, multimodal theorists contend that viewing angles have implications for power relations. Put simply, Kress and van Leeuwen (2006) propose that when the visual constructs a perspective in which the viewer appears to look down upon a represented participant, it affords the viewer power, conversely if the angle requires the viewer to look up, power lies with the represented participant, and when the viewer and the represented participant are portrayed at eye level, no power differential is constructed. Jewitt and Oyama (2001) suggest that viewing angles and points of view create 'meaning potentials' between image producers, the represented participants or objects in the image, and the viewer. Aligning with the work of Kress and van Leeuwen (2006), Jewitt and Oyama

(2001) propose that, in the case of vertical angles, a meaning potential for 'symbolic power' (p. 35) is realised. They make two key points in relation to these theoretical assumptions about viewing angles: 'First 'power', 'detachment', 'involvement', and so on are not 'the' meanings of these angles. They are an attempt to describe a meaning potential, a field of possible meanings'; and secondly, 'Symbolic relations are not real relations and it is precisely this which makes point of view a symbolic resource' (Jewitt & Oyama, 2001, p. 135). Thus, in a cartoon depiction of a religious leader, or a figurehead of Western commerce, viewing angles can as readily imply that, in the context of the discourse, power lies with the viewer when angled as if the viewer is looking down on the represented participant, as they can position power with the represented participant if the viewing angle is upwards.

Relating this to our analysis, viewing angles in the cartoon present Muhammad at eye level with the viewer, hence a meaning potential is afforded in which relations of power are flat. This meaning potential, coupled with the openness of the image achieved through the central perspective, avails a display of equality between Muhammad, as representative of Islam, and the audience, irrespective of ethnic or religious category membership. We now turn to the textual components of the discourse, before drawing our analysis together and further assessing how the 'Survivors Issue' cartoon operates as situated multimodal discourse.

Textual Components

As indicated earlier, alongside the caricature of Muhammad, there are two textual components on the page. The first is a headline, presented in large black handwritten capital letters, located above the head of the prophet. The headline reads 'TOUT EST PARDONNÉ' (ALL IS FORGIVEN). The other appears on the placard which the prophet holds in front of his upper torso. Again, the text is presented in handwritten black capital letters, and reads 'JE SUIS CHARLIE' (I AM CHARLIE). Kress and van Leeuwen (2006) discuss image composition at length, and the ways in which composition of the overall image serves to realise information values. Through detailed examples, they propose that composition serves to connect representational and interactive meanings through three related principles: information value, salience and framing. Drawing on analysis of magazine visuals, Kress and van Leeuwen (2006) demonstrate how information values of the left and right differ, with content on the left typically relating to what is already known, or 'the given', whilst information values on the right communicate new, or key, information. The authors argue that this left (given)/right (new) composition structure is found in all manner of visuals including composite texts, works of classical art, webpages, and diagrams. In addition to the information values that are linked to the left and right, visual elements which occupy a position toward the 'top' of the image are theorised to communicate aspects of the 'ideal', whilst elements located as 'bottom' convey the 'real'. Drawing upon examples as diverse as magazine advertisements, and geography textbooks, Kress and van Leeuwen (2006) demonstrate that information values presented toward the top communicate ideals and ideological assumptions about the matter at hand, whilst information values in the lower part of the image convey more mundane details and assumptions of fact. These, in turn, can often serve as forms of support to underpin the assertions offered in the top of the image. Jewitt and Oyama (2001) state that 'For something to be 'ideal' means that it is presented as the idealized or generalized essence of the information, hence usually also as its ideologically most salient part. The 'real' is then opposed to this in that it is its meaning potential to present more 'down to earth information'' (p. 148). Again, we want to highlight, the concern here is with the meaning potentials which are availed by the composition of the image, irrespective of any assessment of 'truth' which might be levied at the content of the discourse. Applying this to our data enables a consideration of how these two textual objects operate in relation to one another, and helps to examine the activity of the text within the multimodal communication.

The Placard

The message on the placard is located way below the other textual message, and toward the bottom of the overall visual, thus it communicates something which can be assessed as 'real', or dependable information (Kress & van Leeuwen, 2006). The slogan, 'I am Charlie' was originally penned by a French journalist, and appeared on social media in the hours following the attack (Devichand, 2016). It proliferated on social media and was adopted by members of the public and mainstream media in France and the West, both as a symbol of support for all those who died in the attack and as a mark of commitment to maintaining and protecting the rights to free speech, and to a free press. Presenting this message as 'real' within this cartoon constructs an unwavering solidarity with the dominant Western response to the Charlie Hebdo attacks. However, the choice to present this slogan on a placard held by the prophet Muhammad warrants further consideration. Whilst we acknowledge that the represented participant is not the agent, but the medium through which interactive participants (producers and receivers of the visual) communicate (Kress & van Leeuwen, 2006), the visual organisation of the cartoon nevertheless serves to invest a level of agency in the represented participant. It produces a discourse in which Muhammad, both as an embodied Muslim member and as originator of Islam, stands in unity with Charlie Hebdo, and with the ideological values reflected in the phrase 'I am Charlie'. Muhammad and all that he stands for is thus posed in opposition to those individuals who undertook the attacks, thereby refuting any reading of their violent acts as being motivated by genuine Islamic values.

It is here we begin to see the complexity of the multimodal work in the cartoon. For all that this cartoon—produced and published by the French magazine in response to a highly emotive episode of direct violence of which it was the victim— seemingly rejects any temptation to respond with a narrative which positions Islam, or Muslims, as the aggressor, or which seeks violent retribution, it does so via very complex means. Whilst the incorporation of the phrase 'Je suis Charlie' held by

Muhammad might arguably seek to construct Muslims and non-Muslims as members of a universal group who share common values and reject violence in the name of Islam, the underpinning decision to publish a visual portrayal of the prophet Muhammad can equally be read as a provocative act of ideologically driven cultural violence. Indeed, such an interpretation is indicated by the appearance of a counter catchphrase, 'Je ne suis pas Charlie', circulated by both Muslims and non-Muslims who deemed Charlie Hebdo's continued publishing of Muhammad cartoons to be reflective, not of free speech, but of hate speech (Brooks, 2015).

The Headline

Turning to the headline, located at the top of the image, this message of forgiveness is presented as the 'ideal', or the core ideological element of the visual (Jewitt & Oyama, 2001). Whilst there is little ambiguity regarding the absolution offered by the words 'All is forgiven', there is uncertainty regarding who is offering forgiveness, and who it is being offered to. Here the receiving audience must make a judgement about the intent, or modality, of the message. Kress and van Leeuwen (2006, p. 154) state that 'In so far as we are prepared to act, we have to trust some of the information we receive, and do so, to quite some extent, on the basis of modality markers'. Modality refers to the expectations that might be routinely held regarding the 'reality value' of an image (Jewitt & Oyama, 2001). In this sense, naturalistic photographic images have a high modality, as they are widely anticipated to represent 'real life', and reflect 'truth'. Crucially however, modality does not convey certainties of truth or falsehood, rather it constructs shared realities, which variously align or distance members of the audience with aspects of the discourse. Moreover, modality judgements are contextual, 'dependent on what is considered real (or true, or sacred) in the social group for which the representation is primarily intended' (p. 156). The issue of modality highlights how the 'ideal' message of forgiveness in this cartoon is both uncertain and open to varied interpretation. In the given context, category membership as either Muslim or non-Muslim is a central factor which potentially influences how this message of forgiveness might be judged, yet, it is not the only factor at play. As Western media responses to the 'Survivors' Issue' front page highlight, there were varying judgements regarding the modality of the message. Headlines in the days following publication (e.g. 'Is all forgiven now?'[5]; 'Charlie Hebdo's strange cover'[6]) indicate a palpable level of uncertainty and suspicion amongst the Western media.

   This uncertainty reveals an interesting tension between the visual portrayal of Muhammad, and the textual message 'Je suis Charlie', which are treated as relatively straightforward, and the ambiguity of the textual message 'All is forgiven'. This concern with ambiguity voiced by the Western media is both in terms of questioning the credibility of discourse as a genuine message of forgiveness and indicating

---

[5] http://www.bbc.co.uk/news/blogs-trending-30799770

[6] http://www.thecommentator.com/article/5531/charlie_hebdo_s_strange_cover

uncertainty about whom is offering forgiveness, and to whom it is offered. It is also interesting to note that amongst the queries of the Western media, concerns are raised which challenge who has the *right* to forgive on behalf of the dead, particularly if the living are deemed to differ from the dead according to categories of religion (see footnote 6).

Completing the Multimodal Jigsaw

Our analysis reveals that the portrayal of Muhammad in the 'Survivors' Issue' front page differs from other depictions of Muhammad (cf. Müller et al., 2009), and from other portrayals of Muslims in general in political cartoons (cf. Moloney et al., 2013) in ways that construct important affordances for interpretation of the overall discourse. Mazid (2008) notes that the skill of the political cartoon is to arrive at a given perspective in a manner laced with satirical humour, often achieved by destabilising a well-worn schema, or contrasting two schemas to create incongruity. It is notable therefore that this mainstay of political cartoons is largely absent in our data. The lack of incongruity, or humour either in the clothing, the facial features, or the activities of Muhammad, marks this 'Survivors' Issue' front page out. We suggest that this reflects the situated nature of the discourse, highlighting the capacity retained by even the most subversive discourse genre, to respond to events in a manner which are deemed appropriate to achieve particular communicative ends, and, in the case of political cartoons, to avoid overstepping a line between challenging moral boundaries and certain moral alienation. Furthermore, given that satirical cartoons typically portray the prophet Muhammad in ways which are culturally and/or morally offensive, coupled with the fact that conflations between Muslim identity and violent extremism feed a mainstream Western narrative in which Muhammad, and Muslims in general, are routinely othered, a cartoon which seemingly ascends this narrative might be deemed to challenge the mainstream discourse. However, as Galtung (1996, p. 197) notes, one way in which cultural violence operates is by 'making reality opaque, so that we do not see the violent act or fact'. Such insight appears highly relevant here, reminding us that, whilst the carefully constructed discourse of the 'Survivors Issue' front page appears conservative in comparison to other portrayals, the situated layers of contextual meaning are deeper than the components of the page.

Given the explicit reference to forgiveness, we have been concerned to examine how (and if) this cartoon can be understood to communicate a message of peace in the days following the attack on the Charlie Hebdo offices, and to assess how any potential messages of peace might be variously experienced in relation to differing group-based identities. The combination of a 'close-up' which uses direct gaze to communicate an unambiguous emotion of sorrow, coupled with the maintenance of stereotypical facial features which construct a knowable Muslim 'other', affords varying potentials for interpretation linked to ideas about closeness and distance with the represented participant. Furthermore, as Jewitt and Oyama (2001, p. 146) note, a 'close-up' does not require a reading in which the person represented is understood to be actually close to us, but that 'they are represented as though they belong or should belong to 'our group', and the viewer is thereby addressed as a certain kind of person'.

In the context of the events surrounding this cartoon, and with an awareness that a critical group-based category difference amongst the receiving audience is Muslim/non-Muslim identity, we suggest that members of these groups might experience the discourse in broadly different ways. (Note however, to do so is not to suggest that either group is homogenous such that all members will experience the discourse in the same way, or that it is impossible for Muslim/non-Muslim members to interpret the discourse in other ways.) For the non-Muslim audience, the close-up of Muhammad advances a narrative whereby the stereotypical physiognomic portrayal of Muhammad *as* a Muslim elevates and maintains the salience of Muslim category membership. However, the strong emotion communicated by Muhammad is one which promotes a narrative of common morality and shared humanity with the capacity to transcend ethnic, cultural or religious category divisions. This universally accessible moral position offers a potential to act as a pivotal ground in which boundaries between Muhammad *as* Muslim and the non-Muslim audience are penetrable. Here, it is possible to at least partly assess this multimodal discourse as one in which tenets of universal common values are presented to a non-Muslim audience as being similarly upheld by Muslim members, whilst also conveying that such values are compatible with Muslim identity. The content of those universal accessible values express a mutual rejection of forms of direct violence witnessed in the Charlie Hebdo attacks, and thereby signal a collective discourse in which peace and forgiveness are central. From this perspective, the Charlie Hebdo response might be judged to be one of restraint, and one which seeks to bring Muslim and non-Muslims together and put violence behind them with peace at the fore.

For the Muslim audience however, things may be a little different. The elevation of Muslim/non-Muslim category boundaries achieved via the multimodal discourse serves to reinforce the salience of their membership *as* Muslim. The emotional display remains available as a shared resource between the represented participant and the viewer, and as indicated above, this offers a currency of common values to which both Muslim and non-Muslims can align. However, for Muslim members, the deeply held cultural sensitivities to any visual portrayal of the prophet Muhammad cannot be extricated from this discourse, no matter what the unusually conservative stylistic qualities of that portrayal may be. Recognition of the entrenched debates over visual portrayals of the prophet which have repeatedly divided some Muslim and some non-Muslim members cannot be ignored. These issues are at the heart of the continuing arguments, to which Charlie Hebdo contributed by design through their ongoing visual depictions of Muhammad. Galtung's (1996) discussion of democracies and their varying capacity for bellicism (the general propensity toward engagement in war/war-like acts) might offer some guidance as to why Charlie Hebdo chose to respond to the attacks on 7th January 2015 with yet another portrayal of Muhammad. Such a decision was taken with awareness that it would cause further offense and increased controversy at a time when emotions on all sides were already running high.

Galtung (1996, p. 56) notes that members of democracies have a tendency toward extremes of self-righteousness driven by the ideals of the democratic system itself. He states that:

> 'People living in democracies tend to become self-righteous simply for that reason. If we assume that the leading political system is the system of the world's leading countries then to live in a democracy is prestigious. To live in a non-democracy carries a stigma'.

Thus, the cherished values of democracy, including rights to free speech, coupled with heightened self-righteous beliefs whereby the ideals of Western democracy trump those derived from a religious worldview indicate that cultural violence performed by Western states, such as publishing satirical visual depictions of the prophet Muhammad, is justified in and through the ideology of democracy. Of course, a counter argument would maintain that if rights to free speech were outdone by religious beliefs then another form of cultural violence would prevail. In this sense an ideological dilemma comes to the fore. However, if democracy is to be revered by those who live according to it as the leading political system, we suggest it is incumbent upon members of democratic societies to carefully consider the social, moral and political responsibilities that freedom of speech must surely entail. Moreover, they should strive to use the tools of democracy, *especially* the power of free speech, in ways which serve to demystify, and to denounce forms of cultural violence wherever they are found.

Conclusion

Distinguishing between discourses of peace and discourses of violence might, at first thought, appear to be a relatively straightforward matter, particularly when the textual message speaks expressly of forgiveness. However, as our multimodal analysis is at pains to demonstrate, discourses of peace and violence are ideologically formed and thus, situated concepts. What might present itself as forgiveness from one perspective may be experienced quite differently from another vantage. In examining this cartoon, we hope to offer some insight regarding the complex ways in which multimodal discourse can simultaneously communicate forms of peace and violence. We contend that it is through combined textual and visual affordances that the Charlie Hebdo 'Survivors' Issue' front page serves to problematise interpretation; obscure the social, moral and political values embedded in the given ideological stance; and create divisions along the lines of peace and violence.

More broadly, through our analysis, we have strived to demonstrate that there is a need for criticality within discursive approaches to peace psychology which seeks to examine the rhetorical ways in which the language of peace, tolerance, war, and violence is used, with ideology seen as a structuring agent which packages these discourses into recognisable arguments for their situated political ends. Galtung (1996, p. 200) reminds us that, regardless of whether violence is direct, structural, or cultural, 'violence breeds violence'. To this we would add that the same is as true when violence is done in discourse as in any other form.

References

Aboudi, S. (2015, January 14). Al Qaeda claims French attack, derides Paris rally. *Reuters.* Retrieved from http://www.reuters.com

Abu Bakar, M. F. (n.d.). *Colours of Islam.* Retrieved from http://www.academia.edu

Brooks, D. (2015, January 8). I am not Charlie Hebdo. *The New York Times.* Retrieved from https://www.nytimes.com.

Carter, D. (2011). *Multimodal critical discourse analysis of systematically distorted communication in intercountry adoption industry websites* (PhD Thesis, Washington State University).

Catalano, T., & Waugh, L. (2013). The ideologies behind newspaper crime reports of Latinos and Wall Street/CEOs: A critical analysis of metonymy in text and image. *Critical Discourse Studies, 10,* 406–426.

Charlie Hebdo. (2015, January 14). How I created Charlie Hebdo survivor's cover: cartoonist Luz's statement in full. *The Telegraph.* Retrieved from http://www.telegraph.co.uk

Devichand, M. (2016, January 3). How the world was changed by the slogan 'Je Suis Charlie'. *BBC.* Retrieved from http://www.bbc.co.uk

Djonov, E., & Zhao, S. (Eds.). (2014). *Critical multimodal studies of popular discourse.* London: Routledge.

Edwards, D. (1997). *Discourse and cognition.* London: Sage.

Edwards, D., & Potter, J. (1992). *Discursive psychology.* London: Sage.

El Refaie, E. (2009). Metaphor in political cartoons: Exploring audience responses. In C. Forceville & E. Urios-Aparisi (Eds.), *Multimodal metaphor* (pp. 75–95). Berlin: Mouton de Gruyter.

Fairclough, N. (1989). *Language and power.* London: Longman.

Fairclough, N. (2001). Critical discourse analysis as a method in social scientific research. In R. Wodak & M. Meyer (Eds.), *Methods of critical discourse analysis* (pp. 121–138). London: Sage.

Fairclough, N., & Wodak, R. (1997). Critical discourse analysis. In T. van Dijk (Ed.), *Discourse studies: A multidisciplinary introduction* (Vol. 2, pp. 258–284). London: Sage.

Galtung, J. (1996). *Peace by peaceful means.* London: Sage.

Gamson, W., & Stuart, D. (1992). Media discourse as a symbolic contest: The bomb in political cartoons. *Sociological Forum, 7,* 55–86.

Iedema, R. (2003). Multimodality, resemiotization: Extending the analysis of discourse as multi-semiotic practice. *Visual Communication, 2,* 29–57.

Jewitt, C. (1997). Images of men. *Sociological Research Online, 2*(2), 1. Retrieved from http://www.socresonline.org.uk/2/2/6.html

Jewitt, C. (1999). A social semiotic analysis of male heterosexuality in sexual health resources: The case of images. *International Journal of Social Research Methodology: Theory and Practice, 1,* 263–280.

Jewitt, C., & Oyama, R. (2001). Visual meaning: A social semiotic approach. In T. van Leeuwen & C. Jewitt (Eds.), *Handbook of visual analysis* (pp. 134–156). London: Sage.

Kress, G., & van Leeuwen, T. (1996). *Reading images: The grammar of visual design.* London: Routledge.

Kress, G., & van Leeuwen, T. (2001). *Multimodal discourse: The modes and media of contemporary communication.* London: Arnold.

Kress, G., & van Leeuwen, T. (2006). *Reading images: The grammar of visual design* (2nd ed.). London: Routledge.

Leudar, I., Marsland, V., & Nekvapil, J. (2004). On membership categorisation: 'Us', 'them' and 'doing violence' in political discourse. *Discourse & Society, 15*, 243–266.

Levine, P., & Scollon, R. (Eds.). (2004). *Discourse & technology: Multimodal discourse analysis.* Washington, DC: Georgetown University Press.

Machin, D. (2013). What is multimodal critical discourse studies? *Critical Discourse Studies, 10*, 347–355.

Machin, D. (2016). The need for a social and affordance-driven multimodal critical discourse studies. *Discourse & Society, 27*, 322–334.

Machin, D., & Mayr, A. (2012). *How to do critical discourse analysis: A multimodal introduction.* London: Sage.

Mazid, B. (2008). Cowboy and misanthrope: A critical (discourse) analysis of Bush and bin Laden cartoons. *Discourse & Communication, 2*, 433–457.

Meyer, M. (2001). Between theory, method, and politics: Positioning of the approaches to CDA. In R. Wodak & M. Meyer (Eds.), *Methods of critical discourse analysis* (pp. 14–31). London: Sage.

Moloney, G., Holtz, P., & Wagner, W. (2013). Editorial political cartoons in Australia: Social representations and the visual depiction of essentialism. *Integrative Psychological and Behavioral Science, 47*, 294–298.

Müller, G., Özcan, E., & Seizov, O. (2009). Dangerous depictions: A visual case study of contemporary cartoon controversies. *Popular Communication, 7*, 28–39.

Richardson, J., & Wodak, R. (2009). The impact of visual racism: Visual arguments in political leaflets of Austrian and British Far-right Parties. *Controversia, 6*, 45–77.

Richardson, J. E. (2016). Recontextualisation and fascist music. In L. C. S. Way & S. McKerrell (Eds.), *Music as multimodal discourse: Semiotics, power and protest* (pp. 71–94). London: Bloomsbury Academic.

Schegloff, E. A. (1997). Whose text? Whose context? *Discourse & Society, 8*, 165–187.

Taibi, C. (2015, January 7). These are the Charlie Hebdo cartoons that terrorists thought were worth killing over. *Huffington Post.* Retrieved from http://www.huffingtonpost.com

te Molder, H., & Potter, J. (2005). *Conversation and cognition.* Cambridge: Cambridge University Press.

van Dijk, T. A. (2001). Multidisciplinary CDA: A plea for diversity. In R. Wodak & M. Meyer (Eds.), *Methods of critical discourse analysis* (pp. 95–120). London: Sage.

van Dijk, T. A. (2015). Critical discourse studies: A sociocognitive approach. In R. Wodak & M. Meyer (Eds.), *Methods of critical discourse analysis* (3rd ed., pp. 63–85). London: Sage.

van Leeuwen, T. (1999). *Speech, music, sound.* London: Macmillan.

van Leeuwen, T. (2004). Ten reasons why linguists should pay attention to visual communication. In P. LeVine & R. Scollon (Eds.), *Discourse and technology: Multimodal discourse analysis* (pp. 7–20). Washington, DC: Georgetown University Press.

van Leeuwen, T. (2005). *Introducing social semiotics.* London: Routledge.

van Leeuwen, T., & Jewitt, C. (Eds.). (2001). *Handbook of visual analysis.* London: Sage.

Wodak, R., & Meyer, M. (Eds.). (2015). *Methods for critical discourse analysis* (3rd ed.). London: Sage.

Wooffitt, R. (2005). *Conversation analysis and discourse analysis: A comparative and critical introduction.* London: Sage.

Chapter 18
Concluding Remarks: Developing a Critical Discursive Peace Psychology

Stephen Gibson

Introduction

The chapters in this volume have featured a range of analytic materials pertaining to a variety of specific contexts. Far from adopting a uniform analytic perspective, they have been marked by differences in analytic priorities and preferences, from the micro-interactional to a more macro-oriented concern with cultural discourses; and from empirically grounded strategies on which to base practical interventions to a concern for a conceptual expansion of the discursive realm to take in the visual domain. In this brief concluding discussion, I will endeavour to draw out what, for me, seem to be some of the key lessons that we might take from these analyses, and in so doing point the way to further developments in what we might tentatively describe as critical discursive peace psychology.

First, I will consider the essentially contested nature of the objects of peace psychology, most notably 'peace' itself, and suggest that the focus on analysts' definitions of peace (and violence) might usefully be complemented by a greater concern with participants' constructions. Second, I will consider the potential for discursive peace psychology to contribute to the analysis of cultural violence (and, by extension, to the achievement of cultures of peace), as well as suggesting that a unique contribution might come in terms of the analysis of *discursive violence*. Third, I will consider the practical implications for discursive psychology, with the encounter with peace psychology encouraging a more interventionist (in the non-military sense) form of practical engagement. Fourth, I will sketch out some potential obstacles to an integration of discursive and peace psychology, focusing in particular on the incompatibilities between the structural focus of peace psychol-

S. Gibson (✉)
York St John University, York, UK
e-mail: s.gibson@yorksj.ac.uk

© Springer Nature Switzerland AG 2018
S. Gibson (ed.), *Discourse, Peace, and Conflict*, Peace Psychology Book Series,
https://doi.org/10.1007/978-3-319-99094-1_18

ogy and the post-structural orientation of discursive psychology. Fifth, and relatedly, I will suggest that a post-structural positon has advantages in enabling peace psychology to overcome a residual individualism that it shares with much of the broader discipline of psychology.

The Construction of Peace

One of the more striking aspects of the analyses is the extent to which the concern for analysing discursive construction highlights the ways in which many of the objects of peace psychological analysis are themselves available for, and subject to, contestation in the course of debate and interaction. For example, we see how the nature of 'peace' itself is contested. For all that scholars have sought to delineate different forms of peace and violence (e.g. Galtung, 1969, 1990), consideration of the discursive construction and invocation of peace and conflict shows how for speakers and writers in a whole range of contexts, the nature of peace and violence is itself up-for-grabs. Indeed, one of the notable things about peace is that it is not typically something that one finds people arguing against—it is a universal good—and as such it is typical to find people positioning themselves as being in favour of, and/or working towards, peace regardless of the specific course of action that they propose (Gibson, 2011). Indeed, Galtung (1969) observed as much when he stated that,

> 'peace' serves as a means of obtaining verbal consensus – it is hard to be all-out against peace. [footnote omitted] Thus, when efforts are made to plead almost any kind of policy – say technical assistance, increased trade, tourism, new forms of education, irrigation, industrialization, etc. – then it is often asserted that the policy, in addition to other merits, will also serve the cause of peace.
> (Galtung, 1969, p. 167)

Similarly, as we saw briefly in Chap. 1 of this volume, and more fully in Burridge's chapter, even those who argue for military action do not appear to frame their arguments in terms of the desirability of *war*. Being seen to be a 'war monger' is something to be avoided.

In this respect, peace and war can be understood in similar terms to other categories that carry with them connotations that are either overwhelmingly positive or negative. For example, research on prejudice has shown how speakers—even those on the extreme right—orient to the undesirability of prejudice (e.g. Billig, 1988). The analytic focus can therefore be placed on how speakers construct prejudice, and how it is negotiated, avoided, managed, and denied (e.g. Condor, 1988; Condor, Figgou, Abell, Gibson, & Stevenson, 2006). Similarly, as several chapters in this volume attest, there is scope for a discursive peace psychology to focus on the way in which peace and violence themselves are made relevant in discourse. Kirkwood and Goodman's and McVittie and Samabaraju's chapters in particular highlight this idea, and McKenzie's ethnomethodologically inspired analysis developed it by exploring the way in which the distinction between direct and structural violence/peace could be oriented to by aid workers in making sense of their own complex positioning in relation to conflict. A core task of critical discursive peace psychology is, therefore, to explore participants' orientations to, and constructions of, peace and violence.

Cultural and Discursive Violence

Focusing on participants' orientations need not, however, preclude discursive analysis from adopting some of the broad schema of peace psychology, or even from developing some additional conceptual tools. Many of the contributors frame their analyses as highlighting some aspect of how discourse can be used to maintain direct or structural violence, or how it can be used to achieve positive peace. At the conclusion of their chapter, Kilby and Lennon highlight the utility of discourse analysis for deconstructing cultural violence. In this respect, they identify one of the key areas in which discursive psychological analysis can contribute to the aims of peace psychology. In emphasising the close, detailed, analysis of discourse, discursive psychology provides a toolkit for deconstructing those aspects of culture that contribute to the maintenance of direct and structural violence. Indeed, many of the chapters in this volume—whether they orient themselves to this objective explicitly or not—can be seen to be engaged in such an endeavour. This sort of patient, painstaking critical analysis is precisely what is called for if we are to unpick the ideological manoeuvrings that are designed to maintain social injustice and legitimate militaristic ideologies.

Moreover, based on consideration of the analyses as a whole, we can begin to make a case for a new category of violence: *discursive violence.* This concept awaits a fuller working out, but in highlighting the role of discourse in constructing and sustaining violence, the contributors to this book highlight a form of violence that is at once both more specific and more general than cultural violence. If cultural violence can be said to involve 'those aspects of culture … that can be used to sustain or legitimize direct or structural violence' (Galtung, 1990, p. 291), then discursive violence pertains to *those uses of discourse that function to sustain or legitimise violence.* This is not such a radical departure from the way in which the ideological functions of discourse have been theorised in discursive psychology and other fields (e.g. Fairclough, 2013; Henriques, Hollway, Urwin, Venn, & Walkerdine, 1998; Wetherell & Potter, 1992), with a key concern being the way in which discourse is used to legitimate inequality, exploitation, and injustice. But positioning this definition specifically in terms of *violence* highlights also the need for its counterpart, *discourses of peace.* Here, we can begin to consider how discursive analysis might begin to complement the excellent work on the deconstruction of discursive violence with a concomitant focus on how to construct discourses of peace. Stokoe's chapter provides one such example of a practical strategy for how this might begin to be achieved, but by comparison with peace psychology, discursive psychology does not yet have a well-established track record of engaging in such interventions.

The Nature of Intervention

Stokoe's chapter (and the wider body of work that it represents; e.g. Stokoe, 2013, 2014) raises a number of potential opportunities for synergy between peace psychologists and discursive psychologists. In outlining the way in which the detailed analysis of discourse relating to matters of conflict resolution can contribute to practical strategies for overcoming conflict, Stokoe's work chimes with the themes of peace psychologists who have sought to engage with dialogic approaches to conflict resolution (e.g. Kelman, 2010, 2015). Such work has had important and significant impacts, yet there remains potential for it to be extended through the sort of thoroughgoing discursive analysis provided by Stokoe. Equally, whilst there is a developing tradition of applied conversation analysis (Antaki, 2011), on which Stokoe draws heavily, as well as attempts to develop an applied discursive psychology (e.g. Willig, 1999), in truth the practice-oriented elements of a specifically discursive psychology remain underdeveloped.

There is much value to be gained from scholarly analysis in and of itself, and the very conceptual foundations of discursive psychology encourage us to be sceptical of the distinction that is sometimes drawn between words and action, for discourse itself is action-oriented. Equally, in a political context which increasingly exhorts academics to demonstrate their practical and economic utility, there is an important critical task to be performed of challenging the devaluation of scholarship (Billig, 2012, 2013). Indeed, we might follow Žižek's (2008, p. 6) words of caution in suggesting that, 'There are situations when the only truly 'practical' thing to do is to resist the temptation to engage immediately and to 'wait and see' by means of a patient, critical analysis'. I would therefore have no truck with those who simply and uncritically adopt what, in the UK context, is currently known as 'the impact agenda'. Indeed, in her chapter, Stokoe is careful to note that the sorts of interventions in which she has engaged have involved compromises that might be a step too far for some analysts; yet the movement towards a public-practical tradition in discursive psychology need not be seen as existing in competition with the careful, sober analysis of talk and text, but rather as a natural outgrowth of it. As Gergen (1973) argued long ago in his seminal critique of experimental social psychology, most psychologists aim to produce insights that can—in however an unpredictable and ill-defined manner—be of wider benefit in some way, and this should not be seen as troublesome just because present and/or longstanding political imperatives urge us towards particular kind of 'benefits'. In doing this, we open ourselves up to criticism (and, indeed, to deconstructionist analysis), but then this is not that much of a change. Who gets to define what constitutes a practical 'benefit', and in whose interest that 'benefit' might be, are quite properly matters for critical analysis. But the analysis of discourse has always involved the production of texts which can themselves be the subject of analysis (e.g. Ashmore, 1989). Engaging in more public/applied activities is no different—they can, and should be, subject to critical scrutiny, but that shouldn't mean that we don't engage in them.

The Nature of Critique: From the Structural to the Post-Structural

The aim of contributing to attempts at creating a more peaceful and just world is central to peace psychology. The reduction of violence in all its forms—direct, structural, and cultural—is prioritised over and above any attempt at generating the sorts of universal laws of human behaviour that have been prized by the wider discipline of psychology. In this respect, discursive psychology's (sometimes uneasy) foundations within what has been termed 'critical psychology' (e.g. Fox, Prilleltensky, & Austin, 2009; Hepburn, 2003) would appear to offer an obvious point of connection and overlap. Both peace psychology and critical psychology have sought to challenge those uses of psychology which reproduce and exacerbate inequality and injustice, and to bring about a psychology which is committed to action and intervention as much as it is to the standard concern with uncovering general laws of psychological processing.

However, this apparent sympathy obscures some potential obstacles. There are many varieties of critical psychology, and one key tension has been between critical realist approaches, often influenced by some form of Marxism, and relativist approaches which adopt a postmodern and post-structural orientation. In emphasising the structural nature of violence, peace psychology would appear to sit firmly within the realist camp. By contrast, there are discursive psychological perspectives that adopt both critical realist and relativist approaches, and it would therefore perhaps be tempting simply to suggest—as Karlberg (2012) does—that an approach that orients more towards a critical realist position would be best suited to integration with peace psychology. Any attempt to adopt a relativist approach would surely risk conveying the impression that the brutal realities of direct and structural violence were somehow being neglected.

Indeed, many of the criticisms levelled at relativists have involved precisely such an appeal to both direct and structural forms of violence as realities that cannot and should not be denied. In their classic defence of relativism, Edwards, Ashmore, and Potter (1995) cite some examples of such critiques, including one that took issue with a trenchantly relativist text by the sociologist Mike Mulkay (1985), whose playful subversion of conventional literary forms of social scientific writing emphasised the contingency of truth claims. In response, one reviewer claimed the following:

> As I write this, an area of Tripoli has been laid waste by a number of aircraft currently (I hope) sitting on the ground a few miles down the road from my Ivory Tower. Some 100 people (not very many by modern standards) have been killed. They were not killed by words neither are they dead because the rest of the world decides to call them dead. Their death was brought about by the employment of a disproportionately immense amount of scientific and technical knowledge. If we can only see this knowledge as just another story, then we too deserve to fall victim to it.
>
> (Craib, cited in Edwards et al., 1995, p. 33)

Edwards et al. proceed to dismiss such objections by 'turning the moral tables', asserting that realists have no more of a sure foundation from which to participate in political and moral debate than do relativists, and that relativism, in insisting on the contingency of all accounts, is preferable to a realism which can, after all, be used to justify inaction every bit as much as action: 'how does ontological realism, allied with empiricism, sit with moral conviction? What are realists doing in possession of something as irrational as conviction?' (Edwards et al., 1995, p. 35). Fundamentally, their arguments point to the centrality of value commitments:

> Relativists focus analytically on variability and contingency. But they (we) can also *take part in* that variability at least as comfortably as realists can. There is no contradiction between being a relativist and being *some*body, a member of a particular culture, having commitments, beliefs, and a common-sense notion of reality. [footnote omitted] These are the very things to be argued for, questioned, defended, decided, without the comfort of just being, already and before thought, real and true.
> (Edwards et al., 1995, pp. 35–36, italics in original)

A post-structural framing would, if anything, sit more comfortably with the value commitments enshrined at the heart of the peace psychological project. Indeed, such an approach provides a way of overcoming another key tension at the heart of peace psychology, concerning the dualism between the individual and the social. In pointing the way beyond the individualism that is at the cornerstone of psychology and which—for all the focus on macro-social structures—remains at the heart of the *psychology* enshrined in peace psychology, post-structuralism has some significant advantages.

Beyond Individualism

As Christie (2006) makes clear, peace psychology involves an emphasis on the macro-social level of analysis that is not typical in other areas of psychology. The systems-level analysis to be found in recent (especially post-Cold War) developments of peace psychology is an admirable improvement on the individualism of much psychology. To cite just one recent example, in reviewing the potential contributions of positive psychology to peace, Cohrs, Christie, White, and Das (2013) note the individualism enshrined in much positive psychology and suggest that well-being needs to be considered within a global context. Such criticisms echo those of many discursive psychologists (e.g. Billig, 2005), and others influenced by post-structuralism (e.g. Binkley, 2014), who highlight the extent to which positive psychology functions to maintain the status quo by focusing on the individual as the locus of well-being.

Nevertheless, in deriving the specifically psychological aspects of its frameworks from (broadly) cognitivist traditions, peace psychology does not so much challenge the individualism of psychology as suggest that the focus on the individual needs to be complemented by an equivalent (or even greater) focus on the systemic. The challenge of post-structuralism is more radical in that it de-centres the subject (Henriques et al., 1998), dissolving the individual-social dualism entirely (Wetherell, 1996). The individual as currently conceived in much (western) psychology thus comes to be seen itself as a cultural product—as the outcome of a particular set of historically-situated discourses that have arisen in particular places at particular times (Sampson, 1993). This rather more sweeping conception of discourses of the individual can be complemented by the micro-analysis of discursive psychologists who have focused on the ways in which categories usually understood as referring to mental furniture can be usefully re-specified as participants' concerns in the course of interaction (Edwards, 1997; Edwards & Potter, 1992). This ultimately Wittgensteinian position sees no advantage in theorising about the putative mental objects of much of what passes for psychological science (Potter, 2001), and instead focuses on the way in which psychological business gets done in talk and text. For peace psychology, a focus on how these aspects of psychological discourse are made relevant to, managed, and oriented to in discourse concerning peace and conflict would seem to have important advantages. In highlighting the cultural specificity of the conception of the individual, and of the psychological, that peace psychology works with, a discursive perspective founded on post-structuralism dismantles the continued reliance on a set of assumptions that have been used to ride roughshod over alternative (e.g. collective; non-unitary; distributed) conceptions of subjectivity (e.g. Owusu-Bempah & Howitt, 2000; Sampson, 1993). Moreover, insofar as this notion of the individual has been part of a wider ideological apparatus that has underpinned a range of abuses, atrocities, and injustices committed in the name of progress, it can be understood as a form of cultural violence itself. For peace psychology to retain such a conception of the psychological is, therefore, untenable.

References

Antaki, C. (Ed.). (2011). *Applied conversation analysis: Intervention and change in institutional talk*. Basingstoke: Palgrave Macmillan.

Ashmore, M. (1989). *The reflexive thesis: Wrighting sociology of scientific knowledge*. Chicago, IL: University of Chicago Press.

Billig, M. (1988). The notion of 'prejudice': Some rhetorical and ideological aspects. *Text, 8*, 91–110.

Billig, M. (2005). *Laughter and ridicule: Towards a social critique of humour*. London: Sage.

Billig, M. (2012). Undisciplined beginnings, academic success, and discursive psychology. *British Journal of Social Psychology, 51*, 413–424. https://doi.org/10.1111/j.2044-8309.2011.02086.x

Billig, M. (2013). *Learn to write badly: How to succeed in the social sciences*. Cambridge: Cambridge University Press.

Binkley, S. (2014). *Happiness as enterprise: An essay on neoliberal life*. Albany, NY: State University of New York Press.

Christie, D. J. (2006). What is peace psychology the psychology of? *Journal of Social Issues, 62*, 1–17.

Cohrs, J. C., Christie, D. J., White, M. P., & Das, C. (2013). Contributions of positive psychology to peace: Toward global well-being and resilience. *American Psychologist, 68*, 590–600.

Condor, S. (1988). 'Race stereotypes' and racist discourse. *Text, 8*, 69–89.

Condor, S., Figgou, L., Abell, J., Gibson, S., & Stevenson, C. (2006). 'They're not racist': Prejudice denial, mitigation and suppression in dialogue. *British Journal of Social Psychology, 45*, 441–462.

Edwards, D. (1997). *Discourse and cognition*. London: Sage.

Edwards, D., Ashmore, M., & Potter, J. (1995). Death and furniture: The rhetoric, politics and theology of bottom line arguments against relativism. *History of the Human Sciences, 8*, 25–49.

Edwards, D., & Potter, J. (1992). *Discursive psychology*. London: Sage.

Fairclough, N. (2013). *Critical discourse analysis: The critical study of language* (2nd ed.). Abingdon: Routledge.

Fox, D., Prilleltensky, I., & Austin, S. (2009). *Critical psychology: An introduction*. London: Sage.

Galtung, J. (1969). Violence, peace, and peace research. *Journal of Peace Research, 6*, 167–191.

Galtung, J. (1990). Cultural violence. *Journal of Peace Research, 27*, 291–305.

Gergen, K. J. (1973). Social psychology as history. *Journal of Personality and Social Psychology, 26*, 309–320.

Gibson, S. (2011). Social psychology, war and peace: Towards a critical discursive peace psychology. *Social and Personality Psychology Compass, 5*, 239–250.

Henriques, J., Hollway, W., Urwin, C., Venn, C., & Walkerdine, V. (1998). *Changing the subject: Psychology, social regulation and subjectivity* (2nd ed.). London: Routledge.

Hepburn, A. (2003). *An introduction to critical social psychology*. London: Sage.

Karlberg, M. (2012). Discourse theory and peace. In D. J. Christie (Ed.), *The encyclopedia of peace psychology*. New York: Wiley.

Kelman, H. C. (2010). Interactive problem solving: Changing political culture in the pursuit of conflict resolution. *Peace and Conflict: Journal of Peace Psychology, 16*, 389–413.

Kelman, H. C. (2015). The development of interactive problem solving: In John Burton's footsteps. *Political Psychology, 36*, 243–262.

Mulkay, M. (1985). *The word and the world: Explorations in the form of sociological analysis*. London: George Allen & Unwin.

Owusu-Bempah, K., & Howitt, D. (2000). *Psychology beyond western perspectives*. Leicester: British Psychological Society.

Potter, J. (2001). Wittgenstein and Austin. In M. Wetherell, S. Taylor, & S. J. Yates (Eds.), *Discourse theory and practice: A reader* (pp. 39–46). London: Sage.

Sampson, E. E. (1993). *Celebrating the other: A dialogic account of human nature*. New York: Harvester Wheatsheaf.

Stokoe, E. (2013). The (in)authenticity of simulated talk: Comparing role-played and actual interaction and the implications for communication training. *Research on Language and Social Interaction, 46*, 165–185.

Stokoe, E. (2014). The conversation analytic role-play method (CARM): A method for training communication skills as an alternative to simulated role-play. *Research on Language and Social Interaction, 47*, 255–265.

Wetherell, M. (1996). Constructing social identities: The individual/social binary in Henri Tajfel's social psychology. In W. P. Robinson (Ed.), *Social groups and identities: Developing the legacy of Henri Tajfel* (pp. 269–284). Oxford: Butterworth Heinemann.

Willig, C. (1999). *Applied discourse analysis: Social and psychological interventions*. Buckingham: Open University Press.

Žižek, S. (2008). *Violence*. London: Profile.

Index

© Springer Nature Switzerland AG 2018
S. Gibson (ed.), *Discourse, Peace, and Conflict*, Peace Psychology Book Series,
https://doi.org/10.1007/978-3-319-99094-1

Lightning Source UK Ltd.
Milton Keynes UK
UKHW020821171221
395757UK00001B/21